HOLY POWER,

HOLY PRESENCE

Rediscovering Medieval Metaphors for the Holy Spirit

ELIZABETH A. DREYER

Paulist Press
New York/ Mahwah, NJ

Cover art: Jean Poyet, *The Pentecost*. French, c. 1500. Miniature from a Book of Hours. Photo © The Cleveland Museum of Art.

Cover design by Cynthia Dunne

Book design by Sharyn Banks

For a list of credits for the illustrations, please see p. 332.

Library of Congress Cataloging-in-Publication Data

Dreyer, Elizabeth, 1945–
    Holy power, holy presence : rediscovering medieval metaphors for the Holy Spirit / Elizabeth A. Dreyer.
        p. cm.
    Includes bibliographical references and index.
    ISBN-13: 978-0-8091-4485-3 (alk. paper)
    1. Holy Spirit—History of doctrines—Middle Ages, 600–1500. I. Title.
    BT119.D74 2007
    231'.30902—dc22   2007013297

Published by Paulist Press
997 Macarthur Boulevard
Mahwah, New Jersey 07430

www.paulistpress.com

Printed and bound in the
United States of America

CONTENTS

Contents

PREFACE

In the recent past, there have been a lot of complaints about the supposed eclipse of the Holy Spirit in the Christian tradition.[1] Christians talk a lot about Jesus, often address the Father/Creator in prayer, but become vague when it comes to the Holy Spirit. Given that the Holy Spirit is the third person of the Trinity and is at the heart of Christian spiritual life, it is hard to imagine the Holy Spirit as invisible, upstaged, silent, or neglected. And yet, at the beginning of a course on the history of Christian spirituality, when I asked seminary students to engage in an exercise of free association vis-à-vis the term *spirituality*, the words *Holy Spirit* rarely passed anyone's lips.

Theologians continue to speak of the neglect of the Holy Spirit in the Western tradition, in contrast to Eastern strains of Christianity that they see as more faithful to the Spirit. Eastern emphases on *epiclesis*[2] and divinization place the Spirit at the heart of the church and of the Christian life. Yet it seemed strange that medieval theologians, steeped as they were in the Bible and the writings of the fathers of the church, East and West, would ignore or neglect the Spirit. Is the tradition as Spirit-impoverished as contemporary theologians suggest?

This is a book in search of answers to criticism that the Western Christian tradition paid too little attention to the distinctive characteristics of the Holy Spirit. I discovered that these conclusions were based on the examination of a rather narrow range of texts, most of which belong to the genre of fundamental or systematic theology. For example, Augustine's *On the Trinity* is often cited as the primary or only source, while his letters and sermons are not consulted.[3] It is true that medieval theologians were deeply concerned about divine unity. Less clear to them was how the pluralism and diversity of created reality imaged the Creator.

1

My objective, then, is not to deny the medieval importance assigned to God as One, but rather to gather evidence that documents the significant attention given to individual divine persons, in particular, the being and function of the Holy Spirit.

When I began to read infrequently consulted texts—sermons, letters, catechetical and liturgical material, mystical treatises, lives of the saints—I discovered that the Holy Spirit was indeed alive and well for these writers. This material, often composed with an eye to the daily practice of the Christian faith by ordinary people, was communicated in a poetic rather than discursive literary style, and it is filled with symbols, imagery, and metaphor. Thus, this book contributes to the emerging impulse to recover the particular, concrete, and image-laden language about the Holy Spirit in the tradition.[4]

Indeed, these texts reveal that the Spirit was not only alive and well but invoked, described, and celebrated in many and varied ways in the personal and ecclesial lives of medieval Christians. These texts must be considered for us to arrive at a fuller, more accurate picture of the Holy Spirit tradition. In addition to giving us a fuller picture of medieval pneumatology, this material has the potential to enrich and complement contemporary systematic theology.[5] Placed in creative dialogue with more systematic theological approaches, as well as with the experience of ordinary Christians who desire a closer walk with the Spirit, this material carries the promise of renewed consciousness and fresh engagement with the Spirit.

I examine six medieval figures—three men and three women, five of whom lived between the twelfth and the fourteenth centuries. All of the authors are known for their fertile thought about the spiritual life, and most of their works are readily accessible in reliable English translation. While I provide a substantive sampling from their texts, many readers may want to delve more deeply into the primary sources on their own. I begin with Augustine (354–86), in part because he is often blamed for the Western neglect of the Spirit, but also because his trinitarian thought has been so influential in subsequent theologies of the Trinity.

From the twelfth century, I examine the work of the Benedictine abbess and visionary Hildegard of Bingen. Because women were forbidden to preach and teach in public, Hildegard's prophetic voice had to be defended, often by reference to the work of the Spirit within her. The next figure to be considered is Hildegard's celebrated contemporary Bernard of Clairvaux, who was centrally instrumental in the renewal of the Cistercian Order and was judged by many to be an unrivaled master of the spiritual life. Since his theology and spirituality are so intensely focused on Christ, it is understandable that most students of Bernard analyze his Christology. For this reason, it becomes even more important to obtain a better grasp of the less frequently explored topic of the Holy Spirit.[6]

In the thirteenth century, I turn to Bonaventure of Bagnoregio (1217–74), known as the second founder of the Franciscan Order, a model theologian/pastor who was able successfully to embrace and keep in creative and fruitful tension both the ordered expression of systematic theology as a university professor and the more lyrical, poetic expression of the spiritual life as general of the order. From the fourteenth century, I explore the works of a laywoman and an anchorite. Catherine of Siena (1347–80) was dedicated to reconciling warring civic and papal forces and was an advocate for the return of the papacy from Avignon to Rome. She belonged to the Dominican Third Order, called the *mantellate*. Our journey ends in England with Julian of Norwich (c. 1343–c. 1416), a solitary, whose visions of the crucified led to years of reflection during which she produced her major work, *Showings*, which contains a sophisticated theology of the Trinity.

Introductory and concluding chapters form the bookends around these six individual authors. In chapter 1, I locate this inquiry within the broader context of contemporary theological discussions of the Holy Spirit. I assess in detail recent criticism of the Western pneumatological tradition; the turn to history/praxis/narrative; the function of image and symbol in theology; and the relationship between spirituality and theology. A final chapter raises questions about the silences of the Spirit; identifies threads uncovered in previous chapters that can profitably be brought forward; and looks to challenges as we shape future theologies of the Holy Spirit.

I have also included visual material created by artists from the twelfth century to the early seventeenth to give the reader a sense of how the Trinity and the Holy Spirit were portrayed during and beyond the historical parameters of the figures studied. These images include the Trinity imagined as three human persons, a fairly uncommon approach; the Trinity present at the death of Jesus (pietà); the Trinity crowning Mary; and various representations of Pentecost. Also included are four images related to the Spirit from the visions of Hildegard of Bingen. I invite readers to ponder these images and reflect on them as aids to further shaping their personal theologies and spiritualities of the Holy Spirit within the context of trinitarian life.

This book, which emerged out of research and ecumenical conversation, is offered as a tool and an invitation to readers to make their own decisions about the role of the Holy Spirit in theology and spirituality. It will become clear that all of our medieval authors struggled with the challenge to be open to the Spirit's presence and to discern what the Spirit was doing in their lives. We are no different. Part of the Spirit's comforting and consoling presence is knowing that so many of our ancestors in the faith faced challenges we know well: discerning the difference between unity and uniformity, learning how to do a better job judging good spirits from bad, identifying and overcoming our fears that tempt us to squelch the Spirit, and trusting in the Spirit's presence.

Every Christian is accountable for discerning in light of the cross, nurturing gifts and fruits of the Spirit in our daily lives, being willing to work in love within communities of faith, and speaking a Spirit-filled prophetic word for our time. The point of studying the past is to enhance the present and to help us create a Spirit-filled future. Each chapter ends with reflection questions—"Food for Thought"—that invite readers to identify resonances within their experience, to test their understanding of the material, and to discern a new and creative future for life in the Spirit and for theologies of the Holy Spirit. The aim is to invite readers into a creative dialectic between learning about the history of the tradition and making decisions about how we want to appropriate it in our very diverse lives.

The book is structured around the following questions: (1) What specific Spirit language and imagery did medieval authors use? (2) What do these more existential, pastoral texts reveal about how medieval authors understood the being and functions of the Holy Spirit? (3) How did each sociohistorical context affect what these theologians said about the Spirit? When and why did they choose to speak about the Spirit in certain ways? What needs and questions did a given approach address? (4) How can the images, language, and concepts about the Holy Spirit serve as a resource for contemporary pneumatology? (5) How can this material bring new life to our experience of the Spirit, by enhancing our knowledge of the tradition, allowing it to quicken and renew our confidence in the Spirit's power to infuse love and joy into our lives?

My basic approach can be described as a "close reading" of selected primary texts by six leading medieval thinkers. As a way to honor these ancestors in the faith, I attend closely to their words, to the concepts, language, and imagery they use to describe the Holy Spirit. I invite anyone who picks up this book to practice "slow" rather than "speed" reading. In the mode of *lectio divina*, ponder, chew, and digest the world, imagery, poetry, and associations contained in these texts—feel them and allow them to penetrate your own spirit. Although I bring my unique experience, perspective, and limitations to the study of these medieval figures, I have intentionally focused on their words rather than analyzing their texts through the lens of postmodern philosophical, linguistic, or literary hermeneutic strategies. My primary aim is to let each author speak in her or his own voice, to invite the reader to theological and spiritual reflection on the material, and to raise questions relevant to current discussions of the Spirit and to the practice of the spiritual life.

In addition to attending carefully to language, I situate the texts within the social, ecclesial, and intellectual currents in which they were composed. The authors call on the Spirit to address specific, concrete issues of the day, and without knowledge of these contexts, we cannot rightly understand what they say about the Spirit. Historical information is found at the beginning of some chapters and is also woven into the discussion of the various pneumatological themes. For those who wish to pursue issues raised in the book, the endnotes include explanations of terms and historical movements, references to primary texts, and information about secondary literature. This documentation is a way to acknowledge the work of so many scholars who study the various dimensions of medieval life and thought. Other readers may want to focus on the Holy Spirit material alone, bypassing the more academic opening chapter and the endnotes. The chapters may be read profitably either in chronological order, or by dipping into favorite authors separately.

This book appeals to a number of interests. Specialists in the discipline of spirituality can learn how authors in one period of the tradition spoke about the Holy Spirit and assess how this material might be helpful to contemporary expressions of the spiritual life. Ministers may become aware of the rich Spirit tradition in the West that can serve as a resource for contemporary ministerial engagement. Adult Christians who are seeking resources for understanding and nurturing a lively Spirit-filled existence will benefit from a reading of the metaphors and images for the Spirit employed by these ancestors in the faith.

Medieval historians and theologians may be reminded of the ways in which rarely discussed texts can fill out the portrait of medieval theological thought and piety in its existential, practiced forms. Systematic theologians may want to take this material into account as they work to forge language about a trinitarian God and a Holy Spirit that will hold up and be compelling amid the challenges of the twenty-first century. A particularly important group of people are those entrusted with the care and Christian education of the young. Early development of our images of the triune God provides a critical foundation for later spiritual growth. In particular, the potential for bringing the medieval tradition to life again in programs designed to prepare members of the community and their families for baptism and confirmation is promising. Imagine a sacramental program creatively shaped by the images of the Spirit we will encounter in the pages ahead. The following story reminds us of the theological wisdom of children.

Once a week, in an urban evening program, inner-city children aged three to eight gather in a local church for ritual, story, creative activities, and a hot meal (the ritual is modeled on Compline, the evening prayer of the church). The lay catechist uses a feltboard and hundreds of colorful felt figures that provide a highly visual and tactile tool. Watching the storyteller move the pieces around to create tableaux, the children enter imaginatively into the stories of the Christian tradition. As the story is told, the children often interrupt with questions and ideas. When given the opportunity, they play with the tableaux, repositioning the figures and talking about the stories.

The Trinity is represented by a large red heart and two hands for God the Father; the figure of Jesus; and a small dove for the Spirit. These symbols are used to portray the story of Jesus' baptism. Each week, as the group proceeded through the New Testament and imagined the various accounts of Jesus' life and ministry, the catechist continued to place the hands and heart and figure of Jesus at the beginning of each story. Often she neglected to include the dove. Whenever that happened, some child would call out: "Where the bird at?" When it came to Holy Week and the cross, the children responded with a unanimous "Yes" when asked whether the dove should be present with Jesus on the cross. Perplexed, the teacher complied, and told the story of the crucifixion with the dove in place. Then, on a sudden inspiration, she snatched it away at Jesus' words, "My God, my God, why have you forsaken me?" The children silently accepted this action. Several weeks later, during the telling of the story at Pentecost, the dove reappeared on the board, marking the Spirit's presence passing from Jesus to the disciples.[7]

In its own way, this book also asks, "Where the bird at?" By learning about where the Spirit lives and breathes for Augustine, Hildegard, Bernard, Bonaventure, Catherine, and Julian, we may come to our own awareness of the Spirit's power and presence in our lives. By uncovering details of medieval language about the Holy Spirit, I invite further exploration and debate about the ways our ancestors in the faith spoke of the Spirit; how specific historical and ecclesial contexts affected the people who spoke about the Spirit; how this material might enhance contemporary religious experience and understanding of the Spirit's vibrant presence and operation; and how it might contribute to systematic expressions of pneumatology.

The first and final chapters address issues of our present context, including contemporary discussions of pneumatology, and how various communities of faith experience and understand the Spirit's presence in their lives. A major new development affecting both areas is Pentecostalism, the fastest growing branch of the Christian church across the globe. As more and more knowledge and insight about this movement become available, negative stereotypes and simplistic assessments give way to careful historical studies, allowing more informed and honest judgments, and potentially fruitful new questions.[8] In an ideal world, tradition-bound denominations (in which I and many who will read this book are located) and more recent religious movements grounded in spontaneous openness to the Spirit, would remain in dialogue, enriching and stretching each other. Unfortunately, too often fear of the new, or rejection of the old, blocks our openness and ability to learn from each other. But there are reasons to remain open and create opportunities for ongoing conversation. I offer two.

Whether or not history's judgment ends up supporting the claim that the worldwide Pentecostal movement is of such magnitude that Christianity will never be the same again, it is incumbent on us to learn more about this large and diverse movement as it affects established Christian groups and expresses itself in new forms.[9] Second, the universal importance of the Holy Spirit in the Christian faith holds forth an ongoing challenge to Christians to work and pray together so that the Spirit might indeed descend upon us, enlightening, guiding, comforting, inflaming, and renewing us as we work to bring about a world of justice and love. The medieval tradition at the center of this study is the heritage of all Christians. The images and metaphors that are discussed provide room for all to enter and explore how our ancestors might speak to us in the twenty-first century. For some, the impact will be great; for others, less so. But it is my hope that those who read what follows will invite the "other"—Christians who follow a different path and even members of other religions—into a larger conversation about the universal hunger for a renewed, enlivened, and Spirit-filled existence.

The initial impetus for this project came from an invitation from William Thompson, who, as president-elect of the Catholic Theological Society of America, invited me to give a plenary address on the Holy Spirit in the Western Christian tradition at the society's annual meeting in San Diego in 1996. When I began, I could not have predicted the rich vein of Spirit imagery that came to light in the course of my research. Generous grants from the Louisville Institute provided an extended period of time for work on this project and allowed me to engage a group of local pastoral leaders in stimulating and fruitful discussion about the theological, spiritual, and ministerial implications of this work. Six denominations were represented: Anglican, Congregational, Lutheran, Methodist, Presbyterian, and Roman Catholic. Jane Ferreira, William Goettler, Rosemarie Greco DW, Louise Higginbotham, Michael Merkel, Gretchen Pritchard, Brian Schofield-Bodt, Nancy Strickland, and Susan Power Trucksess will all hear their voices echoed throughout the chapters ahead. I am grateful for the ways these dedicated Christian leaders helped me connect history and theology with the spiritual and pastoral life of the church. By sharing their gifts, they helped me shape a more ecumenical voice in the context of a theological, pastoral, Spirit-filled community.

I am also grateful to Fairfield University for research leaves, and to colleagues who read and commented on aspects of this work at early points in its development—the late Walter Principe, Joseph Chinnici, Mark Burrows, Michael Slusser, Elizabeth Johnson, and Nancy Dallavalle. Special thanks to my husband, John Bennett, whose loving companionship, encouragement, and indefatigable editing skills held me up throughout what has been a lengthy, but rewarding, engaging, and enlightening journey.

Elizabeth A. Dreyer
Hamden, Connecticut
May 2006

Chapter 1

THE STUDY OF THE SPIRIT
Context and Method

I begin with the anonymous, ninth-century Latin hymn *Veni Creator*.[1] After combing through medieval texts in search of material on the Holy Spirit, I returned to this short hymn with a new awareness of how it reflects major elements of the tradition in a comprehensive yet economic and poetic way. Beginning with the text of a prayer also underlines the doxological as well as the historical and theological interests of this book.

> Come, Creator, Spirit,
> visit the souls of your own;
> fill with heavenly grace
> the breasts that you have created.
>
> You who are called Paraclete,
> gift of the most high God,
> living water, flame, charity
> and spiritual anointing;
>
> You who are sevenfold in your gift,
> finger of God's right hand,
> you who were rightly promised by the Father,
> enrich our throats with speech.
>
> Inflame the light of our senses,
> pour love into our hearts,

the weakness of our bodies
strengthen with lasting power.

Drive the enemy far back,
and at once grant us peace;
with you going ahead of us,
may we avoid all harm.

Through you may we know the Father
and recognize the Son;
and may we always believe
in you, Spirit of both.

This prayer splendidly captures many of the themes we will encounter in more detail in subsequent chapters. These few stanzas point to the Spirit both as God's gift to us and as finger of God's hand. It reminds us that we belong to God as recipients of the Spirit's gifts of heavenly grace and charity. The hymn calls attention to the traditional images of water, fire, and oil that will come up again and again in the authors examined below. It petitions the Spirit for inspired speech, alert senses, loving hearts, strong bodies, safety, and peace. Finally, it attests to the belief—first articulated in John's Gospel (14:25–26; 16:13)—that the power of the Spirit enables us to know about and live out of God's saving love.

In this opening chapter, I explore the background and context for recent scholarship on the Holy Spirit. To begin, I document recent criticisms of the Western Christian tradition's treatment of the Holy Spirit. Contemporary scholarship is influenced by a number of intellectual, philosophical, and cultural developments that affect how theology is practiced. In particular, I call attention to the turns to history, praxis, and narrative. It is from this perspective that contemporary scholars view and assess the past. An outgrowth of these concerns involves questions about the relationship between *spirituality* (a term we use to describe the practice of the Christian faith) and *theology* (the ordered reflection on this experience). How can we keep these two aspects of the faith in creative relationship? A section on symbols aims to heighten awareness of how symbols function, and to equip ourselves to enter more deeply into the medieval symbols of the Spirit we will encounter in subsequent chapters. The chapter ends with comments about methodology, the specific approach I take in reading and bringing to light material on the Holy Spirit from the distant past of our ancestors in the faith.

Neglect of the Spirit

Criticisms of Western theologies of the Holy Spirit are long-standing and numerous. Descriptors of the Spirit include "personally amorphous, faceless, forgotten, upstaged, ethereal and vacant, unclear, and invisible."[2] Descriptors of pneumatology (study of the Spirit, from the Greek word for spirit, *pneuma*) include "ambiguous, reticent, obscure, neglected, groping, abstract."[3] Talk of the Holy Spirit as the forgotten God goes back to the 1920s,[4] and in 1957, G. J. Sirks wrote an article naming the Holy Spirit the Cinderella of theology.[5] As recently as 2003, Kilian McDonnell noted that in the broad central tradition, the significance of the Son has been consistently robust, but we cannot say the same for the Spirit "because pneumatology has not been integrated in an organic way into the whole theological process."[6]

Are these criticisms justified? One must answer both yes and no. Yes, inasmuch as the personal terms *Father/Mother* and *Son* are indeed more accessible than the abstract term *Spirit*. Most of us know and have relationships with mothers, fathers, sons, or daughters, but rarely find ourselves in conversation with spirits—and if we do, we probably keep it quiet. It is also true that in the early centuries of Christianity, the church's initial theological concerns focused on understanding the God-man, and only later, the being and role of the Spirit. This christological emphasis perdured into the Middle Ages.[7]

Eastern Orthodox theologians criticize the West for neglecting the Spirit in liturgy, spirituality, creedal statements, and theology.[8] The Western commitment to the *filioque* (the doctrine that the Holy Spirit proceeds from *both* the Father and the Son) is seen as a partial culprit, blamed for obscuring the fullness of the Spirit's distinctive role. Still other critics suggest that the Western preoccupation with Christology has caused the Spirit to be eclipsed.

Another major complaint focuses on what is perceived to be an excessive focus on the nature and unity of God at the expense of a full theology of the three persons. In ecclesiology, this over-emphasis on unity is seen to endanger the proper recognition of the Spirit's work in the diversity of the church's individual members (1 Cor 12:4ff). Philosopher, theologian, and cultural analyst Louis Dupré (b. 1925) criticizes the Western practice that privileges the unity over the trinity of God.

> We in the Latin world begin with a theory of the one God and add the "distinctions" later. But by that time they no longer relate to the primary object of spiritual theology, man's approach to God. The Greeks, on the contrary, begin directly with the order of salvation.[9]

When all these elements are taken into account, many conclude that the West has an inadequately developed pneumatology.

But the argument that the Western church has consistently undervalued the Holy Spirit needs to be qualified. For example, if we look more closely at the nuts and bolts of the medieval university curriculum, we discover a little-known but relevant fact. The role of the Spirit was in fact widely taught and debated in the medieval Latin church. Students at medieval universities were required to comment on the four-volume *Sentences* of scholastic theologian Peter Lombard (c. 1100–c. 1160).[10] Students tackling the topic of God in the first volume did not initially encounter material on God's unity, but rather thirty-four "distinctions" (sections) on the characteristics of the individual divine persons.[11] Nine distinctions treat the Holy Spirit as Love and Gift, discuss the Spirit's "proceeding" from the Father and the Son, and enumerate the Spirit's visible and invisible missions. Not until distinction 35 does Lombard take up the more general divine attributes such as knowledge, providence, omnipresence, causation, omnipotence, and will. It is hard to imagine that this formative exercise, undergone by all students from Alexander of Hales to Martin Luther, led to a theology that disregarded the distinctive nature of the persons in the Trinity, as Dupré and others suggest.

A second example of questionable criticism stems from the practice of isolating systematic texts from their various contexts. In her otherwise fine treatment of the Trinity, *God for Us*, Catherine LaCugna writes:

> Even if Augustine himself intended nothing of the sort, his legacy to Western theology was an approach to the Trinity largely cut off from the economy of salvation....When the *De Trinitate* is read in parts, or read apart from its overall context and in light of Augustine's full career, it is both possible and common to see no real connection between the self-enclosed Trinity of divine persons and the sphere of creation and redemption.[12]

At the least, one can question how the *De Trinitate* could be interpreted legitimately *apart from* its overall context and Augustine's full career. In chapter 2, I offer a corrective to this narrow view by presenting a broader range of Augustine's texts on the Spirit, placing them in relationship to what was going on in his life. The results reveal a quite different pneumatology, challenging assessments based on a limited range of documents, abstracted from their sociohistorical location.

How can we further explain these negative conclusions about the place of the Holy Spirit in the tradition? Perhaps there is a modern expectation that earlier theologies exhibit a kind of Cartesian order that is simply not there. This happens when scholars read a text exclusively in terms of a structure it does not have, thereby missing the structure it does possess. Our interpretations also falter when we attend too exclusively to systematic treatments and not enough to sermons, biblical commentaries, letters, and liturgical and catechetical material; or when we fail to appreciate adequately the language and imagery of these texts. Also important are the ways texts functioned in specific historical contexts.[13] Like Christians today, Christians of previous centuries called on the Spirit in a variety of settings and circumstances.

Undue criticism of the pneumatological tradition may also stem from the pressing search for a contemporary pneumatology that responds to needs and questions radically different from those of historically and geographically distant communities. The worldview and problems of the twenty-first century could not be more foreign to those of the twelfth. But it is not time to lose heart about the tradition. I am convinced that the past can provide resources for today. While we cannot step out of our twenty-first-century skin or completely avoid projecting modern sensibilities onto historical material, we can attend to medieval texts without egregiously foisting modern viewpoints upon them. Such a "close reading" allows the discovery of a wealth of creative insight and language that speak to our contemporary situation without undue violation of the historical integrity of the texts. This brief survey of criticisms of the pneumatological tradition reveals both legitimate and problematic factors, highlighting complaints that fail to establish in a convincing way that the Holy Spirit was truly neglected.

The Turn to History/Praxis/Narrative

The rationale and methodology for this exploration into the nature and function of the Spirit echo recent concerns expressed by philosophers, theologians, and literary figures who want to maintain a creative, constructive tension between formal systematic reflection and concrete historical practice. In *Power and the Spirit of God*, Bernard Cooke acknowledges the recent spate of books on the Holy Spirit, but notes that most still concern the Spirit's identity and role within the Trinity. Much remains to be done to clarify what he calls the Spirit's divine outreach to creation.[14] Postmodern thinkers work to correct what they see as an overly theoretical and universalizing approach that does not adequately honor the historical particularity of the *other*.[15]

For instance, philosopher Stephen Toulmin comments on the dead end we seem to have reached after three hundred years of Cartesian theater. For Toulmin, the main question today is what we should be *doing*, not thinking. He wants to give primacy to the practical, placing theory in its service. Philosophy, he says, is not just a mind game. Philosophical theses are not useful unless they *are* useful. Rationality must make way for, and accommodate, the inevitable *complexity* of human existence.[16] Divorced from the practical, systematic thinking alone is inadequate to the task.[17]

Philosopher Pierre Hadot makes a compelling argument for the value of understanding as a "way of life."[18] His focus is ancient philosophy, but I find his analysis instructive and applicable to our own times and to the discipline of theology as well. Hadot argues that ancient philosophy is rightly understood primarily as a choice to live in a certain way—a decision to live a life guided by reason and the practice of virtue. Philosophy as mode of existence is distinct from philosophical discourse, which comes later and functions to justify and provide theoretical foundations for a way of life.[19] Philosophy is a concrete act that changes how we view the world and leads to action in the service of the human community—not the construction of systems. "It is a life, not a discourse."[20] In addition to reason, it requires affectivity and imagination that enable us to view reality from a broad, deep, indeed cosmic, perspective.[21]

Hadot warns against projecting onto ancient philosophical texts our penchant to see philosophy as the construction of abstract systems. In truth, ancient philosophy is more interested in forming and transforming the person than in communicating systematic propositions. Ancient philosophy was primarily oral—it involved dialogue and conversation intended to train disciples to "orient themselves in thought, in the life of the city, or in the world."[22] The goal is not to acquire abstract knowledge but to transform our vision of the world and our very being and personality—intellect, imagination, sensibility, and will.[23]

This understanding of ancient philosophical knowledge is even more applicable to the history of Christian theology. Ancient and medieval Christian authors did theology with one primary goal in mind—to become saints themselves and to help others reach this same goal. While the church engaged reason at every step of its doctrinal journey, and political considerations always had a role, the overall thrust of the development of doctrine was spirituality. The church's mission was to find ways to articulate the faith in every age in challenging and relevant ways, so that ordinary people could be assisted in their baptismal commitment to follow the way of Jesus of Nazareth.

A quite different problem involves the style of theological writing. Historical theologian Michel René Barnes examines how contemporary trinitarian theology uses Augustine.[24] He calls attention to the continuing and unhelpful use of Théodore de Regnon's late nineteenth-century categories that contrast Greek and Latin approaches to trinitarian theology.[25] Barnes criticizes the preference of systematic theologians for what he calls grand, architectonic and idealistic styles of writing. In this approach, details matter less than perspective, and historical facts become secondary considerations, often reduced to ideology. History is treated as the material enstructuring of those themes that are constitutive of contemporary systematics.[26] The requirements of a grand architectonic scheme dictate the interpretation of experience, rather than vice versa. Barnes gives several examples of trinitarian theologies that ignore the broad range of relevant historical texts and/or fail to take their polemical context into account.[27]

I suspect that the situation is even more complex than Barnes allows. Historians too can err by limiting the data on which they reflect or by imposing ideological constructs on them. Some historians also relegate the past to the past, refusing to entertain the kind of dialectic that connects the past and the present in mutual, critical, and meaningful ways. They approach the past as dead and over, rather than as a living resource. Is it not just as legitimate for the past to "read us," as it is for us to "read" the past? David Tracy reminds us: "If the text is a genuinely classic one, my present horizon of understanding should always be provoked, challenged, transformed."[28] In other words, if we invite it, the tradition calls us to account, not primarily by judging us and finding us wanting but by expanding our horizons through exposing us to other ways of seeing, other ways of thinking about God.

Another contemporary criticism points to a penchant for excessive abstraction in current treatments of the Holy Spirit. As a corrective, German theologian Michael Welker advocates a biblical, concrete, pluralistic understanding of the Spirit's work. He rejects language about the Holy Spirit that emphasizes transcendent and otherworldly qualities—what he calls "naked supernaturalness" and the "mysterious numinous quality of much theology of the Holy Spirit."[29]

> Many treatments emphasize the vagueness of the Holy Spirit; you cannot grasp it, it is numinous. Well, if you look at these more than three hundred biblical texts on the Holy Spirit, you do have three or four that emphasize this vagueness and this mysticism. But I thought that it would be wiser to see these three or four sentences in the light of the three hundred others instead of the three hundred others in the light of these three. So here you have my kind of approach, looking at

abstractions, misleading abstractions, and trying to correct them. Here I feel myself very much in agreement with Whitehead, who described the task of philosophy as a critique of abstractions, and I think we need this in theology too.[30]

Asked in an interview whether his choice to begin his systematic theology with the Holy Spirit reflected an antisystematic mood of our time, Welker, a philosophical theologian himself, assures his interlocutor that he is decidedly *not* antisystematic, but he wants to correct what he perceives as reductionistic tendencies in theology.[31] Welker is right in his contention that returning to the complex symbolic resources of the Bible and tradition will help us better work toward solutions to major social and moral dilemmas.[32] Our examination of select medieval traditions on the Holy Spirit is a prime example of what Welker calls for.

Another solution to excessively abstract theology is the examination of narrative as a theological tool. Theology should not obscure the stories that make up our lives, but attend to them and lift them up in the light of God's loving presence. Taking account of narrative includes examining the stories of those seeking to live in the Spirit and the sociohistorical narrative contexts out of which talk about God emerges. Despite the dominance of metaphysical and then scientific analysis in our culture, Christian theology must remain in touch with traditional language of narrative and symbol. Narrative is important because it is the primary language of theology, telling the story of the encounter between God and humans in essentially dramatic ways. But once again, the point is not to take up narrative forms at the expense of the universal, but to keep both in play.[33]

Understanding faith through philosophical analysis plays a necessary and valuable role, but it can never stand alone. Symbols and narrative stand behind all analytic, philosophical, theological expressions. And for Christians, stories about Jesus' life form the concrete, particular, historical core for all belief and language. Ideally, the various understandings that come through narrative or through analysis complement and determine each other. Narrative or personal language recalls us to original insights that empower us. Ontological analysis can refine our understanding of this relationship and correct misleading notions, but it cannot replace the narrative structure.

Other critics of early and medieval pneumatologies point to inadequate attention to, and connection with, the historical contexts. Theologians do not write in a vacuum. They are influenced by the ecclesial, intellectual, political, social, and economic factors that surround them. The world of each author affects her or his choice of language, the concepts emphasized and the metaphors chosen. Conflicts, responsibilities, and setting affect more academic, theoretical genres, but show up most noticeably in sermons and letters addressed to specific individuals and audiences. Thus, Augustine's more philosophical descriptions of the Trinity as one and three in *On the Trinity* must be complemented by his Pentecost sermons. As we will see in chapter 2, Augustine's descriptions of Pentecost reveal a close connection between the Holy Spirit and courage, about which he speaks in a very intense passionate tone. We can better understand his speech about the Spirit when we remember that as bishop of Hippo, he had the responsibility of leading a community of faith in the midst of the trials and tribulations of the North African church in the fourth-century Roman Empire. In his battles with Donatists, pagans, and the Roman Empire, he faced concrete, pressing, and challenging problems that led him to desire the kind of courage displayed by the apostles after the Spirit's descent.

Life is always specific. Theologian of the Spirit Jürgen Moltmann reminds us that whatever we may say in general about ourselves and other people in the light of eternity, the Spirit of life is present always as the Spirit of this or that particular life. Our experiences of the Spirit are as specific and varied as each person.[34] A primary aim of this book is to view what six medieval figures wrote about the Holy Spirit in all their particularity. But in order to make creative, critical use of this tradition, we must reflect on our present context and analyze the complex symbolic resources that operate in church and society, decode them, and reformulate them.

A careful reading of these symbols—many of which come from the Bible—calls reductionist interpretations into question. Welker offers two examples: the theological tradition of "law and gospel" and "creation." A careful analysis of biblical texts reveals multiple complex dynamics that too often are reduced to mere commandment in the first case and the control/dependence in the second. In other words, our theology does not do justice to the biblical narrative.[35] In the church, there are legitimate reasons to seek simplicity of articulation in the interest of dogma and confessional traditions, not to mention as a way of coping with the overwhelming complexity of postmodern culture. But now, he notes (using his work on the Holy Spirit as an example), we need to "go back to the stronger symbolic resources which have been developed over 1500 years."[36]

By attending to the concrete and particular experiences and understandings of the Spirit, this exploration of the medieval tradition combats the undue abstractness of systematic theology that is removed from personal experience and disconnected from scriptural images and metaphors. But unlike Welker, who understands mysticism in a reductionistic way as a force that works against seeing the Spirit in the concrete events of life, I argue that mystical texts not only are grounded in biblical language, providing rich, creative, and imaginative variations on biblical stories and imagery, but also open a window onto the real life concerns and hopes of each age. I suggest that just as we need to plumb the symbolic resources of the Bible, we need also to provide a "rich description" of the subsequent mystical and pastoral traditions on the Holy Spirit.

It is necessary to add that in many segments of world culture, the turn toward history, the affections, and praxis is well on its way. For example, the revolutions of the 1960s, various forms of liberation theology, feminist theology, and the notable growth of charismatic forms of religion on every continent have already begun to rehabilitate the affections and praxis—in some cases eschewing systematic theology in any form. Often history implements its own corrections at a faster pace than scholars can write and publish books. These new developments mean that while we attend to history, the particular, the affections, and praxis, we need to ground them in reasoned discourse, creative theory, and the wide arc of a two-thousand-year-old tradition. The theological tension between these two poles leads to questions about the relationship between spirituality and theology.[37]

Spirituality: Resource for Theology.

Questions about the relationship between theology and spirituality arise logically from the criticisms of pneumatology just discussed. I use the term *spirituality* to refer to the daily, practical, concrete living out of one's faith commitment. *Theology* refers to the reasoned, ordered, systematic expression of this faith experience. The distinctive realms to which these terms relate need not lead to a rigid separation, but rather invite us to explore ways in which each informs and corrects the other. Theory and practice are two indispensable dimensions of Christian existence.[38] The mystical and pastoral texts I have chosen are replete with narrative, practical, poetic, and affective elements that complement more systematic expression. Attending to this material responds to the desire of many Christians to have theology reflect, and contribute to, the existential dimensions of a lively and intentional spiritual life. As a way to honor the methods of the authors treated here, I wish to keep theological and spiritual concerns yoked. The call for this linkage is also present in our own context. Spirituality has become important to growing numbers of Christians, making it imperative to include it in theological deliberations.[39] In addition, a number of theologians have been working to establish spirituality as an academic discipline, initiating dialogue with other branches of theology.[40]

Theology is accountable to ongoing revelation as it is experienced in the community of faith. It is also charged with influencing and correcting that experience in constructive and meaningful ways. In other words, theology's ultimate goal is to nurture holiness in individuals and in the community. Decades ago, German Jesuit Karl Rahner (1904–84) offered an invitation to articulate the doctrine of the Trinity in a way that would touch peoples' hearts and bring vitality to the concrete lives of the faithful. He asks: "How can the contemplation of any reality, even of the loftiest reality, beatify us if intrinsically it is absolutely *unrelated* to us in any way?"[41] When trinitarian formulas become rigid and overly precise in their expression, they lose their ability to be a resource and catalyst for prayer and for kindling the hearts of the faithful.[42]

A disjunction between experience and doctrine is misguided in several ways. It is obvious that theology and doctrine cannot exist without a prior "spirituality" or experience of God. But it is also true that the language of theology and doctrine influences religious practice. We can point to misguided forms of spirituality, such as certain strains of fundamentalism or cults that seem not to have benefited from the kind of ordered reflection systematic theology provides. Spirituality and theology are brought into an even more intimate relationship when we hold together God's gift of Godself to us in grace and the ways we experience this gift in our spiritual lives.[43] When this is our goal, theoretical and practical disciplines in theology operate from different perspectives, but may not ultimately be disjoined. God's self-gift, our individual and communal experience of it, and our attempts at both poetic and systematic expression are not separate entities, but rather different aspects of the same reality.[44]

In an effort to find language to express ineffable experiences of God, spiritual writers turn to narrative, image, symbol, and metaphor. These language forms have the potential to function like a wellspring to which we can return again and again to renew and reinvigorate spiritual experience. In contrast, the purpose of systematic theology is to provide a disciplined, ordered reflection on the community's experience of God. To the extent that systematic theology becomes divorced from its source in experience or mistakes its more abstract language and categories for the reality of experience—what British philosopher Alfred North Whitehead (1861–1947) calls the "fallacy of misplaced concreteness"—it loses its ability to influence and shape the community in fruitful and life-giving ways. Effective doctrines are embedded in a community's experience of the triune God acting in history. As will be illustrated in subsequent chapters, for the majority of Christians, narrative and images have the potential to evoke and transform encounters with God in ways that the concept of *esse*, for example, does not.

Scholars articulate the need to reconnect spirituality with theology from a variety of perspectives.[45] But too often theologians focus on systematic theology and doctrine, forgetting that both depend on the experience of Christians in every age, in the daily workings of their lives, their struggles to love God and neighbor, and their efforts to fight the demons that prevent love from flowering. Thus, we can agree with Michael Buckley's lamentation about the failure of theology to appreciate the relevance of accounts of religious experience, since the saints surely point to the reality of God in compelling ways. After describing the religious experience and witness of Edith Stein, Raïssa Maritain, and Simone Weil, he writes,

> If what these histories point to is true, is it not extraordinary that so much Catholic formal theology for centuries, its divorce between spirituality and fundamental or dogmatic theology, has bracketed this actual witness as of no cogency—aside from polemic allusions to the holiness of the Church? Is it not a lacuna in the standard theology, even of our own day, that theology neither has nor has striven to forge the intellectual devices to probe in these concrete experiences the warrant they present for the reality of God and make them available for so universal a discipline?[46]

Bracketing religious experience or divorcing spirituality and theology, life and thought, appears strange indeed when we remember that Christian theology has always held that God is revealed in the saints' experience of God drawing near. The fruit of the Spirit transforming human affectivity and awareness allows us to recognize in ourselves and in others the image of God, which persons throughout history have found to be both credible and compelling as a testimony to the existence of God.[47]

As a result of this bracketing, theologians have neglected the study of historical texts recounting religious experience in favor of more formal, theological treatises. As we saw above, accounts of Augustine's trinitarian theology are based on this kind of selective reading. But if theology does include sermons, prayers, letters, and spiritual texts, we are faced with the question of how to relate this material to the demands of formal theological expression. In the case of pneumatology, we ask how language and imagery about the Spirit in more explicitly pastoral, mystical texts can enhance and correct conclusions based solely on systematic works. But we often discover that in ancient and medieval material, the very distinction between "spiritual" and "theological" may be misplaced, raising questions about how well we are interpreting even systematic texts on the Spirit. As noted above, Pierre Hadot has cautioned us about projecting a post-Enlightenment interest in abstraction onto a world that would not even have recognized it.

The work of this book aims to keep the marriage of theory and practice intact by examining neglected medieval texts that address or describe the Holy Spirit. The texts I have chosen offer a more direct view into the authors' experience of God in their own lives and in the various communities to which they belonged. We do not have access to the interior lives of our authors, nor can we interview them about their experience of the Spirit, but I am convinced that their choice of images, symbols, and metaphors offers glimpses of the distinctive ways in which they encountered, prayed to, and taught about the Spirit.[48]

Trinitarian theology will become a living force in the Christian community when it stays hinged to religious experience. Language describing the Trinity must not only be linked with language for the Father, Son, and Spirit, and vice versa, but also situated within the context of religious experience. Traditionally, our most intimate experiences of God, most visible in the world's mystical literature, have been attributed to the powerful presence of the Spirit. We need to attend to these accounts if we are to have an adequate pneumatology.[49] Each of the six figures we examine produced accounts of precisely this type of encounter with God.

Images and Symbols

Renewed attention to the role of image, symbol, and metaphor opens the way to a greater appreciation of their usage in medieval texts and their potential relevance for today.[50] Symbol is an encompassing category that can be described as a "complex of gestures, sounds, images, and/or words that evoke, invite, and persuade participation in that to which they refer."[51] Whether symbols take up elements of the natural world such as fire, water, and oil; make use of human artifacts such as a flag or a logo; or are expressed in literary or oral forms such as stories, visions, or poetry, they lend themselves to polyvalent meanings that function to shape our world. Symbols not only reflect the meaning and values of a given community but also function to change them in positive or negative ways. In terms of our earlier discussion on the differences between narrative and ontological statements, we can say that symbol complements dialectic, functioning to reveal the tensions, conflicts, and struggles that logic wishes to streamline.[52]

Since systematic theology cannot adequately translate the meaning of the symbol without reduction, it needs to keep the symbol in view, approximating its meaning in a provisional way. We begin with the stories and symbols of the Bible. Theology reflects on this material in a more analytical way, employing reason to construct an ordered system by which each generation understands and explains the faith. But in the end, we revisit the stories and symbols, hopefully with a deeper, more informed understanding of their meaning. When this process is successful, the task of interpretation and the experience of the symbol are mutually enriching. Since effective religious symbols are transformative, they invite believers to encounter God and be converted to live and love in godly ways. They engage and shape affectivity and thus, value. Like metaphor, they juxtapose dissimilar elements, as in "the Holy Spirit is fire," in order to lead us to new insight, feeling, and behavior. From the earliest days of Christianity, symbols and images were used as catechetical aids in explaining and inviting to faith. For Christians, the incarnate and risen Christ provides the supreme symbol, embodying the truth of the triune God and grounding the meaning of all other Christian symbols and images.

Recent challenges to monolithic language about God (why not speak of God as "Mother," "Sister," or "Nurse" as well as "Father"?), and the broadening of our understanding of the person of Jesus (a poor Jewish male, rabbi, prophet,) are welcome developments, but these efforts to multiply names of God have not often been extended to the Holy Spirit. As a result, our images and symbols of the Spirit remain impoverished. A recovery of the pluralism of Spirit imagery in the tradition will feed a deeper understanding of the Spirit's all-important presence by which Christians first encounter life in God. For "it is in and through the Spirit that we participate in the trinitarian life."[53] We need to uncover and attend contemplatively to the images and stories of the Spirit tradition in order to discover whether they retain an expressive power that resonates with our deepest memories, associations, and longings.

Of course the medieval understanding of symbols was quite different from our own. There is no comparison between the bombarding of images to which we are subject each day and the cultural world of the Middle Ages. Images also functioned differently in the Middle Ages, a world believed to be pervaded by the divine, a world that perceived a spiritual meaning in everything.[54] Gerhart Ladner comments that medieval people understood signifying, symbolizing, and allegorizing functions not as arbitrary or subjective. Rather, symbols were thought to represent reality objectively and to express faithfully various aspects of a universe that was perceived as widely and deeply meaningful.[55] Historical theologian Marie-Dominique Chenu describes the distinctive and even primary role of symbol in relationship to reason in the twelfth century.

> To bring symbolism into play was not to extend or supplement a previous act of the reason; it was to give primary expression to a reality which reason could not attain and which reason, even afterwards, could not conceptualize. Moreover, these symbols claimed to disclose certain intimate relationships—ranging from the psychological import of colors to the sublimated religious value of social acts or to revelations of the divine in nature—which the art of ascertaining multiform truth could not fail to take into consideration.[56]

For medieval mystics and poets, imagery played a crucial role conveying meaning less by argument than by wonder. Writing about medieval literary texts, John Hirsh describes the medieval world as one that included

> the Gothic smile, the delicate tracery, intricate enamels and wood-carving, amazingly graceful flora and fauna, perfection of craftsmanship even to the tiniest detail, accompanied by soaring and grand cathedrals of exquisite, fragile strength and powerful beauty—all these bespeak a lyric freshness of awareness of God's world.

Mosaics and stained glass windows radiated a kind of "mural poetry" that could not have but influenced those who saw them.[57]

In the Middle Ages, symbols carried a weight unimaginable for most of us. In a work tracing the development of a medieval musical form, the sequence, Margot Fassler comments that arguments were won and lost in the Middle Ages through the re-creation of symbols. Indeed the symbolic mode of thought predominated at least up to the thirteenth century. Even then, when formal logic, as Marcia Colish says, "effected a decisive split between reality, thought and language," the symbolic mentality remained of major importance in some quarters and especially with thinkers of the Franciscan school.[58] The symbolic modes of thinking that prevailed during most of the Middle Ages were not less capable as a vehicle of human thought than the rational mode that eventually came to replace it. It was simply different.[59]

Few of us realize the possibilities or even know how to allow symbols to affect and form us at the deepest levels of our being. Advertising alone bombards us daily with so many symbols that any single image is unlikely to capture our imaginations or penetrate our consciousness. More demanding still is the task of discerning which symbols draw us to the good, bring life, and lead to the practice of virtue, and which draw us in the opposite direction. To the extent that we remain unconscious of how symbols affect us, they do their work at subliminal levels. A simple exercise may inform us about our awareness of symbols and how we relate to them. Spend a moment dwelling on the symbol of the Holy Spirit as fire (see figs. 1, 2, and 3). What might it mean at a very personal and concrete level to be "on fire with the Spirit"? Is being enflamed by the Spirit something you desire? If you have already experienced what this age-old Christian symbol means, what fruit has it borne in your life?

In her book *Image as Insight: Visual Understanding in Western Christianity and Secular Culture*, historical theologian Margaret Miles examines the visual arts as a primary means of representing "the nature of reality and the range of human possibilities that intimately informed the emotional, spiritual, and intellectual lives of individuals."[60] This was nowhere more true than in the medieval period and the tradition on which it drew. Miles cites Plato and Plotinus, who note that the experience of beauty need not be limited to conceptual understanding, for it yields a somatic (bodily) religious sense as well. Thomas Aquinas goes further, positing that sensible objects are not just the first step toward knowledge but an enduring foundation for it.[61]

Imagery surrounding the Holy Spirit presents a host of riches, as we will see, but also some problems. We have noted the impersonal, abstract quality of some Spirit imagery, making a relationship with the Spirit distinctly challenging.[62] On rare occasions, the Spirit has been imaged as a person, but it is the exception that proves the rule[63] (see fig. 4). For example, Spanish artist Miguel Ximenez (1466–1503) portrayed the Holy Spirit as a human being in a painting titled *The Trinity*.[64] Another representation of the Spirit as a human being is found in an image of the celestial court in the Book of Hours of John the Fearless, Duke of Burgundy (duke 1404–19). Andrei Rublev paints the three divine persons as the three angels who appeared to Abraham, sitting at a eucharistic table[65] (see fig. 5). One can also point to Master I. M.'s *Coronation of the Virgin by the Trinity* (1457), a French panel painting, in which the three persons are imaged as three men surrounding a kneeling Mary,[66] and a painting in Bavaria (c. 1378–95) titled the *Urschalling Trinity*.[67] In contrast, late-fourteenth-century Spanish artist Rubielos imagines the first two persons of the trinity standing on either side of Mary. The Spirit, in the form of a graceful dove, hovers over her head, with wings touching the mouths of the Father and the Son. As bond of love, the Spirit provides the link that unites the persons of the Trinity around the kneeling Queen of Heaven (see fig. 6).

In spite of few personal images of the Spirit, the tradition has consistently thought of the Holy Spirit in personal terms. Building on biblical roots that support at least three distinct divine functions, the language of the doctrine of the Trinity sets the tone— three persons in one God. And, as we will see, there are many personal functions attributed to the Spirit throughout Christian history. No doubt debate about the advantages of both personal and impersonal metaphors for the Spirit will continue. Theologian Mary Ann Fatula weighs in decisively on the side of a personal Spirit. She cites the wide range of biblical texts that attribute personal characteristics to the Spirit. The Spirit is presented as per-sonified Wisdom (Wis 1:6, 7, 22, 25; Sir 1:1–10; 4:11–19) and as one who groans and pleads for us (Rom 8:26); is referred to as "he" (John 14:17, 26; 16:7–8, 13–14); speaks and gives direction (Acts 13:2–4); helps and teaches (John 15:26; 14:26; 16:13–15).[68]

It would be interesting to survey Christian communities about the impact of imagining the Spirit as a dove. Does it enhance or detract from spiritual growth—or is it simply irrelevant? The biblical tradition on "doves" is well established from Genesis to John.[69] And even a small sampling of representational images of the Trinity underlines the omnipresent depiction of the Spirit as a dove—even though in some instances a magnifying glass is required to locate it[70] (see fig. 7). But the contexts in which this symbol had meaning have changed in significant ways.

In many cultures, birds represented epiphanies of gods, spir-its, or messengers of divine beings, announcing new situations and/or serving as guides. Birds symbolized the freedom and tran-scendence of the human spirit as it was released from the body in ecstasy or death. Birds were associated with divinity, immortality, power, victory, and royalty. The dove was also associated with eroticism and fertility. The dove's softly moaning sound suggested loyalty and the gentleness of love—the dove was sacred to the Greek goddess of love, Aphrodite. In Judaism, the dove points to Israel's status as the beloved of Yahweh. Philo interpreted the dove as a symbol of virtue and reason.[71] We have noted that in Christianity, the Spirit, in the form of a dove, appears at Christ's baptism, and as an impregnating force at the annunciation. In Islam, birds represent human souls that journey through the seven valleys, finally uniting with the divine bird that has a name but no body, a perfectly spiritual being. The dove can also symbolize purity, innocence, or peace.[72] While we still occasionally release large flocks of doves into the open sky at Special Olympics, wed-dings, and funerals, it is safe to say that in contemporary Western culture, the symbol of the dove as visual representation of the Spirit has been largely emptied of its theological and spiritual meaning.

A desired result of the exploration of medieval imagery of the Holy Spirit is to raise awareness of the plurality of Spirit images and to bring new life to them. There is a much broader range of ways in which to imagine, think about, and engage the Spirit than we might think. Some writers make creative use of traditional nature images such as fire and water, while others use a wider range of personal images in which the Spirit is portrayed as nurse, comforter, even waiter. Medieval metaphors for the Spirit include the familiar wind or breath (Gen 1:2), tongues of fire (Acts 2:2–3), and light flowing from and returning to God like a beam of the sun.[73] As we will see, the image of water was important in Bonaventure's portrayal of the Holy Spirit. Bonaventure also speaks of the entire scriptures as the heart, mouth, tongue, pen, and scroll of God—the pen representing the Holy Spirit.[74]

In the east, Ignatius of Antioch employs a construction/building simile that points to the Holy Spirit as the means by which the building of the church is effected. The stones are the faithful; the builder is the Father; the crane is the cross; and the Holy Spirit is the hawser, a large rope used for hoisting or towing a ship.[75] Ambrose sees the Spirit in a more passive role. He conflates images of lilies of the valley and the root of Jesse from the Song of Songs and Isaiah. The root symbolizes the Jews; the rod Mary; and the flower Christ, who thus spreads the good odor of faith throughout the world.

> The flower, when cut, keeps its odor, and when bruised, increases it, nor if torn off does it lose it. So, too, the Lord Jesus, on the gibbet of the cross, neither failed when bruised, nor fainted when torn. When he was cut by that piercing of the spear, he became more beautiful by the color of the outpoured blood. He grew comely again, not able in himself to die, and breathed forth upon the dead the gift of eternal life. On this flower of the royal rod the Holy Spirit rested.[76]

In a quite different metaphor with an oxymoron at the center, in a hymn for Lauds attributed to Ambrose, the Holy Spirit is connected with drunkenness—a motif that runs from the Bible (Acts 2:15; 1 Cor 12:13; Eph 5:18) throughout the mystical literature. He says, "let us happily drink the sober inebriation of the Spirit."[77]

Many of us need help in order to appreciate the role and function of medieval imagery. Since we generally approach texts with conceptual, cerebral tools rather than sensory ones, we can benefit from instruction about how to read medieval texts. Historian Rosemary Drage Hale suggests that when we read medieval mystical texts, "we miss something of the sensory dynamic of the world or culture of medieval mystics if we persist in interpreting their experience solely as 'visions'...perhaps we can begin to do more than translate the words if we take a 'hermeneutical turn'—instead of reading the texts, we could be learning to sense them."[78] Can we learn to slow down, to dwell in a text, to use our imaginations not only to hear the words in the deepest reaches of our being but to feel them, enjoy them, wrestle with them? Rather than demanding "bottom line" conclusions and logical, ordered understanding, can we permit the images to hang in the air, waiting for other types of meaning to break in on us? The symbols and metaphors religious writers use to describe their experience of ineffable deity enlarge ordinary speech—giving it dimensions into which the reader can enter, dwell, and derive renewed meaning.[79]

Like symbols, the point of spiritual writing is not primarily to lead the reader to engage in an ordered, conceptual analysis of the text—helpful as this can be. Rather, the goal is personal transformation. Moral philosopher Edith Wyschogrod reminds us that understanding the works and lives of the saints consists not in recounting their meaning but in being "swept up in their imperative force." Comprehension equals practice. The addressee is "gathered into the narrative to extend and elaborate it in her/his own life."[80] If we engage medieval texts with this awareness, we begin to move beyond analysis and knowledge to a "felt sense" of what the authors are trying to communicate about their experience of being a Christian and also of what it might mean to have the Holy Spirit descend upon us. In turn, the insights thus gained can become a resource for the more rational, ordered, systematic expression that is appropriate to systematic theology and pneumatology.

In different but analogous ways, symbols and images in the Middle Ages and today function as vehicles of deeper meaning, providing a bridge between past and present. Medieval images and metaphors are elusive on one level, since we cannot know in a demonstrably precise way what they meant to the authors or their audiences, but this does not mean that we cannot work carefully to

understand and argue for a text's potential meaning in its past context and for today. When exploring texts and images from distant
historical periods, we must be content with working hypotheses
and a range of possible interpretations rather than "proof" for a
single meaning.[81] And just as formal theological statements can
succumb to undue rigidity, images can also be interpreted in too
literal a fashion, forgetting the caution of the Fourth Lateran
Council that there is greater dissimilarity than similarity between
creation and the Creator.

The goal of metaphoric language is to create space to enter
and "play" with multivalent possibilities. The church continues to
embrace many medieval symbols, but the associations and meanings we attach to them change over time. Each age and culture
reinterprets its symbolic heritage in terms of its own life and
worldview. Unless symbols and narratives relate to the intellectual,
existential, moral, and political horizons of the present, they will
not remain vibrant or authoritative. Our concepts of ultimacy and
our theological notions have meaning for us only if they thematize
and shape our experience and our world.[82] But if they are transformed into a new key, symbols and images remain alive from age
to age, providing a kind of bridge on which to travel between the
worlds of the tradition and the world of today.

The point of mining the tradition for images and metaphors
of the Spirit is not, then, to baptize the tradition uncritically,
much less to absolutize it. The relevance of an image or symbol
across time depends on an act of recognition by the viewer. In
each age, symbols take on new elements of meaning and lose
those that are no longer viable. For example, our awareness of
ecological damage to oceans, rivers, and lakes provides a context
for the symbol of water that would not have existed in the Middle
Ages. And in some cases, symbols that were once positive are
experienced by certain individuals or groups as no longer meaningful or even as oppressive.[83] For example, Catherine of Siena's
image of the Spirit as a waiter at table might be perceived as
threatening or dangerous rather than emancipatory for women
who feel that society has assigned this task to women arbitrarily
and to their disadvantage. The wager of what follows is to test
whether medieval symbols and narratives of the Spirit are out of
touch with modern experience and therefore empty and lifeless,

or whether they have the potential to provide our experience of Spirit with joy, illumination, healing, coherence, and order.

Methodology

My search for material on the Holy Spirit is grounded in the trust that the tradition reveals what Jaroslav Pelikan calls "the living faith of the dead" rather than "the dead faith of the living"— a stance that invites us to discover, name, and bring forward in responsible and creative ways the Christian legacy.[84] We have noted some of the ways in which scholars name the risks, benefits, and methods in examining and retrieving medieval texts. We cannot isolate a text from its original sociocultural matrix, nor from its long trajectory of interpretation down the ages.[85] For example, Augustine's Spirit language needs to be located within the context of his experience and culture—a context that was deeply biblical, ecclesial, and fraught with problems that he was often called upon to solve with the best lights available to him. Attending to a text's particular location mitigates the penchant to assess what Augustine wrote about the Spirit as abstract or theoretical. While Augustine often expressed himself in systematic, philosophical language, his interests, as bishop of Hippo, were eminently soteriological.

Language can be understood as dialogue among persons— each in the fullness of her or his specific time and place. This dialogic context stretches into the past and future. Past meanings born centuries ago cannot be finalized, but are always changed and renewed in the process of subsequent development of the dialogue.[86] Such an understanding of the never-ending flow of language encourages us to try to understand and relate medieval texts to our own time. Elements of this retrieval include the understandings of symbols that were passed down to the Middle Ages; how the medieval community interpreted and used these symbols; and how these symbols function for us now—meanings that will inevitably lead into future understandings. To the extent that we offer to the past the kind of concrete, historical contextualization that we demand for ourselves, we will have more adequate theologies of the Holy Spirit.[87]

Sources for material on the Holy Spirit are diverse. But, as we have noted, *the* primary backdrop for medieval talk about the Spirit is the Bible. Most medieval theologians spent a significant part of their lives commenting on biblical texts, which informed their thinking, their letters, their sermons, and even their more systematic writing of disputed questions and *summae*.[88] Thus, the Holy Spirit is often treated in sections on the annunciation, the baptism of Jesus, and the all-important Spirit passages in John and Paul. Sermons for the feast of Pentecost are valuable inasmuch as they are oriented toward pastoral communication to the broader faith community, revealing how various authors applied the biblical account of the Spirit's coming to their own specific individual and communal settings.

Mystical texts reveal the God met in intense experiences—usually of individuals—and by extension, of the communities and societies in which they lived. Letters show an author's thinking about how the Spirit should function in the lives of others. Prayers reveal images of the God who is addressed and show how the author relates to the Spirit and how the Spirit is seen to relate to the other persons in the Trinity. Other texts include lives of the saints (*vitae*), theological works, and works that are more catechetical in orientation. All of these forms of speech offer distinctive perspectives and reveal different aspects of a community's interpretation of their experiences of Spirit. These genres complement one another, providing a more adequate account of the ways in which a community experienced, thought about, imaged, and wrote about the Holy Spirit.

I share with Barbara Newman, scholar of medieval literature and spirituality, the methodological assumption that religious texts bear witness to religious experience on three counts. First, the subjects of religious experience are persons with developed interiority—conscious and unconscious wishes, anxieties, projects, and beliefs regarding key human concerns such as life, love, and death. Such profound, psychic layers are often affected by, and expressed through, religion. Second, religious experience takes place in complex, dynamic cultures characterized always at some level by struggle. Third, religious experience reveals mysterious, multivalent, often opaque traces of a real and transcendent object.[89] Columba Stewart reinforces this last point by challenging academic colleagues to read spiritual texts more "spiritually." By this he means that students of early texts need to take account of the spiritual concerns of the author as well as the political ones. We need not pray in order to read and interpret texts, but the texts are products of persons who themselves prayed and who wrote texts for others who they believed prayed as well.[90]

Conclusion

The historical theological task is located in the study of the presence of the triune God in history, the contact point where God and humankind "touch" one another. We start with the individual and collective experiences of the Spirit, the gift of God's presence given to us, the fruit of the Spirit's mission.[91] Then we search for metaphors of the Spirit in texts that describe these experiences,[92] thus, taking seriously the faith experience of the individuals and their communities in their social, ecclesial contexts.[93] Authors in the medieval period said more about the Holy Spirit than has been acknowledged. These data give us information, invite to transformation, and also test the criticism that the West's understanding of the experience of the Holy Spirit is disconnected from the Bible, devoid of discussion about the distinct roles of the persons, and unrelated to the ordinary lives of the baptized.

These texts invite us to name our own hungers and questions as citizens of the twenty-first century, for it is from this vantage point that we view and interpret the tradition. While each of us views contemporary needs through her or his own lens, I call attention to a number of key themes. We seek a pneumatology that embraces both intellects and hearts. We value careful systematic reflection on our experience of Spirit and a pneumatology that is theologically and philosophically respectable, intelligible, and coherent. We attend to the concrete, historical unfolding of salvation in everyday life, knowing that the present is held up by past traditions of Bible and Christian history. We resonate with a Holy Spirit who enjoys the fullness of a distinctive role and personhood in the economy (*proprium*), but remains equal and integrally connected within the intra-trinitarian community. We want a three-personed God whose infinite mutual love overflows in relationship to us and the entire universe in our very particular joys and sorrows.

We invite into our lives a Spirit who will bring our spirits to life and transform tendencies in the church to mistrust what Yves Congar calls "the personal principle" (not to be divorced from an "institutional principle" that sees the church as a Spirit-filled communion of persons).[94] We have much to learn from our Quaker and Pentecostal sisters and brothers about trusting the Spirit's voice as it speaks to each person in the community. And beyond Christianity, enhanced knowledge about the particular language and images of the Christian Spirit can enrich interfaith dialogue. Knowledge of our tradition increases the possibility of productive conversation with Buddhists, Hindus, Jews, and Muslims who engage and name their specific understanding of "spirit." At the heart of all religious quests is the desire for fullness of life and justice, the Spirit/spirit's "breath" and "fire" bringing newness to all believers and practitioners of various spiritual paths.

Particularly pressing is the need for the spirit of prophecy. Who among us has the courage to open ourselves to the Spirit's searing invitation to speak truth and peace in humility and simplicity to power, and to pay what is too often the enormous price exacted from prophets and martyrs past and present? Empowered by the Spirit we raise our voices in defense of the poor and marginalized among us and even extend our care to the universe itself. We hunger for a pneumatology that concerns itself with the world on a cosmic as well as a personal level. Finally, we long for a pneumatology that will move us to action, arouse our hearts, and inflame our spirits to become agents of the Spirit, gift and bond of love. Let us turn now to the texts.

∞

Food for Thought

1. What arguments are offered to suggest that current criticisms of past theologies of the Holy Spirit might not be accurate? What have they omitted or misread?

2. What are some strategies that would help systematic theology (theory, abstraction) and spirituality (practice, concreteness) remain more connected? Do you have any ideas of your own to add to what is presented in this chapter?

3. Why does theology need spirituality? Why does spirituality need theology?

4. Discuss an image or a symbol that has significant meaning in your life. Then allow others a chance to comment on this particular image or symbol. Were the associations similar, complementary, or divergent? Did the discussion help elucidate the contribution symbols can make to life's meaning?

5. Language about God is always symbolic. Language functions as our stumbling attempt to catch some small aspect of an ineffably mysterious God. Why do you think people become fearful and angry when new names for God are introduced or recovered from the tradition? Would you like to see the church use a broader range of language about God? Why or why not?

6. What specific language, imagery, and symbolism do you think would best renew our consciousness of the Holy Spirit and motivate us to live our Christian lives more aware of the Spirit's power and presence?

CHAPTER 2

AUGUSTINE OF HIPPO
The Spirit of Courage and Reconciliation

Augustine of Hippo (354–430) set the agenda for trinitarian theology in the West perhaps more than any other theologian. In this chapter, I explore a wide range of texts—many of which have been neglected by systematic theologians—in search of a fuller sense of Augustine's narratives of the Spirit. After a word about the trajectory of pneumatology in the early church, I turn to Augustine's particular interest in the distinctiveness of the trinitarian persons. Then I explore four ways in which Augustine emphasized the action of the Spirit: (1) the Spirit as active principle of church unity and agent of reconciliation; (2) the Spirit as one who helps us overcome fear in order to witness to the gospel with courage; (3) the Spirit as source of intelligent living; (4) the Spirit as love, empowering us to love God and one another, to abide in God, and to enkindle desire that will lead us home.

The Spirit in the Early Church

The early church faced a number of pressing issues related to speech about God.[1] New Testament authors were concerned about the continuity between the Yahweh of the Jews and the emerging God of the followers of Jesus of Nazareth. There was also a need to safeguard monotheism in a world that worshiped many gods. An early issue debated in the church asked whether Jesus was fully divine as well as fully human. Arius, an Alexandrian priest, was worried that if the early church introduced distinctions in God, monotheism would be compromised. This legitimate concern led him to speak about Christ as divine, but not in the same way as the Father was divine. He turned to a common and respected concept of his day—hierarchy—to speak of the Father as first, followed by the Son, a divine but lesser, created being.[2] This often contentious discussion about the divinity of the second person was worked out before, during, and after the ecumenical Council of Nicaea, called in 325 by the first Christian emperor, Constantine. Using technical Greek philosophical language, the council spoke about Christ's relationship to the Father in terms of one substance (*ousia*) and distinct persons (*homoousios*). In this formulation the Father and Son shared both divinity and unity.[3]

It was not until the Council of Chalcedon in 381 that the church addressed the same issue with regard to the Holy Spirit and concluded that the Spirit too was God. In this instance, the church turned to metaphoric language to speak of the Spirit—a language more reminiscent of the Bible. These creedal words are familiar to all Christian worshipers:

> We believe in the Holy Spirit, the Lord, the giver of life,
>   who proceeds from the Father
>   who with the Father and the Son is worshiped
>   and glorified,
>   who has spoken through the prophets.

In the end, the Arians were defeated. Led by Arius's bishop, Alexander, the feisty Athanasius, and the Cappadocian bishop Basil the Great, the church asserted that the Spirit was truly God along with the Son, both equal to the Father.

We need to remember that the issue at the center of these arguments was not some abstract language game. At the heart of these debates were Christian identity and what it meant to be saved, the community's experience of what God had done for the world in Jesus Christ, and how this faith was articulated and passed down to new members of the community. There is a very existential feel to the theological language of the early church. Before there was *doctrine* or *orthodoxy*, there was a community struggling to figure out what it meant to be Christian and to be followers of the "way" of Jesus Christ. Second-century theologian Irenaeus spoke of the Son and the Spirit as the "two hands of God." The Spirit is present in the fluid language of the emerging Christian biblical canon; in catechetical and liturgical formulae; in metaphors of wind and rain, birds and fire; and in the Spirit's effects as the community experienced them. This language offered a freedom of expression and illustration that conveys immediacy and allows a glimpse into the living faith behind the church's early theology.[4]

Augustine's World

In his biography of Augustine, Peter Brown describes Augustine's life and times as characterized by rapid and dramatic change.[5] The superabundant energies of the second and third centuries in Africa had "become a stagnant and affluent backwater" by the fourth.[6] Ordinary folk were oppressed by inflation and high taxes. Augustine and several of his friends escaped to Italy to study and to establish their professions as orators. Eventually Augustine converted to Christianity and later returned to Hippo to take up his responsibilities as bishop at the fringe of the Roman Empire. Augustine would spend eleven years as a teacher of rhetoric, and thirty-five as bishop of Hippo. Brown comments on how Augustine's education helped him develop "a phenomenal memory, a tenacious attention to detail, an art of opening the heart, that still moves as we read his *Confessions*."[7] A seeker of meaning and wisdom, Augustine was drawn to the mysterious, extremist, and persecuted religious movement called Manichaeism.[8] For most of his twenties, Augustine was a "Hearer" in this outlawed sect, which viewed the world in stark dualistic terms of good and evil, light and darkness.

Augustine has become infamous for his youthful affair with a young woman with whom he had a son, Adeodatus, who died at nineteen. But in the culture of the time, such a relationship would not have been unusual. Young men with promising futures might enter a relationship with a less prominent woman and then later "marry up." In the chronology of his new biography of Augustine, James J. O'Donnell lists 371/72 as the year "Augustine marries (wife's name not known)."[9] After his conversion, Augustine divorced himself from sexual activity with some difficulty—visible in the prayer "Lord, make me chaste, but not yet." Perhaps Augustine's perceptions of his failures toward God recounted in his *Confessions* influenced his later understanding of church as a body that includes and welcomes sinners through the power of the Holy Spirit.

In time, Augustine became disillusioned with Manichaeism. In 384, a still-searching Augustine went to Milan, where he heard the sermons of Bishop Ambrose. Prodded by his mother, Augustine eventually turned to the spiritual world of Christianity and was baptized by Ambrose in Milan in 387. In September of the previous year, Augustine had left his job, retired to Cassiciacum with a group of friends, and entered a period of leisure and study that provided the theological backdrop for the rest of his life. His interest in the unity of the human race and in friendship would become more and more pressing when he had to confront divisions in the church as bishop of Hippo. But in the monastic setting at Cassiciacum, Augustine sought to imitate the apostolic community united at Pentecost through the tongues of fire sent by the Spirit—a microcosm of how he would eventually understand the church universal.[10]

However, more change intruded. In 388, Augustine returned to his family's property in North Africa to read and reflect on the philosophical questions that always engaged his inquiring mind. Aware of the custom of conscripting clergy and bishops by fiat, Augustine avoided places where he might have been susceptible to such a mandate. But soon he was thrust into priesthood in Hippo in 391. Burdened with the responsibilities of bishop in a fractious and divided community,[11] Augustine set out systematically to shape the church of Hippo, at times using strong-arm tactics or sarcasm, and even calling out the police to subdue the Donatists, a group within the church who demanded that those who had denied the faith during persecution should be rebaptized before being allowed to return to full standing in the church.[12] We will see below how this elite and perfectionistic concept of church endorsed by the Donatists clashed with Augustine's more inclusive, universal vision.

But Augustine struggled not to despise the sinners in the community. He voiced the conviction—often hard to live out—

that no matter who they were, they remained a part of the community, indeed a part of himself.[13] It is hard not to wonder how Augustine linked the Spirit with his job as a stern but loving figure of authority in the face of "warped, misshapen men."[14] In 410, the Goths sacked Rome, the symbol of culture and stability. In the chaos that ensued, Augustine called for discipline. Using the metaphor of the olive press, Augustine preached, "The world reels under crushing blows, the old man is shaken out; the flesh is pressed, the spirit turns to clear flowing oil."[15]

Augustine's Trinitarian Theology

Augustine's thought is shaped by his concern for an intelligent, persuasive theology and by the pastoral needs of his community. His ideas on the Trinity are perhaps best known through his masterwork, *On the Trinity*. In Augustine's trinitarian theology, he generally speaks first about the one substance of God, and, second, about the divine persons. He turns to multiple sets of triadic analogies as a way to approach the mystery of the three-personed God. Reflecting on his knowledge of human interiority, he employs the language of human memory, intellect, and will to suggest both the unity and the distinctive functions of the three divine persons. Augustine's trinitarian theology is visible also in letters, sermons, and biblical commentaries. Here we see the immediacy and existential quality of his theology, put to use to solve the problems of his community—offering spiritual guidance and settling disputes.

Struggling to explain plurality in God, Augustine portrayed the distinctive roles of the persons in creative and lively ways. Augustine's sense of accountability to the scriptures led him to use language and imagery that point to three persons with quasi-distinct operations, mitigating his preoccupation with establishing the unity of God and God's operations. Augustine called the scriptures the "countenance of God,"[16] and Peter Brown writes that Augustine "had come to believe that the understanding and exposition of the Scriptures was the heart of a bishop's life."[17] Augustine did not easily come to terms with biblical allusions to three persons in God, but he held himself accountable to texts like Luke's description of Jesus' baptism (Luke 3:22). This passage includes the voice of the Father, the human nature assumed by the Son, and the Holy Spirit portrayed as a dove.

In Augustine's world—in which supreme value was given to unity—it would be impossible, except for an explicit revelation, to arrive at a triune God. For Augustine, this revelatory language functions to teach us that while the persons are "inseparable Trinity, yet they are a Trinity." And just as we cannot pronounce all three names at the same time—even though their existence is inseparable—"so in some places of Scripture also, they are by certain created things presented to us distinctively and in mutual relation to each other."[18] For Augustine, the Trinity is not something separate from the God who is revealed. The Trinity *is* the God who is revealed.

Augustine further explains biblical speech about distinct persons in terms of God's need to accommodate human weakness. In true Neoplatonic fashion, Augustine seems embarrassed by the human fall into variety. In a letter written in 389 in response to a question from his friend Nebridius about why the incarnation is ascribed only to the Son, when belief states that all operations in the Trinity are common, Augustine offers a rather "pale" explanation. Augustine held that the human fall from unity to plurality explains why we cannot grasp the unity of operations and thus requires that they be presented in distinct ways.[19] Four years later, in *On Faith and the Creed*, Augustine addresses the difficulty of identifying the uniqueness of the Holy Spirit. He acknowledges that the lack of previous discussion on the Holy Spirit by learned and distinguished investigators of the scriptures makes it difficult to "obtain an intelligent conception of what also constitutes his special individuality (*proprium*): in virtue of which special individuality it comes to be the case that we cannot call Him either the Son or the Father, but only the Holy Spirit; excepting that they predicate Him to be the Gift of God, so that we may believe God not to give a gift inferior to Himself."[20]

On the other hand, Augustine is credited with being the first in Christian history to formulate a theology of the Holy Spirit as Love within the Trinity and therefore as properly Gift to the church.[21] His understanding of intra-trinitarian life leads naturally to the missions of the persons as Word and Love. Augustine's pneumatology thus portrays the Spirit as connected to the community of the faithful in an integral, experiential way. In *On the Trinity*, Augustine also speaks of the special, distinctive nature of the second sending of the Spirit at Pentecost.[22] He says, "But that He was given twice was certainly a significant *economy*, which we will discuss in its place...."[23] Augustine explicitly links the Spirit to both the divine and human realms: "and so the Holy Spirit is not only the Spirit of the Father and of the Son who gave Him, but He is also called ours, who have received him....Therefore the Spirit is both the Spirit of God who gave Him, and *ours* who have received Him."[24] This Spirit is not the spirit by which we are human beings but the Spirit by which we are made holy: "the Spirit is ours in another mode, *viz.* that in which we also say, 'Give us this day our bread.'"[25]

I suggest that Augustine's drive toward precise metaphysical speculation did not preclude discussion about the three persons, especially in reference to the daily life, pastoral needs, and struggles of the community. It is the case that his skepticism about plurality in God led him to emphasize the unity in God and God's operations. But his commitment to the biblical witness and the budding theological tradition of a three-personed God fueled his significant efforts to articulate distinct divine roles in the context of the life of the North African church. We cannot fully grasp Augustine's understanding of God's identity without attending to texts in which he speaks of the divine persons' distinctive activities—language that reveals liveliness, warmth, and engagement.

There has been some debate about when Augustine's interest in the Spirit becomes visible. Patristic scholar J. Patout Burns suggests that "Augustine moves from a mysticism of the second person of the Trinity in his early writings to a mysticism of the third person in the later writings."[26] But Yves Congar sees evidence of Augustine's interest in the Spirit from quite early in his career. Already in 393, in the text *On Faith and the Creed*, Augustine articulated a need for a theology of the Holy Spirit.[27]

> Many books have been written by scholarly and spiritual men on the Father and the Son....The Holy Spirit, has, on the other hand, not yet been studied with as much care and by so many great and learned commentators on

the scriptures that it is easy to understand his special character and know why we cannot call him either Son or Father, but only Holy Spirit.[28]

As noted, Augustine's most fully developed and systematic theology of the Holy Spirit takes shape in *On the Trinity*, begun in 399 but not finished until 419. I suggest that in addition to Augustine's awareness of the late-fourth-century need to reflect theologically on the Spirit, he was led to focus on the Spirit because of the fractious situation of the church at Hippo, for which he was responsible as its ecclesial leader.

Metaphors of the Spirit

Augustine's references to the Holy Spirit are widespread and diverse. Out of this field, I have identified four prominent themes: (1) the Spirit as agent of unity and reconciliation; (2) the Spirit as one who casts out fear; (3) the Spirit as source of intelligent Christian living; (4) the Spirit as love.

The Spirit as Agent of Unity and Reconciliation

We have noted how Augustine struggled in the midst of a failing empire to combat forces that he judged inimical to orthodoxy and the church's integrity. Augustine envisioned a universal church, capable not only of including saint and sinner alike but also of influencing the wider world for the good. At every turn, Augustine invoked the Holy Spirit to support his idea of church against that of the Donatists, who preferred an elite church of the pure and sinless in both head and members.[29] The origin of the Donatist controversy can be traced back to the great persecution of Diocletian in 303–5. As emperor, Diocletian (r. 284–305) instituted a number of measures in a successful attempt to regain control over the Roman Empire, protect its borders from invading enemies, and reestablish unity. In 303, he tried to effect unity by issuing four harsh decrees requiring Christians to participate in the imperial cult and offer homage to the emperor.

During this period of persecution, some Christians capitulated and handed over their Bibles to the persecutors. Others died as martyrs for the faith—one of whom was Donatus, for whom the movement was named. Opposed to any compromise in the Christian community, the Donatists refused to receive back into the Christian community those who had not maintained their loyalty to the faith. Those who did return were expected to undergo a second baptism.

The tension between Augustine's "Catholic" and the Donatist viewpoints was visceral and violent.[30] In Hippo, the Donatists were the majority party, supported by prominent landowners and local officials. At one point the Donatist bishops successfully organized a boycott, convincing local bakers not to bake bread for the Catholics.[31] For Donatists, sinful bishops prayed ineffectual prayers and administered questionable sacraments. Both groups used popular song as a way to influence potential supporters. In 394, Augustine wrote a 297–verse song entitled *A.B.C. Against the Donatists*, which included the metaphor of the wheat and the tares growing together (Matt 3:30) to describe a church made up of both saints and sinners.[32] Augustine's sarcasm was evident when he wrote: "The clouds roll with thunder, that the House of the Lord shall be built throughout the earth: and these frogs sit in their marsh and croak—We are the only Christians!"[33]

Since the early fourth century, African Christians had been divided about how to deal with the split between the ideal holy church and the actual sinful church. Also at stake was the question of the church's stance toward the larger society. The Donatists saw themselves as a new Israel, faithful to the law and called to preserve and protect a community over against a society that in turn either persecuted them or demanded unacceptable compromises. "Innocence, ritual purity, meritorious suffering, predominate in their image of themselves."[34]

Peter Brown describes how the imagination of African Christians had become riveted on the idea of the church as a preserve of safety and cleanliness in a world ruled by demonic powers. Africans came to church, he says, not because they were thirsty and burdened but to survive in a battlefield.[35] Both the Donatists and Augustine compare the church to Noah's ark (Gen 6), but to different ends. W. H. C. Frend notes the presence among the Donatists of Cyprian's popular metaphor of the church as the ark—"within the saved, outside the drowning multitudes." Images of an ark and a dove on a sculptured pillar of a Donatist church in central Numidia portray the church of the saints watched over by the Holy Spirit.[36]

For Augustine, on the other hand, the church lived out of a confidence that it could absorb, transform, and perfect the world around it without losing its identity—an identity that was dependent not on the holiness of its members but on the power of Christ and the Spirit.[37] In *On the Gospel of John*, Augustine says, "if the ark was a figure of the church, you see indeed that in the present deluge of the world, the church must of necessity contain both kinds, as well the ravens as the dove. Who are the ravens? They who seek their own. Who are the doves? They who seek the things that are Christ's."[38]

In an effort to calm the fears and doubts of those wondering about the identity of the true church (and also to threaten them a bit), Augustine calls on the Spirit to support his portrayal of a church with clear boundaries for insiders (Augustine's church) and outsiders (the Donatists). He says, "whoever has the Holy Spirit is in the church...whoever is outside this Church hasn't got the Holy Spirit."[39] Those can be sure of having the Holy Spirit who "consent through sincere charity firmly to attach their minds to the unity."[40] Within the church, Augustine warns those members who belong insincerely by deceit and dissimulation.[41] Those outside the church who "hate the grace of peace and who do not hold on to the fellowship of unity" have "absolutely no share in this gift of the Holy Spirit."[42] Outside the church the Holy Spirit gives life to no one. Outside the church the enemies of unity are blocked from partaking in divine love.

For Augustine, the sending of the Holy Spirit revealed a trustworthy God who fulfills all promises.[43] But he warned his congregation that just as the soul departs from a severed limb, so the Spirit departs from those who cut themselves off from the church.[44] In a Pentecost sermon, he further develops the metaphor of the body.

> It can happen in the human body—or rather from the body—that one part is cut off, a hand, a finger, a foot; does the soul follow the amputated part? When it was in the body, it was alive; cut off, it loses life. In the same way too Christian men and women are Catholics, while

they are alive in the body; cut off, they have become heretics, the Spirit doesn't follow the amputated part. So if you wish to be alive with the Holy Spirit, hold on to loving-kindness, love truthfulness, long for oneness, that you may attain to everlastingness. Amen.[45]

In his commentary on the Gospel of John, Augustine says "there is nothing that a Christian ought to dread so much as to be separated from Christ's body."[46]

When Constantine officially permitted the practice of Christianity within the Roman Empire beginning in 313, Christian leaders could depend on the support of the Roman government against those who developed divergent doctrines and practices. As the violence of the Donatists escalated, Stilicho, the imperial minister at Ravenna issued an imperial Edict of Unity in 403, allowing for punishment of the Donatists as heretics. As Augustine's intolerance for disorder hardened, and in spite of his misgivings about this policy, which contravened his commitment to leniency and open conversation, he enforced the Edict in Hippo.[47] Augustine employs Luke's parable about compelling guests to come to the wedding banquet (Luke 14:23) to force the Donatists into the fold. "Compel them to come in. Use compulsion outside, so freedom can arise once they are inside."[48]

But Augustine's sometimes harsh language about the Spirit's presence or absence to ecclesial insiders and outsiders must be juxtaposed with his struggle with reconciliation. Against the Donatists, Augustine underlined the importance of the forgiveness that can be offered only within the church and only through the power of God. The Holy Spirit is the Gift who enables communion with God and with each other. For Augustine, the remission of sins is the first blessing of God's goodness in the Holy Spirit. In his commentary on Psalm 8, he locates the bowels of the mercy of God in the Holy Spirit.[49] Against this gratuitous gift, the impenitent heart stands as an affront of enormous proportion.

In a number of texts, sermons, and letters, Augustine comments on Matthew 12:31–32: "Therefore I tell you, every sin and blasphemy will be forgiven, but the blasphemy against the Spirit will not be forgiven."[50] Part of the context for Augustine's interest in, and understanding of, the sin against the Holy Spirit was the fierce debate going on about the contrast between the ideal unity and holiness of the church and the often unedifying behavior of its members. In a sermon, Augustine excoriates the recalcitrant individual who remains impassive in the "persevering hardness of an impenitent heart." Such a heart is the "blasphemy of the Spirit which shall not be forgiven, neither in this world, nor in the world to come."[51]

Augustine also spoke of the effects of the remission of sin. In his exposition on the Apostles' Creed, written for the bishops of Hippo-Regius in 393 when Augustine was still a presbyter, he elaborated on the sources and fruits of reconciliation, which he relates to the words in Paul's letter to the Romans: "we rejoice in our sufferings, knowing that suffering produces endurance, and endurance produces character, and character produces hope, and hope does not disappoint us, because God's love has been poured into our hearts through the Holy Spirit which has been given to us" (Rom 5:5)—perhaps Augustine's favorite biblical reference to the Spirit. Reconciliation in love, he says, makes us sons and daughters of God (1 John 4:18); casts out fear (Rom 8:15); fills us with the spirit of liberty by which we cry, "Abba, Father" (Rom 8:15); calls us back into friendship and acquaints us with all the secret things of God (John 16:13).[52]

Almost twenty-five years later, in his *Treatise concerning the Correction of the Donatists*, written to the tribune Boniface in 417, Augustine characterizes the fruits of pardon in this way. "The prince of sin, the spirit who is divided against himself, should no more reign in us...we should thenceforward be made the temple of the Holy Spirit, and receive Him, by whom we are cleansed through receiving pardon, to dwell in us, to work, increase, and perfect righteousness."[53] One is reminded here of Paul's interior struggle in Romans: "For I do not do what I want, but I do the very thing I hate" (Rom 7:15). John Cavadini speaks of Augustine's articulation of the ambiguous, "mixed" character of life as one of his most characteristic and enduring accomplishments.[54] Augustine linked this freedom from inner division to the work of the Spirit, visible in those community members who are no longer slaves to the war within, but experienced fully only in the eschaton.

But in addition to defining the church over against its enemies, Augustine wanted to establish the Spirit's ongoing presence and function in the church. In a Pentecost sermon delivered in

412, he lays down the challenge to those who suggest that the Spirit no longer visits the community. He asks rhetorically, "Isn't the Holy Spirit being given nowadays, then, brothers and sisters? Anyone who thinks that isn't worthy to receive it. It certainly is given nowadays."[55] Evidently, one of the arguments used to suggest the Spirit's absence was the disappearance of the gift of tongues. As part of his response to this complaint, Augustine altered the Pentecost account in Acts 2:3–4, positing that *each* individual spoke in *all* tongues. The reason Christians no longer spoke in tongues was because the promise of Pentecost had been fulfilled. At Pentecost one person speaking in the tongues of all nations pointed to the unity of the church.[56] The sign of the Spirit's presence for Augustine was the unity of a world church that embraced all languages.[57]

> Among you, after all, is being fulfilled what was being prefigured in those days, when the Holy Spirit came. Because just as then, whoever received the Holy Spirit, even as one person, started speaking all languages; so too now the unity itself is speaking all languages through all nations; and it is by being established in this unity that you have the Holy Spirit, you that do not break away in any schism from the Church of Christ which speaks all languages.[58]

The variety of tongues given by the Spirit pointed to the unity of the world church that Augustine envisioned, contrary to what he perceived as the narrow, parochial vision of the Donatists.[59]

The Holy Spirit is also the Gift that makes possible communion with God and with each other. In another sermon, Augustine links the bond of love that is the Holy Spirit within the Trinity with its effects in the community of faith. He says, "The Father and the Son have willed that we enter into communion among ourselves and with them through That which is common to them, and to bind us into one by this Gift which the two possess together, that is by the Holy Spirit, God and gift of God. It is in him in fact, that we are reconciled with the Divinity and take our delight in it."[60]

Augustine's intense drive toward unity and his desire for communion among the faithful was grounded in part in the decidedly mixed character of the church's members and the daily, life-and-death struggle with the Donatists. Using the scriptures as a launching pad, he turns to the Holy Spirit as a force for unity and reconciliation within each individual and within a divided community. He persuades, cajoles, threatens, and anathematizes in the interest of preserving what he sees as the life, integrity, and future of the church. Augustine's talk about the Spirit gives the reader a clear sense that the Spirit was not an abstract principle, but rather a present and compelling force, engaged in the struggle to preserve the church as Augustine envisioned it.

Preaching without Fear

In the accounts of Pentecost, a prominent effect of the Holy Spirit's descent was the elimination of fear and the creation of courage in the hearts of the apostles. The Spirit empowered the disciples to bear witness to the risen Lord.[61] In several instances, Augustine focuses on Peter as an embodiment of this courage. I cite at some length a stirring description from Augustine's commentary on the Gospel of John.

> And then that Spirit, pervading him thus with the fullness of richer grace, kindled his hitherto frigid heart to such a witness-bearing for Christ, and unlocked those lips that in their previous tremor had suppressed the truth, that, when all on whom the Holy Spirit had descended were speaking in the tongues of all nations to the crowds of Jews collected around, he alone broke forth before the others in the promptitude of his testimony in behalf of Christ....And if any one would enjoy the pleasure of gazing on a sight so charming in its holiness, let him read the Acts of the Apostles: (2.5) and there let him be filled with amazement at the preaching of the blessed Peter, over whose denial of this Master he had just been mourning; there let him behold that tongue, itself translated from diffidence to confidence, from bondage to liberty, converting to the confession of Christ the tongues of so many of His enemies, not one of which he could bear when lapsing himself into denial.

And what shall I say more? In him there shone forth
such an effulgence of grace, and such a fullness of the
Holy Spirit, and such a weight of most precious truth
poured from the lips of the preacher, that he transformed that vast multitude of Jews....[62]

In this rhetorically powerful passage, we glimpse how Augustine
envisioned the working of the Spirit, and possibly his own identification with Peter's effective eloquence. One can conjecture that
Augustine identified with Peter, desiring that the Spirit function in
him as it did in Peter at Pentecost. The elements of commonality
are several. I note three. First, the *Confessions* reveal what Augustine
came to regard as his own betrayal of the truth prior to his conversion. His pronounced commitment to proclaiming the truth of
the one true God he had encountered in Christianity can be seen
as a correction of his earlier life.

Second, as a rhetor, Augustine had high expectations of his
preaching skills. In his response to a request for some help in catechizing the uninstructed from a Carthaginian deacon, brother
Deogratias, Augustine writes,

Indeed with me, too, it is almost always the fact that my
speech displeases myself. For I am covetous of something better...when my capacities of expression prove
inferior to my inner apprehensions, I grieve over the
inability which my tongue has betrayed in answering to
my heart. For it is my wish that he who hears me should
have the same complete understanding of the subject
which I have myself; and I perceive that I fail to speak in
a manner calculated to effect that....[63]

Third, Augustine perceived the decadence of his society and the
forces of personal and social evil to be daunting, requiring a super-
human love and intelligence—gifts with which he describes the
Spirit-filled Peter.

For Augustine, the Spirit's distinctive role is as an agent of
visible change and renewal. Frigid hearts, locked lips, diffidence,
fear of speaking the truth, bondage, and mourning for sin—all are
transformed in the power of the Holy Spirit. The Spirit's presence

is described as a fuller effulgence of grace, a presence that compelled Peter to witness to Christ with astonishing ease. Through Peter's words and actions, the truth and power of Christ, given through the Spirit, were visible and effective, leading to the conversion and renewal of those who were once Christ's enemies. One can imagine the churches in Augustine's Hippo in desperate need of the Spirit's gifts, visible in those who could preach and witness to the truth of Christ's redeeming love.

The Holy Spirit as Source of Intelligent Christian Living

For Augustine, the Spirit also fosters understanding.[64] In addition to the traditional connection between knowledge, understanding, and the Word, Augustine also follows the scriptural lead that associates understanding with the Spirit, and love with the Word. In his commentary on John 16:13—the Holy Spirit leads us into all truth—Augustine compares the knowledge that comes from our own spirit with the knowledge of God that is the Holy Spirit. He says,

> So also the things of God know no man, but the Spirit of God. We with our spirit, God with His: so, however, that God with His Spirit knows also what goes on within us; but we are not able, without His Spirit, to know what takes place in God.[65]

In other words, the Holy Spirit is the power—in both God and human beings—that makes it possible for persons, divine and human, to know one another. This bold and provocative expression of divine–human mutuality invites further reflection about how we might be limiting the role of the Spirit in our spiritual lives.

Augustine understands this function of the Holy Spirit to be a completion, a fulfillment, a more mature stage in the experience of faith in which the believer not only has faith, but *knows* it. Commenting on the role of the dove at Jesus' baptism (John 1:32–33), Augustine argues that at the baptism, John the Baptist *learned* something: not that Christ is God, not that he baptizes with the Holy Spirit, but—against the Donatists—that the effectiveness of baptism rests in Christ, not in good or bad ministers.[66]

Augustine also puzzles over the passage in John (14:15–17) in which the Lord says that if the apostles keep the commandments, God will send another Paraclete to abide with them. How can the Spirit be sent a second time, when the prerequisite for the Paraclete's coming—loving and keeping the commandments—demands that the Spirit be already present? Augustine's solution is to understand Pentecost as a fuller possession of the Spirit. Augustine distinguishes between possessing the gift of Love which is the Holy Spirit and the further stage of being conscious that one has the gift. He says,

> We are therefore to understand that he who loves has already the Holy Spirit, and by what he has, becomes worthy of a fuller possession, that by having the more he may love the more....They had Him in a hidden way, they were yet to receive Him in a way that was manifest; for this present possession had also a bearing on that fuller gift of the Holy Spirit, that they might come to a conscious knowledge of what they had.[67]

In this passage, Augustine reveals the importance of both heart and head. Love is primary and enough, but the fullness of God's purpose includes awareness of our love and knowledge of God.

A further instance in which Augustine connects the Holy Spirit with understanding is in his treatise on the Sermon on the Mount. Commenting on Paul's first letter to the Corinthians (12:3), "No one can say that Jesus is Lord except by the Holy Spirit," Augustine describes what must obtain in order to make this statement of faith properly. It requires that the speaker be engaged "with the deliberate consent of the will....But truly and properly those parties say it whose utterance in speech really represents their will and intention."[68] Belief is not intended to be a mindless, empty "going-along," but rather an integral part of one's whole being—mind, heart, speech, and behavior.

We might inquire how Augustine's plea for an intelligent Christianity squares with his commitment to nurture an inclusive church. Against the Donatists, Augustine clearly did not advocate a church of the pure—an intellectual or spiritual elite. He drives this point home in a letter to Bishop Evodius, who asks if the text of 1 Corinthians (14:38), "He that is ignorant shall be ignored," refers to those who cannot comprehend the unity of the Trinity. Augustine responds,

> For if Christ died for those only who with clear intelligence can discern these things, our labor in the Church is almost spent in vain. But if, as is the fact, crowds of common people, possessing no great strength of intellect, run to the Physician in the exercise of faith, with the result of being healed by Christ, and Him crucified, that "where sin has abounded, grace may much more abound." (Rom. 5.20)...many glorying in the cross of Christ, and not withdrawing from that same path, attain, notwithstanding their ignorance of those things, which some with most profound subtlety investigate, unto that eternity, truth, and love—that is, unto enduring, clear, and full felicity—in which to those who abide, and see, and love, all things are plain.[69]

Augustine was wise enough to know that book learning was not the only kind of knowledge when it came to God, but he clearly longed for the ideal Christian who embraced the faith not only in love but also with intelligence.

As philosopher and scholar, Augustine was committed to the "highest peak of human reason" within the realm of faith.[70] He admits that, in the end, the Spirit infuses us who are infirm with a "certain learned ignorance."[71] But in the heat of daily life in the church, he combated the literalism and anti-intellectualism around him: "Far be it from us to think that God would hate in us that which distinguishes us from the beasts....Love understands wholeheartedly."[72] The Holy Spirit played a key role in this loving understanding. Not only was Augustine committed to speculative thought, brilliantly displayed in *On the Trinity*, but he was also intent on inviting others to understand the faith, so that they might open themselves to the Spirit's power and become intelligent Christians in their own right. A good example of this drive to lead his congregation to understanding is found in a sermon on the ways in which faith allows us to see what is unseen in those things that we do see: "God has made you a rational animal, set you over the cattle, formed you after His Own image....Don't be like a horse and mule, which have no understanding" (Ps 32:9).[73]

Thus, without the Spirit's presence, individuals may hear about the good news of salvation, but they would be unable to know the truth about God's life; to realize that God dwells within (1 John 3:24; 4:13); or to proclaim that "Jesus is Lord."[74] For Augustine, the Christian life is a longing for home that admits of growth and development. It is as if he says, Don't be stupid, but rather, live in the Spirit, that is, seek understanding, vision, wisdom, and the joy that accompanies ease in being good. The presence of love and the gifts and fruits are signs of the Holy Spirit's presence, but consciousness of that love is a fuller gift. In a suggestive rather than explicit way, Augustine connects the fullness of the Spirit's truth with a mature faith. Thus, he reminds us that the Spirit not only empowers belief but also enables Christians to come to maturity—that is, to know, to will, and to rejoice in that belief in an intentional way.

The Holy Spirit and Love[75]

Scholars consistently identify Augustine's understanding of the Holy Spirit as the bond of love between the first and second persons in the Trinity as a notable original contribution to the theology of the Holy Spirit. In addition to linking the Father and the Son, Augustine also saw the Spirit as connecting the world with God.[76] Thus, the Spirit is able to bring together things that are different without overshadowing their uniqueness.[77] In *On the Trinity*, Augustine writes, "Therefore the Holy Spirit, whom God has given us, makes us to abide in God and God in us; and this is what love does....Therefore God the Holy Spirit, who proceeds from the Father, when He has been given to humans, inflames them to the love of God and of neighbor and is Himself love."[78] In Sermon 21, Augustine again emphasizes the intimacy of love. "The Father and the Son have willed that we enter into communion among ourselves and with them through the One who is common to them, and to bind us into one by this Gift which the two possess together, that is by the Holy Spirit, God and gift of God. It is in

Him in fact, that we are reconciled with the Divinity and take our delight in it."[79]

Biblically this connection is anchored in Romans 5:5, a passage that runs like a leitmotif throughout Augustine's corpus. As we have seen, in his struggle to maintain the orthodoxy and integrity of the church against what he sees as false competing positions, Augustine literally hammers away at the ways in which the Holy Spirit gathers the church into a unity, reflecting the Holy Spirit's unifying role within the Trinity.[80] At Pentecost, the apostles speak in all tongues because they belong to a church whose unity of members is to be of one mind through charity.[81] And in what today may seem a quaint yet provocative exegesis of Isaiah's description of the Holy Spirit as the finger of God (53:7), Augustine says,

> But inasmuch as it is through the Holy Spirit that God's gifts are divided to His saints, in order that, although they vary in their capacities, they may nevertheless not lapse from the concord of charity, and inasmuch as it is especially in the fingers that there appears a certain kind of division, while nevertheless there is no separation from unity, this may be the explanation of the phrase.[82]

Further, this unifying love bears fruit. In the midst of the struggle of life, the Holy Spirit's love enables believers to love their neighbors as themselves (Gal 5:14). God the Holy Spirit, who is Love, is given to us and inflames us to the love of God and neighbor.[83] The Spirit empowers us to choose the good, draws us toward our true selves in God.

> Free choice alone, if the way of truth is hidden, avails for nothing but sin; and when the right action and the true aim has begun to appear clearly, there is still no doing, no devotion, no good life, unless it be also delighted in and loved. And that it may be loved, the love of God is shed abroad in our hearts, not by the free choice whose spring is in ourselves, but through the Holy Spirit which is given us.[84]

This emphasis on love of neighbor and the common good provides a healthy caution to aspects of the reigning anthropology in the twenty-first century that sees the human person as an autonomous agent, unhinged from others in a *laissez-faire*, "live-and-let-live" world.

In 421, Augustine wrote a theological treatise entitled *Enchiridion*, described as a handbook on faith, hope, and love. At the end of this work, Augustine emphasizes that the aim of all the commandments is love, a love that embraces love of God and love of neighbor, on which hang the law, the prophets, the gospel, and the apostles.[85] But there is more. The Spirit at Pentecost allows Christians to fulfill the law in loving God and neighbor, "not only without the sense of its being burdensome, but even with a joyful mind."[86]

No doubt, Augustine intended this message for himself as well as for his hearers. At times, the weight of his responsibilities must have indeed seemed burdensome. But the Spirit's important role as "keeper of the joy," offers hope that the command to take up the Lord's easy burden in love can be fulfilled and even extended to one's enemies (Matt 11:20).[87] For Augustine, the unity that joins believers together as members of one body can be effected only by the love that is poured out by the Holy Spirit, a love that quickens and enlivens both individual members of the church and the body as a whole. Faith unites. Understanding quickens. Augustine knew this experience of church firsthand, and that is why he felt dread at the thought that anyone would be separated from the body of Christ.[88]

Extending his understanding of the Spirit as bond of love, Augustine speaks of the Holy Spirit's link with human desire. Following on the Spirit's gift of repentance in baptism, the Holy Spirit brings fire and fervor to love.[89] Augustine speaks of the drive that compels us to migrate home, a place of peace symbolized by the dove. The tongues at Pentecost caused the dead in spirit to be "pricked in their hearts and converted."[90] "Therefore, that you may love God, let God dwell in you, and love Himself in you, that is, to His love let Him move you, enkindle, enlighten, arouse you."[91]

Augustine also associates the Spirit of desire with prayer. Paul assured the Romans that in their weakness and inability to pray, the Holy Spirit comes to their assistance (Rom 8:26). Augustine comments that it is not within the Trinity that the Holy Spirit groans, but rather the Spirit groans because he makes us groan. He goes on, "Nor is it little matter that the Holy Spirit teaches us to groan, for He gives us to know that we are sojourners in a foreign land, and He teaches us to sigh after our native country: and through that very longing do we groan."[92]

In a letter to Proba, a widow from a noble and wealthy Roman family, Augustine included a little treatise on prayer.[93] Proba sought Augustine's opinion about Paul's statement in Romans 8:26 that we know not for what we should pray. His response is a reflection on the good and bad desires of the heart. Since Proba is a woman of wealth and position, Augustine attributes the power to extinguish a desire for riches to the Holy Spirit, urging her to thirst and long for God alone (Ps 63:1). "A person lives in those things which he loves, which he greatly desires, and in which he believes himself to be blessed."[94] The image of the Holy Spirit groaning within us comes to life in the following passage:

> To use much speaking in prayer is to employ a superfluity of words in asking a necessary thing; but to prolong prayer is to have the heart throbbing with continued pious emotion towards Him to whom we pray. For in most cases prayer consists more in groaning than in speaking, in tears rather than in words. But He sets our tears in His sight, and our groaning is not hidden from Him who made all things by the word, and does not need human words.[95]

Conclusion

For Augustine, then, the Holy Spirit had a number of important and practical roles in the church and in the believer's journey to God. Contrary to contemporary theological opinion, Augustine did not relegate the Spirit to the wings offstage, but saw the Spirit as an existential force in the life of the individual believer and of the ecclesial community. For Augustine, the Spirit calls and empowers the church to the very difficult task of living in unity—loving and forgiving one another. It is the Spirit, he says, who teaches us the way of charity, bends the knee to God for us so that we may know the amazing knowledge of the love of Christ. The Spirit casts out fear, giving courage to speak and witness to the Word of God in the world. He saw the Spirit as a force leading believers to a full and mature knowledge of the things of God and as the bond of love within the Trinity, in the world and between the two.

What in Augustine's understanding of the Spirit triggers in us a flash of recognition that links his world and church to the world and church of the twenty-first century? We continue to ask: What is the church? Who is the Holy Spirit? Are there postmodern parallels to the Roman Empire, the barbarians, the Donatists? Do we long for a church that is inclusive or exclusive? How do our actions conform to our professed desires? How do we understand individual versus institutional charisms? What does the Spirit teach us about our response to the rampant individualism of our culture?

The Spirit can help us name the divisive tensions that separate us—issues of gender, sexual orientation, literalism, inculturation, tension among world religions, ecological concerns. We call upon the Spirit to shed light and bring unity in the midst of these debates. We need to open ourselves to the Spirit's gifts of discernment that allow us to respond in love when groups lightly claim the authority of the Spirit about deeply divisive issues. The Spirit breathing within us nurtures our abilities to get at the truth and distinguish between good and bad spirits. The Spirit moves us to keep tensions creative rather than destructive.

As a community, we struggle to distinguish genuine unity from uniformity. It is dangerous to claim upon the Spirit to defend the kind of unity that excludes or diminishes others who are different from us. When we feel overwhelmed by the pluralism of the world, it is all too easy to retreat to sameness or to an unexamined past. Our brief examination of Augustine's world should disabuse us of nostalgia for a "golden age" that, of course, never existed.[96] Finding ways to be of one heart with others who see Christianity differently, follow the paths of other religions, or profess no religion at all, is crucial to our survival as a human community. But this pressing need should not distract us from realizing that the Spirit's power functions equally to champion diversity and plurality. Here too, we need to distinguish between a destructive tribal pluralism and one that is life-enhancing because grounded in the Spirit. Process theologian Blair Reynolds notes that Augustine's concept of Spirit reflects not only God's immutability but also God's dynamic relationship with the world. "There is, in Augustine, a strong recognition of the Spirit as the presence of a loving, vital will" that involves contingency, interdependency and novelty, a creative energy that perfects Christians and their world.[97]

Prayerful reflection on themes of unity and diversity suggests that there are threads of continuity between Augustine's times and our own. At the least, we have to acknowledge that Augustine did not stay on the sidelines, but jumped into the fray with both feet and passionately engaged the struggles of his time. While we do not want to imitate him in all his choices, we cannot but admire his love of the church and his wholehearted dedication to shape it as an open, culture-influencing community.[98] It is also clear that he called on the Spirit to accompany him and his church along the way. He challenges us to allow the Spirit to pour forth love into our hearts in our time and place.

In the end, it is the Spirit who finally brings us to rest.[99] In his exegesis of Genesis 1:2 at the end of the *Confessions*, Augustine discusses why the Holy Spirit alone was said to be "borne over the waters":

> In your Gift we rest; there we enjoy you....By your Gift we are inflamed, and are borne upwards; we wax hot inwardly, and go forwards. We ascend your ways that be in our heart (Ps 84.5), and sing a song of degrees; we glow inwardly with your fire, with your good fire, and we go, because we go upwards to the peace of Jerusalem; for glad was I when they said to me, "Let us go into the house of the Lord" (Ps 122:1). There hath your good pleasure placed us, that we may desire no other thing than to dwell there for ever.[100]

⌒⌒

Food for Thought

1. Do you experience the church as basically unified or fragmented? If we live, worship, and converse only with those who hold the same positions as we do, is genuine unity possible? (For example, a pacifist pastor struggles to be open to pro-war members of his congregation,

and vice versa.) How deeply do we really yearn for an inclusive church? Do you believe that the Spirit has the power to connect what is different without overshadowing uniqueness? What have you done recently to nurture unity in the body of Christ?

2. Describe what you have learned about the specific context in which Augustine lived; then note similarities or differences between the church/society of Hippo and the church/society to which you belong. Do you agree with Augustine that the church should strive to influence the whole world?

3. After reading about Augustine's concerns for the church's orthodoxy, inclusiveness, and responsibility to influence the world for the good, discuss the practice in some Christian communities of refusing communion to Christians of denominations other than their own. How do you think the Spirit is leading in such situations?

4. Just like everyone else, Christians disagree with one another. At times, some even feel called in conscience to separate themselves from the church, protesting what they see as sin or simply wrong directions taken in the church. In Augustine's case, the Donatists are likely to have been sincere in their efforts, as was Augustine. Did he do the right thing? What are signs that disagreements are authentic or, instead, driven by ego and material gain?

5. Whether pastoral leader, lay volunteer, or member of a congregation or parish, how does fear operate in your life? How does it block the Spirit's power working within? How would you design an instrument to help a faith community identify and come to terms with its fears?

6. Augustine was determined to invite everyone in the church to an intelligent faith. Some Christian denominations take pride in being thoughtful and intellectually informed about the faith, but lack hearts on fire that are

moved by Spirit; others rely on ritual to nurture their faith and don't feel the need to ask questions, read, study, or seek the Spirit's help in understanding the scriptures and tradition; yet others may lack both a mature, intelligent faith and spiritual enthusiasm. Where are you and your church on this continuum? Where would you like it to be? What advice do you think Augustine might give you?

CHAPTER 3

HILDEGARD OF BINGEN
The Spirit's "Greening" Power

Holy Spirit, making life alive,
moving in all things, root of all creation,
cleansing the cosmos of every impurity,
effacing sin, anointing wounds.
You are glistening and praiseworthy life,
you awaken and re-awaken everything that is.[1]

The World of the Twelfth Century

In this chapter, we leap from the fourth to the twelfth century. The following historical overview provides the context for both Hildegard of Bingen (1098–1179), a Benedictine prioress in the Rhineland, Germany, and Bernard of Clairvaux (1090–1153), a Cistercian abbot in France. The twelfth century was like a bridge, bringing to fulfillment the world of monasticism and sowing the seeds for a future scholasticism. The former prospered on free symbolic associations and employed language laced with biblical allusions. The latter found a home in the emerging university, in which Aristotelian philosophical categories and reason were pressed into service—Thomas Aquinas is perhaps the most well-known exemplar. In the twelfth century, Latin Christendom rediscovered the riches of Greco-Roman philosophy and the theology of the Eastern fathers of the church. Adding to this intellectual ferment was the growing knowledge of Islam, which brought unsettling consequences.

Some scholars have dubbed the twelfth century a "renaissance." Although others quibble with the adequacy of this term, it was a time of reform, renewal, and exploration, characterized by a spirit of questioning and reevaluation of every aspect of life—social, spiritual, and intellectual.[2] About 1050, a world that referred all reality to the supernatural began to give way to curiosity about human experience and capabilities. Analytical introspection became an arena for discovering the truth. The power of the human mind was evident as it moved from discovery by trial and error to knowledge of reality governed by natural law. Technological inventions were abundant: waterpower was harnessed in mill wheels as well as hydraulic wheels that enabled one horse to do the work of twenty-five; windmills; machines that could store power through weights and geared wheels; new armaments and means of transport; draft collars for horses and oxen and the mechanical clock. These discoveries fueled a passion for learning that led to the rapid spread of schools so that laypeople like Bernard and Abelard had access to the study of grammar, rhetoric, dialectic, and Latin authors.[3]

Town life experienced a rebirth, and the middle class began its ascent—a guild system developed and the beginnings of vernacular literature opened learning to greater numbers. The twelfth century was not only a time of growth and rising power for the institutional church, but also witnessed an increasingly active and critical laity. Laypeople participated in the evolution of gothic architecture, building the civic and ecclesial edifices that dominated the landscape, and influenced the way people thought about God, the church, and the spiritual life. While, from a later vantage point, the Crusades have rightly been judged destructive and cruel, they were part of a common medieval ethos of war and provided an opportunity for laypersons to participate in the activities of the church, opening doors into distant geographical cultures.[4] The meaning of "religious" was extended from exclusively explicit religious activity to a broader range of human endeavors. Productive social pursuits became relevant to the religious scheme of things in ways that had not been the case before.

Thus, the possibility of living a full spiritual life was extended to the laity in the twelfth century. Elements included simple living, itinerant preaching, pilgrimage, crusade and gospel piety. Some laity, dissatisfied with the worldliness of the church, joined heretical "protest movements" that not only criticized the church but propagated a return to the sources of Christianity in the form of an apostolic lifestyle. Lay movements included the Waldensians, a group that began in Lyons, France, in the 1170s, and the Humiliati, dating from the early twelfth century in Italy.[5] Both groups lived simply, earning their bread through their own labors, preaching the gospel, and advocating lay preaching and access to a vernacular Bible.

Against the Catholic thesis that only the ordained could preach, Waldensians held that anyone could preach without ecclesiastical ordination, including lay men and women. These groups looked to biblical passages such as Mark 16:5, "Go out to the whole world and preach the gospel to all creatures," and Acts 5:29, "One must obey God more than people." When the church established rules governing preaching—for example, laity were permitted to witness to the presence of God in their lives but were forbidden to preach about doctrinal matters—the Waldensians refused to accept these strictures and were condemned as heretics by 1179. Nevertheless their ideas spread across Germany and central Europe as an underground movement, surviving into the reformist movements of the sixteenth century. The Humiliati had a different fate, being successfully reintegrated into church structure as a religious order.

Another popular heretical movement called Catharism was flourishing first in Germany and then in France in the eleventh and twelfth centuries. The Cathars called themselves the "poor of Christ" and also advocated a return to the apostolic simplicity of the New Testament. They did not own property, performed manual work, prayed, and fasted. Claiming to be the true church, they gained a large number of new members in a surprisingly short time. In 1163, their influence was drastically curtailed by the church. After theological interrogations, a number of influential members were burned outside Cologne.

Cathars also embraced a radical dualism that pitted matter against spirit.[6] They reacted to spiritual crisis with pessimism, fatalism, and a rejection of the physical world. The image of an all-powerful, beneficent God was complemented by an almost equally strong, but utterly dark, evil, and personal devil. The thirteenth-century focus on the devil in art may have been due, in part, to Cathar influence. Hildegard and Bernard's more positive assessment of bodiliness and matter was likely due, in part, to their desire to refute the crass dualism of heresies like the Cathars. In Hildegard's mind, clerical sloth and lack of pastoral care were the reasons for the Cathars' growing influence. She foresaw the existence of a remnant of faithful clergy who would experience what she called the "first dawn of justice," suggesting an idealization of the primitive church.

Medieval theologians, especially those connected with the School of Chartres, developed a fascination with nature and cosmology. By mid-century, the idea of hierarchy—borrowed from the works of fifth-century Pseudo-Dionysius—took hold. This master idea included an image of the world as connected in all its parts—a great chain of being in which reality flowed out from God, ultimately to return to the embrace of the Trinity at the end of time. In a rising spiral movement of recapitulation, lower species would be caught up by higher, as all of reality made its way, emerging finally in a glorious divine totality, the "all in all" *(apocatastasis)*.[7] Medieval historian Marie-Dominique Chenu compares the twelfth-century understanding and use of the all-encompassing principle of hierarchy with our understanding and use of the theory of evolution. Each in its own time provides the overarching framework or set of lenses through which humans view their world.[8]

The cosmos and the individual mirrored each other. Some of Hildegard's images graphically depict the human person as a microcosm reflecting the macrocosm of the entire universe. Curiosity about the world led to new questions related to the meaning and value of matter and the human body. The world was seen as inscribed in the human body, and both reflected divine beauty.[9] A leading thinker in the twelfth century, Alan of Lille, responding to the question of why the human person was created, wrote: "For it was fitting that corporeal as well as incorporeal nature should come to participate in the divine goodness, should relish that goodness and live in joy."[10]

This all-encompassing worldview resulted in a shift of perception about the relationship between the natural and the supernatural. Nature and grace became connected in new, more integral ways. Interest in the dramatic breaking-in of the supernatural in the form of miracles and wonders waned, replaced by a more scientific, reasoned approach. Hildegard's writing embraced both this more scientific approach to reality (a probing interest in natural and medical questions), and a symbolic view of the world (the theological, allegorical analysis of her visions). This tendency to value the world as good and beautiful minimized but did not eliminate the tension with an opposing, dualistic stance of contempt for the world *(contemptus mundi)*.

The twelfth century also had a great interest in anthropological questions. Theologians pondered: Who is the human person? How does one attain union with God? They were inquisitive about interiority, about intention and personal conscience, about experience. And in all the major religions, twelfth-century authors focused on love.[11] The symbolist mentality of the twelfth century envisioned the world on two levels: an outward literal level, and a "second level lying beneath the surface and becoming accessible through transposition, via imagery, onto the first."[12] This sacramental view of reality involved the perception of a deeper, hidden truth, the kernel within or beneath the literal surface or shell of things. Someone like Bernard exemplifies this symbolist approach to reality in his reflections on spousal intimacy as a metaphor for humanity's relationship with God.

Like the language of scripture, the meaning of reality was penetrated through the imaginative use of symbols, metaphors, analogies, and allegory. There was a mysterious kinship between the physical world and the realm of the sacred.[13] Animals, nature, color, numbers, art, the human person, names, virtues, vices, even history contained hints of the sacred.[14] This style is prominent in the writing of Bernard and Hildegard, who makes extensive use of allegory. Referring to the sermons of Bernard of Clairvaux, Chenu notes that the symbolist mentality "dwelt fondly, got carried away as it read, discovered, and divined at the heart of the most lowly things and the most simple events those signs and invitations and direct messages which came to it out of the most hidden recesses of love."[15]

Perhaps the most central issue in the twelfth-century church was reform. The eleventh-century reform under Gregory VII (r. 1073–85) sought to free the church from secular evils and clerical vices. This reform reached its culmination in the twelfth century. Bishops, clergy, religious, regular canons, and laypeople participated, fueled by a desire to return to the purity of the early church, a search for order, and the need to renew integrity and virtue in the church. The success of the reform has been attributed to several factors: (1) the foundation of new religious orders; (2) a shift toward personal piety; and (3) the emergence of new heresies.

Heresy was not just a threat to Christian unity. Dissenters' stringent ideals of asceticism and poverty not only attracted serious Christians but also shamed and bewildered adherents to the mainline church. In her four preaching tours, Hildegard promoted reform, calling the church back to the poverty and singleness of purpose of the early church. The spiritual and doctrinal malaise that was the object of these efforts was complex and widespread. Hildegard describes the evils of her time in graphic terms:

> The streets of certain cities are filled with mud, and the pathways of some men are filled with slime. Justice has grown dark with iniquity, and the precepts of the law are violated by abandonment of the laws of God. Therefore, let the shepherds wail and sprinkle themselves with ashes (Jer 25:34), because although established as the "steps" of the Church, they do not seek to know what they are. For the head has no eyes, and the feet no paths, since the shameful deeds of man's iniquity have not yet been fully purged by the hand of God.[16]

The buying and selling of church offices revealed an inordinate concern with power and money. The ideal of celibacy was yet to become fully established—clergy had wives, children, and concubines.[17] Church leadership suffered from the widespread vice of its pastors. The engagement of the church with secular pursuits such as armies and war, political machinations, and court intrigue led it further and further from the vision of Christ's early followers of a church that would shine as a beacon in the world, witnessing to the life of the Spirit.

In Germany, there were growing conflicts over land, money, and power between local rulers and the crown; between the crown and the papacy; and among powerful, aristocratic families that required both church and state to amass armies and raise funds to fuel the costs of war. The papacy exercised power by anointing the German king as Holy Roman Emperor. In turn, monarchs were deeply implicated in the appointment and consecration of popes and bishops. This latter power struggle, known as the investiture controversy, was eased—but only briefly—by the Concordat of Worms in 1122 under Henry V and Callistus II, a valiant but, in the long run, ephemeral attempt to restore order. During her lifetime, Hildegard witnessed some dozen popes and ten antipopes elected/appointed to the See of Peter.[18]

The Holy Spirit was explicitly associated with a number of key ideas and movements in the twelfth century. In addition to seeing the renewal of the apostolic life as the work of the Holy Spirit (Acts 4:32), Christian thinkers borrowed the idea of the world-soul from Plato's dialogue, the *Timaeus*. Since the world was seen to have an integrity and harmony that allowed it to be studied in and of itself, it seemed logical to surmise that, like human beings, the world also contained a soul that was initially linked with the Holy Spirit.[19] In addition, a new awareness of history led twelfth-century thinkers to link historical events with salvation history. The march of history was interpreted through various templates. For example, time was divided into six ages or eons modeled on the six days of creation. Toward the end of the century, Joachim of Fiore described history in three stages, reflecting the Trinity. The age of the Hebrew Scriptures was the age of the Father; the time of the incarnation was the age of the Son; and his own age, marked by renewal, inaugurated the third and final age of the Holy Spirit.

Life and Writing

Hildegard's gifts and energy were truly remarkable. Medieval scholar Peter Dronke writes: "Hildegard of Bingen still confronts us, after eight centuries, as an overpowering, electrifying presence—and in many ways an enigmatic one."[20] Prophet, scientist, mystic, author, visionary, poet, dramatist, and musician—Hildegard was the quintessential renaissance woman of the twelfth century. She was born into a noble German family to Mechtild and Hildebert at Bermersheim in 1098, the youngest of ten children. Two of

Hildegard's brothers, Hugo and Roricus, were priests, and one of her elder sisters, Clementia, became a nun at the convent Hildegard founded at Rupertsberg.[21] We know little about the details of her early life except that she began to have visions at a very early age, visions that she later described as "the living light"—not ecstatic but interior—visions that did not interfere with her normal physical sight or consciousness.

It was not unusual for wealthy, devout families to "tithe" a child to the church. When Hildegard was eight years old, she was sent to a local anchoress, Jutta of Spanheim, to be tutored. Hildegard's education likely involved learning to pray the psalms in Latin and to chant the divine office. It is possible that she also learned to sew or weave.[22] Formal education available to monks would have been off limits to these holy women. As a result, there has been a good deal of speculation about how Hildegard came to know so much about music and medicine and theology. Hildegard herself speaks of receiving direct divine inspiration from "the living light" through the power of the Holy Spirit.

The community grew, and at the age of fourteen or fifteen, Hildegard chose to live under vows according to the Benedictine Rule. In 1136, when Jutta died, Hildegard succeeded her as abbess of the convent at Disibodenberg. She was thirty-eight years old. In 1141, Hildegard was told in a vision to "tell and write" what she "saw and heard." With the help of her close friends—the monk Volmar (d. 1173), and Richardis of Stade, a sister in the monastery—Hildegard began to write her first book, *Scivias*, or *Know the Ways of the Lord*. In 1146, Hildegard wrote to Bernard of Clairvaux to seek his opinion about her visions. He responded in a guarded letter affirming that her visions were authentic. The following year, at the Synod of Trier, Pope Eugenius III approved Hildegard's visions and sent her a letter of apostolic blessing authorizing her "in the name of Christ and St. Peter to publish all that she had learned from the Holy Spirit."[23]

Under divine inspiration, Hildegard later decided to move her convent from Disibodenberg to Bingen on the Rhine. Because of her reputation and the income it produced for the monastery, Abbot Kuno was reluctant to let her go. Hildegard enlisted the support of the Archbishop of Mainz and the mother of her friend, Richardess, the Marchioness of Stade, who had been a loyal patron of the convent. After much negotiation and in the wake of a serious illness that sent Hildegard to bed (she suggested that the illness was a sign of God's disapproval of Kuno's refusal to allow the sisters to depart), the abbot relented, and twenty nuns moved to Rupertsberg in 1150. Her secretary, Volmar, was the only male to accompany the community to the new location.

It took until 1158 to establish her monastery firmly as an independent and viable enterprise. Hildegard struggled under the strain of the new venture. Some sisters complained of the unaccustomed hardships; others chose to leave. Still plagued by illness, Hildegard undertook a major preaching tour at the age of sixty. In the span of twelve years, she made four preaching tours, proclaiming God's word to clergy and laity, in churches and chapter houses of religious communities. In 1165, she founded a second monastery across the Rhine at Eibingen. She visited the sisters there twice a week, trying to assist them through a number of difficulties that resulted in the departure of some of the sisters who returned to life in the world.

Texts by and about Hildegard reveal a woman who could be doubtful and confident, determined and flexible, harsh and tender, a tireless worker who was plagued by illness, respectful and condescending, willful and prayerful, joyful and dejected, extravagant and parsimonious. She struggled with what to do about her visions until later in life, when she felt God calling her to "go public" and write them down for others to read. But then she threatened with divine retribution anyone who dared tamper with her words, since she claimed they were divinely inspired. She excoriated an effeminate clergy for their failure to live up to their gospel calling, exercising her prophetic vocation with courage and conviction.[24]

Hildegard's strong will was visible to the end of her life. When the bishop wanted to exhume the body of an excommunicated nobleman buried in the convent cemetery, Hildegard insisted that he had repented before he died. Since she had promised him a Christian burial, she obliterated all evidence of the grave, making it impossible for the authorities to find it.[25] As a result of Hildegard's stubbornness, the bishop imposed an interdict on her convent, effectively silencing the liturgy and the chanting of the divine office in her community. Through the influence of Archbishop Christian of Mainz, the interdict was eventually lifted. Shortly after this incident, Hildegard died in 1179, past eighty years of age.

Since Hildegard was from a wealthy family and moved comfortably in the higher circles of society, she was consulted by, and corresponded with, popes, bishops, priests, monks, nuns, and laypeople, including princes and Emperor Frederick Barbarossa. In one letter, Hildegard chastised the emperor for his recalcitrant position against the papacy—he had appointed three antipopes! She also corresponded with Bernard of Clairvaux, Thomas Becket, a younger mystic named Elisabeth of Schönau (1129–64), four popes (Eugene III, Anastasius IV, Adrian IV, and Alexander III), and several royal families (Henry VI of Germany, Henry II and Queen Eleanor of England, Emperor Conrad II and Empress Berta of Greece). She was involved in the major political and religious issues of her day—the Crusades, the struggle between empire and papacy, and the Cathar heresy.

"Hildegard's longevity is surprising since she was ill much of her life. Since the day of her birth, she has been entangled, as though in a net, in the afflictions of her infirmities, so that she is troubled by continual pains in all her veins, marrow and flesh" (*Book of Divine Works*, Epilogue). Hildegard's visions tired her, often to the point of exhaustion.[26] But in spite of these difficulties, she lived an amazingly productive life. During her lifetime, she supported her friend Elisabeth of Schönau when Elisabeth reported having visions, and after Hildegard's death, her writings influenced several women mystics of the next century, including Mechthild of Magdeburg (1210–95), Mechthild of Hackeborn (1241–99) and Gertrude the Great of Helfta (1256–1302). Her canonization process was initiated not long after her death, but was never formally completed because of administrative difficulties. In 1324, Pope John XXII allowed her "solemn and public cult." In the German liturgical calendar, her feast is celebrated on September 17, the anniversary of her death.[27]

Hildegard was a prolific writer on many topics. With the help of several secretaries, she wrote three major theological works. The first is titled *Scivias*, which is an abbreviation for the Latin *Scito vias domini*, or "Know the ways of the Lord." This work, written between 1141 and 1151, is her most important work. It is a comprehensive account of salvation history from creation to the end of time, illustrated with colored images produced by sisters in her community under her direction. Some scholars consider this work an important early medieval *summa* because of its scope and comprehensive nature. The images were inspired by Hildegard's visions and modeled on the then fashionable style of manuscript illuminations.

Scivias contains a foreword and three parts, following a trinitarian pattern. In part I (six visions), Hildegard describes the work of God and the ways in which God relates to humanity and the world. In part II (seven visions), she focuses on the Savior and the process of redemption, the church, and the sacraments of baptism, confirmation, priesthood, penance, and Eucharist. The female figure *Ecclesia* dominates. Part III (thirteen visions) highlights the Holy Spirit, and the role of the virtues in the journey of salvation. The text reveals a double structure: historical and moral. The building metaphor symbolizes salvation history.[28] This "edifice of salvation" is inhabited by personified virtues that map out a theology of the moral life. In each section, Hildegard offers a detailed description of each vision followed by theological explanation. The last of these visions includes the texts of fourteen liturgical songs composed by Hildegard, and a rudimentary version of a morality play—what eventually became her *Ordo virtutum*. The text ends with an apocalyptic vision of the final judgment, divine victory, and the praise offered by the host of heaven.

A second theological work completed in 1163 is the *Book of Life's Merits (Liber vitae meritorum)*. This is a book of six visions detailing the ethical life of virtues and vices, describing in colorful imagery and compelling prose the realities of purgatory and hell. Hildegard holds out to the reader both the judgment of God and the glory of heaven. Scholars contrast the tone of the *Scivias*, in which Hildegard paints the image of a tumultuous world in flux, with that of her third major theological work the *Book of Divine Works (De operatione Dei)*, completed in 1173 or 1174. This treatise is a very structured account of the relations in the universe—delineated in detailed, static imagery bordering on the mathematical. The book has been described as prophetic proclamation, allegorical vision, exegetical study, theological summa, and multimedia work! In this text, Hildegard imagines the universe as a cosmic egg, containing a human person resting within the womb of God. Part 1 (four visions) deals with the creation of the world and human beings. Part 2 (one vision) explores human beings as moral agents. Part 3 (five visions) treats salvation history, the incarnation, and the end-time. Humans are invited to work with God toward the perfection of creation.

Hildegard also composed a number of scientific works. Her *Natural History* or *Book of Simple Medicine (Physica, 1151–58)* has nine sections that name and describe the healing qualities of plants, trees, precious stones, fish, birds, animals, reptiles, metals, and the elements. Yet another work, *Causes and Cures* or *Book of Compound Medicine (Causae et curae)* is a categorization of certain physiological and psychological temperaments. In this book, Hildegard addresses specific female issues such as menstruation and gestation as well as home cures for common ailments.

Reading Hildegard's vast and diverse corpus is a daunting undertaking.[29] The reader is easily overwhelmed by the magnitude of her vision. It pulls us out of the narrow confines of daily, mundane existence into the realm of the cosmos and the entire sweep of salvation history. Hildegard sees the world as a cosmic struggle between the powers of good and evil. She puts her intellectual genius at the service of her prophetic vision.

Hildegard also composed seventy-seven liturgical songs collected in a cycle entitled *Symphony of the Harmony of Celestial Revelations (Symphonia)* completed by 1158. Specialists in twelfth-century musicology note the originality of Hildegard's music. There are few precedents to explain the unusual intervals and haunting tone of her compositions. An article on medieval music in the *Washington Post* reports:

> Hildegard von Bingen, virtually unknown a few years ago, is now one of the hottest composers on record, partly as a feminist icon but mostly for the sheer, simple beauty of her works. Purists treasure her limpid plainchant melodies and mystical Latin texts in chastely correct recordings by medieval specialists. The Now Generation has put her at the top of the crossover charts in modern arrangements with drum tracks and environmental sounds overlaid on the ancient vocal melodies.[30]

Her CD *Vision* has been advertised with full-page ads in both the *New Yorker* and *Rolling Stone* magazines. One can only muse about what Hildegard might make of these developments.

Hildegard's writing is a prime example of literature that weds text and imagery—each shedding light on the other. There are three elements: the text itself; the images Hildegard creates with words; and the actual portraits of her visions. There is a certain primitive quality to her images, yet they need to be understood in tandem with her quite sophisticated theological explanations.[31] Ideally, Hildegard's images become part of the cognitive process of understanding her thought. In some cases, the images go beyond the text, as in her images of the praying women *Ecclesia* and *Zion* that privilege the feminine in a powerful, visual way.

In *The Cloister Walk*, poet Kathleen Norris compares the way a poet acquires knowledge with the way Hildegard spoke of her visions. Norris cites a letter Hildegard wrote to a monk late in her life: "I see, hear, and know simultaneously, and learn what I know as if in a moment."[32] Norris speaks of the poet's knowledge as a process in which "thoughts and images constellate, converging, sometimes violently, in the subconscious. The sounds of words and the silence of images are more important at this stage than sense or 'meaning.' In composing a poem, one often seems to move directly from ignorance to revelation, instantly from a muddled sense of things to a clear picture, with only a vaguest sense of how it happened."[33] While eventually we articulate what we see to create meaning, a poetic way of knowing privileges "image over idea, the synthetic over the analytic, the instantaneous over the sequential, the intuitive and associative over the formal and prescribed."[34]

Norris's comments remind us to keep Hildegard's images as well as her text before us. Each enriches the other in ways not visible if we focus only on one form of her expression. Hildegard's creativity and boldness, the energy of her writing, and the subtle ways in which her own language is steeped in the language and imagery of the Bible provide testimony to her originality and literary skill. Peter Dronke says of Hildegard:

> Her approach to every problem—human, scientific, artistic, or theological—was her own. She took nothing ready-made. Her conviction that she *saw* the answers to

the problems in her waking vision meant that she did not have to defer to established answers. Often we see she does not give a damn about these, however powerful their proponents. Many times she expresses herself courteously and modestly; yet when it comes to asserting what she believes to be right, she will do it bravely, outfacing all opposition.[35]

Trinity of Persons

Hildegard's theology and spirituality are deeply trinitarian (*Scivias* II.2; III.7).[36] The very structure of her theological works follows a trinitarian pattern. She experienced the triune God as a pillar filled with a providential strength, the power ultimately to overcome evil—"the ineffable Trinity stands against the darkness of the world" (*Scivias* III.7.3) and "cuts down and burns all who raise the aridity of heterodoxy" (*Scivias* III.7.4; see fig. 8). She weaves portraits of the three persons interacting with each other and with the world—prodding, demanding, consoling, loving. God is a master artist, architect, builder, and gardener. The church is the visible sacrament of the true Trinity (*Scivias* II.3.10). None of the persons exists without the others—they are a dynamic unity engaged together in the act of redemption (*Scivias* III.7.9–10). The first person creates the world that is redeemed by the second person, who became human through the power of the third.[37]

Consonant with the themes of light and darkness that infuse all her thought, Hildegard describes the persons of the Trinity as light/power/heat; brightness/radiance/ fire; power/will/fire. In the following passage, Hildegard links the Trinity with the sweep of salvation history:

> Again, as the flame of a fire has three qualities, so there is one God in three Persons. How? A flame is made up of brilliant light and red power and fiery heat. It has brilliant light that it may shine, and red power that it may endure, and fiery heat that it may burn. Therefore, by the brilliant light understand the Father, who with paternal love opens his brightness to His faithful; and by

the red power, which is in the flame that it may be strong, understand the Son, who took on a body born of a virgin, in which His divine wonders were shown; and by the fiery heat understand the Holy Spirit who burns ardently in the minds of the faithful. (*Scivias* II.2.6)

This image of light and fire is surprisingly juxtaposed with Hildegard's christological image, known as the "Blue Christ" (see fig. 9). A series of circular lines in the form of a mandala is located within a square, decorated border. In the center of this double mandala is the figure of Christ in sapphire blue, "surrounded by brilliant light suspended before a fiery gold disk."[38] While this unusual image of the Trinity underlines the christocentric preoccupations of the twelfth century, it provokes reflection, since the Trinity is rarely portrayed as a single individual, Christ. Thus, it is necessary to read this image in tandem with Hildegard's explanation. The bright light surrounding the figure symbolizes the Father; the man the color of sapphire designates the Son; the Son's blazing with a gentle glowing fire is the Spirit. "And that bright light bathes the whole of the glowing fire, and the glowing fire bathes the bright light; and the bright light and the glowing fire over the whole human figure, so that the three are one light in one power of potential" (*Scivias* II.2.2.). It is instructive and potentially transforming to sit before this image in a quiet, prayerful posture, much as one might approach an icon, and to allow its power and energy to inform our experience and understanding of the Trinity.

In a letter to the bishop of Bamberg, Hildegard offers a mini-treatise on the Trinity extending the range of the Trinity's activities.[39] In response to his queries about the Trinity, she explains the essential quality of the Father, eternity, as a wheel without beginning or end. The Son's primary characteristic, equality, involves Christ's giving physical form to the eternal idea of humankind in the mind of the Father. While the Son empties himself, taking on human form and a kind of equality with creation, the Spirit's role is to bind them together, permeate them, revealing eternity and enkindling equality. She explains the Spirit's role in homey analogies: a person binding together a bundle of sticks, which if not bound, fly asunder; a blacksmith who unites the two materials of bronze, making them one through fire. Likely inspired by Paul's letter to the Ephesians, "Take the helmet of salvation and the sword of the Spirit, the Word of God" (6:17), Hildegard compares the Spirit to a "sword brandished in every direction." The metaphor conjures up images from films that showcase the martial arts—truly a new and provocative image of the Spirit to ponder.[40]

In an antiphon for the Trinity, Hildegard associates God's gift of life with music.

> To the Trinity be praise!
> God is music, God is life
> that nurtures every creature in its kind.
> Our God is the son of the angel throng
> and the splendor of secret ways
> hid from all humankind,
> But God our life is the life of all.[41]

Since Hildegard relies so heavily on imagery, it may not be easy at first blush to decipher her theology. But her texts are rich in theological material, and Bernard McGinn is correct to suggest that Hildegard "can well be called the first great woman theologian in Christian history."[42]

Metaphors of Spirit

Like the theology of her contemporary Bernard of Clairvaux, Hildegard's theology is largely christocentric, even though interest in the stories of Jesus' life is marginal. But our focus is her material on the Holy Spirit and the role Hildegard assigns the Spirit in her vision of God and salvation history. Hildegard is not alone in giving the Spirit theological attention. Other twelfth-century authors delved into the ways the human person is an image of the Trinity (*imago trinitatis*), and two commentaries on the Song of Songs connect the Spirit with charity and knowledge of God. William of St. Thierry (1085–1148), monk and friend of Bernard of Clairvaux, wrote: "O Holy Spirit, we beg you to fill us with your love—O Love!—so that we may understand love's song and ourselves be made in some way participants in the dialogue of the Bride and Groom."[43] And in a text written for a monastery of

Benedictine nuns in Germany, *A Teaching of the Loving Knowledge of God*, the author refers to the Spirit as Creator, Redeemer, Lover, and Mother. The prologue is structured around the seven gifts of the Holy Spirit (Isa 11:2): "We wish to speak of the highest joy, the greatest grace, the most restful sweetness that is the Holy Spirit."[44] Like Hildegard, the author of this work places the virtues and the gifts of the Spirit at the heart of his description of the spiritual life.

Let us turn now to Hildegard's words in her *Sequence for the Holy Spirit.*

> O fire of the Spirit, the Comforter,
> Life of the life of all creation,
> Holy are You, giving life to the
> forms.[45]
>
> Holy are You, anointing
> the mortally broken;
> Holy are You, cleansing
> the fetid wounds.
>
> O breath of sanctity,
> O fire of charity,
> O sweet savor in the breast
> and balm flooding hearts
> with the fragrance of virtues:
>
> O limpid fountain,
> in which we can see
> how God gathers the strays
> and seeks out the lost:
> O breastplate of life
> and hope of the integral body,
>
> O sword-belt of honor:
> save the blessed!
> Guard those the foe holds
> Imprisoned,
> Free those in fetters
> Whom divine force wishes to save.

O current of power permeating all—in the heights,
upon the earth,
and in all deep:
you bind and gather
all people together.
From you clouds overflow, winds
take wing, stones store up moisture,
waters well forth in streams—and
earth swells with living green.

When by his Word God
fashioned the cosmos—
founded sky and earth and sea—
You, Spirit,
brooded over the waters,
unfolded your deity.
You make waters
fruitful to give
life to creatures:
You breathe on men
to make mortals
living spirits.
You are ever teaching the learned,
made joyful by the breath
of Wisdom.
Praise then be yours!
You are the song of praise,
the delight of life,
a hope and a potent honor
granting garlands of light.[46]

Before turning to a more detailed analysis of specific Spirit metaphors in Hildegard's work, I note how others perceived the Spirit working in Hildegard. References to Hildegard as inspired by the Spirit are common. First, her contemporaries saw the Spirit as an agent of revelation in her life. In her *Life* and in numerous letters addressed to Hildegard, there is reference to her access to the Spirit, through whom she discovered the secret things of God; saw into the past, present, and future; and guided others in God's ways.[47] Bishops write to her as "wondrously infused with the Holy Spirit"[48] and number her among the prophets (Amos) in whom the Spirit breathed, distributing gifts as She wishes (John 3:8; 1 Cor 12:11; Amos 7:14).[49]

It is through persons like Hildegard that the Holy Spirit is brought down to earth.[50] Helengerus, Kuno's successor as abbot of Disibod, writes to Hildegard: "Although the whole world rightly proclaims that you are enriched with the joy of the Holy Spirit, I (who should have been the first to invite others to come to you, blessed lady), have remained hidden in my sloth. But now seized by fear and love, I have found it necessary to address you in this letter."[51] Acknowledging that Hildegard has privileged access to the Spirit's voice, people seek her counsel and consolation. In another letter, Helengerus describes how Hildegard becomes a medium for the Spirit's presence.

> We know, beloved mother, that you recently came to us at the prompting and indeed at the command, of the Paraclete, the holy spirit of Almighty God....And thus we offer our ceaseless, though unworthy thanks, thanks to that Paraclete as best we can, because, to confess the truth, we have become fully aware of the burning power and strength of His illumination among us and indeed within us.[52]

Helengerus goes on to refer to the specific, concrete, unifying effect of the Spirit's presence—a theme dear to Augustine. Hildegard's decision to move away from Disibod to found a new monastery created a long-standing rift between the two communities. Helengerus notes that because of Hildegard's Spirit-filled visit to Disibod, he has "cast off the inveterate hostility and animosity that we have nurtured for many years now, and we have come together fully unto the unity of genuine divine love, as with one body and one spirit."[53] Through Hildegard, the Spirit is given credit for a change of heart in a painful and difficult human situation.

The vision with which the *Scivias* begins contains an image of Hildegard receiving revelation from the Spirit—an excellent example of how text and image need to be read in tandem (see fig. 10). She is seated, her feet on a stool, writing on a slate with a stylus.

Reminiscent of Paul's description of the Spirit being poured forth into our hearts (Rom 5:5) and Luke's story of Pentecost (Acts 2:3), Hildegard is portrayed as a recipient of the inflowing Spirit. Inverted tongues of fire reach out from the top of an arch under which she sits and surround the top of her head like a crown. From a side panel, the monk Volmar protrudes his head into the drawing's primary central space, occupied by Hildegard. His pose suggests that this dedicated secretary is anxious to assist her but also belies his curiosity and his desire to be part of the Spirit activity surrounding Hildegard.[54] A similar image is found in the *Book of Divine Works*. In this image, a river of fire flows from a small window at the top of the image onto Hildegard's head as she writes. Her dear friend Richardis of Stade stands behind her, and on the other side of a wall, Volmar sits at a desk writing her visions on parchment.[55]

In a second common role assigned to the Spirit, Hildegard connects the Spirit with what she calls "works"—action usually related to virtue or justice.[56] Works should shine before others with the Spirit's fire; the divine voice of mercy gathers to itself the poor and lame, seeking the Spirit of good works. The Spirit's coming as "the burning sun poured into the apostles" empowers them—even to pour out their blood in martyrdom.[57] In her discussion of the church, Hildegard emphasizes works. The church is a birthing mother who through the power of the Holy Spirit at baptism conceives and brings forth the faithful; she is also the mother who laments the children who have abandoned the Spirit to become filthy with sin (*Scivias* II.3.12, 15, 26, 28). Through faith, the Spirit revives the life of the soul, providing the breath that enables believers to "fly in the heights of Heaven" (*Scivias* II.2.30). Hildegard's interest in physical and spiritual healing leads her naturally to link the work of the Spirit's anointing with healing.[58] She turns to plague-like symptoms to describe the evils of sin.

> For I do not find it loathsome to touch ulcerated wounds surrounded by the filthy, gnawing worms that are innumerable vices, stinking with evil report and infamy, and stagnating in habitual wickedness. I do not refuse to close them gently up, drawing forth from them the devouring poison of malice, by touching them with the mild fire of the breath of the Holy Spirit. (*Scivias* III.8.8)

The Spirit also warns the world and the church of impending danger. Hildegard looks to the story of the flood in which Noah embodied the Spirit's presence and power against the forces of evil—a role later assumed by the church (*Scivias* II.3.19).

Holy Spirit and "Greening"

Hildegard imagined the outpouring of the Spirit in natural rather than cultural metaphors. Our first image links the Holy Spirit with what Hildegard calls "greening." She combined images of planting, watering, and greening to speak of the presence of the Holy Spirit. Hildegard linked the flow of water on the crops with the love of God that renews the face of the earth, and, by extension, the souls of believers.[59]

Scholars explain the prominence of the color green in Hildegard's work in a number of ways, one of which suggests that she may have been influenced by the lush green countryside of the Rhineland Valley. But "greenness" *(viriditas)* plays a larger role in Hildegard's theology. In the English-language edition of her letters the translators lament, "This *viriditas*, this despair of translators, this 'greenness' enters into the very fabric of the universe in Hildegard's cosmic scheme of things. In Hildegard's usage it is a profound, immense, dynamically energized term."[60]

Viriditas expressed and connected the bounty of God, the fertility of nature, and especially the presence of the Holy Spirit. Hildegard wrote to Abbess Adelheid, "May He anoint you with the ointment of His mercy....May He anoint you with the viridity of the Holy Spirit, and may He work good and holy works in you...."[61] Barbara Newman comments about this aspect of Hildegard's thought, "If you are filled with the Holy Spirit then you are filled with *viriditas*. You are spiritually fertile, you are alive."[62] Commenting on the annunciation, Hildegard imagines Mary as the grass and the green earth; the Spirit is the dew that made her womb fruitful.[63] In a letter to Abbot Kuno, Hildegard described Rupert, a man of exceptional virtue and the patron of her monastery, as the "greenness of the finger of God" *(viriditas digiti Dei)*.[64] In contrast, Hildegard described the prelate who is filled with weariness *(taedium)* as lacking in *viriditas*, and counsels the neophyte in religious life to strive for "spiritual greenness."[65]

In addition to life and fertility, the *viriditas* of the Spirit points to a life of virtue, the active fruit of the Spirit's gift. Hildegard imagines that a garden imbued with *viriditas* allows the virtues to grow.

In one of her many descriptions of the Trinity in the *Scivias*, Hildegard connects the Holy Sprit with the flowing freshness of sanctity. It is rare for a medieval author to expend more ink on the Spirit than on the first two persons of the Trinity as Hildegard does here.

> And so these three Persons are in the unity of inseparable substance; but They are not indistinct among themselves. How? He Who begets is the Father; He Who is born is the Son; and He Who in eager freshness proceeds from the Father and the Son, and sanctified the waters by moving over their face in the likeness of an innocent bird, and streamed with ardent heat over the apostles, is the Holy Spirit. (*Scivias* III.7.9)

Like a fallow field, a person with a good heart receives the seed of God's word and is granted the gifts of the Holy Spirit in superabundance. The person who sometimes accepts and sometimes refuses God's word has some greenness, though "not much," she says. But one who never chooses to hear the word or waken the heart to the admonition of the Holy Spirit dries up and dies completely (*Scivias* III.10.4; III.10.7).[66]

Holy Spirit as Timbrel Player

> Praise to you
> Spirit of fire!
> To you who sound the timbrel
> And the lyre.
> Your music sets our minds
> ablaze! The strength of our souls
> awaits your coming
> in the tent of meeting.[67]

Music was central to Hildegard's psyche and to the liturgical life of her Benedictine community.[68] She experienced music as a healing medium; its harmonies brought order and well-being to human life. "For each element has its own particular sound, a primordial resonance emerging from the order of creation. All these sounds come together in one great concordance and unique harmony."[69] Hildegard imagined heaven as a joyous "symphony of the Holy Spirit."[70] Peter Dronke explains how Hildegard not only linked the music of the divine office with the cosmic music of the spheres, but saw music as a key to understanding salvation history.[71] Adam's disobedience caused him to lose the "voice of the living Spirit" with which his voice "blended fully with the voice of the angels."[72] The Spirit inspired the prophets to "compose psalms and canticles (by which the hearts of listeners would be inflamed)" and also to construct various kinds of musical instruments.[73] Human beings filled with zeal and wisdom imitate this musical behavior, "so that they might be able to sing for the delight of their souls, and they accompanied their singing with instruments played with the flexing of the fingers, recalling...Adam, who was formed by God's finger, which is the Holy Spirit."[74]

This exalted plea for the necessity and beauty of music in the spiritual life is found in a letter Hildegard wrote to the bishops of Mainz. As mentioned above, Hildegard's monastery had been placed under an interdict for her refusal to exhume the body of a nobleman who was thought to have died in sin—despite Hildegard's protests to the contrary. An interdict was a common sanction used by the medieval church to correct and chastise dioceses or monastic houses that were judged to be in error. In Hildegard's case, it meant the silencing of music, the lifeblood of her community.

Hildegard was a composer who saw the chant of the divine office as an act of imitation of the heavenly choirs of angels ceaselessly praising God. Indeed, she names the Holy Spirit as the ultimate songster. Referring to St. Rupert, she wrote:

> In you the Holy Spirit makes symphony,
> for you are joined to the angelic choirs
> and adorned in the Son of God.[75]

The Spirit not only sings but also plays the timbrel and the lyre.[76]

Hildegard's theology may not have broken new ground, but her treatment and style are strikingly original. Barbara Newman describes Hildegard's hymn-writing:

> Her poems, even apart from their musical settings, leave an indelible impression of freshness and power. What she lacked in fluency, Hildegard made up in sheer immediacy. Not words but images formed her native idiom, and in her lyrics these images can leap out of their verbal wrappings to assault the mind with all the force and inevitability of a Jungian dream. Startling at first, even incoherent, they slowly or suddenly explode into sense, revealing the lineaments of a patterns that—if one is a twelfth-century Christian—one has always known."[77]

Holy Spirit as Fire and Warmth

Hildegard makes creative use of traditional biblical imagery linking the Holy Spirit with fire and warmth. But she also puts her own stamp on this Spirit imagery, mingling medical and theological idioms. In a text on the Trinity in which she imagines the persons as spirit/water/blood, Hildegard refers to the Spirit as blood that "surrounds and warms people...arousing and enkindling the brightest human virtues" (*Scivias* III.7.8). Hildegard often cuts a steely, matter-of-fact figure—she is very cerebral—but close attention to her ideas reveals her preoccupation with desire, with the *eros* that reaches out to good or evil. Commenting on the event of Pentecost, she says,

> And so, because the true Word had become incarnate, the Holy Spirit came openly in tongues of fire; for the Son, who converted the world to the truth by His preaching, was conceived by the Holy Spirit. And, because the apostles had been taught by the Son, the Holy Spirit bathed them in Its fire, so that with their souls and bodies they spoke in many tongues; and because their souls ruled their bodies, they cried out so that the whole world was shaken by their voices. (*Scivias* III.3.7; see fig. 13).

Hildegard's discussion of confirmation also provides ample opportunity to describe the Spirit's work (see fig. 11).[78] She imagines a huge tower that "represents the flaming forth of the gifts of the Holy Spirit, which the Father sent into the world for love of His Son, to enkindle the hearts of his disciples with fiery tongues and make them stronger in the name of the Holy, True Trinity." Hildegard weds contrasting images of fire and water and brings other opposites into coincidence in her description of the sweetness of the Holy Spirit given at confirmation. The Spirit is serene as well as boundless, swift to encompass all creatures in grace. She continues, "Its path is a torrent, and streams of sanctity flow from it in its bright power, with never a stain of dirt in them; for the Holy Spirit Itself is a burning and shining serenity, which cannot be nullified, and which enkindles ardent virtue so as to put all darkness to flight" (*Scivias* II.4.2).

In a quite different setting, in a vision on the three orders in the church, Hildegard explores the elements of nature required for crops (and the spiritual life) to prosper—a variation on the theme of *viriditas*. In this passage, Hildegard is discussing the problem of parents coercing children to become nuns or clerics. We noted above that as the last of ten children in an aristocratic family, Hildegard herself was "tithed" to religious life at the age of eight. Later, as abbess of two Benedictine convents, she was well aware of the difference between a coerced following of Christ and a genuine conversion. She employs the analogy of a field to which only God can give dew and send rain, on which only God can confer fresh moisture, and for which only God can draw warmth from the sun. God says: "So too, you can sow a word in human ears, but into his heart, which is My field, you cannot pour the dew of compunction, or the rain of tears, or the moisture of devotion, or the warmth of the Holy Spirit, through all of which the fruit of holiness must grow" (*Scivias* II.5.46). This text is a good example of the twelfth-century interest in internal intention over external observance, a preoccupation visible as well in the Spirit's role in helping us appropriate the Word of God.

Holy Spirit and Understanding the Things of God

The Holy Spirit is also the means by which the believer understands the things of God—the Spirit writes true doctrine in human hearts.[79] The Western Christian tradition has commonly linked the human experience of understanding with the Logos, or second person of the Trinity, and love with the third. But in the Gospel and letters of John these roles are reversed. The Spirit is identified with the truth, teaches the truth, and bears witness to Jesus, especially in the context of persecution (1 John 5:7–8). For John, the Holy Spirit not only teaches what Jesus taught but causes this teaching to enter and take root in hearts. In a letter to the shepherds of the church, Hildegard described them as teachers whom the Holy Spirit had inspired by "writing true doctrine in their hearts."[80] The Holy Spirit's task is to make the disciples understand internally the words of Jesus, to make them grasp the message in the light of faith, to perceive all the possibilities and importance of such words for the life of the church. The message of Jesus is not far removed from us because the Holy Spirit helps us to internalize it, to grasp it spiritually, and to discover in it a word of life. The Holy Spirit's doctrine is not new doctrine but a deeper understanding of the mystery of Jesus.

Hildegard embroiders this biblical insight in new patterns. To begin, she turns to the Holy Spirit to ensure that her readers will absorb the message God is sending through her. In part I of the *Scivias*, Hildegard concludes each of the six visions with the same sentence. God says,

> Therefore, whoever has knowledge in the Holy Spirit and wings of faith, let this one not ignore My admonition, but taste it, embrace it and receive it in his soul.
> (I.6.12)

The repetition of this phrase—to taste, embrace, and receive this knowledge into one's soul—functions like a mantra. Repetition is aimed at effecting in our lives what we are saying with our lips. As we read the words over and over, they penetrate more and more deeply into our psyches, making it possible to appropriate and absorb the truth that the Holy Spirit desires for us.

In her descriptions of Pentecost, Hildegard suggests that although Jesus taught the disciples at great length, his words did not have the power he wanted them to have. Jesus even shows frustration with their slowness of understanding. But after the infusion of the Holy Spirit at Pentecost, these same slow disciples spoke with deep understanding of the purposes of God and the kingdom. While Jesus supplied the words, the Holy Spirit's presence brought change, making it seem as though the disciples had heard them for the first time—with understanding. Hildegard writes,

> And the Holy Spirit took their human fear from them....And then they remembered with perfect understanding all the things they had heard and received from Christ with sluggish faith and comprehension; they recalled them to memory as if they had learned them from Him in that very hour....And thus they brought back many of this throng to the knowledge of God.
> (*Scivias* III.3.7)

In all of these texts, we see Hildegard carrying out her agenda of reform of the clergy and correction of heretics; neither group had allowed the Spirit to work in them so that the Word might penetrate their hearts.

Hildegard comments negatively on the role of Christ's flesh as something that blocks our ability to receive the Spirit. In the next chapter, we will see how Bernard of Clairvaux assigns a much more positive role to what he calls "carnal knowing." Still speaking about confirmation and Pentecost, Hildegard suggests that knowing Jesus in the flesh prevented the apostles from seeing his inner, spiritual meaning. God says,

> Because the disciples had seen My Son *in the flesh*, their inner vision was unopened and they loved Him in the flesh, and thus did not yet see the bright teaching that afterward, when they were made strong in the Holy Spirit they spread abroad in the world. (*Scivias* II.4.1)

Hildegard sees a similar broadening of understanding on the wider canvas of salvation history. At the beginning of the church and at its end, she says, understanding is narrow and cold. But when the

> Gospel was spread, the wisdom of the saints broadened; they burned in the Holy Spirit, seeking It in depth so as to find through It the deepening of their understanding of the Word of God....And so the sense of the Scriptures that went forth from the mouth of the holy doctors broadened too; they searched the depths of the Scriptures' astringency and made it known to the many who learned from them, and thus they too enlarged their senses by knowing more of the wisdom and knowledge of the divine writings. (*Scivias* III.4.12)

The unlettered Hildegard explained her understanding of the scriptures, of theology and doctrine, of medicine and music, through the unmediated tutoring of the Holy Spirit. In her letter to Bernard of Clairvaux, asking for his counsel about her visions, Hildegard appealed to his own similar experience. She wrote, "In your piety and wisdom look in your spirit, as you have been taught by the Holy Spirit, and from your heart bring comfort to your handmaiden."[81]

Hildegard's message about knowing in the Spirit invites us to reflect on how deeply we hear the divine word. Does Pentecost happen in our lives, so that like Archimedes, we experience an "Aha" experience of discovery and insight into the Word of God? Does the Spirit cause the "light to go on" so that we *know* the love of God and live out of it in the concrete circumstances of our everyday lives? We may hear the Gospel every Sunday, or engage in prayer every day, but do these moments lead to a new level of realization of the existential meaning of the good news so that it begins to take root and bear fruit in a new way? There is a crucial difference between hearing the Gospel simply in our ears or also in our hearts.

This awareness can be difficult for those of us who are "cultural Christians," that is, Christians who are born into Christian families, are baptized as infants, and who live in a culturally Christian society, and perhaps even are active within a church in either a formal or an informal way. In this situation, it is very easy to think that we understand God, just because we have been hearing about God for as long as we can remember. This is quite different from actually letting the reality of God penetrate our inmost being. It is all too easy to think we are spiritual pilgrims, when in reality, we have never even gotten on the road.[82]

At the height of the spiritual life, the Spirit's power leads to ever more profound understandings of God and the world. Life becomes an ongoing conversion in which the Spirit penetrates more and more deeply over a lifetime. The Spirit leads us from glory to glory, to an ever deepening grasp of the things of God and the committed living out of this meaning in our everyday lives. Hildegard speaks to those who penetrate the true meaning of the Word, but do not have the courage to preach it. At the very outset of the *Scivias* she writes,

> And behold, He Who was enthroned upon that mountain cried out in a strong, loud voice saying, "O human, who are fragile dust of the earth and ashes of ashes! Cry out and speak of the origin of pure salvation, until those people are instructed, who, though they see the inmost contents of the Scriptures, do not wish to tell them or preach them, because they are lukewarm and sluggish in serving God's justice. Unlock for them the enclosure of mysteries that they, timid as they are, conceal in a hidden and fruitless field. Burst forth into a fountain of abundance and overflow with mystical knowledge, until they who think you contemptible because of Eve's transgression are stirred up by the flood of your irrigation."
>
> (I.1)

Holy Spirit and Prophetic Power

Hildegard is often described by scholars primarily as a visionary and a prophet, since she does not fit neatly the "type" later identified as "mystic." Hildegard sees herself as a prophetic reformer, and her acute sense of the battle between good and evil influences her to view what is going on around her in apocalyptic terms. Known as the "Sibyl of the Rhine," she describes herself as wisdom's mouthpiece, "the trumpet sound of the Lamb, destined to resound a little, like a small trumpet not from the living brightness." As we have often noted, Hildegard views the spiritual life from the perspective of a cosmic struggle between light and darkness. In her eyes, there is a war going on. Sin and evil loom large, and she is inflamed to confront, to chastise, to encourage, and to fight. In the introduction to the *Scivias*, Hildegard witnessed to her prophetic call to write and announce whatever she saw and heard from the "Living Light."

Her ministry was to inflame church leaders with a profound consciousness of the justice and compassionate love of God. Her task was twofold: to criticize the evils she saw around her and to energize church leadership for reform. While Hildegard preached clerical chastisement, she also held out the promise of renewal. The clergy, she preached, would be reduced to small numbers, stripped of their wealth, and utterly humbled. Only the devout would survive. In the midst of all this ferment, it is no wonder that a reformist visionary like Hildegard, although herself a member of the Benedictine Order, began to anticipate sweeping changes that would call the complacent clergy to apostolic rigor.

Hildegard played an explicit, public role as prophet and seer in the twelfth-century church. And yet she struggled to overcome doubt and fear to speak about her visions and to assume the strange role of female prophet in the church. Later in life, her fear of speaking about her experiences eventually made her ill, and she recovered only when she had the courage to make her visions public. Like many medieval figures, Hildegard identified the tensions of her world with those of the apostles. In the *Scivias* she spoke of how the Trinity was declared openly in the world by the verdant virtues and tribulations of the apostles. She described how ravening wolves sought to tear them apart, but how their various calamities strengthened them for the struggle. It was through the inspiration and anointing of the Spirit that the church was able to build up its faith (*Scivias* II.4.3, 6).

Like Augustine, Hildegard spoke eloquently of how the Spirit conquered the fear of the apostles at Pentecost. In her vision entitled "The Pillar of the Trinity" in part III of the *Scivias* (see fig. 8), she writes:

the Holy Spirit came openly in tongues of fire...the Holy Spirit bathed them [the apostles] in Its fire, so that with their souls and bodies they spoke in many tongues; and...they cried out so that the whole world was shaken by their voices....And the Holy Spirit took their human fear from them, so that no dread was in them...all such timidity was taken from them, so ardently and so quickly that they became firm and not soft, and dead to all adversity that could befall them. (III.7.7)

As Caroline Walker Bynum notes, "it is hard not to see in [Hildegard's] parable of the apostles a description of her own prophetic role."[83]

But as a woman, Hildegard had to defend her right to speak. It is impossible to know her motivation for referring to herself so often as a "poor little woman speaking...in the Spirit."[84] Hildegard and her supporters had to engage in a number of "creative bypasses" to explain the anomaly of a female, Spirit-inspired prophet.[85] On the one hand, the monk Guibert of Gembloux, Hildegard's devoted disciple and later secretary, defended her right to teach:

The Apostle does not allow a woman to teach in church (1 Tim 2.12), but through the gift of the Spirit, this woman is absolved from that prohibition, and having been taught by His instruction, she has come to know that Scripture very well in her heart: "Blessed is the one whom thou shalt instruct, O Lord: and shalt teach out of thy law" (Ps 93:12)....The Apostle also commands women to cover their heads with veils (1 Cor 11:5ff). Yet this woman is not obliged to wear the kind of veil that wives commonly wear, although some kind of veil is required. For in her great loftiness, she transcends the lowly condition of women. And she is compared to the most eminent of men for "beholding the glory of the Lord with unveiled face, she is transformed into the same image from brightness unto brightness, as by the Spirit of the Lord" (2 Cor 3:18).[86]

But he also felt compelled to address the limits of her femaleness:

> But although the divine anointing teaches her within about all things, and commands her, as we find in her writings, to disclose faithfully and openly for the instruction of her hearers what the Spirit intimates to her secretly, she nevertheless bears in mind her sex, her appropriate condition, and especially the Apostle's aforementioned prohibition. She is obedient to the Spirit, and does not contradict the Apostle sent by the Spirit, but rather, she educates the Church with books and sermons wholly consonant throughout to the Catholic faith, teaching in the Church, but not after the fashion of those who are accustomed to harangue the people.[87]

Hildegard confidently turns culturally accepted limitations on women into assets. She explains that while women's softness may make them more vulnerable to the power of evil spirits, that same softness also functions to make them more receptive to the Holy Spirit. According to Hildegard, the devil tempted Eve precisely because she was the easier target. But this same quality in Eve allows God to effect redemption with similar ease. If the devil had succeeded with Adam, she says, God would have had a terrible time communicating grace through male solidity and hardness (*Scivias* I.2.10). Barbara Newman notes Hildegard's sensitivity to storms and wind, which, in Hildegard's view had a silver lining, making her more receptive to the Holy Spirit—the mighty wind from heaven.[88] Hildegard's femaleness became her personal claim to that divine foolishness that is stronger and wiser than the wisdom of men.[89]

We have noted that Hildegard described this period as "effeminate." Since male leadership was in disarray, God commissioned a woman to speak out against the evils in the church. The Spirit is repeatedly named as the source of Hildegard's inspiration and the authorization of her speech. In the second book of the *Scivias*, Hildegard is addressed by God:

> O you who are wretched earth, and, as a woman, untaught in all learning of earthly teachers and unable

to read literature with philosophical understanding, you are nonetheless touched by My light, which kindles in you an inner fire like a burning sun; cry out and relate and write these My mysteries that you see and hear in mystical visions. So do not be timid, but say those things you understand in the Spirit as I speak them through you.   (II.1)

In the *Book of Life's Merits*, Hildegard recalls that in 1158, at the age of sixty-one, she heard a heavenly voice that said, "From infancy you have been taught, not bodily but spiritually, by true vision through the Spirit of the Lord. Speak these things that you now see and hear....Speak and write, therefore, now according to me and not according to yourself."[90]

But Hildegard is not above invoking the Spirit to get her way. When her good friend and secretary Richardis von Stade was summoned as the newly elected abbess of Bassum, Hildegard refused to let her go. In response to a letter from the archbishop of Mainz, commanding her to release Richardis, Hildegard wrote: "The Spirit of God says earnestly: O shepherds, wail and mourn over the present time, because you do not know what you are doing when you sweep aside the duties established by God in favor of opportunities for money and the foolishness of wicked men who do not fear God."[91] Once again, there is question about Hildegard's motivation. Was she calling on the Spirit simply because she was angry about losing a friend and assistant, or was she lamenting the possibility that Richardis's family had purchased this office—an abuse against which Hildegard had protested often and vigorously.

There are other parallels between Hildegard's portrayal of the Spirit and her own prophetic role. For the most part, Hildegard's texts reveal a critical, confident, thundering prophet. The Spirit plays a key role in her call to the church to repent, and it is the Spirit who warns those who choose the path of iniquity (*Scivias* II.4.14). It is through the Spirit's fiery gift that the church builds up its fortitude so that it can never be thrown down by an error of wickedness (*Scivias* III.4.4). In her vision on confirmation (see fig. 11), Hildegard writes,

> Therefore this tower that you see represents the flaming forth of the gifts of the Holy Spirit, which the Father sent into the world for love of His Son....Before the coming upon them of the Holy Spirit in fire, they were sitting shut up in their house, protecting their bodies, for they were timid about speaking of God's justice and feeble in facing their enemies' persecution....But by Its [Holy Spirit] coming they were so confirmed that they did not shrink from any penalty, but bravely endured it. (*Scivias* II.4.1)

But Hildegard, the thundering prophet, also gave voice to the passive dimensions of the Spirit's presence. In a well-known image, Hildegard speaks of God's elect as wind instruments that remain silent until the divine musician plays them. The prophet sings not with her own voice but with that of Another.[92] In Hildegard's discussion of baptism, the Holy Spirit appears in the form of a gentle animal, "whose place is held by the man who speaks to and teaches the person to be baptized in simplicity of heart" (*Scivias* II.3.32). In a letter to Pope Eugenius III, Hildegard imagined her vocation as a small feather, touched by the king so that it flew miraculously, sustained by the Spirit so that it would not fall.[93]

How are we to think about prophecy today? In an article on Hildegard, Colman O'Dell describes the prophet's role as one that hinges on personal encounter.[94] The prophet receives a special summons and undergoes an unforgettable experience that convinces her that she must reveal with voice and deed the word God has entrusted to her. The prophet is one who yields herself to the experience of deity as handmaid, witness, or sign. Prophets do not speak in generalities but always address persons in concrete historical situations. They speak of God in times of crisis when they perceive that God's interests are at risk. The need for prophets is often answered in a way that seems unlikely to produce success—that is, through the weak or unlettered.

The prophet is one who lives in submission to the Holy Spirit in order that, by her life, actions, and words, she may be a sign of God to the world. Prophets have neither vague ideas nor ready-made solutions. Rather, by the vigor of their ideas, the intensity of their contemplation, and the forcefulness of their words, they compel others to act, giving them worthy reason for doing so. Abraham Heschel describes the prophet as one who intensifies responsibility; who is impatient of excuse and contemptuous of pretense and self-pity. He calls them exegetes "of existence from a divine perspective." The prophet is sensitive to evil and feels fiercely. Heschel queries about prophets: "What gave them the strength to 'demythologize' precious certainties, to attack what was holy, to hurl blasphemies at priest and king, to stand up against all in the name of God?" The prophets, he says, "must have been shattered by some cataclysmic experience in order to be able to shatter others."[95] Hildegard easily takes her place in this company. In many ways in her struggle for ecclesial justice and orthodoxy, Hildegard, the Sibyl of the Rhine, called upon the Spirit, whose testimony, she says, is this: "death cannot resist the justice of God" (*Scivias* II.4.8).

These Spirit narratives provoke us to delineate the sources and contours of our fears and to petition the Spirit for release from them. They also lead us to identify destructive forces in church and society and to examine why we do or do not work against them. Who are our prophets—those who open themselves to the Spirit and witness to God's presence by their words and above all, by their actions? The sources of the prophet's courage are multiple—openness to the Spirit; summons from God; a sensitive conscience; the ability to "cross over" imaginatively to the sufferings of others; boldness of feeling that has the potential to engage others in the struggle.

Like the era of twelfth-century Bingen, our time calls for a prophetic word to real persons in concrete historical situations of sin and suffering.[96] Hildegard invites us to examine our fears and timidities, to allow the grace of God to work freely within us, and to pray for the courage of the Spirit, so that we might open ourselves to grace and have the courage to speak our own prophetic word.

Conclusion

Hildegard's imaginative, symbolic mode of discourse comes from a world that is both distant in time from and alien to our own. Medieval symbolism appears imprecise, ambiguous, hidden to our empirically driven, "bottom-line" culture. And yet symbolic thinking can provide an opening into the Spirit's presence among us. Like symbols, the Spirit provides room to maneuver, to find our own way amid the different paths the Spirit takes in our lives. Hildegard's theology awakens our creativity, defrosting our frozen imaginations about who God might be for us.

Hildegard's Spirit is full of energy, life, vitality, *viriditas*. She offers a model of Christian humanism that bears careful consideration. The Spirit's living voice speaks, luring us to the things of God, challenging us to make these divine realities our own. There is a primordial aspect to Hildegard's Spirit, linked to the natural processes of earth and cosmos. This energy force assumes two important forms. First, Hildegard seems to have known intuitively that a faith without works is a clanging symbol (1 Cor 13:1). Among the many fruits and gifts the Spirit brings, love of justice for our neighbors is front and center. While Hildegard does not place the Spirit at the center of her thoughts on discernment, she is clear about the Spirit's power as the force enabling us to engage in good works and practice the virtues. Surrounded by bad works, Hildegard is adamant and hopeful about conversion, urging her listeners to turn to the Spirit in order to bear witness in daily life to the fruits and gifts in concrete, particular ways.

Second, the Spirit brings us close to God's earth with an intensity and an immediacy that awaken us to wonder at cosmic beauty and to embrace the responsibility of caring for a fragile humanity and endangered ecosystems.[97] Hildegard's worldview reminds us of the aesthetic dimension of the faith—to see God, each other, and the world in terms of their sheer beauty and loveliness. How can we read her and not recall images of the earth's glowing presence from space? Matter—bodies, fields, earth, air, water, and fire—bodies forth the Spirit's presence to us. Science and spirituality meet in openness and engage in serious conversation.

Hildegard's openness to the Spirit's voice and her willingness to name and condemn the greed, arrogance, lying, hypocrisy, and cowardice of her church and world challenge us to be honest about the evils of our own situation. To the cynics among us, Hildegard would no doubt send a letter warning about these dangers, offering solutions, cajoling and threatening us to live in the Spirit, to give the Spirit's healing balm a chance to win out over sin. It is only in the light and warmth of the Spirit's presence that we can muster the courage necessary to speak a prophetic word to ourselves, the world, and the church.

And what about a Spirit who sings and plays instruments? The Spirit binds together in love the sounds of the cosmos, from the heavenly spheres, to the praise of the angels and the hymns of the earth and of humanity. Music is a powerful force in our society. Hildegard helps us realize that music can provide entrée to the Spirit's power and presence, especially to many young people, for whom music is so important. Recall the sound and the accompanying feelings of a great symphony or chorus, the soothing rhythms of country and western; the energy of rock and rap—even the dissonances of recent New Age music, of innovative classical forms or the unusual intervals of Hildegard's own plainchant. How might the Spirit speak to us through these harmonies and disharmonies? Music is an important part of Hildegard's legacy. She invites us through this medium to reconsider aspects of the Spirit's identity we may not have considered before.

God's desire to communicate Godself to the human community is evident in the person of Hildegard, who opens herself to the Spirit, voice of the Living Light (see fig. 10). In her and in so many others, past, present, and future, the Spirit mediates and binds the conversation and love within the Trinity, between the Trinity and the world, and among ourselves. There is urgency and intensity in Hildegard's voice as she speaks to us in our own time of war, famine, genocide, and the potential for nuclear disaster. And yet she is ever hopeful, ever confident, because she trusts that God's love cannot fail. The Holy Spirit has the power to draw us "into the power and patterns of divine love."[98]

Hildegard's texts need to be read and reread until we see her not only as a historical figure but as a lively source of meaning and inspiration.[99] She places the joys and sufferings of existence in an eternal frame, whose center contains images of a loving, creative, three-personed God working in harmony with all of humanity and all the forces of the universe. It remains an inspiring and compelling vision. Hildegard's prayers to the Spirit of life are worthy to be added to our familiar repertoire of prayers of praise.

Holy Spirit, making life alive,
moving in all things, root of all creation,
cleansing the cosmos of every impurity,
effacing sin, anointing wounds.
You are glistening and praiseworthy life,
you awaken and re-awaken everything that is.[100]

⌥

Food for Thought

1. Find a recording of a favorite musical selection. Locate a quiet place and take a few moments of silence. Take some deep regular breaths. As you absorb the sound, melodies, and rhythms of the music into your body and spirit, turn your mind to the Spirit's breath and power and allow the Spirit's presence to touch you through the music. Afterward, reflect on the experience. What was it like? Did you experience the Spirit as close, distant, puzzling, welcoming? Did you discover any new insights into the identity of the Holy Spirit and the Spirit's role in your life?

2. There is a long-standing tension between the charisms and prophetic inspiration of individuals and groups, on the one hand, and the church's official voice, on the other. Both are entrusted with being open to the Spirit and building up the body of Christ. Do you have any awareness of this tension? Can you give specific examples of times when the tension became destructive? How might this tension be put to creative use for the benefit of the church and the world?

3. Hildegard speaks about the Christian faith in cosmic terms. She has a deep interest in natural processes and the rhythms of the universe. She experienced God as Creator, Sustainer, and Friend of the world and wished that the church and each person in it might be touched by the "greening" finger of the Spirit. Our ability to view the earth from outer space and our growing awareness

of ecological destruction allow us to identify with Hildegard's vision over eight hundred years later. Do you ever link the Spirit with the cosmos and ecological responsibility? Is Hildegard's image of "greening" helpful? Is there another metaphor that comes to mind?

4. Hildegard wishes for everyone in the world the gift of *viriditas*—a dynamic quality in which our lives are metaphorically warmed by the sun, moistened by the dew, growing in grace and virtue, alive to the dynamics of authentic relationships. The opposite, *ariditas*, symbolizes those aspects of our lives that are dried up, without water or sun, atrophying or dying. In this state we close ourselves off from others, from God's offer of grace, and from the Holy Spirit, refusing to use our talents, practice virtue, or work for justice. We are bored, indifferent, apathetic, and cynical. Reflect on these two images and on where you find yourself alive or dead in the Spirit.

5. Hildegard writes of justice on almost every page of the *Scivias*. How do you link the Spirit's presence with your energy and creativity for bringing about a more just world? How are/might you become an instrument of the Spirit's healing power for the world's suffering and hurts?

6. Confirmation is the church's sacrament that initiates young Christians into the adult phase of their faith. Reflect on your experience of this sacrament. Then identify Hildegard's Spirit images that you think might be used in confirmation preparation and why. For starters: cosmic web, living light, edifice of salvation, cosmic egg, and so on.

CHAPTER 4

BERNARD OF CLAIRVAUX
The Spirit as Kiss

Bernard of Clairvaux, Hildegard's contemporary, was a celebrated figure of the twelfth-century church.[1] In addition to his key
role in the renewal of Cistercian monasticism (he founded seventy
Cistercian monasteries)[2] and his preaching of the Second Crusade,[3]
Bernard is known especially for his eighty-six *Sermons on the Song
of Songs*, on which he worked for eighteen years, beginning in 1135,
leaving the text unfinished at his death in 1153. This text is considered one of the great mystical classics in the Christian tradition.[4]

Like the other authors we are treating, Bernard did not write
a formal treatise on the Holy Spirit. In fact, the unity of God, preoccupation with the Word, and intense interest in Christ as bridegroom are his overriding concerns. Nevertheless, as we will see,
the Spirit is central to Bernard's conception of the spiritual life,
and material on the Spirit is found throughout his writings. It is
instructive to explore Bernard's pneumatology in light of his very
prominent Christology. The themes we will explore include the
Spirit in the spiritual life; the Spirit as kiss; Bernard's understanding of the relationship between "spirit" and "Spirit"; and the Spirit
as guide to the church.

In the twelfth-century church, Bernard saw himself as a
guardian of the tradition. He worked to correct heresies and was
wary of some of the new theological developments, concerned that
they would confuse and undermine the faith of ordinary people.
But in addition to being an advocate of the theologically "tried and
true," he forged new paths in his understanding and articulation of

the spiritual life in personal, affective terms. His insight into the incarnation as authorizing what he calls "carnal" bodily knowledge of God was truly revolutionary in the monastic world in which he lived. Not only is Christ's body a way for humans to know God, but the incarnation provides an additional concrete, bodily way for God to know the human race.

Bernard's theology has deep roots in the patristic tradition and in the monastic practice of *lectio divina*,[5] rather than in the newly emerging theology of the schools.[6] He did not call on the Spirit to question the status quo but had great confidence in the Spirit's ability to "make all things new" in terms of turning away from sin toward the love of God. We will explore how he understood the Spirit; the images he assigned to the Spirit; and the functions he attributed to the Spirit in the Christian life, monasticism, and the church. As we will see, Bernard took most of his cues about the Spirit—and about most other theological categories as well—from the Bible.

Bernard's poetic, suggestive language often points to the Spirit indirectly. Many Bernardine preoccupations highlight qualities traditionally associated with the Holy Spirit. Even when the Spirit is not explicitly mentioned, the informed reader will recognize language that evokes a Spirit presence. For example, the tradition links the Spirit with the bond of love, fire, peace, the will, the gifts and fruits, anointing, and the flowing of grace—all themes dear to Bernard.[7] Reminiscent of the passage from Romans 5:5, "The Spirit has been poured forth into our hearts," Bernard emphasizes the fluid, affective response to God. The metaphor of the Spirit as the bond of love between the first and second persons of the Trinity echoes in the love language that dominates Bernard's thought—charity *(caritas)*, delight *(dilectio)*, love *(amor)*. God and the soul become bridegroom and bride. The text from the Song of Songs, "Your name is as oil poured out" (1:2), leads Bernard into a labyrinth of images of anointing indirectly alluding to the invocation of the Spirit at baptism and confirmation. Bernard's imagery of hearts on fire with fervent love echoes the imagery of tongues of fire at Pentecost. His insistence that the heights of ecstatic love steer us outward and open us to service in the world emphasizes the important role played by the fruits and gifts of the Spirit.

After a good work one rests more securely in contemplation, and the more a man is conscious that he has not
failed in works of charity through love of his own ease,
the more faithfully will he contemplate things sublime
and make bold to study them.   (SC 47.4)

Bernard's monasticism was no comfortable, ivory-tower existence.
The test of its authenticity was always how the monks loved one
another within and beyond the monastic walls.

Life and Works

Bernard was born in Fontaines, near Dijon, France, in 1091 into a
noble Burgundian family of five brothers and one sister. He seems
to have been a pious child and decided to become a monk at
Cîteaux in 1112 at the age of twenty-three. His enthusiasm for this
way of life was contagious—he persuaded thirty relatives and companions to enter the monastery with him. Only three years later,
Bernard became abbot of the newly founded monastery of Clairvaux
and subsequently presided over the significant growth and renewal
of the Cistercian Order.[8]

Bernard's personality has been a long-standing interest of
scholars. In addition to his gifts of speech, his unremitting zeal for
reform, and his love of friends, evidence suggests that he was also
prone to sulks when he did not get his way; had to be excused from
manual labor because of ineptitude; could be confusing, demanding, and scrupulous; and pushed asceticism to extremes.[9] On the
other hand, there is abundant testimony to his personal attractive-
ness. People loved him, were inspired by him, called upon him for
help, and chose to follow him into monastic life.[10] Throughout his
life, Bernard experienced tension between his choice of the silence
and invisibility of the monastery and his public role in church and
society—a role that seems to have been inflated after his death.[11]

It was not until the 1930s that Bernard was acknowledged as
a theologian in his own right by medieval scholar Étienne Gilson.[12]
Although Bernard's passion was the spiritual life rather than dog-
matic theology per se, that he was clearly a theologian of note is
evident in his many writings as well as his involvement in doctri-

nal disputes with Arnold of Brescia, Abelard at the Council of Sens in 1140, and Gilbert of Poitiers at the Council of Reims in 1148. Bernard lived through five papacies.[13] He supported Innocent II against Anacletus II in the schism that divided the church between 1130 and 1138.[14] Bernard died in 1153, was canonized by Alexander III in 1174 (feast day, August 20), named a doctor of the church by Pius VIII in 1830, and given the title *Doctor mellifluus* by Pius XII in 1953.

Bernard of Clairvaux spoke about the spiritual life in exalted, poetic language.[15] Constant reading, memorizing, and preaching on biblical texts affected his own writing, which is steeped in biblical language and imagery.

> What then, O Bride, will you do?…Where he [Bridegroom] is, you cannot come now, but you shall come hereafter (John 13:36). Come then follow, seek him; do not let that unapproachable brightness and glory (1 Tim 6:10) hold you back from seeking him or make you despair of finding him. "If you can believe, all things are possible to him who believes" (Mark 9:22). "The Word is near you, in your mouth and in your heart" (Rom 10:8). Believe, and you have found him. Believing is having found. The faithful know that Christ dwells in their hearts by faith (Eph 3:17). What could be nearer? Therefore seek him confidently, seek him faithfully. "The Lord is good to the soul who seeks him."
> (Lam 3:25; SC 76.6)

He uses this material in creative ways, associating biblical ideas and images in a free and rhetorically compelling style. At times, the level of detail and the endless lists of metaphorical associations can be dizzying or even numbing. But there are rewards when we manage to cross over into Bernard's world, accept him for who he is, and listen attentively to his wisdom. Bernard makes abundant use of metaphors in which he moves the reader from a concrete object of experience to spiritual realities. Fragrant flowers, breasts, ointments, kisses, arms, and feet point to virtues, support, purification, divine embrace, and merciful judgment.[16] He turns to images of breasts/lactation/milk/suckling/weaning to describe the intimate nature of the spiritual life (SC 9.7). In prayer, the Holy Spirit is the force that fills breasts with divine consolation so that the "milk of sweetness" can be passed on to those who need it.[17]

The primary setting for Bernard's spiritual writings is monastic life. It is important to keep this historical context in mind, but it need not limit application of his thought to other groups in the church. With some adjustment, there is wisdom here for Christians in all walks of life and in all periods of history. In fact, Bernard envisioned the divine marriage as a possibility for all Christians, although he saw monasticism as a special, privileged opportunity for union with God. Bernard's first significant work was *On the Steps of Humility and Pride* (1124). Other treatises include *On Loving God* (1126) and *On Grace and Free Choice* (1128), a more doctrinal work in which Bernard discusses his understanding of the harmony between God's work in us and our free human response to this gift.[18] In 1145 Bernard's novice and fellow monk was elected to the papacy as Eugenius III. Bernard wrote *On Consideration* in 1149 to encourage Eugenius to hold fast to the monastic way of life in spite of the demands and pressures of the papacy. Through his influence on Eugenius, Bernard was also instrumental in the church's endorsement of the Spirit's activity in Hildegard of Bingen, whose works were read and blessed at the Council of Trier. In a now famous letter to Hildegard, Bernard writes, "For you are said to be so favored inasmuch as the hidden things of heaven are revealed to you, and the Holy Spirit makes known to you those things which pass human understanding." When Hildegard is united to God in the Spirit, Bernard writes, she will be able to help the church greatly (*Letter* 366; *Opera* 8:323–24).[19]

In addition to *The Life and Death of St. Malachy*,[20] Bernard left a significant body of letters and sermons that follow the liturgical seasons.[21] In his letters, many of which are public and political in nature (although not lacking in expression of the strong personal emotions for which Bernard is famous), Bernard mentions the Holy Spirit infrequently. In contrast, the term *spiritus* occurs over two hundred times.[22] But his most well-known work is *Sermons on the Song of Songs*—eighty-six sermons in which he interprets the biblical text of the Song of Songs (1:1 to 3:1) as a template for monastic life.[23] Part of a long tradition of such commentaries beginning with Origen in the third century and reaching back into commentaries by Jewish exegetes, this work reveals many of Bernard's key preoccupations. Like commentators before and after him, Bernard used the Song of Songs to underscore the most important features of his spirituality and theology, including his understanding of the Holy Spirit.[24]

Bernard's Theology of the Trinity

Bernard's contemplative, monastic theology would later be contrasted with theological developments in the thirteenth century and would eventually be overshadowed completely by the steady drift of theology toward reason and logic. Bernard was wary of those who would later be identified as precursors of scholasticism—applying grammar and logic to biblical and theological questions. He judged much of the free-ranging intellectual curiosity around him to be fueled by hubris and therefore dangerous to the faith. Bernard regularly distinguished between knowledge sought via the senses out of vain curiosity and that which is sought in the Spirit (Gal 5:16).

But it would be a mistake to paint Bernard as inimical to reason. He steadfastly holds together head and heart. His constant attention to the affections should not mislead the reader into thinking he is anti-intellectual. Correct doctrine and theology were important to him, provided they did not overstep what he saw as the boundaries of reason, and were rightly directed toward union with God. For Bernard, the primary fruit of genuine intellectual work is to grow in the knowledge that we are beloved by God. In *Sermons on the Song of Songs*, the bride asks for a kiss, calling on the Spirit to give her both the taste of knowledge and the savor of grace so she can understand with love and love with understanding (SC 8.6).

For Bernard, the unity of the Trinity is founded on love, that is, on community. Love, he says, is the "law that somehow holds the Trinity together and binds it in the bond of peace" (Eph 4:3).[25] Bernard speaks explicitly about the Trinity in its unity and its plurality of persons, and about the properties of the persons. He addresses the need to keep these aspects in creative tension—

resisting the temptation to minimize or nullify one at the expense of the other. But the tradition's preoccupation with divine unity is evident in Bernard's thought—only the Trinity possesses a "pure and unique simplicity of essence" (SC 80.5). Bernard cautions against assigning gifts to individual persons in the Trinity. We need to beware of excluding any of the persons from any proper gift, he writes, "lest the distinction of Persons should diminish the divine fullness proper to each of them" (SC 11.6). In a sermon on the feast of Pentecost, Bernard speaks of this relational fullness. He envisions Pentecost as the culmination of Christ's resurrection, ascension, and enthronement. The Spirit comes because of the Father's largesse, bestowing charismatic grace.[26]

Bernard pays careful attention to both the Trinity in itself (immanent) and the Trinity as it operates in human life (economic). On the one hand, the eternal ways of generation and procession within the Trinity remain mysteries to the human mind; but these movements are visible to us through divine action and grace.[27] Through creation, incarnation, and the infusion of the Spirit, humans reflect the image of God and are called to union. But this intimacy should not lead to confusion about the utter otherness of God. He writes,

> O truth! O love! O eternity! Oh blessed and beatifying Trinity! To you the wretched trinity that I bear within me sends up its doleful yearnings because of the unhappiness of its exile.[28] Departing from you, in what errors, what pains, what fears it has involved itself! Unhappy me! What a trinity we have won in exchange for you!...O trinity of my soul, how utterly different the Trinity you have offended in your exile.   (SC 11.6)

In his defense of the doctrine of the Trinity against Abelard, Bernard appears as defender of the Spirit's rightful place in the Trinity. If Abelard was teaching that the Holy Spirit does not proceed from the substance of the Father and the Son, then does the Spirit proceed from nothing? If so, Abelard is saying that the Spirit is created—an Arian position rejected by the church. When Abelard used the metaphor of a brass seal and the brass from which it is made to explore the relationship of the Son to the

Father, Bernard accuses him of "grading" the persons in the Trinity—the Father has full power; the Son has some power; and the Holy Spirit, then, must have no power at all. Bernard attacks Abelard, accusing him of being worse than Arius, of introducing profane novelties into the tradition (*Letter* 190.1.2).

At the beginning of *On the Steps of Humility*, written for Godfrey of Langres, who was then abbot of Clairvaux's second house, Fontenay, Bernard describes the threefold way in which truth is perceived—each linked to a person of the Trinity. Christ provides a model for truth about oneself (humility); truth in one's neighbor points to the Spirit, who as brother and friend empowers us to love and console others (compassion); the Father, eternal Truth, beatifies souls in glory (contemplation).[29] Each step is linked with a Beatitude: the meek, the merciful, and the pure of heart.[30] The Spirit is associated with compassionate love of neighbor, mercy, love, and consolation of others.

In the end, Bernard appeals to faith to hold with firm conviction to the mystery of the Trinity, which reason cannot plumb. He writes, "This is a great mystery, worthy of all veneration, not to be keenly scrutinized....To closely examine the fact is rashness, to believe it is piety, to know it is life, and eternal life" (*On Consideration* 5.8.18; *Opera*, 3:482). Bernard immediately declines his own advice, however, and proceeds to an analysis of eight different ways to think about unity, none of which, he says, begins to compare with the unity of the Godhead.

Metaphors of the Spirit

We have seen that Bernard held the traditional Augustinian theology of the Spirit: the Spirit proceeds from the Father and the Son;[31] knowledge of the Father and the Son presupposes knowledge of the goodness of both, which is the Holy Spirit (SC 8.4); the Holy Spirit is the mutual love between the Father and the Son (SC 8.2, 4, 6). In addition, Bernard's complex development of the themes of will and desire, often associated with the Spirit, point to the importance of pneumatology in his thought. Echoes of Augustine, who developed a sophisticated analogy between the Spirit and human will, resound everywhere.

One function of the Spirit that permeates Bernard's entire corpus is the Spirit's assistance in interpreting revelation. Everything that Bernard wrote involved probing the meaning of God's word to the human community. According to Bernard, it is the Spirit who opens to him the depths of the mysteries of God. The Spirit is like the fuel that enables Bernard to probe the spiritual meaning of the Word of God—the heart of his vocation. Not only is the Spirit the author of the sacred text (SC 55.2; 56.1), but Bernard regularly invokes the Spirit to help him understand, especially when faced with a particularly difficult passage (SC 53.3). Bernard goads the monks to follow the Spirit into more and more secret divine places to search for meanings that may yet be attained (SC 17.1). Two hundred years later, Dante chose Bernard to escort him to the throne of the Trinity in *The Divine Comedy*.[32] It was an apt choice, for Bernard functioned for others as Spirit-filled teacher and guide throughout his life.

As noted above, Bernard respected intellectual work when it was grounded in the Spirit—in grace, in the affections, in the will. He was wary of individual interpretations, "for the Spirit teaches not by sharpening curiosity but by inspiring charity" (SC 8.6; 17.1; 14.8; 15.1).

> It is scarcely possible to avoid doubts about the truth when we lack the light of the Holy Spirit; but it is another thing to hanker after erroneous opinions which a man might easily guard against if he would acknowledge his ignorance, as Job did....When the Holy Spirit speaks, both of these yield [falsehood and doubt], for he speaks not merely the truth but the certain truth. He is the Spirit of truth (John 15.26) with whom falsehood cannot be reconciled....When this Spirit is silent we must be alert and hold falsehood in abhorrence, even if bound in the clutches of perplexing incertitude....Either let the Holy Spirit always speak, a procedure that no influence of ours can procure; or let him at least warn us when he withdraws into silence, that his very silence may then be our guide; otherwise, mistakenly thinking he is still leading us on, we shall pursue with disastrous assurance an erroneous course of our own.   (SC 17.3)

The Spirit functions as Director (1 John 2:27; SC 17.2, 4), Instructor (SC 1.3; 16.1), Revealer of meaning and certain truth (SC 8.7; 17.3, 8), Artist (SC 17.2). In all these ways, the Spirit "lights the fire of love" (SC 8.5; 17.3).

In a striking image, Bernard refers to the Spirit as a condiment. Medieval monastics often spoke of meditation on the Word in terms of eating. One ingests it, tastes it, chews it, and digests it so that its nourishment flows into one's being and, over time, shapes the identity of the monk in the image of Christ. In a long alimentary metaphor, Bernard offers this provocative and original image of the Spirit. He writes, "Let us with the Apostles offer a honey-comb at the table of the Lord in the heavenly banquet. As honey flows from the comb so should devotion flow from the words; otherwise if one attempts to assimilate them without the condiment of the spirit/Spirit 'the written letters bring death'" (2 Cor 3:6; SC 7.5).

This reference to the spirit/Spirit is a good example of Bernard's style of exposing layers of meaning in a single text. To begin, Bernard recommends reading the text spiritually rather than literally—a feat made possible only with the help of the Spirit's guidance. Second, medieval Europeans thought of condiments and spices not only as adding flavor to food but as necessary aids to digestion.[33] Without the Spirit, the Word cannot be absorbed and assimilated into one's being and behaviors. The tradition has consistently held that the Spirit's gifts provide a "fluid mobility" to moral action, in contrast to the slow, plodding nature of our efforts to be good.[34] Third, the flavor of the spirit of God is sweeter than honey—a prod to entice the monks to indulge in the rewards of contemplation. Fourth, some spices, like salt, were used to preserve food and many also had medicinal uses. Fifth, there are overtones of the eucharistic table, in the present and at the eschatological, heavenly banquet. Finally, the Spirit functions like glue. His phrase, "without the condiment of the Spirit" reads in Latin *absque spiritus condimento glutieris.* The term *glutieris* has a range of connotations, including glue or paste; pasting together strips of paper to make a sheet of papyrus; to close a wound; to unite, grow together, knit.

The monks' daily exposure to the Word of God in liturgy, reading, and private prayer would have made the Spirit a daily, hourly companion. Bernard's references to the Spirit as the source and goal of breaking open the meaning of the sacred text are too numerous to list. "The Spirit of Jesus, the Good Spirit, the 'Perfect Spirit' (Ps 50:12, 13) will make broad and easy whatever appears narrow and hard in this wicked world....Let us rejoice the more abundantly on the approaching solemnity of the Holy Spirit, Who will teach us all truth, as the Son of God promised" (John 16:13).[35]

> Let us invoke the Spirit of truth (John 14:17), let us call to him from the deep into which he has led us, because he leads us on the way by which we discover ourselves, and without him we can do nothing (John 15:5). Nor should we be afraid that he will disdain to come down to us, for the contrary is true: he is displeased if we attempt even the least thing without him. For he is not "who passes and does not return" (Ps 77:39), he leads us on from brightness to brightness because he is the Spirit of the Lord (2 Cor 3:18). Sometimes he fills us with rapture by communication of his light, sometimes he adapts himself to our weakness and sends beams of light into the dark about us (Ps 17:29). But whether we are raised above ourselves or left with ourselves, let us stay always in the light, always walk as children of the light (Eph 5:8).   (SC 17.8)

Let us turn now to five specific ways Bernard calls on the Spirit.

The Spirit in the Spiritual Life

Bernard's theological spirituality is centered on themes of love, grace, redemption, mercy, compassion, and the gifted nature of existence. It is in this context that we must search out the meaning of his pneumatology. The Spirit works internally to strengthen virtue and externally to endow us with gifts to serve others (SC 18.1). In fact, the entire journey toward holiness depends on the Spirit—the reason monks should avoid self-congratulation—a theme with which Bernard seems preoccupied (SC 13.7). The Spirit links earth to heaven inasmuch as the Spirit who gives life to our spiritual journey is the same Spirit who empowered Jesus to exclaim, "Abba Father" (SC 8.9).

In his Pentecost sermons, we meet a Bernard who cannot contain himself—his lists of the Spirit's functions mimic the pouring out of the Spirit's love (Rom 5:5), a theme we will meet again in the chapter on Bonaventure. The Spirit's power leads the disciples from timidity to steadfastness; helps their weakness by offering compunction, petition, and forgiveness (Rom 8:26); through fire leads the soul to repentance, to hope, and to asking for forgiveness, groaning "Abba, Father." Through loving trust and mercy, the Spirit lifts us up and inclines God toward us.[36] The Spirit admonishes memory by suggesting good thoughts and banishing listlessness; instructs reason to lead us to act on our inspired thoughts; and assists the will to influence us to the good.

In other words, the Spirit is always speaking in our thoughts so that we may hear what God speaks within us. True understanding and speech about God, however, are inadequate without action. In an article on Bernard's rhetorical epistemology, Luke Anderson traces Bernard's rhetorical concern for enlightenment that leads to action. For Bernard, cognitive union is absolutely inadequate when it is separated from affective union. Bernard wants to *move* the audience/reader *to do the truth*.[37] He appeals to the affections that, when enflamed, lead to virtuous behavior. For Bernard, practical truth is ultimately ordered not to theological systems but to the contemplative vision and the authentic virtue that flow from it. In the end, the Spirit will come in fullness to all the saints after death.[38]

In a sermon for the feast of the Ascension, Bernard reminds the monks that this feast is a time for them to grieve Christ's departure, but also to pray that they will be made worthy of the Spirit's coming. The Spirit will fill the whole house (Acts 2:2); grace will teach them all things (1 John 2:27); they will not have to labor to understand (Isa 28:19); with enlightened intellect and purified will, the Spirit will come into their hearts and make his abode with them (John 14:23).[39]

1. Bernard's Christian Anthropology

Bernard was acutely aware of the enormous potential of the human person for good, in spite of sin. In order to convince the reader that God's power to heal is without limit, he creates a list of sins that may be unparalleled in the spiritual literature.

> We have seen how every soul—even if burdened with sin (2 Tim 3:6), enmeshed in vice, ensnared by the allurements of pleasure, a captive in exile, imprisoned in the body, caught in mud (Ps 68:3), fixed in mire, bound to its members, a slave to care, distracted by business, afflicted with sorrow, wandering and straying, filled with anxious forebodings and uneasy suspicions, a stranger in a hostile land (Exod 2:22), and, according to the Prophet, sharing the defilement of the dead and counted with those who go down into hell (Bar 3:11)— every soul, I say, standing thus under condemnation and without hope, has the power to turn and find it can not only breathe the fresh air of hope of pardon and mercy, but also dare to aspire to the nuptials of the Word, not fearing to enter into alliance with God or to bear the sweet yoke of love (Matt 11:30) with the King of angels.
>
> (SC 83.1)

If this plea does not touch the heart of the most sinful among us, nothing is likely to inspire the kind of confidence Bernard feels about the power of God's mercy to remedy sin. The extensive prevalence in our society of brokenness, alienation, and addiction should cause us to identify with Bernard's lament and be challenged to share in his confidence in God's grace.

The way to God requires humility, perseverance, and generosity, but with God's grace, conversion is possible for everyone. This list of sins does not suggest that Bernard's spirituality was centered on human failing. Quite the contrary. He presented the spiritual life as a collaborative process between God's grace and human effort (1 Cor 3:8–9; SC 71.5). The entire journey is rooted in the love of Christ and the power of the Holy Spirit (SC 23.8).[40] Human beings are flesh-and-blood creatures of the earth, born of the desires of the flesh, but when correctly ordered by grace, they end up consumed by the Spirit.[41]

Bernard refers to a wide range of the Spirit's fruits—signs that the seeker is on the right track. A generous God never tires of offering gifts in abundance. For example, the work of the Spirit-filled monk is the praise of God; he lives in continence and practices contemplation, fortitude, and singleness of purpose; he is eager to discover the fruit of wisdom (SC 7.6). In another passage the works of the Spirit produce compunction of heart, fervor of spirit, labor of penance, works of charity, zeal for prayer, leisure for contemplation, love in its fullness (SC 18.6). All of these fruits and gifts are given to be shared with fellow monks and the wider church. Clairvaux became known as the "school of spiritual studies"—a school of Christ whose true master was to be found in the Holy Spirit's anointing (*Vita* 8, 38; PL 185:250).[42]

While Bernard was concerned about guarding orthodoxy, it is clear that his thought was deeply fueled and shaped by religious experience.[43] When Bernard and William of St.-Thierry were both ill, they used their time in the infirmary to read the Song of Songs together. William, judged by many to be the more astute theologian, later commented that Bernard taught him about "his intellectual convictions and experiential feelings...making every effort to teach my inexperienced self the realities that can be learned only by experiencing them" (*Vita* 1.12.59; PL 185:227).

For Bernard, experience is a concept whose meaning he takes for granted—he does not define or describe it in detail. Our understanding of experience as a discrete human encounter with our environment (e.g., "I met a friend downtown for coffee.") is not Bernard's. His "book of experience" points to a deepening understanding of our identity as we move toward or away from God. It is a capacious idea encompassing understanding, struggle, disappointment, desire, delight, love, awe, wonder, and anticipation.[44] Bernard's monastic surroundings also mean that all life experience was communal—a marked contrast to our understanding of experience as primarily individual. What was important about human experience was its relationship to the redemptive process: sinfulness, redemptive insertion into Christ, and the journey toward holiness guided by the Spirit.[45]

Bernard writes, "Today the text we are to study is the book of our own experience. You must therefore turn your attention inwards, each one must take note of his own particular awareness of the things I am about to discuss" (SC 3.1; see also 1.9). Experience precedes and leads to understanding (SC 22.2).

Commenting on Paul's statement about the inscrutability of God's ways and judgments (Rom 11:33), Bernard says, "If you are holy, you understand and you know; if you are not holy, be holy, and you will understand by experience" *(On Consideration* 5.30; *Opera* 3:492.10–11).

In *Sermons on the Song of Songs,* Bernard cites John 3:8 five times: "The wind blows where it wills, and you hear the sound of it, but you do not know whence it comes or whither it goes; so it is with everyone born of the Spirit." The task of the spiritual life, for Bernard, is to follow the Spirit's promptings, whether these lead into the secret places of our hearts or into the heart of God (SC 17.1). With grace, the monks will grow in the ability to discern good from evil promptings; attune themselves to the Spirit's voice (SC 32.7); and share in the bride's happiness that is celebrated by the Spirit (SC 46.5). It is voice that signals the Spirit's presence, and each monk hears a voice ordered to the common good. Because of the Spirit's power, the monks can be sure that the groaning of that Spirit within them comes from, and goes to, God (Rom 8:26; SC 59.6; see also 61.2). At times Bernard refers to his own experience of the Spirit. He says that he has never been conscious of the moment of the Spirit's coming; at times he has a presentiment and later a memory, but he was "never conscious of his coming or his going" (SC 74.5).[46]

For Bernard, it is the Spirit who awakens experience and draws us into union with God. But those guided by the Spirit do not always remain in the same state. No doubt as a way to encourage monks at all stages of the spiritual life, and also those who struggled with dryness and slow progress, Bernard notes that the Spirit sets the pace, "sometimes torpidly, sometimes blithely" helping the monk to forget the past and look to the future (SC 21.4). He counsels those who do not know this experience to "burn with desire" that they might not only know but also feel and touch God (SC 1.11). I cite the following extensive passage about the Spirit's power to draw believers into God's ambit as an example of Bernard's sensual, soaring, biblical poetry.

> "Draw me after you; we shall run in the odor of your ointment" (Song 1:3). It is indeed necessary that we be drawn, because the fire of your love has quickly cooled

within us. We cannot run now, because of this cold (Ps 147:17), as we did in former days. But we shall run again when you restore us to the joy of knowing you are our Savior (Ps 50:14), when the benign warmth of grace will have returned with the renewed shining of the Sun of Justice. The troubles that hide him from us like clouds will then pass, the soft breath of the caressing breeze will melt the ointments and the perfumes will rise to fill the air with sweet odor. Then we shall run, run with eagerness where the wafted perfumes draw us. The lethargy that now numbs us will vanish with the return of fervor, and we shall no longer need to be drawn; stimulated by the perfumes we shall run of our own accord. But now again, "draw me after you." (SC 21.4)

But in spite of his literary skill, Bernard is not taken with his own artistry. It is clear that he took language seriously and enjoyed playing with words, but then he asks, "where is all the seriousness in these words? The external sound is not worth hearing unless the Spirit within helps our weak understanding" (SC 61.2).

Bernard is unusual in his constant concern to link the Christian story with human experience in an explicit way. The monks are not merely to learn about union but to desire it and experience it (SC 1.11). In the context of silence and calm, he says, they can consult their experience and open themselves to the gift of God's presence in faith. Spirit-filled experience yields several truths. For example, experience is crucial to understanding sinfulness.[47]

But experience also teaches spiritual aliveness and growth in the heart, allowing us to realize that it is the Spirit bearing witness with our spirit that we are children of God (Rom 8:16).[48] In *On Conversion*, we find a clear, succinct statement of Bernard's conviction about experience. Bernard describes the comfort and the kindling of desire that follow the experience of grief.

The sweet, inner voice of the Comforter brings joy and gladness to the ears (Ps 50:10). You do not need any speech of mine to commend this to you. The Spirit reveals it himself (1 Cor 2:10). You do not need to look it up in the pages of a book. Look to experience instead.

> Man does not know the price of wisdom. It comes from
> hidden places and it has a sweetness with which no sweet-
> ness known to living men can compare. It is the sweetness
> of the Lord, and you will not recognize it unless you
> taste it. "Taste and see," he says, "how sweet the Lord
> is" (Ps 33:9).   (*On Conversion* 13.25; *Opera*, 4:99.17)

Indeed, Jean Leclercq notes that for Bernard, "everything begins
and ends with experience and, in between, experience is the object
of reflection."[49] Although Bernard's theology involves speculative
thinking, it is above all a practical theology, rooted in everyday life.

At times, Bernard claims inadequacy in speaking about the
highest reaches of the spiritual life (SC 69.1; 71.6; 74.1), but in
other passages he confesses that he is revealing to the monks what
he himself has experienced (SC 51.3; 73.10; 74.5). In many passages the sheer force and clarity of what he says suggest that he
knew firsthand that of which he writes:

> We may even find ourselves at times living beyond our nor-
> mal powers through the great intensity of our affections and
> our spiritual joy, in jubilant encounter, in the light of God,
> in sweetness, in the Holy Spirit (2 Cor 6:6), all showing
> that we are among those envisioned by the Prophet when
> he said: "Lord, they will walk in the light of your favor; they
> will rejoice in your name all day and exult in your righ-
> teousness" (Ps 88:16–17). (SC 13.7; see also 51.3 and 74.5)

His defense of practical knowledge was also, in part, a
response to what he saw as the growing encroachment of dialectic
on theological method. As noted above, knowledge was not to be
sought for its own sake, but only in the interest of wisdom and holiness of life. Truth was to be known, but ultimately it was to be lived.
In a sermon for the feast of Sts. Peter and Paul, Bernard reminds
his listeners that the early disciples were teachers who instructed
not in the art of fishing, or of reading Plato, or of tangling with the
arguments of Aristotle, or with endless searching without ever
coming to know the truth. Rather they teach us how to live.[50]

This evidence documents Bernard's spirituality as full of
hope.[51] For him, the human person is filled with beauty and

endowed by nature with the potential for God—in spite of sin and a lack of gratitude. Grace unleashes freedom to link our wills to God's. "God is present in a man in such a way that he causes an effect...this occurs in such a way that someone need not fear to say that God is one spirit with our spirit, even if he is not one person or one substance with us....Who adheres to God is one spirit with him" (*On Consideration* 5.5.12; *Opera* 3:476; see also SC 82.8; 71.6). And again: "He who is united to God is one spirit with him. On this matter let us listen to [the Spirit] who by his anointing and by constant familiarity has become our teacher above all others" (1 Cor 2:7; 1 John 2:27) (SC 83.6).[52]

2. Love of Neighbor

In Bernard's trinitarian schema, the Spirit is associated with traditional attributes—love, consolation, compassion, and tenderness. While the Father operates in rapture that makes us sons and daughters, and the Son leads us to understand that we are beloved disciples, the Spirit functions in the will to make us friends. The Spirit has everything to do with engaging our affections in love of neighbor, a necessary prerequisite for contemplative encounter with God. The centrality Bernard gives to love of neighbor is visible in a twofold pattern found in many of his sermons. For example, in the body of Sermon 47, Bernard waxes eloquent on the grace required to do God's work and love the neighbor. But when he reaches the culmination of the text he turns to specific problems within the monastery such as drowsiness and singing the divine office in weak and broken tones. It is here, in the nitty-gritty of monastic life that Bernard invokes the Spirit—three times in one paragraph (SC 47.8).

Echoing Gregory the Great's treatment of the gifts of the Spirit, Bernard brings his own brand of order to these gifts. Wisdom, understanding, and knowledge are given for the benefit of the neighbor. To hoard them for oneself is to lack charity. The other gifts are given to nurture one's interior life through compassion and forgiveness, patience and forbearance. To parade before others the secret things of God is to lack humility.[53]

Would that I possessed an abundance of these trees that grow so thickly in the Bridegroom's garden (Song 1:15–16),

121

the Church: peace, goodness, kindness, joy in the Holy
Spirit (Gal 5:22), cheerful compassion, open-hearted
almsgiving (Rom 12:8), rejoicing with those who rejoice,
weeping with those who weep (Rom 12:15). (SC 46.9)

If we allow the Spirit to work in us, love does not move us
away from others but toward them.

"Our God is a consuming fire" (Deut 4:24), and when
the Prophet feels inflamed with divine love he describes
it as a fire sent from heaven into his bones (Lam 1:13).
So when fraternal love gives you gentleness like oil, and
divine love inspires you with zeal like wine, you may feel
secure in your purpose to heal the wounds of the man
who fell among brigands, you are equipped for the work
of the Good Samaritan (Luke 10:30–37). (SC 44.8)

The chambers of love into which the bride is led (Song 1:3) are
none other than the hearts of our neighbors.[54] Ordered love
extends to the neighbor, and even to enemies, to whom love
demands "some feeling, however small" (SC 50.7; 12.7).[55]
Authentic contemplative love arouses the affections and nurtures
the virtuous life—active love in the world.[56] In a Pentecost sermon,
Bernard describes the Spirit as reflecting the perfect sweetness and
kindness of God. What we can know of the Spirit is in the Spirit's
breathing—coming forth from the Father and the Son and proceeding toward humanity.[57]

The Spirit as Kiss

Bernard's poetic gift for expressing the experience of love
was influenced by twelfth-century expressions of chivalry and
courtly love. But he also made his own distinctive contribution to
this tradition, articulating a faith-filled love inspired by the erotic
love language of the Song of Songs.[58] Throughout the tradition,
the imagery of a passionate love affair was used to articulate the
experience of spiritual marriage between God and the soul/church.
For Bernard, the Song of Songs is such a magnificent text that it
could only have been written through the Spirit's presence and

power. "Only the touch of the Spirit (1 John 2:27) can inspire a song like this, and only personal experience can unfold its meaning" (SC 1.11).[59] The Song of Songs, says Bernard, was composed through the art of the Spirit, inspiring its author, Solomon, to write a joyful song out of the experience of exulting in the Spirit (SC 1.5 and 1.8).[60]

Since Origen's third-century commentary on the Song of Songs, Christians have imagined mystical union in terms of the marriage relationship. Bernard writes: "For if marriage according to the flesh constitutes two in one body, why should not a spiritual union be even more efficacious in joining two in one spirit" (SC 8.9)? The language of the Song prompts Bernard to create an elaborate exegesis of the kiss. The first eight sermons of *Sermons on the Song of Songs* explore the text "Let him kiss me with the kiss of his mouth" (Song 1:2). Bernard's fluid, associative style leads him to assign many meanings to the kiss. It is a token of peace (SC 1.6); a sign of reconciliation (2.5). It refers to the Word (2.2), to Jesus, mediator between the divine and the human (2.3); it is the mutual knowledge between Father and Son (8.1); a sign of the fullness of human participation in the divine life (8.8; 9.1). But the kiss is also the Holy Spirit breathed on the apostles (John 20:22).

"He breathed on them," according to John, "and he said: 'Receive the Holy Spirit'" (John 20:22). That favor, given to the newly-chosen Church, was indeed a kiss. That? you say. That corporeal breathing? O no, but rather the invisible Spirit, who is so bestowed in that breath of the Lord that he is understood to proceed from him equally as from the Father (John 15:26), truly the kiss that is common both to him who kisses and to him who is kissed. Hence the bride is satisfied to receive the kiss of the Bridegroom, though she be not kissed with his mouth. Father it is no mean or contemptible thing to be kissed by the kiss, because it is nothing less than the gift of the Holy Spirit. If, as is properly understood, the Father is he who kisses, the Son he who is kissed, then it cannot be wrong to see in the kiss the Holy Spirit, for he is the imperturbable peace of the Father and the Son, their unshakable

123

bond, their undivided love, their indivisible unity.
(SC 8.2; see also 8.5 and 8.7)

While Bernard understood the biblical text of the Song ("Let him kiss me with the kiss of his mouth") primarily in christological terms (SC 2.3), his poetic style and vision do not limit him to this association.[61] For example, in Sermon 8, the kiss of the mouth becomes a gift of the Spirit, with two primary roles (8.2). First, the Spirit makes the knowledge of revelation possible, and, second, the Spirit represents the intimacy of love within the Trinity and between God and believers. Bernard reminds us of the crucial role of the Spirit, without whom we would not be able to participate in the intimate love of Father and Son—the inner dance (perichoresis) of love at the heart of a relational God. Indeed, the Spirit that moved Jesus is the same Spirit that moves believers (8.9; 16.13).

To help him develop the idea that the spiritual journey encompasses various levels of intensity (and is not without setbacks), Bernard imagines three different kinds of kisses. Moving beyond the text of the Bible, he describes the spiritual journey as kissing Jesus' feet (forgiveness of sin), hands (the grace of good deeds), and mouth (contemplation; 4.1). Bernard uses the kiss between the Father and the Son to establish their equality and to contrast the immediate inner experience of the trinitarian persons with that of the human spouse who has access to this knowledge only through the Holy Spirit (Matt 11:27; 1 Cor 2:9).[62] Through this amazing gift of the kiss, Bernard expressed his understanding of the mutual nature of this spiritual union. God's two lips symbolize knowledge and love of virtue—the Word of God which is wisdom. The two lips of the soul refer to human reason and will, through which we are able to return God's kiss. The kiss requires the integrity of the whole person: it is not complete unless wisdom illumines reason and virtue seizes the will. When either reason or will stands alone, one has but a "half-kiss."[63]

The bride realizes that this kiss is no small thing, for to be kissed by the kiss is to be given the Holy Spirit. The kiss is the source of the bride's outrageous boldness toward God, and the object of the bride's desire when she asks for a kiss (SC 8.3). For Bernard, the higher reaches of the spiritual life are characterized by joy, confidence, and boldness. The successful monk develops ease in virtue, ebullience in praising God, boldness like that of the bride in the Song who asks for a kiss. It is the Spirit "who inspires the daring spirit of the bride...therefore she dares to ask for this kiss, actually for that Spirit in whom both the Father and the Son will reveal themselves to her" (8.3; 9.1–2; 10.9; 14.5).

I wonder if Bernard's preoccupation with confidence was intended for himself as a way to reinforce his own courage to engage in a demanding ministry? Or did he find that his spiritual life did indeed give him confidence, and he wanted to pass this wisdom on to his monks? Perhaps he had disdain for those who lacked courage? We do not have access to his inner thoughts, but he does go to say, "From all this we may conclude that the poor, the needy and the pusillanimous cannot prepare an ointment of this kind. Confidence alone can lay hold of its spices and ingredients, a confidence that is itself the fruit of liberty of spirit and purity of heart" (SC 10.9; see Acts 2:4, 11; 1 Cor 1:4–7).

The bride's confidence leads her to ask for a kiss that involves the entire Trinity. Even when scripture mentions only the first and second persons (John 14:9; 1 John 2:23), Bernard insists that the Spirit is implied, for the Spirit is their very love and goodness (8.5) and the sole witness to the embrace of Father and Son (8.6). Therefore, when the bride asks for a kiss, she is asking for the grace of trinitarian knowledge. The revelation of Father and Son is given through the Holy Spirit (1 Cor 2:10), who not only illumines the understanding but also fires the spirit with love (SC 8.5; Rom 5:5).

Bernard creates a distinction between the "kiss of the kiss" and the "kiss of the mouth." The first refers to the relationship of the Trinity to the world—the tie that binds the bride to God in Christ. The "kiss of the mouth" suggests the fuller, more intimate kiss of the bonds within the Trinity, a kiss that is beyond the claim of any creature. This kiss is the Spirit binding the Father and the Son together (John 10:30; 14:10). The kiss of the kiss is what humans receive from the fullness of the kiss of the mouth. "Instead of the spirit of the world, we have received the Spirit that comes from God, to teach us to understand the gifts that he has given us" (1 Cor 2:12; 8:7–8). Since the kiss is common to the one who gives and the one who receives, it must be the Holy Spirit, says Bernard. In his fluid, synthetic approach to contemplation, Bernard associates the Spirit's kiss with a kind of knowledge that always embraces love. The Spirit's kiss is the crucial element that allows humans to receive the revelation of God (1 Cor 2:9).[64]

Entrance into the meaning and role of the Spirit through the metaphor of the kiss may be a stretch for many of us. The surprise or shock of the metaphor may prompt us to make light of it or to reject it. But a good decision about what this metaphor might hold for us today (or not) requires reflection. Think about how the kiss functions in our culture and the network of human experiences related to it—touching, embracing, intimacy. There are profoundly moving and loving kisses, passionate kisses, and "Kiss and Ride" kisses when we drop loved ones off at school, work, or the train station. Some experience genuine kissing every day. Others go decades with nary a peck on the cheek. What are the differences between a phony or manipulative kiss and a genuine, loving kiss? It takes two persons to kiss—bringing us back to community. In some religious rituals, people of faith kiss the cross, icons, or sacred statues. What insights emerge when you bring these many humans experiences of kiss into contact with the Spirit of God?

Spirit/ʃpirit—Boᵭy/carnal/fleʃh

For all his attention to experience and his use of erotic imagery to describe the heights of the spiritual life, Bernard remained a man of his times, that is, one who saw the world in categories that privileged Spirit over spirit and both over the bodily condition of humanity.[65] Imagine the effect of his counsel to novices to "leave their bodies outside the monastery where only spirits lead" (*Vita* 1.4.20; PL 185:227). Humans have ties to both earth and heaven, but Bernard is clear about which is the stronger. In an exploration of the Adam/Christ typology, Bernard associates Adam with sin, guilt, and desires of the flesh. But for those who have the mind of Christ (1 Cor 2:16), the Spirit gives witness (Rom 8:16) and pours out love (Rom 5:5). We are "more closely related to God by our birth than to Adam by the flesh, since we were spiritually present in Christ long before our existence in the flesh of Adam."[66]

In the opening paragraph of *Sermons on the Song of Songs*, Bernard strikes the keynote of what is to follow. He cites Paul, "We teach not in the way philosophy is taught, but in the way that the Spirit teaches us: we teach spiritual things spiritually" (1 Cor 2:13; SC 1.1). The material in the Song of Songs is intended for mature monks, those who are able to eat solid food (1 Cor 3:1–2), who have moved from the carnal to the spiritual.[67] "It is the Spirit," Bernard writes, "that gives life, the flesh has nothing to offer" (John 6:64; SC 10.8).[68] The trajectory of the spiritual journey begins with carnal attachment to Christ's humanity and then advances to spiritual attachment to Christ's spirit/Spirit. How are we to sort out the various meanings Bernard attaches to these terms?

Bernard often associates "Spirit" with "spirit."[69] In addition to being the third person in the Trinity, the Spirit also lies behind Bernard's multiple and complex understanding of "spirit." For example, the link that ties human life to God and the saints includes both "Spirit" and "spirit." He writes: "Therefore let this union be in the spirit, because 'God is a spirit' (John 4:24), who is lovingly drawn by the beauty of that soul whom he perceives to be guided by the Spirit, and devoid of any desire to submit to the ways of the flesh, especially if he sees that it burns with love for himself" (SC 31.6).[70] Leaving behind the country of bodiliness, the soul enters heaven, the realm of the divine Spirit, and joins the spirits of the blessed (*On Consideration* 5.1.2; *Opera* 3:468). It is God the Spirit who bestows the variety of angelic gifts and graces (*On Consideration* 5.5.11; *Opera* 3:475); each person receives a manifestation of the Spirit distinct to her/him and for the profit of all (1 Cor 12:7; *On Consideration* 5.5.12; *Opera* 3:476).

Bernard plays on the tension between Spirit/spirit and body/carnality. While he sees Spirit/spirit as the higher value, the body is not without worth. Perhaps in part as a reaction to the dualistic, anti-matter tendencies of the flourishing and extremely dualistic Cathar heresy, Bernard takes care to laud the positive contributions the body makes in the spiritual life.[71] Devotion to the humanity of Christ is a "great gift" of the Spirit—and love of Christ is not possible at all without the Spirit, whether we love in the flesh or in the fullness of the Spirit (SC 20:7–9). Mortal bodies are needed as the vehicles through which the soul operates and serves the neighbor. How can you instruct the listener, he writes, if you have no tongue, or receive it if you have no ear? (SC 5.5).[72] Since no created spirit can act directly on our minds, the body is required to acquire or increase knowledge or virtue. Only the Holy Spirit can communicate directly to the mind, and since it is the Spirit who uses Bernard's tongue to instruct his disciples, there is no reason to boast or take the credit himself (SC 5.8–9). In the end, soul and a spiritualized body will be united in eternity in imitation of Christ's own glorified body.

Echoing Paul's analogy of the many gifts in the body of Christ (1 Cor 12), Bernard offers this realistic description of the human body in his sermon at the funeral of Bishop Malachy. It is a powerful and unified passage that I cite at length.

> Our very love for this holy father compels us to grieve more deeply along with that people and to shudder more violently at the cruelty of death which has not refrained from afflicting the Church with so terrible a wound. Death surely is awful and inexorable....Blind and improvident, it has tied Malachy's tongue, shackled his footsteps, relaxed his hands, and closed his eyes. Those faithful eyes, I say, which by their tender, loving tears used to bring divine grace to sinners. Those undefiled hands which had always loved to be exercised in laborious and humble deeds, which had so often offered up for sinners the saving host of the Lord's body and were lifted up to heaven in prayer without anger or contention; which are known to have conferred many blessings on the sick and to have shone with various signs. The feet so often wearied in the eagerness of loving mercy. Those footsteps, always worthy to be pressed with devout kisses. Finally those holy lips of the priest which guarded knowledge; the mouth of the just which shall meditate wisdom and his tongue which shall speak judgment, yes, and mercy too. By these he used to cure great wounds of souls.[73]

It is clear from this eulogy that Bernard treasured the physical human body and grieved its loss. But his explicit interest is in its spiritual value and function.

In other passages, Bernard frequently juxtaposes "spirit" (and occasionally "Spirit") with "flesh" or "corporeality." Jean

Leclercq explains, "All of Bernard's teaching is concerned with this passage from 'flesh' to 'spirit' in the Pauline sense, and from self-centeredness to an openness to the whole of creation as the result of going beyond oneself, of surpassing that instinctive self, as yet unliberated by grace."[74] Complaining about someone who had lured his nephew away from religious life as a Canon Regular, Bernard cites 1 Corinthians 2:14—"the carnal person does not receive the things of the Spirit for they appear as foolishness."[75] Even if we allow that Bernard is following Paul in his understanding of "flesh" as sin, statements such as the following place a great burden on bodiliness. "For a perishable body presses down the soul, and this tent of clay weighs down the teeming mind" (Wis 9:15; SC 16.1). "In prayer, one drinks the wine that gladdens a man's heart (Ps 103:15), the intoxicating wine of the Spirit that drowns all memory of pleasures of the flesh" (SC 18.5).

Bernard favored this verse from the Book of Lamentations: "Christ the Lord is a Spirit before our face" (Lam 4:20; SC 3.5; 20.3, 7). He saw the incarnation as an accommodation to human fleshly ways of knowing. Since the human race was too frail to return God's glorious, unapproachable love, God sent the Son to accommodate this weakness. God "wanted to recapture the affections of carnal men, who were unable to love in any other way, by first drawing them to the salutary love of his own humanity, and then gradually to raise them to a spiritual love" (2 Cor 5:16; SC 20.6). Even though Bernard does not dwell on the concrete events of Jesus' life,[76] he describes how human hearts are attracted to Christ's humanity and the works he performed while in the flesh (SC 6.3).[77] But this mode of knowing God must be superseded. Spiritual love *(amor spiritus)* is superior to carnal affections *(carnis affectus)*.

In a sermon on the feast of the Ascension (a favorite of Bernard), he described Christ's being assumed as "the crown and consummation of all the other festivities" that bring the journey of the Son of God to happy completion. When Bernard asks why the Spirit could not be present until Christ had departed from the earth (John 16:6–7), he replies that it was certainly *not* because the Spirit abhorred the companionship of Jesus' flesh. Rather, the Spirit was to teach the community how to walk by faith rather than sight after Jesus left them. Bernard laments that by becoming attached to Jesus' flesh, human minds block the fullness of heavenly grace. The Spirit was sent to transform affections, that is, the will, "so that they who before would have retained their dear Master among them, were now better pleased that He had ascended to the Father." Thus was fulfilled the promise that their sorrow would be turned into joy (John 16:20).[78]

Bernard goes on to apply the experience of the apostles to that of the monks. In Bernard's schema of the spiritual life, there is a clear pattern that begins with sensible love and progresses to rational and then spiritual love (SC 20.9).[79] If the apostles, because of their attachment to the flesh of the Lord, could not be filled with the Spirit until the flesh had been withdrawn from them, how can monks expect to receive the Spirit of infinite purity while they are still attached to their own corrupt flesh?[80] He warns, "Shall he who is always clinging to the dunghill, who fosters his flesh, who sows in the flesh and reaps in the flesh (Gal 6:8), have the boldness to expect the comfort of that heavenly visitation, to look for that 'torrent of pleasure' (Ps 35:9), that grace of the 'mighty Spirit'" (Acts 2:2)?[81] If the Spirit delays, Bernard entreats the brothers not to lose heart, for the Spirit shall surely come and shall not be slack (Hab 2:3). Bernard recommends earnest prayer. He says, "learn to pray, learn to ask, to see and to knock, until you receive and find and it shall be opened to you" (Matt 7:7).[82]

Sorting out Bernard's understanding of the various meanings of "flesh" and spirit/Spirit is not an easy task. It helps to remember that he is certainly using the term *flesh* but not as repudiation of the body in Paul's sense of things that move us away from God.

> For "so long as we are in this body we are exiles from the Lord" (2 Cor 5:6). Not because we are embodied, but because we are in this body which has a sinful lineage, and is never without sin. So you may know that it is not our bodies but our sins that stand in the way, listen to what Scripture says: "it is our sins that raise a barrier between us and God" (Isa 59:2).   (SC 56.3)

Addressing monks, many of whom came to religious life after marriage and child-rearing, Bernard does not deny or reject human, physical love. He assigns significant, positive value to desires directed toward the carnal love of Christ's humanity, even though, ultimately, they are to be directed toward the spiritual realm. The important role Bernard assigns to Christ's flesh has some kinship with Catherine of Siena's description of Christ as the "bridge" connecting earth and heaven. As a twelfth-century person, Bernard could not have embraced what we see as the intrinsic value of, and appreciation for, the body—in itself gift and blessing, made holy by its participation in the incarnation. Today physicality is seen as an integral part of the spiritual journey. But given the medieval monastic worldview, Bernard's positive assessment of the role of the body in the spiritual life is nothing short of astounding. Somehow he gained insight into the incarnation that allowed him to value, even treasure, Christ's bodily nature and the ways in which it identifies us with Christ.

Many in our society neglect or abuse their bodies. Others become obsessed with appearance and health. Excessive consumerism in developed nations breeds the need to compete, which is rarely good for bodies. Some of us work too much, sleep too little. Others exert little effort and end up as couch potatoes. Destructive habits of eating, drinking, sexual excess, and drugs (legal or otherwise) wreak havoc on the body. Bernard's reminder to keep Christ's body before our eyes can help us develop a reverence and care for our own bodies. The Spirit has the power to transform us in the totality of our existence if we will allow it.

Some of us may describe "spirit" as our particular energy or aura—what we communicate when we enter a room. It is the source of our thoughts, creativity, passion, decisions, perceptions. It is what makes us alive in physical, emotional, spiritual, and intellectual ways. It is what disappears when we die and become an inert body. Spirit is also tangible in communities. We talk about school spirit, or the lively or dead spirit in families, churches, workplaces, schools, or neighborhoods. Bernard's attention to spirit/Spirit can help us sort through confusion about how these two realities are distinct (they are not simply interchangeable) and yet related. For believers, spirit of life is linked to the divine Spirit, to incarnation, to God's presence within the world and each of us.

The Spirit and Church Business

We have noted the crucial role Bernard's location within monasticism and the larger church played in his thought. As a reformer and monk, he was called upon to settle disputes, refute heretics, consult with popes, and serve as spokesperson for a range of ecclesial initiatives. His letters reveal that he upheld the charism of office but also demanded leadership that flowed from gifts received directly from God through the Spirit.[83]

Bernard had a focused idea of the proper order and functioning of the church and worked tirelessly to bring it about. Medieval theology was captivated by the concept of hierarchy, powerfully articulated by the fifth-century author Pseudo-Dionysius.[84] Bernard viewed the church as a well-ordered community with monks at the top, followed by clerics, and then laypeople—all of whom were called to holiness through distinct roles in the body of Christ.

> Just as the soul sees with her eyes, hears with her ears, smells with her nose, tastes with her mouth, touches with the rest of her body, so God accomplishes different ends through different spirits....In some he shows himself loving, in others perceiving, in still others doing other things—just as the manifestation of the Spirit is given to each for his or her own good (1 Cor 12:7). (*On Consideration* 5.5.12; *Opera* 3:476).

Bernard was not shy about calling attention to the church's evil and sinfulness, but he also expressed great hope in the church's possibilities. "Yet there is one who truthfully and unhesitatingly can glory in this praise. She is the Church, whose fullness is a never-ceasing fount of intoxicating joy, perpetually fragrant. For what she lacks in one member she possesses in another according to the measure of Christ's gift and the plan of the Spirit who distributes to each one just as he chooses" (Eph 4:7; 1 Cor 12:11; SC 12.11). Even when he does not explicitly refer to the church, everything Bernard says about the Spirit includes the community of faith.

1. The Spirit Guides the Church

Bernard invoked the Spirit to guide the church in various situations (Gal 5:16, 25; SC 11.5). In his treatise *On Consideration*,

Bernard warns Pope Eugenius against getting caught up in the worldly affairs to which he must attend as pope—Eugenius needs to keep his eye on *spiritual* things (*On Consideration* 1.5–7; *Opera* 3:399–404). During the schism, Bernard writes to the bishop of Aquitaine, supporting Innocent over Anacletus. "Whether we will it or not, the truth of the Holy Spirit will necessarily one day be fulfilled" (*Letter* 126.8; *Opera* 7:315).

In a letter to Bruno, who is discerning whether or not to accept nomination as bishop of Cologne, Bernard links the Holy Spirit with vocation. He writes, "Whether the calling is from God or not who can know, except the Spirit who searches even the deep things of God (1 Cor 2:10–12), or one to whom God has revealed it" (*Letter* 8.8; *Opera* 7:47). Often Bernard calls on the Spirit to help him recruit others to religious life. To Geoffrey Perrone and his friends, Bernard writes, "You also, brothers, are 'changed into the same image from glory to glory even as by the Spirit of the Lord'" (2 Cor 2:18; *Letter* 102.2; *Opera* 7:258). In another letter, Bernard encourages Romanus, a subdeacon of the Roman Curia, to enter religious life by reflecting on death: "O how blessed are the dead who lie in the Lord (Rev 14:13) for they hear from the Spirit that 'they may rest from their labors'" (*Letter* 105; *Opera* 7:265).

In a number of instances, Bernard calls on the Spirit to bless elections. The Spirit will assist the prayers of those electing a new prelate in the Archdiocese of Sens in 1144 (*Letter* 202; *Opera* 8:62); those monks electing a new abbot at the Abbey of Fountains are to have one mind and are not to be divided since they "dwell in the school of Christ, under the leading of the Holy Spirit" (*Letter* 320; *Opera* 8:254); and in the disputed election of the bishop of Langres, in which Cluny was pitted against Clairvaux, Bernard counsels the participants to invoke the Holy Spirit (*Letter* 164; *Opera* 7:373). To the monks of the Abbey in the Alps, who had associated with Cîteaux and who were in the process of electing a new abbot, Bernard writes, "Our Order is lowliness, humility, voluntary poverty, obedience, peace and joy in the Holy Spirit....No words can express the mutual charity that exists between us and which works in a marvelous way by the pouring forth of the Spirit. It only remains, brethren, that after invoking the Holy Spirit, you hasten to elect an abbot" (*Letter* 142.1.3; *Opera* 7:340–41).

2. The Spirit of Unity and Peace

Like Augustine, Bernard desired peace and unity in church and monastery, but the tone and emphasis are different. Bernard speaks of the Spirit's unifying presence primarily in the context of monastic life, and I do not sense the intense, almost desperate preoccupation with church unity exhibited by Augustine. Bernard counsels the monks to "be eager always to preserve unity in the bonds of peace, exhibiting toward all the humble love which is the bond of perfection" (1 Pet 4:8; *Letter* 345.1; *Opera* 8:287). In a Pentecost sermon Bernard writes: "Let us pray, brothers, that...the Holy Spirit may always find us all in the same place (Acts 2:1) not only by bodily presence because of our promised stability but also by unity of hearts."[85]

As abbot, Bernard found himself riding herd on what must have been at times boisterous, even violent behaviors.[86] In addition to the common practice of imagining the spiritual life as ceaseless warfare against temptation and sin (SC 1.9), Bernard portrays in realistic and psychologically insightful terms a world of angry, slanderous, wounding, verbal assaults, sneering contempt, and complaints that required a firm hand and careful diplomacy (SC 29.3–5). In the midst of monastic failings and foibles, court intrigue, and ecclesial rivalries, Bernard invoked the Spirit of unity and peace along with the virtue of gentleness (SC 12.4). From his desire that the monks be one as Christ and the Father are one (1 Cor 12:31) to his counsel on the smallest mundane detail, Bernard longs for oneness in the spirit. He wrote to the monks at St. Anastasius in 1140 to commend their zeal for monastic life (and to discourage their use of medicine when they are ill). He exhorts them to strict observance citing Ephesians 4:3, "preserving the unity of the Spirit in the bond of peace" (*Letter* 345; *Opera* 8:287; also *Letter* 65; *Opera* 7:160).

Other references to the Spirit as the source of unity include a letter to Pope Celestine in which Bernard argues against Abelard, whom he sees as tearing the robe of Christ—a robe that symbolizes the unity of the church, which is made firm by the Holy Spirit and cannot be divided (*Letters* 358 and 333; *Opera* 8:272–73, 303).[87] Bernard conveniently appeals to unity in a letter to an abbot who is upset that one of his monks plans to transfer to Clairvaux. Bernard argues that the monk, Thomas, has to follow the Spirit's call, and since it is from God and not Bernard, it is better not to interfere (*Letter* 372.2.3; *Opera* 8:347–48).

In what is perhaps Bernard's most moving letter to the abbots assembled at Cîteaux, he begs them to maintain their unity and have compassion on his labors that necessitate his being away from home. His complaint of not having the Spirit himself is his way of lamenting his physical absence from the gathering of the monks in whose midst the Spirit resides.

> ...a man miserable and born to suffering, yet your brother. Would that I might merit to have now the Holy Spirit, in whom you have met together, as my advocate to your whole body, that He might impress upon your hearts the trouble that I am suffering and bring before you brotherly affections my sad and suppliant countenance just as it now is....Before all things endeavor to keep the unity of the Spirit in the bond of peace, and the God of peace shall be with you. (*Letter* 145; *Opera* 7:347)

Bernard alludes here to the ill health that plagued him all his life—he fears the possibility that he will die away from the brothers.

Don't Quench the Spirit

Bernard cites 1 Thessalonians 5:19, "Quench not the Spirit," in a number of letters, warning those who may have strayed from gospel living not to close themselves off from the Spirit's movements. In a letter to a young man named Fulk, who had been a Canon Regular before being persuaded by his uncle to return to the world, Bernard chastises the uncle, who by luring Fulk away from monastic life is found "to have resisted the Holy Spirit with all his power" (*Letter* 2.3; *Opera* 7:14). To another who delayed entering the monastery for a year—Thomas of St. Omer—Bernard also writes a chastising letter. He describes this delay as a wrong to God, a seedplot of discord, an incentive to wrath, a food of apostasy, "such as must quench the Spirit" by shutting off grace and producing lukewarm feelings. God had bestowed the Spirit of vocation, but by using his freedom badly, Thomas grieved the

Spirit, and so it was withdrawn (*Letter* 108.2.3; *Opera* 7:278–79). Another letter written in 1125 chides Haimeric, chancellor of the Holy Roman See, to stand firm against opponents in the interest of the good of the church. In addition to citing "Quench not the Spirit," Bernard cites Acts 7:51, "You stiff necked people...you always resist the Holy Spirit" to warn the chancellor about the need to make good choices (*Letter* 311; *Opera* 8:239).

But at other times, the Spirit simply seems absent—even in monks who practice prayer faithfully. Bernard wants to help them deal with dryness in prayer and lack of virtue in life by pointing out that such experiences can be used to protect themselves against haughtiness, to attract grace, and to prepare for the "leap-ings of the bridegroom." As is his custom, Bernard refers to very specific faults likely to show up in community life—"repugnance for work, drowsiness at vigils, quickness to anger, obduracy in hatred, over-indulgence of tongue and appetite, greater indiffer-ence and dullness in preaching" (SC 54.8).

> That sorrow from which tears spring I cannot find, such is my heart's hardness (Mark 16:14). The psalms are stale, reading is disagreeable, prayer is devoid of joy, the accustomed meditations irretrievable. Where now that intoxication of the Spirit (Eph 5:18)? Where that seren-ity of mind, and peace, and joy in the Holy Spirit?
> (Rom 14:17; SC 54.8)

The witness of others and the memory of being drunk in the Spirit are important. By facing honestly the first signs of lukewarmness or arrogance, the monks open up the possibility, once again, of standing in awe at God's presence. Like the disciples at Pentecost who appear to be drunk, the monks are called to holy inebriation (Acts 2:16–17; SC 49.2).

Conclusion

In some ways, Bernard seems more relevant to our twenty-first century consciousness than the scholastics who came after him.[88] He can rightly be called a Christian humanist, given his profound sense of the beauty and capability of the human person. He teaches us how to integrate better our deep sense of dignity and freedom with a theism centered in a trinitarian God—Creator, Redeemer, and empowering Spirit. Bernard communicates a strong sense of confidence and hope that the transforming love affair he describes is possible for everyone. He passes on to us what had been engraved in his own heart: the gospel comes not only in word, but also in power and in the Holy Spirit with full conviction (1 Thess 1:5). Hope does not disappoint us because God's love has been poured into our hearts through the Holy Spirit (Rom 5:5). All the monks need to do is ask for the Spirit with urgent prayer and God will grant it.[89]

A second aspect of Bernard's legacy revolves around the polyphonic texture with which he weaves themes of love and binding to describe the Spirit's work. Alongside Christ the Bridegroom, the Spirit is given a role in the Trinity as bond of desire and mutual love. Through the metaphor of the kiss, Bernard invites us to reflect on the spiritual life in ways that may be foreign territory for us. If we trust his direction, Bernard can help us rehabilitate our erotic drives by blessing our desires for holiness in all areas of our lives, challenging us to purify them of egoism and compulsions. He invites us to reflect deeply on the question: What makes me happy?—a tall order in our rampantly consumerist society. He reminds us that the point of the spiritual life is not to curb desires but to purify and deepen them. The Spirit guides our hunger for meaning and fulfillment, helping us to lift it up and order it toward love of God and neighbor.

But our understanding of the Spirit's role in the twenty-first century must also move beyond Bernard. Today, we invite the Spirit to help us treasure embodiment and the material world as a reflection of the divine. We petition the Spirit to bless our physical, sexual selves in all their richness and confusion in ways not possible in the twelfth century.[90] We call upon the Spirit to infuse all aspects of our spiritual and material existence with Spirit power and presence as we struggle to deal with the complexities and agonies of our global village filled as it is with violence, hate, and indifference toward other people and the earth.

Incarnation functions in harmony with the Spirit. It causes us to see every molecule infused with inherent beauty and holiness.

We see our bodies or the material world no longer as obstacles to the spiritual life but as vehicles to its fulfillment. It is clear that Bernard did not suffer unduly from dualist strains in the tradition. He did not disdain matter or the body. But the general medieval penchant to associate flesh with sin no longer serves contemporary Christians. We are more attuned to the intrinsic goodness of Spirit-filled matter, resisting opposition between earthly historical existence and heavenly eternal life. The enemy remains sin, but we struggle to locate sin within the complex networks of human life in ways quite different from medieval consciousness.

It is the case that Bernard, like all the authors discussed in this volume, used the Spirit to support his own opinions about the behaviors of others and about how the church should be run. Jean Leclercq remarks that in certain cases, Bernard seemed to insinuate that people who agreed with his position had a monopoly on the Holy Spirit.[91] In any age, human beings face vexing moral, social, and spiritual problems with the best light available. Like us, Bernard was responsible to absorb the tradition and to open himself to the Spirit's voice. It is safe to say that he did a better job than most, but this did not free him from blind spots. We may raise questions about some of the ways Bernard put the Spirit to work in the very particular situations he faced.[92] Hindsight gives a certain advantage. But Bernard was certainly a model of one who paid attention to God, who opened himself to the Spirit's power and mustered as much prayerful honesty and insight as he could in his attempt to discern good spirits from bad.

Bernard's concluding comments in a Pentecost sermon provide a fitting end to our exploration of his pneumatology. He offers a mini-portrait of the deeply desired ideal of Spirit-filled community life.

> Let us pray, brothers, that the days of Pentecost be fulfilled in us, the days of forgiveness, the days of exaltation, the days of truest jubilee (Lev 25:10), and that by our bodily presence and equally our oneness of heart, the Holy Spirit may always find us in one place (Acts 2:1) because of our vowed stability, to the praise and glory (Phil 1:11) of the Church's bridegroom, Jesus Christ our Lord, who is over all, God forever blessed (Rom 9:15).[93]

◎∕◎

Food for Thought

1. When you read the scriptures, do you consciously call upon the Spirit to be present as you discern their meaning for your life and our times? What was your reaction to Bernard's metaphor of the Holy Spirit as "condiment" as an aid to absorbing the Word of God?

2. Bernard's understanding of the Spirit was centered in his life as a member of a monastic community. Does what he says about the Spirit's role in the Christian life translate for you? Were you able to apply any of his ideas to your own situation of community life—whatever form that might take?

3. Bernard may be the only individual in the Christian tradition to identify the Holy Spirit as a "kiss." How did you react to this metaphor? What associations with "kiss" do you bring to this discussion? Do you think we should retain and use this metaphor or discard it? Why?

4. What relationships do you see between "Spirit" and "spirit"? How do you define your "spirit" and how might you connect your "spirit" with the Holy Spirit?

5. Reflect on ways that our society encourages neglect or abuse of the body. How are you influenced (or not) by these values in your own life? Do you think about your body as a temple of the Holy Spirit? If you truly believed that your body is a repository of the divine presence, how would your concrete daily life change?

6. Bernard's writing is filled with references to feelings and emotions. When you reflect on your prayer, how would you describe it in terms of the balance of feeling/affect and reason/intellect? Are there changes you would like to make in this regard? Do you associate thinking and feeling with a particular person of the Trinity? How might Bernard be helpful?

Figure 1: Duccio (di Buoninsegna) (c. 1260–1319), *Pentecost*

Figure 2: Andrea Orcagna (c. 1308–c. 1368), *Pentecost*

Figure 3: El Greco (1541–1614), *The Pentecost*

Figure 4: Mexican (n.d.), *Holy Trinity*

Figure 5: Andrei Rublev (1360–c. 1430), *Trinity of Uglic*

Figure 6: Rubielos Master (c. 1400), *The Coronation of the Virgin with the Trinity*

Figure 7: Jean Malouel (c. 1370–1415), *Pietà with God the Father*

143

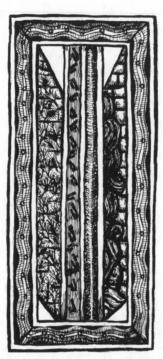

Figure 8: Hildegard of Bingen (1098–1179), *Trinity*

Figure 9: Hildegard of Bingen (1098–1179), *The Blue Christ*

Figure 10: Hildegard of Bingen (1098–1179),
Hildegard Inspired by the Spirit

Figure 11: Hildegard of Bingen (1098–1179), *Confirmation*

Figure 12: Laurent Girardin (c. 1460), *The Trinity*

Figure 13: Jean Fouquet (c. 1420–c. 1480), *The Hours of the Holy Ghost: Pentecost (Prime)*

Figure 14: Nicholas of Verdun (1130–1205), *Pentecost* (detail)

Figure 15: José de Ribera (1588?–1652), *Holy Trinity*

Figure 16: Bohemian/Prague (c. 1410) cutting from an Antiphonary, initial "G" [loria tibi Trinitas], *The Trinity*

Figure 17: Masaccio (Maso di San Giovanni) (1401–28), *The Holy Trinity*

Figure 18: Albrecht Dürer (1471–1528), *The Holy Trinity*

Figure 19: Limbourg Brothers (fifteenth century), *Pentecost*

149

Figure 20: From the Psalter of Ingeborg of Denmark,
Queen of France (c. 1200), *Pentecost*

Figure 21: Flemish-Liege Leaf from a Psalter (c. 1260), *The Pentecost*

CHAPTER 5

BONAVENTURE
OF BAGNOREGIO
The Spirit of Divine Abundance

Life and Times

Bonaventure of Bagnoregio (1217–74), identified by many as the second founder of the Franciscan Order after Francis of Assisi, had a dual career—first as a student and professor at the University of Paris and then as Minister General. Given his stature in the church, it is strange that we have little biographical information about Bonaventure, although some fondly attribute this lack to his characteristic humility. He was born in Bagnoregio, a town in Tuscany, Italy, to Maria di Ritello and John di Fidanza, a physician. It is likely that he received his early education from the Franciscans in his native town. When Bonaventure was seventeen, he went to Paris to study with Alexander of Hales, who had decided to become a Franciscan, bringing his Chair of Theology into the order. In an age in which many stellar universities were founded, Paris shone as the jewel of medieval intellectual life. It was there in 1243 that Bonaventure entered the Franciscan Order. Although Bonaventure never met Francis—Francis died when Bonaventure was nine—he recounts a story of being saved from death through Francis's intercession.[1] Perhaps this early experience at an impressionable age was the foundation for Bonaventure's sense of intimate connection with the Poverello. Bonaventure became Master in Theology in 1254 and taught at the University of Paris until 1257, when he was elected Minister General of the order, a post he held for seventeen years.

The challenges Bonaventure faced in the church and in the order were considerable, given the strife and division of the period. The thirteenth century began with the storming and destruction of Constantinople by western Crusaders (1204), and a massacre of Albigensian heretics in southern France (1209). Throughout the century, control of the Holy Land continued to shift between Christians and Muslims.[2] At century's end (1290) church and state joined forces to burn books and expel Jews from England.

Heresies such as Catharism and Albigensianism continued to challenge the church.[3] Ecclesial abuses and scandals did not abate, and Bonaventure found himself exhorting the friars to remain loyal to a church riddled with scandal and resistant to the pastoral reforms initiated by the Fourth Lateran Council in 1215.[4] Clashes between civil and ecclesial powers intensified, with the hegemony over the Papal States and Sicily in the balance.

The thirteenth century also witnessed positive developments. Innocent III spearheaded what some have called a "pastoral revolution." The Fourth Lateran Council mandated that every Christian take communion and make confession at least once a year; clergy were encouraged to improve their knowledge to preach and teach; a system of synodal meetings was established to ensure that reforms went forward. Innocent oversaw the founding and flourishing of the Franciscan and Dominican medicant orders established to preach against error, serve the needs of the urban poor, and assist in the reform of the church. The Franciscans in particular were deeply engaged in implementing the pastoral reforms of the council and inspired a range of new devotions for ordinary Christians.[5]

But the new group of friars encountered challenges. Especially neuralgic was the debate about the meaning of poverty. Some friars were living a lavish lifestyle. Others were so intent on evangelical perfection that they publicly criticized bishops who were dragging their feet in the implementation of the pastoral reforms of Lateran IV.[6] This council also curtailed the foundations of new religious orders, which were proliferating. New groups were required to adapt an already existing rule. The ministries of the mendicant orders were seen by many as "new" and therefore illegitimate. Secular clergy and bishops lobbied hard to close them down. This threat led Bonaventure to argue for papal power that could protect his order. At the same time, Bonaventure had to consider the very practical needs of expanding ministries. A mission that involved schools and ministries not envisioned at the beginning required advanced education.[7]

To deal with these difficulties, when he became Minister General, Bonaventure made a trip to Mount Alverna, where Francis had received the stigmata, hoping to imbibe Francis's spirit and inspiration in order to heal divisions and lead the order in positive directions. There was acrimonious competition between the newly formed Franciscan and Dominican orders on the one hand, and between the friars and secular bishops and clerics on the other. Issues involved the right to preach, the mendicant practice of poverty, and turf wars over who had the right to engage in various pastoral ministries. Some ministries involved money—funds that ordinarily went to secular clerics ended up in Franciscan hands.[8] Bonaventure reminded the friars of the first line of Francis's Rule: "to observe the Holy Gospel of Our Lord Jesus Christ by living in obedience, without anything of one's own, and in chastity."[9] Since there were both internal and external factors threatening to divide the order, unity must have been a serious preoccupation for Bonaventure. It is true that he connects church unity to the Spirit, but he does not emphasize this function of the Spirit in the same way or to the same extent as we saw in Augustine.

The first of several conflicts over authority and obedience began the year Bonaventure joined the order. In addition to conflict with bishops about whether the Franciscans had a legitimate mission in the church, there were internal conflicts among Franciscans. Splinter groups ("Spirituals" or "Zealots") who were adamant about maintaining the original rigorous tenets of Francis's Rule were fomenting dissent within the order.[10] Others were influenced by the thought of an Italian monk, Joachim of Fiore (c. 1132–1202), who preached a theory of history that was later used to interpret Franciscan life as the inauguration of a new age of the Spirit.

Joachim held that there were three states of the world, corresponding to the three persons of the Trinity. The first age was ruled by the Father, who represented power and inspired fear—this was the time of the Old Testament. In the second age, the period of the New Testament, the wisdom hidden through the ages was revealed in the Son. A third period, the kingdom of the Holy Spirit, would inaugurate a new dispensation of universal love, proceeding from the gospel of Christ but transcending the letter of it, abrogating the need for disciplinary institutions. Joachim held that the second period was drawing to a close and that the third epoch (already in part anticipated by St. Benedict, and later linked with Francis of Assisi) would actually begin after some great cataclysm, which he tentatively calculated to take place in 1260.[11] Conflict over these issues created an atmosphere of contention and disobedience, with dissenters claiming the guidance of the Spirit as justification for their insubordination.[12]

The conflict with the Spirituals is an example of an issue relevant to Bonaventure's theology of the Holy Spirit. Marjorie Reeves notes that Bonaventure both condemned and embraced various aspects of this prophetic tradition. No doubt aware firsthand of the dangers of some aspects of apocalyptic thought, Bonaventure is anxious to dissociate himself from the Joachite trinitarian conception of history and from ideas about the Holy Spirit that eclipse Christ in any way.[13] Joachim's ideas on the Trinity had been condemned at the Fourth Lateran Council in 1215.[14]

Given the intense emotions associated with the prediction that the year 1260 would inaugurate the third age of the Holy Spirit—one can safely wager that Bonaventure would practice restraint and weigh carefully *any* talk about the Holy Spirit. On the other hand, Bonaventure seemed to have sympathy with some of the ideas generated in this conflict. For example, he identifies Francis with the end of the world, the "Angel of the Sixth Seal" of Apocalypse 7:2.[15] He speaks of the ages of history in terms of the three persons of the Trinity,[16] and toward the end of his life, he read the "signs of the times" as ripe for impending crisis.[17] But C. Colt Anderson has argued convincingly that Bonaventure used some of the language and imagery of the Joachites as a way to steer the community away from Joachite positions.[18]

Bonaventure faced other conflicts as well. At a provincial synod at Reims, legislation was passed that went against the Franciscans. The number of friars who could preach and hear confessions in France was restricted. In 1267 before going to Rome to appeal this legislation, Bonaventure wrote his *Collations on the Seven Gifts of the Holy Spirit (Collationes de septem donis)*, in which he reflected on the Spirit's gifts in light of the tensions in the order, appealing for peace and unity.[19] Given Bonaventure's strong christological interests, it is no surprise that he presents the Spirit as the power that joins us to Christ in grace (2 Cor 13:13).[20]

Bonaventure's written corpus is extensive and varied. Scholars classify his works in three categories, reflecting the various "hats" Bonaventure wore in his life: theologian-scholar, mystic-pastor, and leader-defender of the faith.[21] As a student and professor, Bonaventure wrote scholastic works including a *Commentary on the Sentences* of Peter Lombard; disputed questions on the *Mystery of the Trinity, Knowledge of Christ,* and *Evangelical Perfection; A Brief Summary of True Theology (Breviloquium);* and biblical commentaries on Luke, John, and Ecclesiastes. Beginning in 1257 when Bonaventure was elected Minister General of the order, he wrote works aimed at the spiritual and pastoral needs of the order: *The Soul's Journey into God (Itinerarium mentis in Deum); The Tree of Life (Lignum vitae); The Triple Way (De Triplici Via); The Major and Minor Lives of Saint Francis (Legenda maior* and *Legenda minor).* After 1260, he wrote a series of polemical sermons *(Collationes)* to address specific problems the order confronted.[22]

In 1273, Bonaventure was named cardinal bishop of Albano by Pope Gregory X and worked on the preparations for the Second Council of Lyons the following year. He died at this council on July 15, 1274. He was canonized on April 14, 1482, by Pope Sixtus IV and declared a Doctor of the Universal Church by Sixtus V on March 14, 1588, with the title "Seraphic Doctor."

While his texts reveal little autobiographical material, Bonaventure was remembered as a man of great gentleness and humility. The bull of canonization reads, "Bonaventure was great in learning, but no less great in humility and holiness. His innocence and dove-like simplicity were such that Alexander of Hales, the renowned doctor whose disciple Saint Bonaventure became, used to say of him that it seemed as though Adam had never sinned in him." And an account of his funeral reads, "Greeks and Latins, clergy and laity followed his bier with bitter tears, grieving over the lamentable loss of so great a person."

Bonaventure's Literary Style

Thirteenth-century theology can be characterized by two distinct but tightly related strains: the development of "scientific" interests visible in the scholastic method; and an understanding of theology's ultimate goal as holiness—the practice of a contemplative and moral life. Bonaventure embraces both of these aspects in a thoroughgoing way, and like the thought of all medieval theologians, his work is permeated throughout with the language of the Bible.

Like Bernard, he takes pains to distinguish between knowledge that is puffed up and knowledge grounded in the Sprit. In his commentary on the Gospel of John 16:13, "When the Spirit of truth comes, he will guide you into all truth," Bonaventure asks how the Holy Spirit can teach since to teach is an act of wisdom and therefore belongs to the Son, not the Spirit. Bonaventure responds that the act of teaching belongs to the entire Trinity but that sometimes it is linked with the Son and other times with the Spirit. The knowledge that is speculation is attributed to the Son, while that which belongs to experience and devotion—the latter a prerequisite for contemplation—is attributed to the Holy Spirit.[23]

But perhaps more than some of his university peers, Bonaventure wanted to preserve the practical, pious orientation of theology that marked the monastic schools of the twelfth century. For Bonaventure, theology is above all a practical science whose overriding purpose is to assist the faithful to achieve loving union with God. Thus, while he acknowledges, appreciates, and uses rational argumentation with great skill, he has a "tendency to prefer opinions which seem more religious even though other opinions are logically possible."[24] Bonaventure's practical bent serves as an important foundation in our textual search for Spirit imagery, providing a lens through which to view his understanding of the Spirit's active role in the spiritual life.

Bonaventure's Spirit language and imagery are profoundly biblical and inspired by Francis, who seemed almost obsessed by the Spirit's presence and power.[25] Bonaventure describes the inspired scriptures as the heart, mouth, tongue, and pen of God.[26] The Word of God is like the sea, whose depths can be endlessly plumbed.[27] Like Bernard, Bonaventure's knowledge of the Bible is wide and deep. One image leads his biblical imagination to another, and he weaves them together in fluid and provocative ways.

In the volumes celebrating the seventh centenary of Bonaventure's death in 1974, Marigwen Schumacher suggests that Bonaventure's word choice and images in his sermons suggest that he was in touch with his own religious experience.[28] Schumacher investigates the poet-preacher-mystic's personal, intuitive, inspired, nonrational contact with deity. She cites the article on Bonaventure from the *Dictionnaire de spiritualité:*

> Throughout the periods of religious history, there has perhaps never been found a saint who has made the world hear an invitation to mystical union as broad and as urgent as the Seraphic Doctor. For these reasons, among many others, the spiritual doctrine of St. Bonaventure, totally infused as it is with unction and poetry, constitutes a unique monument in mystical literature.[29]

A renewed valuation of image and metaphor in theology can lead to a greater appreciation of Bonaventure's use of these literary devices even though his context and ours differ considerably.

Schumacher writes: "to touch—to probe—in a way, invade the mythic impulses of Bonaventure's heart and mind, is, I feel and think, an as-yet-unexplored path into his contact with God." She sees "an intrinsic, inescapable relationship between the 'what' of Bonaventure's thought and the 'how' of his expression—mysticism tangible through metaphor."[30] Bonaventure's vividness of expression and sensitivity to nuance and cadence pull the reader into the beauty and thence into the spiritual depth of what he is saying.[31]

Bonaventure's Trinitarian Theology

Like Thomas Aquinas's *Summa theologiae,* Bonaventure's theology and spirituality are structured around a threefold movement of emanation, exemplarity, and return. Everything comes forth from God, mirrors the person of Christ in time, and returns to divine fullness at the end of history. Bonaventure's theology is deeply trinitarian, christocentric, and focused on the living of the

Christian life, especially after he became Minister General of the order. Like Bernard's writings, Bonaventure's work reflects the importance of affectivity and the integration of head and heart. But unlike Bernard, Bonaventure does not emphasize the spiritual journey as one that moves from carnal to spiritual love, nor does he place the same emphasis on the role of the will in the spiritual life. In Bonaventure's image of the human person, both body and soul play an integral part in the spiritual journey, and his emphasis on the cross produces a spirit quite different from Bernard's preference for the glorified Christ of the ascension.[32]

For Bonaventure, Christ is the absolute center of creation, history, and the spiritual life. Christ is the exemplar of all reality, the source of all knowledge, the revealed fullness of the Father, the one mediator between God and the world. The essence of the spiritual life is to follow in the footsteps of the humble Christ. Bonaventure views Francis as the epitome of the imitation of Christ, an *alter Christus*. Creation and incarnation provide the foundation stones of his thought, along with historical and cosmological interests. Although Bonaventure's theology is christocentric to the core, a wide sampling of texts reveals that he had a clear agenda regarding the Holy Spirit. Christ pours forth the Spirit into the members of his Body, and while we have noted a range of circumstances that would have caused Bonaventure to be cautious about references to the Spirit, these issues did not prevent him from frequently calling on, and describing, the Spirit's role in the Christian life.

Like Augustine, the starting point for Bonaventure's trinitarian theology is the unity of God, from which he moves to consider the persons in God.[33] Bonaventure complements his dependence on Augustine with ideas from the fourth-century Greek Cappodocian fathers, who emphasized the personal nature of the three divine persons.[34] Bonaventure chooses Gift as the primary name for the Holy Spirit—the first Gift or grace from which all virtues, gifts, and beatitudes flow. The context for understanding the Spirit as Gift is Bonaventure's appropriation of Pseudo-Dionysius's concept of the self-diffusive nature of the good.

Through his teacher, Alexander of Hales, Bonaventure was exposed to the work of Pseudo-Dionysius[35] and Richard of St. Victor,[36] whom Bonaventure incorporates into his own creative synthesis based on the concepts of the good and love—elements that are central to his understanding of the Spirit. From Pseudo-Dionysius, Bonaventure appropriated the idea of self-diffusive goodness *(bonum diffusivum sui)* to describe God.[37] Bonaventure sees positive qualities in "unbegottenness"—the first person is the fountain of all fullness, the fecund source from which flow all goodness, immanent processions, and external productions.[38] The centrality of the concept of hierarchy to Bonaventure should be understood in this context.

From Richard of St. Victor, Bonaventure borrows the analysis of love, personalizing it and transforming it by placing it within the Dionysian concept of the good. Beyond specific elements of his trinitarian theology, one can say with confidence that Bonaventure's entire understanding and practice of theology reflect the Trinity. For him, theology encompasses the science of scripture, the science of faith, and the wisdom of faith. This latter knowledge orients the whole of theology toward contemplation of God in ecstatic love.[39]

Not just theology but all reality reflects its trinitarian exemplar in vestige, image, and similitude. Zachary Hayes comments about Bonaventure, "His is a view that may be seen as a consistent economic trinitarianism for which the world and its history is a vast symbol of the trinitarian God who communicates [God]self in being, in grace, and in consummation."[40] Inasmuch as human persons reflect the divine being as *imago Dei*, they possess in their very beings a desire to see and to be one with the Trinity. Bonaventure writes, "nothing less than the Trinity can fill the soul that is capable of the entire Trinity...nothing satisfies the thirst of the human soul but the Trinity."[41]

For Bonaventure, the Son emanates by nature *(per modum naturae)*, the Holy Spirit by will *(per modum voluntatis/liberalitas)*.[42] The divine generosity finds its perfection in producing a personal Gift. Bonaventure connects the Spirit with love, which is the perfect actuality of a personal God, the primary affection and the root of all others, since it involves true liberality and generosity.[43] Bonaventure shows interest in the economy by emphasizing the correspondence between the mission of the Spirit in the history of grace with the Spirit's eternal emanation.[44] Mission is an aspect of emanation, revealing to the senses the historical effects of the eternal processions and manifestations of the Trinity.[45] The Father generates; the Spirit receives; the Son does both.[46] The Holy Spirit, proceeding from Father and Son actively united in love, is called "bond"—not because the Spirit gives something to the other persons but because the Spirit is *fully receptive*.[47] The attribution of certain characteristics to each person helps believers know the persons in their distinctive modes of being. Zachary Hayes offers the following schema.[48]

Father	Son	Holy Spirit
Unity	Truth	Goodness
Eternity	Beauty	Delight
Principle	Exemplar	End
Efficiency	Exemplarity	Finality
Power	Wisdom	Goodness

Another trinitarian schema is outlined in C. Colt Anderson's analysis of *Bonaventure's Collations on the Six Days*.[49]

TRINITARIAN Relations	PRIMARY Appropriations	MONARCHIAL Appropriations	ANGELIC Orders
Father in himself	Eternity	Stability	Thrones
Father in the Son	Beauty	Wise	Cherubim
Father in the Holy Spirit	Joy	Holy	Seraphim
Son in the Father	Power	Authority	Dominations
Son in Himself	Wisdom	Virility	Virtues
Son in the Holy Spirit	Will	Triumphant	Powers
Holy Spirit in the Father	Piety	Leading	Principalities
Holy Spirit in the Son	Truth	Teaching	Archangels
Holy Spirit in Himself	Holiness	Protecting	Angels

We see in these schemata that Bonaventure associates the Spirit with the traditional qualities of goodness, holiness, and finality. The Spirit as related to the Son is linked to truth, while the Spirit's functions include leading, teaching, and protecting (often assigned to the Father). In terms of hierarchical organization, the Spirit's location is at the bottom, represented by the lowest choirs of angels. Nevertheless, Bonaventure associates the Spirit's procession from the Father and the Son with the exalted qualities of freedom, generosity, and liberality.

The Spirit as Companion on the Spiritual Journey

Two major contexts for Bonaventure's talk about the Holy Spirit are ecclesial ministry and the spiritual life. The first is most prominent when he speaks about the friars, the order, and the church. In these contexts, the Holy Spirit assists in the proper living of the vows, in holding the community together in unity,[50] and in prayer.[51] The context for the Holy Spirit's role in the spiritual life is broader, focused on the goals of a moral life and union with God. The soul's journey, which is open to everyone, begins in faith, develops into a virtuous life, and is fulfilled in the gifts of the Holy Spirit.[52] When the soul opens itself to wisdom, the intellect becomes beautiful, the affections delightful, and the will strong. Then the soul is grounded on the solid foundation of rock, like a house built on seven columns which symbolize the seven gifts of the Holy Spirit.[53] Whether referring to the church or to individual spiritual life, Bonaventure counsels church leaders and the faithful about the importance of humility, without which leadership flounders[54] and salvation is jeopardized. Humility, Bonaventure says, is the basis "of complete spiritual health."[55] Humility is a *sine qua non* of the gift of leadership.[56]

The one text Bonaventure devotes explicitly to the Holy Spirit is the *Collations on the Seven Gifts of the Holy Spirit*, a series of sermons delivered to the friars in 1268 shortly before he departed for Italy to see if he could get Rome to restore banned Franciscan ministries in France.[57] Thus, Bonaventure's admonitions involved pressing issues—the brothers needed to correct what was obviously problematic behavior in order to preserve their ministries in the church. Bonaventure needed to correct the lax as well as the overly zealous. Perhaps it was in the interest of these needs that

Bonaventure reverses the order of the gifts found in Isaiah 11:1–3. He begins with fear of the Lord and ends with wisdom.

Bonaventure aimed to change the minds of many: those who were skeptical about the value of study; those who placed too much trust in philosophy; and those who were impatient about the slow pace of reform. He accomplishes these objectives by reminding the friars that the Spirit has a life-giving role in the institutional church and by calling them to the center, Christ. As Franciscans called to follow the poor Christ to the cross, he says, they should expect pain, suffering, and resistance as part of their vocation and bear it with patience and joy. Bonaventure encourages the brothers by reminding them that God will bring justice and consolation to the oppressed, and that being open to the Spirit's gifts will enable the community to flourish.

Bonaventure upholds the tradition in which the gifts of the Holy Spirit build on and complete the virtues.[58] The gifts of the Spirit function as the height or consummation of the spiritual life. They are not only a sign of God's acceptance and a privilege of adoption, but "a ring of espousal, for He made the Christian soul His friend, daughter and bride."[59] The gifts function to help us comprehend and elucidate what has been accepted in faith. Humans must cooperate with the Holy Spirit, intentionally participating in various spiritual disciplines that lead us to "good" control of our lives.[60] In a bold statement about the Spirit's role, Bonaventure writes: "Whatever therefore the Father does and the Son suffers, it is nothing without the Holy Spirit. For he joins us to Father and Son."[61]

Bonaventure relates the gift of piety to patience and charity toward others. Piety nurtures a life free from pride, envy, anger, harsh judgment, laxity, greed, gluttony—a life of poverty, obedience, mercy, meekness, righteousness, purity of heart, and peace. Mercy and compassion accompany piety—and Christ, once again, is the model—assuming human flesh and dying on the cross, the great sacrament of piety.[62] In this discussion, Bonaventure fends off acrimonious divisions by reminding the friars that it is the Holy Spirit who makes of the church one body. "We are one body, we ought to be piously concerned for one another…we ought to have compassion for one another."[63] The Spirit who conceived Christ in Mary's womb is the same Spirit who conceives believers in the uterus of the church. The gifts of the Spirit are shared in a community of sisters and brothers who share the same mother, the same food and have the same inheritance.

The Spirit's gifts provide spiritual strength. In his discussion of fortitude, Bonaventure cites models of strength—Saints Catherine and Lucy, and above all, the Virgin Mary. These gifts allow us to progress in the spiritual life and bring ease to what otherwise would be arduous.[64] Likewise in his discussion of the gift of counsel, Bonaventure names as models the apostles and saints— Anthony, Basil, Augustine, Martin, Gregory, Benedict, Dominic, and Francis. Counter-models include the Pharisees and a host of unnamed culprits who maligned various aspects of the Franciscan Order.[65]

The gift of wisdom builds the individual soul, the order, and the church into loving dwelling places of God, resting on seven pillars: chastity, innocence of mind, moderation in words, docility toward good things, generosity in action, maturity in judgment, and simplicity of intention without pretense. By exhorting the brothers to greater fidelity to the Rule they had promised to keep, he offers a recipe for a healed and renewed Franciscan community.[66] Bonaventure does not mention the Spirit in his treatment of wisdom, choosing rather to link it with the wisdom of Christ, the cross, and the throne of God. But the Spirit is implied when Bonaventure describes wisdom, infused with mercy and humility, as the gift that brings light to the mind, the heart, and action.[67] In this text, Bonaventure's pneumatology is inseparable from his trinitarian theology and Christology. The Spirit's bestowal of grace and love involves the overflowing fullness of the Father, binds us to Christ, and makes us members of his Body.

Bonaventure relates the spirit of gratitude to the virtue of humility, which he sees as not only the proper response to God's love but also as a necessary disposition to receive the Spirit's gifts.[68] Once again, the primary exemplar for this humility is the Christ of Ephesians, who "descends and ascends that he might fill all things" (4:9–10). For the faithful to descend in imitation of Christ means to recall their fragility (Isa 47:1), blindness (Jer 18:2), and slavery (Exod 19:24).[69] The poor and lowly Francis is the secondary exemplar.[70] Francis was anointed, inspired, and taught by the Spirit; his words were full of the Spirit's power, causing amazement in his hearers; he and his followers were often blessed with the consolation of the Spirit; the reception of Eucharist made Francis drunk in the Spirit.[71] Bonaventure reminds his listeners that the transformation from death to life is a gift of trinitarian love. The faithful, therefore, have no cause to boast about their free will or their good works.[72]

Other exemplars are the apostles, who did not presume to face the powers of the world on their own but only when fortified by the tongues of fire sent by the Spirit. The mission of the Holy Spirit to be carried out by them is "sweet"; that is, it is devoid of haughtiness. The anti-exemplar is Simon the Magician of Acts (8:9–24), who thought he could buy the gifts of the Holy Spirit with money.[73] A century later, Catherine of Siena will use the image of a meal to make a more direct connection between the Holy Spirit and humility. She imagines the Spirit as the waiter at table serving the Lord's food of enlightenment, namely, hunger for souls and blazing desire for the church's reform.

The Holy Spirit belongs especially to the world of affective dispositions. Love heads the list, described by Bonaventure as sweetness, touch, delight, fire, charm, ecstasy, inebriation.[74] We turn now to four specific themes: the Spirit as God's liberality (flowing water), the transformation of the affections, contemplation, and love of neighbor. My primary, though not exclusive, referents are *The Soul's Journey into God*, ten sermons for the feast of Pentecost, and two sermons on the Trinity.[75]

Holy Spirit as Flowing Water

As noted above, in that strain of the tradition referred to as Neoplatonic emanationism, God is imagined as the *fons plenitudo*, the "fountain fullness" or primal source from which love and grace overflow to Son and Spirit and thence to creation.[76] This idea pervades Bonaventure's entire theology and his image of God.[77] In christological terms, Bonaventure imagines the garden of the soul watered by Christ's blood and the Spirit pouring forth from Christ's side at the crucifixion.[78] This image of flowing liquid is given a distinctive pneumatological thrust when linked with Paul's famous phrase in Romans 5:5: "God's love has been poured into our hearts through the Holy Spirit who has been given to us." We have seen how important this passage in Romans was to Augustine, but Bonaventure made use of it in ways quite different from Augustine. Bonaventure turns to biblical imagery of moving, flowing, rippling, cascading fluids to communicate a powerful sense of the Spirit's presence. This imagery has given birth to a certain way of understanding the Trinity and salvation history, in which the Spirit functions as the culmination in a process that begins with the creator God and ends in a kind of Spirit fullness.[79] But we also know that the Spirit is active from the very first moment of faith and at every stage along the way.

For Bonaventure, the central symbol of God's generous love is the cross.[80] In later chapters we will see how Julian of Norwich and Catherine of Siena also underline this theme and relate it to the Spirit. Bonaventure had an acute sense of sin,[81] but an even keener awareness of God's loving generosity. Sin is horrid, but it takes on even more sinister dimensions because it is a negative response to this overwhelmingly gracious love. Theologically, Bonaventure's appropriation and transformation of the idea of the self-diffusive quality of the good suggests that it was not an abstract idea for him, but one that was alive and functioning—an idea that he clearly wanted to communicate to others.[82] In a Pentecost sermon delivered in 1253, he says, "Who has a heart so unyielding that, when he reflects and considers the generosity which the Lord manifests in creation, in redemption, in calling us individually...he is not wholly touched and transformed into love for God?"[83]

This liberality is manifested primarily in the incarnation, cross, and the sending of the Holy Spirit, but also in endless gifts, virtues, fruits, beatitudes—all gratuitously given.[84] These generous acts of God are related in a special way to the third person, to whom is appropriated the name Gift, who comes in fire at Pentecost to bestow a host of charisms on the church.[85] A contemporary of Bonaventure, Mechthild of Magdeburg (c. 1208–c. 1282 or 1297), also employed the metaphor of flowing liquids to speak of the Spirit's revelations to her. She calls this communication a gifted address, and she titles the text describing her experience *The Flowing Light of the Godhead*. She writes: "I, unworthy sinner, was so flowingly greeted by the Holy Spirit." Like Bonaventure, Mechthild's "bewildering fertility" in her use of the theme of "flowing" finds its center in her understanding of the Trinity, and in particular in the outpouring of the Holy Spirit.[86]

In another Pentecost sermon delivered in Paris to the Friars Minor, Bonaventure invited his Franciscan brothers "to gather in, ruminate on, and embrace with affection the unparalleled event of Pentecost, since it revealed so clearly the divine mysteries."[87] He wanted not only to arouse gratitude in their hearts but also to offer instruction on how to be good friars and ecclesiastical leaders. Bonaventure not only speaks of the overwhelming outpouring of God's generous goodness in the sending of the Spirit, but also conveys a "felt sense" of this goodness by "piling on" biblical imagery that describes fluids (mostly water) flowing, gushing, and bubbling.[88] We have noted how this style, common in medieval sermons, is foreign to us, but attention to sound and imagery as well as to content allows us a glimpse into how such a literary technique might have functioned.

This literary form is especially evident in Bonaventure's sermons for Pentecost. I offer two examples. The first is from a sermon delivered in Paris to the Friars Minor, who, according to Bonaventure, were singled out especially to receive the graces of religion and salvation.[89] Multiple iterations of moving water press home his point: the river flowing out of the garden of Eden represents the Holy Spirit's exuberance of life, joy, fruition, and consummation (Gen 2:10); rivers flowing out of Eden water the garden, which becomes four rivers (Gen 2:10); "a spirit of compassion and supplication will be poured out on Jerusalem" (Zech 12:10); a little spring becomes a river and there is water in abundance (Esth 10:6); the response to their cries was like a great river brimming with water that came from a little spring (Esth 11:10); "the river of the water of life, bright as crystal, flowing from the throne of God...was shown" (Apoc 22:1); "the well where God made a covenant with Hagar" (Gen 16:4); "a garden fountain, a well of living water, and flowing streams from Lebanon" (Cant 4:15); "I will make this dry stream bed full of pools" (2 Kgs 3:16); Gideon discovers who is to fight with him by observing how they drink water (Judg 7:5); "clean water will be sprinkled" (Ezek 36:25); "spirit will be poured out" (Joel 2:28); Wisdom is infused into all God's works (Eccl 1:9); a fountain will be opened to cleanse the house of David (Zech 13:1); a spirit of judgment and burning will wash away the filth of Jerusalem (Isa 4:4).[90]

Read the following Latin sounds aloud slowly to hear the flow of the language: *effundam, effusam, fluvium paradisum irrigantem, per fontem scaturientem, fluvium…procedentem, per puteum viventis et videntis me, per puteum aquarum viventium, per alveum torrentis, per aquas Gedeonis, distributam, opulentam, fructuosam, infusio, diffusionis, abluerit, mirabiliter largiflua, amplificata.*

Bonaventure's construction of this sermon was intended either to show off his biblical virtuosity, to make a plug for the thoroughness of medieval biblical aids and concordances, or, as I prefer to think, to move and compel the brothers to pay attention to the incredible, wondrous, amazing God of Pentecost and to allow the Spirit to influence them in their religious lives. Bonaventure wanted to convince his audience that through the Spirit, God was offering them the power to repent; to renew commitments; to understand the mysteries of God; and to be unified, tranquil, inflamed by desire, and made beautiful by being conformed to the light.

A second example of this "piling on" technique comes from the fifth sermon for the feast of Pentecost. Bonaventure begins,

> It seems good to me to reflect devoutly on the ways in which the Holy Spirit replenishes his disciples today with such abundant wonders. The Spirit does this by most fervent clarity of light to understand spiritual truth; by the freshest [*vernantissima*] piety of the divine majesty; by the most charming sweetness of goodness in which we participate in heavenly unction; by most generous charity of love that promotes praise of God and the enflaming of the soul; by the most constant magnanimity of liberality to wipe out sin and vice. It seems to me that on this day we should be totally aroused to the love of God; totally attracted to the unction of grace; totally offer up our activities to heavenly contemplation; and be totally enflamed to attend to the divine herald.[91]

Then he lists *fourteen* kinds of grace that flow from the Holy Spirit: sanctifying, radiant, diffusive, inflaming, imploring [*impinguantis*], renewing, fecund, beautiful, arousing, strengthening, ordering, supportive, conserving, and perfecting. These graces are linked to particular aspects of faith that Bonaventure associates with the Holy Spirit: wisdom, outpouring love, fervor, unction, sweetness, devotion, angelic conversation, contemplation, perseverance, and glory.[92]

The effects of God's generosity in the broader community are also multiple. The faithful become more confident as they become aware of God's largesse.[93] Confidence also comes because the Spirit helps them understand the mysteries of the scriptures and the ways of God.[94] The Spirit teaches all truth (John 10:6), making it possible to say, "Jesus is Lord" (1 Cor 12:13).[95] An environment of gratitude is needed to welcome the Holy Spirit into one's life.[96] Bonaventure counsels his audience to trust the truth of the Holy Spirit rather than the words of those who have the potential to lead us astray—"the stories of old men, the sophisms of the philosophers, the illusions of the magicians."[97]

As we have seen, for Bonaventure, God's generosity elicits from the faithful a disposition of humility. The humble in heart not only avoid the fires of hell,[98] but ready themselves for the Spirit's gifts by repentance,[99] by attending reverently to the scriptures, and by disposing themselves totally to divine counsel.[100] Humility is the condition of the possibility to receive the Spirit's gifts. It is not only a proper response to God's love, but functions as a necessary predisposition to receive the gifts of the Holy Spirit.[101] Bonaventure seems amazed that so few have the Holy Spirit when so many believe in Christ. The reason for this, he says, is that since they do not realize how much they owe to God's generosity, they do not approach the fountain and, thus, remain thirsty.[102]

Holy Spirit as Transformer of the Affections

In the *Collations on the Six Days*, Bonaventure devotes a collation (conference or lecture) to the ways in which the scripture sustains affective dispositions.[103] One of Bonaventure's goals in these sermons, delivered at Paris, was to nurture harmony in the order. We have discussed the various internal divisions in the community. One group of friars was intent on a strict following of Francis's Rule (which involved disparaging scholastic study at the university). Others, engaged in study, were using Aristotle's ideas in ways that seemed not only arrogant but unorthodox. Bonaventure is worried about how to keep the intellect in line when it is tempted by vain curiosities, but he also wants to support the legitimate study needed for the mission of preaching and teaching.

To respond to this dilemma, Bonaventure underlines the importance of enlightened affections. The intellect is ordained toward the affective dispositions, which, when enlightened, allow the intellect to pass from the speculative to the practical. The most exalted affection is charity, which arises out of the fruits of the Spirit and is the goal of the scriptures and life. The proper function of charity for Bonaventure is to rectify the affective power and make it capable of loving everything that has being, and attaching itself to the highest Good.[104] "Neither acts of justice, nor miracles, nor the understanding of mysteries are of any use without charity." Echoing the biblical story of the widow's mite (Mark 12:38–43; Luke 21:1–4), Bonaventure offers the example of "a little old woman who owns a small garden." Even if she has nothing but charity, she will bring forth better fruit than "a great master who owns an enormous garden and knows the mysteries and natures of things."[105]

Jean-François Bonnefoy has written a detailed account of Bonaventure's understanding of the gifts of the Holy Spirit, and there is no need to rehearse that material here. It is helpful, however, to mention how Bonaventure distinguishes among the virtues, gifts, and beatitudes. Virtues belong to a basic state of development and function to rectify our acts. Gifts belong to a middle stage of growth and function to infuse our acts with new energy. Beatitudes belong to the highest stage of development and lead to consummate grace.[106] Taken individually, charity is better, but the gifts presume charity and add something new to it. They expedite the practice of the virtues by eliminating obstacles and accommodating the faculties to the higher good.[107] Of the gifts, Bonaventure names wisdom, fortitude, piety, and fear of the Lord as belonging to the affective domain. All the gifts are aimed at perfection, at the imitation of Christ.[108]

Elsewhere, Bonaventure speaks of the Holy Spirit in terms of intimate affections. The spiritual senses of smell, taste, and touch (the highest), belong to the affective order and communicate the sensuous quality of life with God.[109] He plays on the images of fire and breath, associated with the Spirit at Pentecost, in multiple keys. Fire is bright in appearance, warm in effect, and quick in movement. Love is like breath that exhales warmth. Through love, grace warms and arouses the heart.[110] The context for speaking of the Holy Spirit as "transcendent intimacy"[111] can be ministry, but more often it is prayer or contemplative union.

The Spirit and Contemplative Ecstasy

According to the Joachites, the impending age of the Spirit would be characterized by contemplation as well as new insight into the meaning of scripture.[112] Operative in contemplation are the spiritual senses bestowed by grace as gifts of the Spirit.[113] In *The Triple Way*, in the chapter on prayer, Bonaventure underlines the importance of the intense desire generated by the Spirit, who pleads for us with unutterable groanings (Rom 8:26).[114] And in the final chapter of *The Soul's Journey into God*, Bonaventure links the Holy Spirit with the more advanced stages of the contemplative life, in which affect transcends reason.[115]

For Bonaventure, the Holy Spirit always functions in the context of the entire Trinity, whose traces are visible in the cosmos and the human mind. At the end of chapter 4 of *The Soul's Journey into God* ("The Consideration of God in His Image Reformed Through the Gifts of Grace"), Bonaventure speaks of the mind as the house of God inhabited by Divine Wisdom, daughter, spouse, friend of God; member, sister, co-heir of Christ; temple of the Holy Spirit. Following Augustine closely, Bonaventure cites Romans 5:5 and 1 Corinthians 2:11—the Spirit pours forth love into our hearts and is the means by which one can know the things of God.

However, it is in the final, culminating chapter, in which Bonaventure describes the soul's mystical transport through the cross of Christ, that the Holy Spirit makes a dramatic appearance.

> In this passing over,
> if it is to be perfect,
> all intellectual activities must be left behind
> and the height of our affection
> must be totally transferred and transformed
> into God.

This, however, is mystical and most secret,
  which *no one knows*
except him who receives it (Apoc 2:17),
    no one receives
    except him who desires it,
    and no one desires it except him
who is inflamed in his very marrow by the fire of the
    Holy Spirit
  Whom Christ sent into the world (Luke 12:49).
  And therefore the Apostle says that
  This mystical wisdom is revealed
    by the Holy Spirit (1 Cor 2:10–11).[116]

The text builds in a crescendo toward the transforming power of
the cross (see fig. 12). The entire Trinity has been a part of the
journey—the Father, who creates; the Son, who is the way, the
door, the ladder; and the Spirit, who inflames the very marrow of
our bones with fire. Understanding is left behind so that the
Spirit's prayer might groan within us. Ask for "grace, not instruction…the Spouse not the teacher, God not man, darkness not clarity, not light but the fire that totally inflames and carries us into
God by ecstatic unctions and burning affections."[117]

Through prayer, desire is enkindled by the fire of the Holy
Spirit. And while Christ is the way, the vehicle of this mystical
transport is the Spirit, the Gift who makes it possible.[118] Thus, for
Bonaventure, one of the distinctive activities appropriated to the
Holy Spirit has to do with the final contemplative goal of life. This
final mystical transport is adumbrated in the prologue, where
Bonaventure says without explicitly referring to the Holy Spirit:

First, therefore, I invite the reader
  to the groans of prayer
through Christ crucified,
  through whose blood
we are cleansed from the filth of vice—
  so that he not believe
that reading is sufficient without unction,
    speculation without devotion,
    investigation without wonder,

observation without joy,
work without piety,
knowledge without love,
understanding without humility,
endeavor without divine grace,
reflection as a mirror without divinely inspired wisdom.[119]

In the final pages of the *Breviloquium*, written around 1255–57, Bonaventure describes the final judgment, the cosmic dénouement of salvation history with its rewards and punishments. In the concluding chapter, "On the Glory of Paradise," he speaks of three types of reward: the vision, fruition, and possession of the supreme Good; bodily glory; and the special rewards of preachers, virgins, and martyrs. He comments specifically on the glorified state of the body, that dimension of existence that has always been closely linked with the affections. In the section on bodily glory,[120] Bonaventure reveals his Aristotelian sympathies, noting that the soul cannot be fully happy without the body, since they are naturally ordered to each other.

Interestingly, the Holy Spirit is mentioned only once in this chapter, in connection with the rewards of a glorified body. Since the soul is enlightened with the vision of eternal Light, Bonaventure says, the body also must shine with great splendor; display subtlety and spirituality; be beyond suffering; and possess supreme agility. These gifts allow the human body to assimilate to heavenly bodies. "Hence, this fourfold gift to the human body not only perfects it in itself but also conforms it to the heavenly dwelling and the Holy Spirit. Through Him, the fullness of delights and the rapture of bliss flow from God the Head down upon the skirt of the garment, the body of man" (Ps 132:2).[121] Bonaventure's theological poetics puts before us an image of the Spirit as the inspiration for mystical death with Christ on the cross and as the light and life of our bodies in glory.

Love of Neighbor

Bonaventure's genius is notable in his ability to keep in creative tension the utter heights of mystical contemplation and the honorable but often mundane command to love others. The overflowing fullness of the Godhead does not stop at the processions of Son and Spirit, but continues its course to the created world and every creature in it. The spiritual journey is not a flight from the world but a flight into the world. The burning, compassionate love of the mystical death described in the final chapter of *The Soul's Journey into God* is the same love with which we turn to our neighbor. Perfect love is reached when we find our hearts "not merely willing, but intensely longing, to die for our neighbor's salvation."[122] When the "Spirit of self-giving love takes root within the human soul, then that same Spirit of love can heal the world."[123]

When our affections are transformed, he writes, love proceeds not out of our superficial selves but out of the innermost marrow of our being, broadening our affections, expanding our hearts, moving us to love our neighbors and even our enemies.[124] In his *Life of Francis*, Bonaventure writes about how the gift of piety empowered Francis to offer extraordinary love to friends and enemies alike.

> This is what
> drew him up to God
>   through devotion,
> transformed him into Christ
>   through compassion,
> attracted him to his neighbor
>   through condescension
> and symbolically showed a return
>   to the state of original innocence
> through universal reconciliation
>   with each and every thing.[125]

Bonaventure links activity on behalf of the neighbor to the entire Trinity, but in distinctive ways to the Spirit. The "footprints" (1 John 5:7–8) of the Trinity include the Father's creative power; the Son's divine/human existence; and the Spirit's activity in the world.[126] Bonaventure understands performance or the living of a moral, virtuous life as empowered by the Spirit.[127] The general rationale for love of neighbor lies in the biblical testimony that we are made in the image and likeness of God. Christ on the cross is the exemplar of genuine, selfless love. Bonaventure's conviction that everything comes forth from and returns to God *(exitus/reditus)* entails a responsibility to reach out and "catch up" those below us on the various hierarchies of life (recapitulation). Thus, we are responsible for our neighbors, and since Bonaventure includes everyone in the term *neighbor,* the road taken for the journey into God will be crowded.[128]

Thus, Bonaventure's theology is markedly "this-worldly." Since God's essence is relational, Bonaventure envisions the spiritual life in terms of mutual action—as the soul ascends to God, it simultaneously descends to the neighbor and the created world.[129] The loving union of the persons within the Trinity generates the love of Christ crucified, which is extended to the entire universe through the power of the Spirit. "As we are restored in the image of Christ and thus conformed to him, we are impelled to express the image in our relationship with others."[130] The love visible on the cross is the same love that carries the soul to mystical transports and to care for the neighbor.

In a Pentecost sermon, Bonaventure calls on Gregory the Great: "there is great activity where there is love; if one refuses to be active, then love is not present."[131] He also cites Paul: "Love one another with fraternal affection; outdo one another in showing honor. Never flag in zeal, be aglow with the Spirit, serve the Lord" (Rom 12:10). Good actions, Bonaventure says, relate to love just as firewood to fire and "just as a fire cannot continue without more wood, neither can the grace of God which is love, without good actions."[132] As good actions nourish the fire of love between us and God, so, too, a gentle disposition nourishes it between us and our neighbor, both those who are friendly and those who are unfriendly.[133] Bonaventure understands love of neighbor as a specific fruit of the Spirit's gifts.[134] We exercise mercy when we are moved by our neighbor's misery. We exercise the gift of piety when we are moved by the recognition that the one who suffers is *imago Dei.*[135] When the generous love of God is expressed through the Holy Spirit, we no longer simply "talk the talk" but are also able to "walk the walk."[136]

Bonaventure's own life is perhaps the most powerful witness of his openness to the Spirit's promptings to activity. Both as a university professor and as Minister General of the order, he concerned himself with behavior toward others—in the order, in the church, and in their ministries to the needy. His ability to make himself available to the Spirit is evident in his constant concern that the friars live lives of virtue—humility, balance, love, patience, obedience, wisdom, and fear of the Lord. He wanted the friars to live the gifts and fruits: to be intelligent about their work but not puffed up about what they knew; to be kind to each other; to be generous in their service to the church. He did not live in easy times, but in spite of significant difficulties and responsibilities, he preached about, and witnessed to, a trinitarian God who condescended to walk among us, whose Spirit allowed him, and us, to aim for the heights when it comes to having a love affair with God.

Conclusion

Bonaventure associates the Holy Spirit with giftedness, liberality, generosity, desire, the body, the affections, savoring, bondedness, receptivity, and wisdom. The wisdom that is the final goal of both theology and life begins in knowledge and ends in affection. The gift of wisdom is an experiential knowledge of God's sweetness, a pleasant taste of the goodness of God.[137] Love proceeds where knowledge leaves off; unction fulfills speculation.[138] Like all the mystics, Bonaventure projects a sense of confidence in God's role as giver of gifts. The faithful need only recognize and acknowledge God's generosity, and above all, pray for and trust that all gifts will be given.

In the history of Christianity, the laity have not often been viewed as capable of desiring, or enjoying, the highest reaches of the spiritual life. In our time, it is not only wrong but dangerous for church leaders (or the laity themselves) to constrict the charisms of the laity, whether in the arena of holiness or church ministry. The flowing waters so prominent in Bonaventure's texts remind us that in baptism, we are called to abandon ourselves to the prayer in which the Spirit groans and to follow Jesus to the cross. This is a universal call, a universal gift.

As we interpret Bonaventure's theology of the Spirit for our time, we are challenged not to hang back, not to make excuses, not to set up barriers to God's desire that we become disciples, friends, and lovers in the adventure of allowing the Spirit free reign in our lives and in our world. Bonaventure's deeply incarnational spirituality is "user friendly" to a world that struggles to respect our bodies and the material world, and to a church that needs to be reminded of the Spirit's presence in every atom and molecule. Bernard Cooke writes of Bonaventure: "From his 'father in God,' Francis of Assisi, Bonaventure had inherited a contemplative awareness of the pervading divine presence. This mystical consciousness caused every detail of experience to be Word of God, to speak of God's loving blessing of human life…the symbol world of Franciscan spirituality has a freshness that springs from its discovery of the mystery dimension of the ordinary."[139]

At the close of his final sermon for Pentecost, in which he focuses on the role of the preacher, Bonaventure cites Wisdom 7:7: "Therefore I prayed and prudence was given to me; I called for help and there came to me the Spirit of Wisdom."[140] Bonaventure speaks of the goal of theology and life as peace,[141] as a certain learned ignorance,[142] as charity.[143] In each case, wisdom and the Spirit's presence make it possible to taste the sweetness of God.[144] But the sweetness of which Bonaventure speaks is not to be confused with the saccharine. The final words of *The Soul's Journey into God* remind us of the importance of the coincidence of opposites—the sweetness of which he speaks is fused with death, love, and fire.[145] The Spirit is present in this passage in the imagery of fire and the conviction of Christ's freedom.

> This fire is God
> and his furnace is in Jerusalem (Isa 31:98)
> and Christ enkindles it
> in the heat of his burning passion,
> which only he truly perceives who says:
> "My soul chooses hanging and my bones death" (Job 7:15)
> …
> Let us, then, die
> and enter into the darkness;
> let us impose silence
> upon our cares, our desires and our imaginings.

With Christ crucified
let us pass out of this world to the Father (John 13.1)
so that when the Father is shown to us,
   we may say with Philip:
"It is enough for us" (John 14:8, 7:6; see figs. 12, 15,
16, 17, 18).[146]

❧

Food for Thought

1. Bonaventure's water imagery invites us to reflect on the cleansing, healing waters of baptism. What does your baptism mean to you? Is it a conscious factor in the way you live your life each day? Do Bonaventure's texts help you to discover new creative ways to get in touch with the overflowing graces of your baptism? If you think of the Spirit in terms of flowing liquids, what do you discover?

2. Bonaventure was inspired by the founder of his order, Francis of Assisi. What associations do you have with Francis that might enhance your awareness of the Holy Spirit in your life and in the world?

3. Bonaventure presided over an order that was caught in a web of contentions and divisions. His job must have been a bit like "herding cats." What advice would you give him in terms of prayer to the Holy Spirit? How should the Spirit direct church leaders today? How does the church fail the Spirit and close itself off from the Spirit's guidance and power?

4. Medieval authors situated their pneumatology within their trinitarian theologies. Does your awareness of the Spirit draw you into the loving ambit of the trinitarian relations, into their dance of communion *(perichoresis)*? Do you find it startling to imagine the entire Trinity at the cross? How would you express this presence of the fullness of God at Christ's death?

5. Are you an "either-or" or a "both-and" type of person? What effect did Bonaventure's insistence on a coincidence of opposites have on you? Is life more truly captured by both light and darkness, life and death, beginning and end—and if so, does this create tension, struggle, joy, relief, challenge for you? Does awareness of a coincidence of opposites inform your work, your ministry?

CHAPTER 6

CATHERINE OF SIENA
The Spirit as Waiter

The two women mystics treated in chapters 6 and 7 lived in the fourteenth century: Catherine of Siena in Italy and Julian of Norwich in England. Although the specific facts of their situations are different—Catherine was a laywoman with a very public ministry, and Julian was an enclosed anchoress—both milieux shared common elements of a contentious and violent world, surprisingly coupled with an amazing flowering of mysticism. In the intellectual realm, the pendulum swings from scholastic syntheses and methods based heavily on reason to a focus on human will, the absolute will of God, and individual, subjective perspectives, especially in their personal, affective dimensions. Fears about mystical heresies emerged around 1300 and would wax and wane for four hundred years.[1]

Life and Times

The fourteenth century was a time of crisis and turning points for church and society.[2] Most portraits of the fourteenth century are painted with dark, calamitous, and foreboding strokes. The list of ills is long and serious, affecting all aspects of family, society, economy, and church. In a widely read book, *A Distant Mirror*, Barbara Tuchman sees the fourteenth century as a mirror of our own. She calls it a "violent, tormented, bewildered, suffering and disintegrating age." The fourteenth century "suffered so many

179

strange and great perils and adversities that its disorders cannot be traced to any one cause...plague, war, taxes, brigandage, bad government, insurrections, and schism in the Church."[3] The list of woes goes on: economic chaos, social unrest, high prices, profiteering, depraved morals, lack of production, industrial indolence, frenetic gaiety, wild expenditure, luxury, debauchery, social and religious hysteria, greed, avarice, maladministration, decay of manners.[4] An eyewitness from the fourteenth century captures the misery in a poem:

> Time of mourning and temptation,
>   Age of envy, torment, tears,
> Time of languor and damnation
>   Age of last declining years,
> Time of falseness, full of horror,
>   Age of lying, envy, strife,
> Time without true judgment, honor,
>   Age of sadness, shortening life.[5]

Bad as it must have been, history is always more complex than such characterizations allow—there is always a "normal" side to life, even in the harshest of times. Catherine and her family suffered from this chaos, but they also escaped some of the worst of it because of their middle-class standing and position.

Perhaps the greatest scourge of the century was the Black Death. Brought to Italy on ships from the East, this frightening disease is said to have taken the lives of one-third to one-half of the population of Europe during one of its most virulent visits in 1348–50. During Catherine's lifetime, the plague struck twice, in 1348 and 1374. It is hard to imagine the suffering of those afflicted with the plague and the effect on those responsible for their care and burial. Imagine a third of the population of New York City wiped out in a short span of time. The sickness was no respecter of persons—rich, middle class, poor, men, women, and children succumbed to its power. Businesses were abandoned, wealthy estates left vacant, basic services interrupted. In addition, the psychological toll on those who survived must have been high. Robbers and marauders would have had a field day.

Civilized ways of doing business were compromised. Many would lose the will to live and to hope, much less work for a better tomorrow. In addition to her exposure to death caused by plague, Catherine experienced many deaths close to home. Her twin sister died shortly after birth; in 1362, her beloved sister Bonaventura died in childbirth; a year later, another younger sister died; and in 1368, when Catherine was twenty-one, she lost her father. And, of course, Catherine herself died at the young age of thirty-three.

On the civic front, Italy was racked by tensions and violent confrontations. Powerful dukes, desiring to extend control over north and central Italy, sent armies to capture new land. After 1350, many of the great banking houses of Italy went bankrupt, largely because of the default of their chief debtor, Edward III of England. In the summer of 1373, there was a bad harvest in Tuscany that resulted in famine. In addition, the newly emerging professional guilds fought with each other for power and wealth. Warehouses were sacked and contents destroyed. The lower classes rioted and went on destructive rampages. Merchants lived in the daily uncertainty of war, pestilence, famine, and insurrection. The labor shortage caused by the plague revived the demand for slaves. By the end of the fourteenth century, there was hardly a well-to-do household in Tuscany without at least one slave.

Some Italian cities fought not only among themselves but against the papacy. There was constant strife between the merchant Guelphs, who supported the papacy (Catherine was part of this group), and the aristocratic Ghibellines, who stood with the empire. Florence was at the center of this controversy, and Catherine was early drawn into it as mediator and peacemaker. In response, Florence created an emergency government of eight, got most of the central Italian cities to join them, expelled papal vicars, and declared war on Gregory XI; this was nicknamed the War of Eight Saints. The pope responded with an interdict in 1376, calling Florentines heretics and ordering all Christian rulers to expel Florentine merchants and confiscate their property.[6] It is hard to imagine a pope announcing publicly that God would not be offended if one were to rob Florentine merchants! Of course, this only made the Florentines more resentful of what they perceived as the greed and arrogance of high church prelates.

When Catherine went to Florence in the spring of 1378 to negotiate peace on behalf of Gregory XI, members of the lower classes rioted, brutally attacking several wealthy Guelph families. Catherine had suggested that some of Florence's leaders who were against peace with the papacy be deprived of their offices. When this information was circulated to the "ignorant rabble in the streets," they cried out: "Let us capture her and burn her, this most wicked woman or put her to the sword!" Catherine's host expelled her from his premises for fear of having his house burned to the ground. She and her companions went to a garden to pray. Soon the rioters arrived with swords and clubs, shouting, "Where is that wicked woman? Where is she?"[7] Mary Ann Fatula writes of the incident: "As the assassin drew near, Catherine's joy and courage at the thought of martyrdom disarmed him; he turned away, leaving her to weep at the dream that had slipped from her hands."[8] A peaceful, retired life was not Catherine's way.

Things within the church were not much better. The pope had taken up residence in Avignon, France, and was deeply enmeshed in the power struggles of the French monarchy. Catherine traveled to Avignon and worked tirelessly to convince the pope to return to Rome. The papacy also suffered from its conflict with Florence and other central Italian cities. In 1378 Gregory XI died and Urban VI was elected. The new pope's desire for reform took a tyrannical turn. The French cardinals protested by declaring his election invalid and naming instead the ruthless Cardinal of Geneva, who took the name Clement VII. Urban sought Catherine's help in November of 1378, and she traveled to Rome with twenty-four of her disciples. But in the end, her efforts to resolve the disagreement faltered. The forces of disunity and violent antagonism weakened both her body and spirit, which led to her death in Rome on April 29, 1380.

In the midst of this chaos and uncertainty, there arose in Italy a number of saints, many of them women. Some, like Catherine and Angela of Foligno were linked to third orders.[9] Birgitta of Sweden spent many years in Rome, fighting against some of the same abuses that engaged Catherine. Germany boasted Meister Eckhart, Henry Suso, and Johannes Tauler. England also enjoyed a flowering of mysticism. Julian was part of an English school of mysticism that included the anonymous author of *The Cloud of Unknowing*, Walter Hilton, Margery Kempe, and Richard Rolle.

Catherine Benincasa was born a twin in March 1347, to Lapa di Puccio Piagenti and Jacopo Benincasa—the twenty-fourth of their twenty-five children. They lived on the Vicolo del Tiratoia in Siena. Catherine's mother was the daughter of a poet and a quilt maker, and is described as having a talkative and explosive disposition.[10] Since Lapa was able to nurse only one child, Catherine's twin sister, Giovanna, was sent to a local woman who served as a wet nurse. Sadly, Giovanna died in infancy, leaving Catherine the darling of the family. In her novel about Catherine, Sigrid Undset imagines that the aging Lapa must have loved Catherine with a special, demanding, and well-meaning mother-love that may have contributed to frequent heart-rending misunderstandings.[11] Catherine's father was a prosperous dyer, endowed with a generous and calm nature. Lapa later told Catherine's biographer, Raymond of Capua, that her husband was so even-tempered and so controlled in speech, that no unmeasured word ever passed his lips. Catherine's older sister, Bonaventura, recounts how hard it was for her to listen to the foul language of her husband and his friends. Growing up, Jacopo had forbidden the use of such language in the Benincasa home.

When Catherine was six, she experienced what she would later describe as a vision of Christ. Suzanne Noffke says of this experience: "After that day she became increasingly introverted and quiet, obsessively pursuing whatever her young mind and the society around her considered to be the marks of holiness. She even made a vow of virginity, since that was to the prevailing spirituality the one sure way to belong entirely to God."[12] She cut off her hair and later joined a group of lay Dominican women called the "mantellate" when she was about sixteen.[13] This group was made up of older women (widows for the most part) who lived in their own homes, wore a form of the Dominican habit, and lived lives of prayer and service to the poor. Some of the mantellate were skeptical about admitting this much younger, volatile woman to their ranks. But after three years of seclusion and prayer in the family home, Catherine dedicated herself to the care of the poor in her local neighborhood from 1367 to 1370. Catherine's engagement in prayer and ascetic practices was one cause for Mamma

Lapa's frustration. She wanted to see Catherine happily married and a mother like herself.

But Catherine's solitary pursuits were balanced by her large family. Anyone who has experienced a reunion of a large family understands the complexity, the diversity, and the chaos of such gatherings. They usually include several generations, ranging from the very old to the very young. There may be a stray cousin or two—like Tommaso della Fonte, who came to live with the Benincasas after he was orphaned. Catherine always had a special affection for Tommaso, who later became a Dominican priest and Catherine's spiritual director. Tommaso introduced the Dominican priest Bartolomeo de' Dominici to Catherine, and he became one of the first to join Catherine's circle of friends and disciples. Each person in a family has her or his own story, joys, successes, and hurts. Each person is bound to the other through a unique history and often linked in a common future.

During her short ministry, Catherine continued to be surrounded by people. Her followers grew in number. Catherine is said to have possessed a warm, spontaneous, talkative disposition. She loved her nieces and nephews, wrote many letters, spoke often in public, and confided in those closest to her. There must have been something compelling about her person, her words, and her activity that made others want to join her. Commentators use terms like *vivacious, affectionate, warmth of feeling, bright, sociable, spontaneously loving.* She traveled with a group of favorite disciples, who called her "Mama" and saw themselves as her "family." Her prayers are laced with the phrase "those you have given me to love with a special love." She established close and loving bonds with all her followers. During her work with plague victims, Catherine met the Dominican Raymond of Capua, who would later become the head of the Dominican Order, her lifelong confidant, and her biographer. Catherine was criticized for traveling freely and for keeping company with men, but she did not let such talk deter her from the mission that she felt God had entrusted to her.

The record shows that Catherine had a forceful side to her personality. Authors comment on the frequent use of *"Io voglio"* (I will it) in her writings as a sign of her strong will and staunch commitment to carry out what she thought God was directing her to do. In a letter to Raymond of Capua, she speaks of her vocation to seek God's honor, the salvation of souls, and the renewal of the church: "And by the grace and power of the Holy Spirit I intend to persevere until I die" (LT219/93).[14] She clung to the truth, lived by the truth, and sought after the truth throughout her life. She challenged the powerful and the wealthy as well as the simple. She was what we might call a "one-tracker"; that is, she did everything with drive, conviction, and a refusal to compromise.

Gradually, from about the age of twenty-five, Catherine was drawn into the public arena of both church and state. She was deeply concerned about the open conflicts among Italian city states and between these local governments and the papacy. As we have seen, she often acted as ambassador and mediator in ecclesial and civic disputes. Dealing with so much conflict wore Catherine out. She became ill and weak, unable even to drink water. By February of 1380 she could no longer walk and was forced to stay in bed. She spent her last days with her "spiritual family." In spite of great suffering, Catherine offered her companions spiritual counsel, encouraging them to free themselves from clinging attachments, to trust in God's care for them, and above all, to love one another. To the last, she was giving directions and encouragement to each of her followers, both those present and those at a distance. Finally, she asked their pardon for any offenses she may have committed against them. On April 29, 1380, she died in the arms of her good friend, Alessa, with her followers around her. Catherine was canonized in 1461 by Pope Pius II; proclaimed co-patron of Italy with Francis of Assisi in 1939 by Pope Pius XII; and declared Doctor of the Church in 1970 by Pope Paul VI, an honor held by only two other women, Teresa of Avila (1515–82) and Thérèse of Lisieux (1873–97).

Catherine shares with several other medieval women mystics in England and the Low Countries the distinction of being the first woman to write in the vernacular—in Catherine's case, in her local Italian dialect. Her written legacy can be grouped under three headings. Her major theological work, *The Dialogue of Divine Providence*, was written between 1377 and 1378 when she was immersed in her ministry. We also have twenty-six prayers recorded by friends while Catherine was rapt in an ecstatic state. Most of these prayers date from the last seventeen months of her life. Finally, there are 382 letters, written throughout her lifetime to a wide range of persons.

Catherine's Trinitarian Theology

Catherine's spiritual theology is thoroughly and explicitly centered on the Trinity. Her texts reveal that she is familiar with key aspects of the trinitarian theological tradition, upon which she places her own distinctive stamp. Perhaps in an effort to protect trinitarian orthodoxy in a time of strife and danger, she often reminds her readers that the Holy Spirit is God and that the Spirit proceeds from both the Father and the Son. She notes the Spirit's hand at work in Mary's conception of the Word, a mystery, she says, that is so great that only the Spirit's grace and mercy could have brought it about (P18/158; P23/202–3).[15] Here is how she expresses it: "He [Christ] now has the form of flesh, and she [Mary] like warm wax has received from the seal of the Holy Spirit the imprint of loving desire for our salvation" (L1/38). Catherine consistently used imagery to express her understanding of the events of the Christian story.[16]

Since Catherine is not writing a *summa* in the technical, scholastic sense of that term, she is less concerned to make sharp, defining distinctions among the divine persons and more interested in recording how she experiences the persons at work in the world. For Catherine, the entire Trinity works together in both the creation and the redemption of the world.[17] God speaks in the *Dialogue:* "For the Holy Spirit did not come alone, but with the power from me the Father and with the wisdom of the Son and with his own mercy. So you see, he returned, not in the flesh but in his power, to firm up the road of his teaching" (D29/70; D63/119).[18] Later, she employs the metaphor of bread-making to link the three persons in a very intimate way. God speaks to her:

> My power is not separate from his [Christ's] wisdom;
> nor is the heat, the fire of the holy Spirit separate from
> me the Father or from him the Son, for the Holy Spirit
> proceeds from me.... The person of the incarnate Word
> was penetrated and kneaded into one dough with the

light of my Godhead, the divine nature, and with the
heat and fire of the Holy Spirit, and by this means you
have come to receive the light. (D110/206)

Like her English counterpart, Julian of Norwich, Catherine
experienced each person of the Trinity as deeply related to the
other two persons, with all three involved in encounters with the
world. While both follow the tradition of assigning certain functions to one or another of the divine persons, they interweave
these functions in a way that implicates each person in every act.
It is clear that Catherine does not limit any given activity to one
person. She prefers to assign a distinct activity to one person in
particular and then extend it to the other two persons. For example, usually the medieval metaphor of nursing at the breast refers
to Christ, but Catherine extends this metaphor to the Holy Spirit.
"Such a soul [wholly surrendered to God's love] has the Holy
Spirit as a mother who nurses her at the breast of divine charity"
(D141/292). In another passage describing Pentecost, Catherine
assigns to the Holy Spirit the title "Teacher," a name usually associated with Christ. For Catherine, the living bridge of Christ's
body is gone, but the bridge of Christ's teaching remains and is
held together by the joint work of the three persons (D29/70).
Thus, the Spirit becomes the Teacher who "came to make even
more firm the road my Truth had left in the world through his
teaching....The Holy Spirit's mercy confirmed this teaching by
strengthening the disciples' minds to testify to the truth and make
known this way, the teaching of Christ crucified" (D29/69).[19]

This more fluid approach to the trinitarian relations and
functions provides a resource for twenty-first century theologians
working to create a more compelling trinitarian theology. One
such perspective has come to be called "Spirit-Christology."[20]
The trinitarian theologies of medieval mystical writers provide
pointers as we work to recover the Spirit dimension in Christology.
Catherine links the incarnate Word and the Spirit in many creative
ways. In Catherine's terminology, every attribute of the Spirit is
also attributed to the blood of Jesus. Suzanne Noffke notes, "The
passion of Jesus is in fact, for Catherine, as intimately the work of
the Holy Spirit as is the incarnation itself."[21] Catherine captures
the force of this collaborative relationship through compressed

symbols: "there is no blood [Christ] without fire [Holy Spirit]" (LT80; LT153/365 n. 7; see figs. 7, 15, 18).

This imagery of blood and fire is further developed in a letter to Angelo da Riscasoli, in which Catherine describes how the Holy Spirit taps the cask of Jesus' body to set his blood flowing for us: "His humanity is the cask that enclosed the divine nature, and the cellarer, the fire and hand that is the Holy Spirit, tapped that cask on the wood of the most holy cross" (LT136). Using another metaphor, Catherine links "mother charity" with both the Holy Spirit and the crucified Christ. And from numerous other references in her texts, we discover "that the fountain is the heart of Christ, and the love that we drink in perfect friendship is his blood, the fire of charity, the Holy Spirit of God."[22]

Catherine's trinitarian focus extends from her theology to her anthropology, in which she relies heavily on Augustine. She builds on Augustine's analogy between the three persons of the Trinity, and human memory, intellect, and will (D165/365) and on his understanding of the Holy Spirit as the bond of love between the Father and the Son (D13/49). The Spirit has a key role in the extension of this divine loving bond to humanity. The Holy Spirit functions as "an intermediary binding our soul with our Creator, and enlightening our understanding and knowledge so that we can share in the wisdom of God's Son" (L61/195). A classic statement of Catherine's theological anthropology is found in one of her prayers.

> You made us in your image and likeness so that, with our three powers in one soul, we might image your trinity and your unity. And as we image, so we may find union: through our memory, image and be united with the Father...through our understanding, image and be united to the Son...through our will, image and be united with the Holy Spirit, to whom is attributed mercy, and who is the love of the Father and the Son.
>
> (P4/42)

For Catherine, the incarnation radically deepens the truth articulated in the creation story in Genesis that we are made in the image of God. God speaks to Catherine: "Member for member he

[Christ] joined this divine nature with yours; my power, the wisdom of my Son, the mercy of the Holy Spirit—all of me, God, the abyss of the Trinity, laid upon and united with your human nature" (D140/289). In a letter to Pope Gregory XI that sounds very unlike Augustine; however, Catherine articulates her vision of the exalted nature of every human being. "This seems to be why human beings love so much, because they are made of nothing but love, body and soul. In love God created them in his own image and likeness, and in love father and mother conceive and bring forth their children, giving them a share in their own substance. So God, seeing that humankind is so quick to love, throws out to us right away the hook of love, giving us the Word, his only-begotten Son....With love, then, he has so drawn us and with his kindness so conquered our malice that every heart should be won over" (LT196/19–20). In this letter, Catherine's psychology emphasizes the power and potential of human love in order to remind Gregory that this kind of love will enable him to do the right thing and return to Rome.

But, for Catherine, the truth that we are made in God's likeness and destined for mystic union is inseparable from human suffering. In a letter to her sisters of the Mantellate in Siena, Catherine offers an especially lyrical and poignant passage describing union with the triune God. "Your will will be bound with the bond of the Holy Spirit, abyss of charity, and in this charity you will conceive a gentle, loving, tormenting desire for God's honor and the salvation of souls. Being so sweetly raised into the midst of the Trinity, sharing as I've said in the Father's power, the Son's wisdom, and the Holy Spirit's mercy, you will weep in burning love and boundless sorrow with me, your wretched and worse than wretched foolish mother, over the dead child, humanity, and over the mystic body of holy Church" (L57/178–79).

In the midst of war and plague, it is easy to imagine that Catherine witnessed mothers weeping over dead children. Her words to her sisters witness to Catherine's powerful and compelling vision that juxtaposes heavenly ecstasy with the depths of human and ecclesial suffering, binding us across the centuries. In our time, we too may find ourselves calling upon the Spirit of compassion to rest on mothers in Argentina, El Salvador, Nicaragua, Rwanda, Afghanistan, and all around the world who witness in solidarity on behalf of the hungry, the imprisoned, the tortured and the "disappeared."

Metaphors of the Spirit

We turn now to the ways in which Catherine and those who knew her spoke about the Spirit's role in Catherine's vocation. The rubric I have chosen is that of "voice" and "pen," which encompasses her theological work, her letters, and her prayers—all influenced by the Spirit's presence and power (2 Cor 3:3–6). In the second part of the chapter we reflect on the following metaphors for the Spirit: gift of charity, mercy, one who casts out fear, fire, and waiter/servant.

The Holy Spirit and Catherine's Vocation

In general, Catherine speaks of the call of God's servants as the fruit of the Spirit's law, which is quite different from human law (LT204/80; LT189/135; LT114/341; LT8/359; LT44/581). She seems to be inspired by Jesus' message to his disciples: "for it is not you who speak, but the Spirit of your Father speaking through you" (Matt 10:20). When she or any of her followers encounter opposition, disapproval, or ridicule—as they often did—she accuses her detractors of laying down their own law in opposition to that of the Spirit (LT247/257; LT123/374). In response to local citizens who disapproved of Catherine's being away from her monastery at Belcaro for long periods of time, she accuses them of "opinionated presumption," judging her by their standards rather than by God's mysteries and holy ways. She writes, "Let it [pride] not try to make rules for the Holy Spirit, who is himself both rule and giver of the rule" (T294/380).

As with other authors we have discussed, Catherine is not beyond calling on the Spirit to justify her view of the situation against critics. She writes to a follower, Caterina di Ghetto: "See that you do not act like those stupid and senseless people who want to appoint themselves as both investigators and judges of what God's servants do and how they live....Realize that wanting to make God's servants walk the same way we do is nothing less than an attempt to regulate and legislate for the Holy Spirit—which is absolutely impossible" (LT50/595).

In contrast to her detractors, many in Catherine's community acknowledged that the Spirit was given an active role in empowering Catherine to identify and then live out her particular charisms.[23] In addition to Catherine's works, we examine Raymond of Capua's *Life of Catherine* to see how at least one outsider who knew her well and wanted to see her canonized called upon the Holy Spirit to describe her life.[24] After overcoming some doubt, Raymond was convinced that it was the Spirit who led Catherine from the beginning, giving her a sense of how she was called to serve God in perfect purity (*Life*/I.3.35). At one point, he cites the *Dialogue* to underline the way in which Catherine's gifts were a participation in the very life of the triune God. Catherine says to God, "For you endowed me with something of the Power which is proper to yourself, Eternal Father; and you endowed my intellect with something of your Wisdom, that Wisdom which belongs by appropriation to your Only-begotten Son; and the Holy Spirit, who proceeds from you and from your Son, has given my Will, the faculty which makes me capable of love" (*Life*/III.3.356).

Capua recounts that after Catherine's childhood vision of Christ, the Spirit led her back home because her time had not yet come (*Life*/I.2.34): "The little one grew and waxed strong, in readiness for the day when she would be filled with the Holy Spirit and the wisdom of God." He compares Catherine to a seedling that would grow into a lofty cedar because watered by the fountain of the Holy Spirit (*Life*/I.2.28). As a young girl, the Spirit helped her fight temptation by establishing a cell within her heart through which she was able to hold fast to the truth in times of sorrow (*Life*/I.4.49; I.4.50; I.11.107). Later in life, her "wise insight into the things of the Spirit" permitted Catherine to react to taunts and criticism as Jesus did—with patience and forbearance (*Life*/II.5.176). The Spirit taught her the heroic virtues exemplified in the ancient Egyptian fathers of the desert and the lives of the saints (*Life*/I.2.31; II.4.162). Throughout her childhood, Catherine refused to "quench the Spirit" (*Life*/I.3.35), keeping her eye on the prize which the Holy Spirit set before her (*Life*/I.4.51).

According to Raymond, Catherine's family struggled to come to terms with her "unorthodox" vocation. They put obstacles in her way until one night when her father came upon Catherine praying in her brother Stefano's room, he saw a "small snow-white dove" over her head, which flew out the window when he approached (*Life*/I.5.52). Jacopo Benincasa responds by telling Catherine to do as she sees fit and as the Holy Spirit will direct her (*Life*/I.5.55).

Raymond also links the Holy Spirit with Catherine's reception of the Eucharist. Catherine often requested frequent communion, a practice that was not common in her time.[25] He defends her indirectly by citing *On the Ecclesiastical Hierarchy* by the fifth-century author Dionysius the Areopagite: "in the early church, when the fervour of the Holy Spirit still abounded, the faithful, both men and women, used to receive Holy Communion daily" (*Life*/II.12.312). Earlier in the text, Raymond noted the Spirit's presence to Catherine at communion, when "the supernatural vitality of the Holy Spirit imparted to her took possession of her whole being" (*Life*/II.5.170; II.6.194). Metaphors of eating and drinking play a major role in Catherine's life and in the church of the fourteenth century. Later, we will examine Catherine's image of the Spirit as a waiter at table, and Raymond also employs a well-worn metaphor from the tradition to describe Catherine's ecstasies as inebriation. Catherine becomes "intoxicated by the Spirit of God" (*Life*/II.6.200).

Catherine's Gifts of Voice and Pen

Medieval society assigned women certain roles and spheres within which it was acceptable for them to operate. When women departed from these roles, society had to find an explanation for the exception.[26] Since women were not permitted university education, their knowledge of philosophy, theology, and scripture had to be explained in other ways. Catherine was criticized for engaging in the intellectual life, which involved her in preaching and writing and brought her into the public sphere.

Raymond begins the *Life* with a summary description of Catherine's Spirit-filled charisms of speech.

For the Lord had endowed her with a most ready tongue,
a charism of utterance adapted to every circumstance, so

that her words burnt like a torch and none who ever heard her could escape being touched by at least some spark of her burning eloquence…no one ever came to hear her but he went away moved wholly or in part to compunction, or without finding himself instructed to his betterment, at least in some degree. Who can deny that this is a proof of the fire of the Holy Spirit present within her? (*Life*, First Prologue.9)

When Raymond lauds Catherine for these charismatic gifts, he is obliged to offer "proof" that what she is doing has been legitimated by God. Raymond reports this message to Catherine from God: "You will give proofs of the Spirit that is in you, before the small and the great, before layfolk and clergy and religious, for I will give you a mouth and a wisdom which none shall be able to resist" (*Life*/II.6.216). Raymond goes to even greater lengths to convince readers that Catherine is Spirit-inspired. He tells us that he "tested" Catherine by having her ask for the grace of contrition. Her awareness of her own sinfulness, to which she attests frequently, was put forward by Raymond as an "unmistakable sign that her manner of life was from no one but the Holy Spirit" (*Life*/I.9.87). He concludes his account of Catherine's life by calling attention to the lofty spiritual goals she assigned to each of her followers before she died. For Raymond, this advice to live lives of generous virtue "was a clear proof that her advice was given under the guidance of the Holy Spirit" (*Life*/III.4.363).

Throughout the *Life*, Raymond calls attention to Catherine's intellectual gifts. One day, when Catherine was at prayer, Raymond describes "a ray of brightness from the Holy Spirit [that] shone upon her and flooded her mind with light" (*Life*/I.11.109). Another time when she and Raymond visited a Carthusian monastery, the abbot asked Catherine to speak to the monks. Raymond reports that at first she demurred out of humility (a woman presuming to teach monks!), but eventually, "yielding at last to the most pressing entreaties, she opened her mouth and spoke according as the Holy Spirit gave her to speak." Raymond adds, "By this it is clear to me that she is filled with the spirit of prophecy, and that it is the Holy Spirit who speaks in her" (*Life*/II.10.296).

Catherine herself acknowledges the Spirit's role in the lives of her followers. To Stefano Maconi: "Do whatever the Holy Spirit prompts you to do" (L87/164). To a young Florentine who was considering joining the Crusade: "Do what the Holy Spirit inspires you to do with the advice of Don Giovanni" (L50/152). And to encourage Pope Gregory XI to return to Rome from Avignon, she writes, "Respond to the Holy Spirit who is calling you! I tell you: come! come! come!" (L64/202). She later reprimands him, "Don't make light of the works of the Holy Spirit that are being asked of you. You can do them if you *want* to" (L71/202; also L77/236). Catherine was able to be pointedly directive—at times, even imperious—and yet also encourage people to rely on their experience of the Spirit to guide their lives. Her particular personality allowed her to harmonize what she saw as the right thing to do with the Spirit's wishes and guidance—a risky business for anyone, but especially for a fourteenth-century woman.

Writing for public consumption was another role that was off-limits for medieval women. It was generally understood that, given women's weak rational capacities and their dangerous proclivity to be emotional, they were incapable of thinking or speaking as teachers or theologians. As a result of these prejudices, Catherine's production of *The Dialogue* had to be explained in terms other than her "mere natural power." It had to be attributed to another source, most often, the Holy Spirit. Thus, Raymond writes that Catherine composed it "in her own vernacular, manifestly at the dictation of the Holy Spirit" (*Life*/First Prologue.8; III.1.332).

The Spirit: Gift of Charity

Catherine was a "doer" as well as a thinker. At the end of the *Life*, Raymond compares Catherine to a sturdy dwelling, reminiscent of the biblical allusion to the house built upon rock (Luke 6:48). He says, "She was a steadfast pillar, solidly fixed by the weight of the Holy Spirit in a charity so firmly based that she could not be moved even so much as to change the expression of her countenance, by any tempest of persecution" (*Life*/III.6.415). In Raymond's eyes, the Holy Spirit is the "weight" that allows Catherine, the pillar, to remain steadfast in charity. He also applies to Catherine the gospel test of the Spirit's presence, namely, the gifts of charity, joy, and peace, and does not find her wanting. (*Life*/II.5.175).

Catherine's care and concern for others are characterized by a spirit of energy and an indefatigable vitality that cause people to marvel at her. Her life stands in stark contrast to the widely held notion that mystics are turned in upon themselves and uninterested in the welfare of the world. Her unabated energy, even when she was seriously ill, is explained only by the Spirit's power—yet another proof of her authenticity. Raymond writes, "Did it not come from that Holy Spirit who exults in such works of charity?" (*Life*/II.5.171). To her disciple Bartolomeo she writes that the pounding thrusts of the world, the flesh, and the devil can never penetrate the garment that is the Holy Spirit "because the garment of charity repels them—for love, that is, the Holy Spirit, sustains everything" (L29/103).

Raymond traces the Spirit's guidance from Catherine's earliest moments to her life's culmination. T.S. Eliot echoes this sense of life as a whole—"the end is in the beginning." In the end, believers experience the fullness of the Spirit in harmony with the incarnation. In Catherine's schema, the Christ-bridge effects a final union in the Spirit, uniting the visible and invisible, the earthly and heavenly. Raymond writes that "her soul passed from her body and mounted upward to enter at last into the nuptial union of spirit with Spirit" (*Life*/III.3.359). Catherine herself articulates this all-encompassing role of the Spirit. She writes to a group of male religious, "This Spirit is our beginning, our rule, our intermediary and our end" (L84/257). As we see below, Catherine connects charity with mercy. God speaks: "Sometimes they seek me in the mercy of the Holy Spirit, and then my goodness lets them taste the fire of divine charity by which they conceive true and solid virtues grounded in pure charity for their neighbors" (D61/116).

Holy Spirit as Mercy

We have noted Catherine's appropriation of distinct qualities to the persons in the Trinity—power to the Father, wisdom to the Son, and mercy to the Holy Spirit (D119/227; D135/277; D142/295). But while mercy is a hallmark of the entire Trinity, she associates it most frequently with the Holy Spirit.[27] When Catherine attended liturgy, the repetition of the words of the Kyrie, "Lord have mercy, Christ have mercy, Lord have mercy," and of the Agnus Dei, "Lamb of God who takes away the sin of the world, have mercy on us," would have seeped deeply into her psyche. In addition, her theological understanding of the gulf between a God who was madly in love with the world and a world filled with sin and suffering led to her awareness of the acute need for forgiveness and mercy.

In a paen to mercy, Catherine writes that mercy covers over the faults of creatures; prayer brings forth mercy on sinners; mercy created and preserves the world, making it new in Christ's blood. Mercy conquers death, gives life, shines forth in the saints. Mercy brings food to strengthen us in our weakness. Catherine prays, "O mercy, my heart is engulfed with the thought of you! For wherever I turn my thoughts I find nothing but mercy" (D30/71–72). Later in the *Dialogue* God says to Catherine, "Never relax the desire of asking for my help, nor lower your voice from crying to me to have mercy on the world" (D107/201; see also LT158/307).

The settings in which Catherine mentions the Holy Spirit's mercy are many and diverse. Gentle Truth sends the "fiery mercy of the Holy Spirit" to seize Catherine's sacrifice of desire (D3/28). Those who do not resist the Holy Spirit's mercy are able to accept correction (D4/31). Paul, says Catherine, was bound and chained with the mercy of the Holy Spirit, the fire of charity (D83/152). The Holy Spirit's mercy confirms the teaching of Christ by strengthening the disciples' minds at Pentecost to testify to the truth (D29/69). It is the mercy of the Holy Spirit that allows believers to seek God and develop true and solid virtues (D61/116). To a persecutor of the church, Bernabo Visconti, Catherine writes, "Respond to the call and loving mercy of the Holy Spirit who summons you gently, who makes God's servants raise their voices in your behalf" (L17/72; L18/77). In all these instances, believers share in the mercy and burning love of the Holy Spirit (D119/227).

Mary O'Driscoll suggests that in Catherine's theology, this emphasis on asking for God's mercy reveals her care for the world. God does not wish us to "leave, abandon, or forget the world and the men and women who inhabit it."[28] For Catherine, the mercy of the Holy Spirit is linked especially to divine providence, another commanding idea in her theology. It is important to remember that Catherine experiences a chasm between the divine and the human, making it necessary for God to send Christ as the bridge. She describes the bridge as having stone walls of "true solid virtue" and a "roof of mercy" (D27/66). Without the bridge, there would be no way for humans to return to God. Through the incarnation, grace is restored to us through the clemency of the Holy Spirit (L17/67).

After Christ ascended to heaven, the Holy Spirit became the means of God's merciful activity toward the world. No matter how much suffering is involved, Catherine explains and accepts everything that happens to her because she sees the hand of God, that is, the work of the Holy Spirit, behind each event. Sometimes the Spirit's mercy operates directly, as when the Spirit provided Dominic and the brothers with a miraculous provision of food (D149/314). When the ministry becomes difficult, Catherine exhorts her disciples to trust "that the Holy Spirit will do what seems impossible to you" (L8/54). At other times, the Holy Spirit works indirectly, calling other human beings to come to the aid of those in need. Catherine herself is implicated in both modes of the Spirit's work. God says to Catherine, "You know how often I have pulled you out of your cell to satisfy the needs of the poor. Sometimes to help you when you were in need, and even when creatures failed you, I your Creator did not. In every way I provide for [my poor]" (D151/323).

As the merciful one, the Spirit assumes the roles of gentle caregiver/nurturing mother, nurse or reliable leader/captain of a ship. For example, the Spirit faithfully nurses the souls and bodies of poor hermits who have given up everything for God. God says of them, "I hold them to my breast and give them the milk of great consolation. Because they leave everything they possess and possess me completely" (D151/323). Comparing religious life to a ship that receives souls who want to race to perfection and the port of salvation, Catherine reminds those who live virtuous lives that the Spirit, the captain of this ship lacks nothing and will provide for them (D158/335–36).

The Spirit Casts Out Fear

We see once again in Catherine that the story of Pentecost in Acts functions as a touchstone to speak about the grace that casts out fear (see fig. 14). This dramatic biblical depiction of the Spirit's influence on the attitudes and behaviors of the disciples provides an antidote to the universal human experience of being afraid. Catherine entreats her readers constantly to overcome their fears. Catherine is keenly aware that Jesus' life of witness to the truth ended in the cross. At Pentecost, the disciples "mounted the pulpit of the blazing cross....Their words came forth as does a red-hot knife from a furnace, and with its heat they pierced their listeners to the heart and cast out the devil. Since they had lost themselves, they saw not themselves but only God's glory and honor and our salvation" (LT198/84). Catherine associates the Holy Spirit's courage-producing fire with ecstasy. She writes, "When we look to ourselves and see there such marvelous strength as is this fire, the Holy Spirit, we become so drunk with love for our Creator that we completely lose ourselves" (L84/255).

Like Hildegard, Catherine identifies with the disciples. The sign that she has attained perfect love is the same sign that was given to the disciples after they had received the Holy Spirit. God speaks: "They left the house and fearlessly preached my message by proclaiming the teaching of the Word" (D74/136). Catherine goes on to apply this text to herself, describing God's message to her and speaking of herself in the third person. "I gave her a share in this love, which is the Holy Spirit, within her will by making her will strong to endure suffering and to leave her house in my name to give birth to the virtues for her neighbors" (D74/136).

For some, the Spirit makes hearts strong; for others the Spirit melts hearts. But the end result for both is strength and courage. A letter to Bartolomeo Dominici, her friend and confessor, exemplifies Catherine's penchant to create a collage of mixed images, metaphors, and theological concepts: "I long to see you so strong and filled to overflowing with that Holy Spirit who came upon his holy disciples....After the fire of the Holy Spirit had descended on them they mounted the pulpit of the blazing cross where they felt and tasted the hunger of God's Son, his love for humankind" (L4/46; LT198/84; see figs. 19-21). From what we know, it seems clear that Catherine's very presence to her disciples gave them courage to face the difficult work before them. But when she cannot be with them, the Holy Spirit comes to her aid. In another letter to Bartolomeo Dominici, she writes, "Don't look at your weakness, but realize that in Christ crucified you can do everything. I will be at your side, never leaving you, with that invisible presence which the Holy Spirit makes possible" (L9/55).

In another text, Catherine emphasizes not only how the disciples were freed from fear, but also underlines one of her favorite themes—patience in perseverance. "Peter and the others hid away at home and waited for the Holy Spirit to come…they persevered in watching and in constant humble prayer until they were filled with the Holy Spirit. Then they lost all their fear, and they followed and preached Christ crucified" (D63/119). In addition to freeing the disciples from fear, the Holy Spirit also confers on them the important gift of discernment (D85/156).

Holy Spirit as Fire

Like her personality, Catherine's spirituality reflects a pattern of superlatives, an "all-or-nothing," totally engrossing encounter with God. Her expressions carry momentum—"zeal," "run swiftly," "run free," "run like an untethered horse" dot the landscape of her texts (L147, 210, 211, 217, 230). Perhaps Catherine felt that she did not have much time to complete the tasks God had given to her. Other expressions that communicate her intensity include "become all flame," "engulfed," "plunged," "drowned," "clothed in grace." Catherine speaks of being "clothed and drowned in the Holy Spirit's strength and fullness" (L29/103).

The image of fire is omnipresent in Catherine's texts. It is a commanding metaphor for all aspects of the spiritual life. One particular expression she uses repeatedly in relationship to the Holy Spirit is "blazing charity."[29] In yet another letter to Bartolomeo Dominici, she writes, "I long to see you swallowed up—drowned—in the fire of God's blazing charity, stripped of your unfit clothing and completely covered, clothed in the fire of the Holy Spirit" (L29/103).[30] Catherine's image of the Holy Spirit as fire is a reversal of Hildegard's imagery of greenness to describe the Holy Spirit. Catherine writes to a disciple: "In him [the Word] all the dampness of selfishness is dried up, and we take on the likeness of the Holy Spirit's fire" (LT228/15). The following passage reflects a mosaic of several Spirit images used by Catherine.

> O eternal Trinity!
> Eternal Trinity!
> O fire and deep well of charity!
> O you who are madly in love
> with your creature!
> O eternal truth!
> O eternal fire!
> O eternal wisdom
> given for our redemption!
> But did your wisdom come into the world alone?
> No.
> For wisdom was not separate from power,
> nor was power without mercy.
> You, wisdom, did not come alone then,
> but the whole Trinity was there.
> O eternal Trinity,
> mad with love,
> of what use to you was our redemption? (P10/78)

In this same prayer, Catherine uses the metaphor of fire to speak of desire, union with God, the love that brought about redemption. "And you set their hearts [of the virtuous] ablaze with the Holy Spirit's fire, with desire to love and follow you in truth" (P10/79). In another prayer the Spirit's mercy inflames hearts: "And I proclaim, eternal gentle goodness of God, that the mercy of the Holy Spirit, your blazing charity, wants to enflame my heart and everyone's and unite them with yourself" (P5/48).

Catherine's espousal of the atonement theory of redemption is evident in a letter to the monks of San Girolamo in which she writes, "This fire is the love that is the Holy Spirit, for love was the hand that pierced God's Son and made him shed his blood" (L84/255). In a letter to Queen Elizabeth of Hungary, Catherine sums up many of these themes.

I am writing to you in the precious blood of God's Son, longing to see you set all ablaze with the gentle loving fire of the Holy Spirit. I think of the Spirit as the love that dissipates all darkness and gives perfect light that supplants all ignorance with perfect knowledge. For those who are filled with the Holy Spirit, the fire of divine charity, are always aware that they have no being of themselves, and they recognize within themselves that non-being, sin. (L40/130)

When the flame becomes dim or seems to die out, Catherine returns to the theme of patient perseverance. When God seems to withdraw from her soul, she does not turn back. She perseveres in humility in the cell of self-knowledge where "she waits for the coming of the Holy Spirit, the flame of love" (D63/120). Catherine counsels waiting in patient fidelity for the Spirit to blow where She will and warns against imposing one's own will by "trying...to impose rules on the Holy Spirit" (D68/129). Perhaps Catherine's followers were not unlike ourselves in our desire for the Spirit's presence to empower us *now* and *in the way we desire*. At once, she helps us imagine the intensity of the fire and desire its presence.

No doubt, Catherine often witnessed the warming, softening, melting capacities of fire. In a letter to an abbess in Siena, she writes, "I beg you in the name of Christ crucified; let this stone be melted in the hot overflowing blood of God's Son, in that blood whose warmth is enough to melt the hardness and frigidity of any heart! How does it make us melt? Only in the way we've been talking about—with hatred and love. This is what the Holy Spirit does when he enters the soul" (L1/39). This letter is another good example of the way in which Catherine applies the image of blood to both the second and third persons of the Trinity. The Spirit's warmth can also work on unbelievers. To Pope Gregory XI, she writes: "And once the Holy Spirit's warmth and light had, through holy faith, displaced the chill of unbelief, they would produce flowers and fruits of virtue in the mystic body of holy church" (L74/230).

In the tradition, the metaphor of fire also points to purification (LT335/583).[31] The Spirit's fire consumes selfish love, removes any unwillingness to suffer (LT335/583), and casts out fear, discouragement, and dejection (LT335/588). Although Catherine has a very positive, hopeful view of the human person—evident in her confidence in the human will to say no to sin, and in her dogged expectation that the church could reform itself—she also has a vivid sense of sin and of the nothingness of creation in light of the fullness of God's being. In fact, she seems at times preoccupied with sin. In her prayers, she repeats like a mantra, "I have sinned against the Lord, have mercy on me" (P 11/95; P13/111, etc.). For Catherine, the very heart of self-knowledge is the truth of God's goodness in contrast to human selfishness and nothingness. She describes those guilty of abusing God's grace as resistant to the Holy Spirit, due to their uncircumcised hearts (P25/216).[32]

Being purged of sin is a constant challenge. "Burn with the fire of your Spirit," she prays, "and consume, root out from the bottom up, every fleshly love and affection" (P7/59; P23/203; D29/70). When sinful dispositions are purified, the soul is "warmed" with the Spirit of God's love (P24/214). Another function of fire is that it produces light. Catherine's strong intellectual interests and her exposure to the Dominican way of life with its emphasis on truth provide the context for comments on the light of the Spirit—without this light, she writes, "we cannot walk" (L53/162).

Inspired by the text of Romans 8:26, "the Spirit himself intercedes for us with sighs too deep for words," Catherine refers to the Holy Spirit's fire in conjunction with her discussion of tears.[33] In the *Dialogue*, Catherine describes five stages by which the soul progresses from shedding imperfect tears whose source is fear and disordered love, to the fifth stage, at which one sheds perfect tears as a result of union with Truth and a burning flame of holy desire (D88/161; D90/167). Catherine then goes on to articulate what happens when a soul who wants the perfection of tears cannot have it. She describes an alternate way of tears as "a weeping of fire, of true holy longing" that consumes in love (D91/168). "I tell you," she says, "these souls have tears of fire" (D91/169). I quote at length a section in which she links these tears of fire with the Holy Spirit. God speaks,

In this fire the Holy Spirit weeps in my presence for them and for their neighbors. I mean that my divine charity sets ablaze with its flame the soul who offers me her restless longing without any physical tears. These, I tell you, are tears of fire, and this is how the Holy Spirit weeps. Since the soul cannot do it with tears, she offers her desire to weep for love of me. And if you open your mind's eye you will see that the Holy Spirit weeps in the person of every one of my servants who offers me the fragrance of holy desire and constant humble prayer. This, it seems, is what the glorious apostle Paul meant when he said that the Holy Spirit weeps before me, the Father, "with unspeakable groaning" for you (Rom 8:26). (D91/169)

I wonder what the import of prayer with tears was to Catherine and whether she writes to address her own experience of dryness or simply to encourage others who lacked the gift of tears. At the stage of the spiritual life she describes—"blessed and painlessly tearful"—the soul nevertheless continues to offer to God her desires. Since physical tears have "been dried out in the furnace," the "Holy Spirit's tears of fire" replace them (D92/171).

Finally, at the end of the *Dialogue*, Catherine speaks of tears in the context of mercy—two aspects of the spiritual life that Catherine associates with the Holy Spirit. God speaks: "Now I invite you to weep, you and my other servants. And through your weeping and constant humble prayer I want to be merciful to the world" (D166/363). Catherine spoke constantly of God's mercy and of humanity's need of that mercy. "In prayer after prayer, she pleaded for God's mercy for a needy world, a needy church, a needy neighbor."[34]

Holy Spirit as Waiter

As we have seen over and over again, the Spirit imagery employed by our authors emerges primarily from the Bible. In one instance, Catherine combines her own experience with a number of traditional themes to create a fresh metaphor for the Holy Spirit as a waiter at table. Possible biblical and traditional material in the background include: general references to service in the New Testament; Jesus washing the feet of the disciples; dining at the Passover meal; celebration of the Eucharist; Irenaeus's comment that the Son and the Spirit are the two hands of God, and so on. In addition to these textual traditions, Catherine no doubt relies on her own personal experience of serving at table in her home, feeding the sick and poor in her neighborhood, as well as participating in Eucharist. She imagines the persons of the Trinity as table, food, and waiter.

Service is among the most important activities for Catherine and she uses the metaphor of the Spirit as servant to reinforce the need for selfless service. She admonishes an Augustinian friar, Frate Jeronimo, to be careful to avoid undue emotional attachment with those he serves. Since the Spirit's love is boundless, no other is allowed to serve the Word as food to us. "The waiter, the Holy Spirit—and because of his boundless love he is not satisfied to have anyone else wait on us but wants to serve as waiter himself" (LT52, 120). In another letter, Catherine writes to persuade the Countess Bandeçça Salimbeni to become a member of a new community Catherine had founded in 1377 at Belcaro, just southwest of Siena. Catherine speaks of the importance of "sweet" service (to serve is to reign), which, in turn, leads gradually to becoming a spouse of Christ. Then "the bride is welcomed by her bridegroom and led into the room where table, food, and waiter are found" (LT112/336).

In a letter of condolence to the nuns of San Gaggio and Monte San Savino, Catherine envisions both the living and the dead as being served by the Spirit now and at the heavenly banquet.

> Run on courageously then, because you have the path, the way, and the place where you can find the bed on which to rest, the table where you may find enjoyment, and the food with which you can satisfy yourselves. For he has made himself our table, our food, and our servant....I hear that your very dear mother and mine, Monna Nera, has found her place at the table of everlasting life, where she is enjoying the food of life. She has found the spotless Lamb as her reward. Just as I told you before that he is table, and food and servant, so I am telling you now that she, as a true servant of Christ crucified, has found the eternal Father as her table and her

bed....The Father is her table. The Son is her food, for through the mediation of the incarnate Word, God's Son, we can all reach the port of salvation we so desire. The Holy Spirit waits on her, for it was through love that the Father gave us his son as food, and through love the Son gave us life while taking death for himself. (L62/199)[35]

In another letter, Catherine describes a eucharistic experience on the feast of St. Lucy in which the saint allowed Catherine to taste the fruit of her martyrdom—a desire Catherine harbored for herself.[36] In this context Catherine hears God say to her, "I am table and I am food." Catherine continues, "The hand of the Holy Spirit was dispensing this food, sweetly serving those who relished it" (L47/145). Through her experience of receiving food from the hands of the Holy Spirit, Catherine's spirit was renewed, motivating her to serve courageously, even if it involved sacrifice and suffering. This is the standard that she held out to her followers.

In the *Dialogue*, Catherine describes the fourth and highest stage of the spiritual life as that in which individuals enjoy the indwelling of God in a steady, ongoing way. The rest that these souls experience at this high stage of perfection includes access to the Trinity as "table and food and waiter." The Father is their bed and table. The Word is their food, and the Holy Spirit, God's loving charity, is the waiter who serves God's gifts and graces. God speaks: "This gentle waiter carries to me their tender loving desires, and carries back to them the reward for their labors, the sweetness of my charity for their enjoyment and nourishment. So you see, I am their table, my Son is their food, and the Holy Spirit, who proceeds from me the Father and from the Son, waits on them" (D78/146). The Spirit functions as the "go-between" in this exalted yet deeply reciprocal relationship between God and the soul. The fruits on this table are the "true solid virtues" (L6/49).

In other instances, Catherine speaks of the table of the cross.[37] To Raymond of Capua, Catherine writes about service to God and neighbor: "And we are brought to dwell within the cell of self-knowledge, within which is encompassed the cell of the knowledge of God's goodness to us. There we become fat; there we are happy. Within that cell we eat souls as our food in our suffering, having made the cross our table" (LT104/655–56). Christ too "took his place at the table of the cross" (LT124/696). It is clear that Catherine sees a connection between service in the Spirit and suffering. Eating and savoring food for God's honor cannot be done anywhere but at the table of the cross because eating "in truth" involves suffering. Catherine's acute awareness of sin leads her to beg her followers to persevere in their efforts to work for the salvation of their neighbors. She writes, "Let sighs be our food, and tears our drink at the table of the cross" (LT296, 533, 535; see also LT309/538). The only way to eat at the table of the cross is to light the fire of our desires and allow the cross to be planted in us. The tree of the cross bears fruit, especially when we develop the virtues of obedience, patience, and humility (LT52/121).

Catherine's consciousness of the Trinity and the intimate interaction among the persons is visible in the following citation from a letter to an unspecified group of her disciples.

> Charity is a food that nourishes our soul at her breasts. This divine charity is waiter, table, and food because of the fire of the Holy Spirit. [But the Holy Spirit] is not separate from the power of the Father or the wisdom of the son; they are one and the same thing. This is why I said that the Holy spirit is table and food and waiter. So it is true: the Father is table, and the Son is food roasted on the wood of the most holy cross, and the Holy Spirit waits on us. We see that this dear waiter serves us our being and every grace we have received over and above our being. This means that God gives and is given to us continually, and not out of any obligation but out of love, as a free favor. (Letter 15/663)

Knowing that Catherine's experience of waiting on table likely gave rise to her portrayal of the Spirit as waiter grounds this image in the very concrete, mundane world of everyday living. The image gives rise to thoughts about God's hospitality, not as an abstraction, and not only in a ritual sense, but in the very real, routine things we do for each other. Catherine's imagery of a hospitable Holy Spirit calls to mind another powerful text that draws us into the ambit of God's gracious hospitality, a poem by the Anglican divine George Herbert (1593–1633).[38] Echoes of

Catherine's images of the Spirit and the human sense of inadequacy and unworthiness reverberate in this text.

> Love bade me welcome: yet my soul drew back,
>   Guilty of dust and sin.
> But quick-eyed Love, observing me grow slack
>   From my first entrance in,
> Drew nearer to me, sweetly questioning
>   If I lacked anything.
>
> "A guest," I answered, "worthy to be here."
>   Love said, "You shall be he."
> I, the unkind, ungrateful? Ah, my dear,
>   I cannot look on thee."
> Love took my hand, and smiling did reply,
>   "Who made the eyes but I?"
>
> "Truth, Lord, but I have marred them; let my shame
>   Go where it doth deserve."
> "And know you not," says Love, "who bore the blame?"
>   "My dear, then I will serve."
> "You must sit down," says Love, "and taste my meat."
>   So I did sit, and eat.[39]

The Holy Spirit serves not only food for the soul but also food for the intellect in the form of teaching, and food for the neighbor in the form of charity.[40] In one of her prayers, Catherine says, "And the Holy Spirit is indeed a waiter for us, for he serves us this teaching by enlightening our mind's eye with it and inspiring us to follow it. And he serves us charity for our neighbors and hunger to have as food souls and the salvation of the whole world for the Father's honor" (P12/102). Especially arresting in this sentence is Catherine's final juxtaposition of opposites—the Holy Spirit serves us hunger. Not exactly what one expects to be served at table. But for Catherine being hungry for souls and for the world's salvation goes hand in hand with being fed charity for these same neighbors. Such hunger motivates action for justice.

In a rare instance, Catherine shows how great God's love is by referring to the love God extends to the worldly or ungodly.

God speaks, "For the Holy Spirit, my mercy, waits on these and gives them love for me and warm affection for their neighbors, so that with immeasurable charity they seek their salvation" (D143/297). Even though the abyss that separates even the perfect from God is greater in the case of the worldly, the Spirit still deigns to serve all. The awesome nature of God's condescending love is visible in God's choice to construct a bridge that reaches out to those who are the least deserving of God's tender care. And in every case, the Spirit's merciful service is ultimately ordered to love of neighbor, not personal holiness.

Catherine also extends the "waiter" image to include the Spirit as laborer, gardener, and cellarer. She prays, "Oh gentle fire of love! You have given us as servant, as laborer, the most merciful free-flowing Holy Spirit who is love itself!" (L55/171). In another letter, Catherine offers encouragement to Abbot Giovanni, who wrote to Catherine that his garden (monastery) had no plants (monks). She says, "Take heart, and do what you can, for I trust that in God's goodness the gardener, the Holy Spirit, will adorn the garden and provide for this and every other need" (L67/212). It is the Spirit "who turns over the soil of our perverse sensual will" (LT72/331) and sows seeds of virtue (LT391/395). In a letter to a Florentine bishop, Catherine gives the Spirit an unusual role in the process of redemption. Imagining the Spirit working in a wine cellar, she writes of the Son on the cross: "Bleeding from every member, he had made himself cask and wine and cellarer for us. Thus we see that his humanity is the cask that encased the divine nature. The cellarer—the fire and the hands that are the Holy Spirit—tapped that cask on the wood of the most holy cross" (L37/126). As the blood flowed from Christ's side, it was "heralded with the trumpet of mercy, with the fire of the Holy Spirit as trumpeter, so that whoever wants some of this blood can come for it" (LT87/632).

In the section in the *Dialogue* on divine providence, Catherine often speaks of the Holy Spirit as "servant," providing whatever is needed to individuals or communities. At times the Spirit works through others; in other instances, the Spirit intervenes directly. The services the Holy Spirit performs in the lives of those who have given up worldly concerns are many. God speaks,

Then I become their spiritual provider, and materially I employ a special providence beyond the general: my mercy, the Holy Spirit, becomes their servant....Such a soul has the Holy Spirit as a mother who nurses her at the breast of divine charity. The Holy Spirit has set her free, releasing her, as her lord, from the slavery of selfish love....This servant, the Holy Spirit, whom I in my providence have given her, clothes her, nurtures her, inebriates her with tenderness and the greatest wealth.

(D141/292)

The soul also comes to know the Truth through the "light from the Holy Spirit, whom I have given her as a servant" (D141/293). In this part of the *Dialogue*, Catherine is wrestling with her intense desire to receive frequent communion; with the ways in which God thwarts this desire in order to enhance her hunger; and with the final resolution in which God provides for her. In Catherine's interpretation, the goal of this "cat and mouse" game is to get her to trust "that the Holy Spirit, her servant, would nourish her hunger" (D142/296). The Spirit even pricks the conscience of the priest who refuses Catherine communion (D142/294)!

Among other things, the Holy Spirit serves grace. In one instance, Catherine writes that the Holy Spirit serves us God and "every grace and gift, spiritual as well as material" (L53/161). Catherine is angry at the abuses in the church, in particular at those who "sell" the Holy Spirit's grace like a piece of merchandise (LT 219/92). The vices that cause ministers to do this are impurity, bloated pride, and greed (D126/244). "Not only do they not give what they are in duty bound to give to the poor, but they rob them through simony and their hankering after money, selling the grace of the Holy Spirit" (D114/213; 119/221; 121/232; 127/247–48; L28/101; L65/207). When the church administers the sacraments worthily, the Spirit is able to serve those who partake. God speaks to Catherine of the Eucharist, in which God provides for the soul's growth in hunger and "within the soul's emotions by administering grace through the service of the Holy Spirit" (D146/307).

Catherine interprets life's obstacles and suffering in terms of a loving God who sends hardships in order to test faith and strengthen love. God makes things difficult in order to teach a lesson. Growth in trust that God can and will provide whatever is needed for holiness is the desired outcome. God speaks about bringing souls to the brink "so that they will fall in love with my providence and embrace true poverty as their bride. Then their servant, the Holy Spirit, my mercy, when he sees that they lack anything that is necessary for their bodies, will light a nudging spark of desire in the hearts of those who are able to help, and these will come to help them in their need" (D149/314). Love of neighbor is always the final test of an authentic spiritual life.

In a context of direct exchange between Catherine and the Holy Spirit, Catherine assigns an unusual type of service to the Spirit. She places the Spirit at the cross as the strong hand that holds up the world by holding fast the nails in Jesus' hands.

> The Holy Spirit is the light that banishes all darkness, the hand that upholds the whole world. In that vein I recall his saying not long ago, "I am the One who upholds and sustains the whole world. It was through me that the divine and human natures were brought together. I am the mighty hand that holds up the standard of the cross; of that cross I made a bed and held the God-Man nailed fast to it." He was so strong that if the bond of charity, the fire of the Holy Spirit, had not held him, the nails could never have held him.
>
> (L29/103; see also LT226/8; P24/207)[41]

Catherine's point is that the bond of love binding humanity and divinity is so strong that nothing, even death, can break it. Catherine varies the metaphor—at times it is the bond of love that holds the nails in Christ's hands (LT256/323–24; LT292/599); in other instances it is the heat of divine love (D14/52), charity (LT226/8; D77/143), or Christ's love for the Father (LT253/423; LT38/549); or the love that is the Holy Spirit as bond between the first and second persons. She also extends the bond to those in the Christian community who love (LT292/599). We are "engrafted into the tree of life, Christ gentle Jesus, who will bind you with the same strong bond that held him nailed fast to the cross" and to our neighbors (LT253/425; see also P17/148–52; P24/207–8). Since, for Catherine, humans are made of love, we cannot be drawn to God in any way other than love (LT285/289).

Through this metaphor of the Holy Spirit as waiter, Catherine ties together themes of charity, service, the cross, suffering, and love of neighbor. She also underlines the intimate bond within the Trinity that is extended to all believers. By assigning to the Spirit/love/bond/charity the unusual role of holding the nails in place, Catherine gives the Spirit a significant role in the redemptive action of Christ on the cross. The passages in which Catherine describes the Spirit's role at the cross provide a rich Holy Week meditation that sheds new light on the relationship between the Trinity and the cross. In Catherine's theology, the Holy Spirit is not on the sidelines in God's relationship with the human community (see figs. 7,12, 15–18).

Conclusion

Like so many medieval texts, Catherine's corpus features the commanding presence of the second person of the Trinity, especially the Jesus of the cross. Catherine experienced life as filled with sin and suffering. But the love manifested on the cross not only gives meaning to our suffering but also reveals a divine love beyond all imagining. Her response was to live in virtue, and love others with enthusiasm, immediacy, drive, and joy, refusing to allow sadness, defeat, or discouragement to hold sway. She encouraged others to allow their hunger for souls to banish all fear and to act with courage as did the apostles at Pentecost. Her deeply trinitarian theology leads her to feature the Spirit in ways that awaken the imagination about the Spirit's identity and deepen our understanding of the prominent roles the Spirit plays in the drama of redemption. To a group of monks, Catherine writes, "So we have seen how we find God in time of darkness, how in bitter things we find sweetness—only through the impassioned, consummate love we conceive and continually discover in this baptism of the blood and of the fire that is the Holy Spirit. This Spirit is our beginning, our rule, our intermediary, and our end" (LT189/136).

Let us close with one of Catherine's prayers—a short invocation to the Trinity, notable for its succinct expression and lyric form. Notice the rare reversal of the order in which the trinitarian persons are usually presented and for the inversion of attributes normally assigned to each person.[42]

> O Holy Spirit, come into my heart;
> by your power draw it to yourself, God,
> and give me charity with fear.
> Guard me, Christ, from every evil thought,
> and so warm and enflame me again
> with your most gentle love
> that every suffering may seem light to me.
> My holy father and my gentle Lord,
> help me in my every need.
> Christ love! Christ love! (P6/54)

❧

Food for Thought

1. Catherine is unique in her portrayal of the Trinity as table, food, and waiter. Reflect on and assess this metaphor. Is it shocking, inviting? Focus especially on the image of the Holy Spirit as a waiter at table. Have you ever been a waiter or do you know someone who is? What value does our society place on waiting table? What are some of the implications of thinking about God as a waiter?

2. Either in your mind or on paper, paint an image of the crucifixion in which the cross becomes a bed with the Spirit holding the nails in place as Christ lies on it. What does such an image say about God? What kind of prayer does it inspire? What theological conclusions might you draw from it?

3. Catherine sees the Holy Spirit as the epitome of mercy, empowering us to reach out to our neighbors in need. In prayer after prayer, Catherine pleaded for God's mercy for a needy world, a needy church, a needy neighbor. Discuss Catherine's words: "Then their servant, the Holy

Spirit, my mercy, when he sees that they lack anything that is necessary for their bodies, will light a nudging spark of desire in the hearts of those who are able to help, and these will come to help them in their need" (D149/314). How often do we speak about mercy, recalling the Beatitude, "Blessed are the merciful, for they shall obtain mercy?" Do we allow the Spirit to transform our hearts to work for justice? How do we block the Spirit's "nudge" toward being merciful?

4. Catherine speaks of the Holy Spirit as the One who serves us charity for our neighbors and instills in us hunger for their salvation. We know that Catherine engaged in severe fasts that had a deleterious effect on her body. We are also aware that many young people today, especially women, suffer from anorexia nervosa and bulimia. Discuss the relationship between physical and spiritual hungers. How might we approach eating disorders from a spiritual perspective? How should members of affluent nations think about love of neighbor in relationship to unbridled capitalism, consumerism, and greed? How might the Spirit empower us to find ways to redistribute resources to feed those who are physically hungry and support those who are spiritually hungry?

5. Catherine links the Holy Spirit with the gift of tears that includes sorrow for sin and compassion for the sufferings of others. Read through the following passage slowly and then discuss it. What meaning does Catherine attach to tears? What is your experience of tears? How is the idea that the Spirit helps us weep, grow in compassion, and act for justice important for spirituality today?

> In this fire the Holy Spirit weeps in my presence for them and for their neighbors. I mean that my divine charity sets ablaze with its flame the soul who offers me her restless longing without any physical tears. These, I tell you, are tears of fire,

213

and this is how the Holy Spirit weeps. Since the soul cannot do it with tears, she offers her desire to weep for love of me. And if you open your mind's eye you will see that the Holy Spirit weeps in the person of every one of my servants who offers me the fragrance of holy desire and constant humble prayer. This, it seems, is what the glorious apostle Paul meant when he said that the Holy Spirit weeps before me the Father, "with unspeakable groaning" for you (Rom 8:26). (D91/169)

CHAPTER 7

JULIAN OF NORWICH
"Sweet Touchings": The Spirit and Grace

Our last, shortest—but not least—exploration of the Holy Spirit turns to Julian of Norwich, a fourteenth-century English mystic. In contrast to the previous authors we have studied, Julian's corpus is quite small—two versions of a single text in which she probes the meaning of a series of visions she had of the crucified Christ. But her notable trinitarian theology and creative use of metaphor make her an apt candidate to cap this excursion into metaphors of the Spirit in the Middle Ages.

Life and Times

In the last chapter, we noted the political, economic, demographic, intellectual, and ecclesial ferment of the fourteenth century.[1] In England the chaos took the form of war, failed crops and famine, schism, plague, exorbitant taxation, peasant revolts, and ecclesial corruption. Norwich was struck by plague five times between 1348 and 1406. Fifty percent of the clergy are said to have perished. Thus, Julian of Norwich lived in a world characterized by fear, doubt, guilt, and instability. Official explanations for the plague were either that it was caused by the stars—a malign conjunction of planets or the "drying" effects of comets that affected the air—or by human sinfulness. Both enlightened and corrupt bishops pointed to sin as the cause of God's wrath. Thomas Brinton (1320–89), bishop of Rochester, well-known preacher and staunch defender of the poor, castigated those who subscribed to cosmic causes. In a sermon he says, "since the corruption of lust and the designs of wickedness are greater today than in Noah's time—for a thousand forms of vice are practiced today which did not exist then—let us not impute the scourges of God to planets but rather to our sins."[2]

Evidence suggests that Brinton's contemporary, Norwich's bishop Henry Despenser, was a harsh, arrogant, ruthless individual, given to ostentatious wealth. He viciously quelled a peasant revolt in 1381, executing a delegate who had come to ask for pardon. Since 1369 poor farmers had rebelled against heavy taxation and the burden of being tied to service on land owned by gentry, church, and monasteries. During this uprising, the peasants burned and pillaged the land and even chopped off the head of Simon of Sudbury, archbishop of Canterbury. While unsuccessful, the revolt revealed the intensity of the unrest of the lower classes. In his sermons, Despenser also pointed to the sins of the people as an explanation for the scourges of the day. This context is important if we are to understand the goals and hopes Julian articulates in her book *Showings*, Julian's only work, written in long and short versions.

Concerns about orthodoxy were also prominent. Oxford professor John Wycliff challenged the church in England on a number of fronts. The Lollard movement spawned by his writings attracted both powerful patrons and simple folk who supported criticism of the wealth and corruption in the church; desired that the Bible be available in the vernacular; questioned the role of sacraments; denied the existence of hell and purgatory; and held that the "perfect" were no longer capable of sin. Wycliff was first investigated around 1377 and then banned from Oxford in 1382.[3] All of these issues provide the backdrop for Julian's text. In addition, women who dared to preach or teach were always vulnerable to accusations of heresy.[4] Joan Nuth suggests that Julian's obvious concern about orthodoxy may have been due to her awareness of the church's prosecution of heresy on the continent. After a lull, the Inquisition took on new fervor between 1353 and 1377 and again in the 1390s, when Julian would have been writing her texts. While there is little evidence that England experienced the kind of heretical movements and ecclesial sanctions that were found on the Continent, it does not seem likely that Julian would have been totally ignorant of these developments.[5]

Although there is no precise way to measure social violence, there are good reasons to believe that late medieval Europe was particularly marked by it.[6] England battled with Scotland on one side and France on the other. In 1334, the Scots and the French made an alliance, which spelled trouble for England. Pope John XXII and his successor, Benedict XII, tried to avert a conflict by proposing that France lead a crusade in which England would participate. Philip IV of France agreed, but the pope demurred. Philip diverted his waiting ships to the English Channel and the Hundred Years' War erupted and was waged on and off from 1337 to 1453.

The city of Norwich is located on the eastern side of England in a region known as East Anglia. It lies on a large river, the Wensum, twenty miles from the coast on a highway running directly to London. In the fourteenth century, Norwich was a large, prosperous, and cosmopolitan city, not unlike London. Since trade with Flanders flourished—first wool, then cloth and other commodities—Flemish workers settled in Norwich. Julian makes many detailed references to cloth, which suggests that she was familiar with this trade, either through family or location. The Church of St. Julian is a few hundred yards away from the main road that linked the center of Norwich to Conisford, near a bend in the Wensum River, making it a natural docking place with lots of traffic.

Yet in the midst of such unsettledness, there was an intellectual and mystical flourishing. Norwich had a large number of parish churches and three colleges for secular priests. It was also home to an impressive Benedictine cathedral and priory, whose library was one of the finest in late medieval England. Franciscans, Dominicans, Carmelites, and Augustinians had houses and produced an impressive number of scholars, suggesting that Julian may have had access to large book collections. Norwich was a "feeder" to the universities at Oxford and London.[7] Mystical strains emerged in what some have called an "English school"—in addition to Julian, we have works by Richard Rolle, Walter Hilton, Margery Kempe, and the unknown author of *The Cloud of Unknowing*.[8]

In addition, Norwich was an important center of devotional painting and sculpture. Its churches were filled with religious art, with many examples of wall paintings that were popular at the time. This art provided a simple, direct, moral, and emotional appeal. It was not erudite or allusive. Much art in the churches was "Franciscan" in tone, that is, devotional and affective, with explicit depictions of the crucifixion. It is likely that, in her text, Julian worked with the images surrounding her. The result is clear, detailed, colorful images that appeal to the reader's imagination but, above all, communicate profound and complex theological teaching.

There can be no doubt that Julian was formed in significant ways by the character of Norwich, with its many venues for religious training and the various modes through which doctrine and devotion were communicated to all levels of society. Julian was also obviously influenced by preaching. Although we know no details about Julian's education, her texts reveal a broad and sophisticated acquaintance with theological and liturgical traditions.[9]

Our knowledge of Julian's life is sparse—we do not even know her given name.[10] What we know of her comes from three sources: her writings—a scribe's note in the text says she was alive in 1413; a reference to a visit by Margery Kempe (1415), a married woman who came to consult with Julian;[11] and several wills which suggest that she may have still been alive in 1416 (a man named John Plumpton left Julian forty pence and twelve pence each to Julian's unnamed maid and also a former maid, Alice). Since there is evidence of many "Dame Julians" in local wills, it is difficult to know for certain the identity of the referent. Anchoresses and anchorites often took the name of the church to which they were connected, which is the case with Julian.

Born at the end of 1342, Julian became ill in May of 1373 when she was thirty and a half years of age (3/179).[12] Near death, she experienced a series of sixteen revelations.[13] Her mother was present, as was a priest, who placed a crucifix before her eyes (2/77). The first fifteen visions occurred between 4 a.m. and 3 p.m. (65/309–10) with a final vision the following night (66/310). The primary visual focus of these visions is the body of Jesus on the cross. Julian recovered, wrote a short text recounting her experience, followed decades later (after 1393) by a much longer version of the visions and their meaning.[14] In her account, Julian suggests

218

parallels between her own ordeal and Christ's experience on the cross—similar age, abandonment to God's will, marking the hours of the ordeal.[15] Julian's style is both image-laden and driven by her quest for intellectual understanding. She is a careful thinker and writer. While her mental processes are fluid, the text is carefully organized with intratextual references and attention to detail. Her brilliant and searching mind and her great literary skill have led some to compare her to Chaucer.[16]

Scholars debate whether Julian became an anchoress at the Church of St. Julian before or after her visions. The word *anchoress* comes from Greek and Latin terms meaning "to retire."[17] It was a somewhat common and revered way of life in the fourteenth century that brought prestige and grace to the church with which an anchoress was affiliated. With the approval of the bishop, a male (anchorite) or female (anchoress) agreed to live a life of solitude and prayer.[18] The liturgy of enclosure was a Requiem Mass, symbolizing death to self and world. There was a solemn procession to the anchorhold; the anchoress received extreme unction (the sacrament of the dying); the bishop scattered ashes; and the door was ritually bolted or sealed.

Anchorholds were usually small dwellings of two to four rooms (often with a garden) built on the side of a church or in the eaves under the roof with a view to the sanctuary. An anchoress generally had a servant or two to attend to household tasks and business outside the anchorhold. Often there was a window that opened onto the street or a parlor where the faithful could come to receive spiritual counsel. The lifestyle of an anchoress involved chastity, prayer, moderate asceticism, a simple but nourishing diet and adequate warm clothing. Some women earned a living (needlework, for example), while others were supported by gifts from the community.

The Spirit within the Trinity

The God whom Julian encountered in her visions is thoroughly trinitarian. Her discussion of the Trinity is more prominent in the later Long Text, suggesting that as Julian's reflection on her vision of the crucified matured, she linked the love visible

in the cross with the entire Trinity. As Kerrie Hide notes, Julian
has no separate theology of the Trinity, Christology, theology of
nature and grace, pneumatology, ecclesiology, or eschatology.
Rather, she weaves all of these perspectives, using them to communicate what she had learned about the historical, everyday journey of redemption. Thus, her descriptions of the Spirit's work
have a "vital, existential character."[19]

Her portrayal of the Trinity is also the centerpiece of her
Christian anthropology.[20] "And so in Christ our two natures are
united, for the Trinity is comprehended in Christ in whom our
higher part is founded and rooted; and our lower part the second
person has taken, which nature was first prepared for him"
(57/291). Her theology of the Trinity is informed by Augustine
and the later tradition, but it comes alive in her own experience of
the crucified Jesus.

> And so in our making, God almighty is our loving
> Father, and God all wisdom is our loving Mother, with
> the love and goodness of the Holy Spirit, which is all
> one God, one Lord. And in the joining and the union he
> is our very true spouse and we his beloved wife and fair
> maiden, with which wife he was never displeased: for he
> says: I love you and you love me, and our love will never
> divide in two. (58/293)

Like much late medieval mystical literature, Julian's text is also
overwhelmingly christocentric, centered on her graphic vision of
Christ's wounds and suffering. But her method and the context of
her Christology are trinitarian. Julian's lists of triads call to mind
Augustine's *On the Trinity*. Her explicit treatment of the persons of
the Trinity in chapter 58 reveals the following breakdown:

Father/Creator	Mother/Son	Holy Spirit/Lord
Being	Increase	Fulfillment
Nature	Mercy	Grace
Protection	Perfection	Reward
Natural substance	Sensuality	Gift for living
Might/Power	Wisdom	Love
	Reform/Restore	Goodness

Her basic triads are power/wisdom/goodness; protection/restoration/fulfillment; nature/mercy/grace. But these distinct personal divine qualities should not distract us from the basic fluidity of Julian's theology.[21] The medieval monastic penchant to avoid rigid divisions is dramatically pronounced in Julian's thought processes. Roles and titles (grace, Lord, mother) assigned to Christ in one context are applied to the Spirit in another. The work of salvation is deeply shared by the entire Trinity.

Julian's interest is almost exclusively on the economic Trinity—the Trinity for us (51/278; 55/286). The very first sentence of the Long Text reads:

> This is a revelation of love which Jesus Christ, our endless bliss, made in sixteen showings, of which the first is about his precious crowning of thorns; and in this was contained and specified the blessed Trinity, with the Incarnation, and the union between God and man's soul, with many fair revelations and teachings of endless wisdom and love, in which all the revelations which follow are founded and connected. (1/175)

She views the framework of the Christian tradition on the Trinity through the lens of her visionary experience and using her ordered, reasoned, mental processes, she produced a compelling account of the astounding divine love that lies behind this doctrine.[22]

She sees herself as a medium whose call was to communicate to a suffering community that God's trinitarian love is available and trustworthy. The Trinity is not a mathematical puzzle but an inviting, inclusive love. God the Father is the almighty One who creates and preserves us and the world in all its fragility. God the Son is the wisdom who makes us and restores us to God by wisely and courteously attracting us to himself. God the Holy Spirit is the goodness, comfort, and delight necessary for our healing and fulfillment.

Like Bonaventure and Catherine, Julian places the Trinity at the center of redemption—at the cross (see fig. 16). These mystics realize in their own distinct way that there is no way to heaven except through the cross (19/211–12).[23]

> And in the same revelation [of the crucifixion], suddenly
> the Trinity filled my heart full of the greatest joy, and I
> understood that it will be so in heaven without end to all
> who will come there. For the Trinity is God, God is the
> Trinity. The Trinity is our maker, the Trinity is our pro-
> tector, the Trinity is our endless joy and our bliss, by our
> Lord Jesus Christ and in our Lord Jesus Christ. And
> this was revealed in the first vision and in them all, for
> where Jesus appears the blessed Trinity is understood,
> as I see it. And I said: Blessed be the Lord! (4/181)

Julian's image of the crucified contains and specifies the Trinity.
The face of Jesus on the cross gave her access to trinitarian love.
Like Bonaventure, Julian is careful to include the body as well as
the soul in the journey toward God (58/293–95). When the soul is
breathed into the body we are made sensual, and mercy and grace
begin to work. The Holy Spirit works to care for and protect us
with pity and love, leading us into the power of Christ, "increased
and fulfilled through the Holy Spirit." Sensuality is founded in
nature, mercy and grace, which foundation "enables us to receive
gifts which lead us to endless life." In her visions, Julian saw that
our substance is in God and God is in our sensuality (55/286–87).

Julian is well known for her theology of the Motherhood of
God. The divine mother looks and acts with mercy on children
who are receptive to her.

> From this it follows that as truly as God is our Father,
> so truly is God our Mother. Our Father wills, our
> Mother works, our good Lord the Holy Spirit confirms.
> And therefore it is our part to love our God in whom we
> have our being, reverently thanking and praising him
> for our creation, mightily praying to our Mother for
> mercy and pity, and to our Lord the Holy Spirit for help
> and grace. (59/296)

For Julian, Motherhood *is* God, since mothering describes God's
identity and activity, not only giving birth and nurturing, but also
as filled with power and wisdom.[24] "So in our true Mother Jesus
our life is founded in his own prescient wisdom from without

222

beginning, with the great power of the Father and the supreme goodness of the Holy Spirit" (63/304). This Trinity is a working community, engaged and delighted in bringing about the salvation of souls. Julian's interests are strikingly soteriological—she experienced a Trinity who cares intensely about, and is deeply involved in, the lives of believers. Julian stands out, however, in her ability to bring together the immanent and economic aspects of the Trinity by portraying the intensity, intimacy, and dynamism of divine love, which always includes creation. It is through the Spirit's work that the immanent and transcendent aspects of God are brought together.[25] While Bonaventure's image of the Trinity as the overflowing fountain of goodness produces an image of water pouring out from above to the earth, Julian's imagery suggests an atom teeming with inner life, whose energy bursts forth into the whole world.

Metaphors of the Spirit

In the Long Text, Julian refers to the Holy Spirit explicitly about fifty times. Kerrie Hide calls attention to the fact that, in a text filled with imagery, Julian offers no visual description of the Holy Spirit. She does not use the common image in medieval art of the Spirit as a dove, nor does she mention Pentecost.[26] Nevertheless, she assigns many key tasks to the Spirit's energy and activity, which are dynamic, personal, relational, and intimate.[27] Above all she associates the Spirit with divine love.

> Truth sees God, and wisdom contemplates God, and of these two comes the third, and that is a marvelous delight in God, which is love. Where truth and wisdom are, truly there is love, truly coming from them both, and all are of God's making. For God is endless supreme truth, endless supreme wisdom, endless supreme love uncreated. (44/256)

Julian makes only two references to the Holy Spirit in the context of the immanent Trinity. Both are found in her famous parable of the lord and the servant. In the first, she speaks of the

Holy Spirit in traditional fashion as the equal love that is in both the Father and the Son (51/274). In the second, she describes the Son, sitting in the eternal rest and peace prepared by the Father. In mutual coinherence, the Father is in the Son and the Holy Spirit is in the Father and the Son (51/278). All other references to the Holy Spirit refer to God's activity in history.

The list of virtues, gifts, and dispositions Julian associates with the Holy Spirit is long and diverse. For Julian, the procession of the Holy Spirit acts as a further stage in the divine self-gift.[28] As Bonaventure built on images of flowing water, Julian focuses on the flow of blood from the body of the crucified. Both images convey to the reader the unending plenty of God's love, which is poured out on the faithful (12/199–200). Julian employs a string of terms—fill, fulfill, flow, overflow, beflow, overpass, passover—connecting the hot, flowing blood of the passion with God's love and the eternal generosity of Christ.[29]

But in Julian's mind the Spirit is associated, above all, with grace (7/189). The richness of this concept is visible in the following: "through grace we are touched by sweet illuminations of the life of the Spirit, through which we are kept in true faith, hope and love, with contrition and devotion and also with contemplation and every kind of true joys and sweet consolations. The blessed demeanour of our Lord God works this in us through grace" (71/319). To understand her pneumatology, then, it is profitable to examine briefly her anthropology—how she describes the human person in relation to grace.

In her revelations, Julian meets a God whose love is startling and disconcerting. Not only is this God intimate and familiar, but the divine joy is anchored in creation and especially in human beings (53/284). Julian uses an unusual metaphor to express the effect of God's gaze on humanity. "For it was revealed that we are his crown, which crown is the Father's joy, the Son's honour, the Holy Spirit's delight, and endless marvelous bliss to all who are in heaven" (51/278). In other words, Julian sees humanity as the "feather in God's cap," the children to whom endless gifts are given, and about whom God delights in bragging.

To convince her readers of the potential for intimate union with God, Julian turns to images of clothing, knitting, dwellings, and cities (68/313; 81/337) to express how we are enclosed in God and God in us (53/283). Early on, she mentions the now famous image of the fragile hazelnut that lies secure in God's hand. God made it, loves it, and preserves it (5/183–84). Julian wants her readers to rely on the steadfast rock of divine providence, based in a gentle, tender, committed love.

> For the almighty truth of the Trinity is our Father, for he made us and keeps us with him. And the deep wisdom of the Trinity is our Mother, in whom we are enclosed. And the high goodness of the Trinity is our Lord, and in him we are enclosed and he in us. We are enclosed in the Father, and we are enclosed in the Son, and we are enclosed in the Holy Spirit. And the Father is enclosed in us, the Son is enclosed in us, and the Holy Spirit is enclosed in us, almighty, all wisdom and all goodness, one God, one Lord. (54/285)[30]

God sits in our soul, Julian writes, because it is God's delight to "reign blessedly in our understanding, and sit restfully in our soul, and to dwell endlessly in our soul, working us all into him" (57/292). The point of this indwelling is that we become co-workers with God in the process of redemption (56/289).

> The place which Jesus takes in our soul he will nevermore vacate, for in us is his home of homes and his everlasting dwelling. And in this he revealed the delight that he has in the creation of man's soul; for as well as the Father could create a creature, and as well as the Son could create a creature, so well did the Holy Spirit want man's spirit to be created, and so it was done. And therefore the blessed Trinity rejoices without end in the creation of man's soul, for it saw without beginning what would delight it without end. (68/313; see also 58/293)

Julian imagines all Christians as knitted to Christ by a "subtle and mighty knot...united in this union, and made holy in this holiness" (53/284).

Julian does not stop at the metaphor of clothing in her efforts to describe divine–human intimacy. God is even like our skin: "For as the body is clad in the cloth, and the flesh in the skin, and the bones in the flesh, and the heart in the trunk, so are we, soul and body, clad and enclosed in the goodness of God" (6/186). The saved are in Christ, Christ is in the saved, and Christ is in God. This mutual coinherence of the persons of the Trinity includes all of creation and is the source of joy, honor, and delight for all (55/286). Mary is also regularly inserted into this close-knit community. Julian is aware of the theological role Mary has in the incarnation. But there is also a sense in which Julian cannot imagine the happiness of either God or humans without her. "So our Lady is our mother, in whom we are enclosed and born of her in Christ, for she who is mother of our saviour is mother of all who are saved in our saviour" (57/292).

The gifts that are the fruit of the Holy Spirit's work include the virtues, especially faith, humility, and mercy (54/285; 10/196; 57/292; 77/330); the power to know God and oneself (56/288); reconciliation (48/262); the power to join one's will to God's (41/249); renewal (57/292); the power to be Christ's children and to live Christian lives (54/286). Julian's eschatological interests are revealed in her frequent references to the Spirit's work, which will ensure heaven (40/246; 55/287; 58/295). The final reward is described in terms of reconciliation, protection, peace, and being at ease (48/261). As noted above, the Holy Spirit's presence is not limited to the soul, but reaches into our sensuality as well. Although our sensuality is assumed only by Jesus, the Father and the Holy Spirit are in Christ, working together to lead us in our totality to our final end (58/295).

> And when our soul is breathed into our body, at which time we are made sensual, at once mercy and grace begin to work, having care of us and protecting us with pity and love, in which operation the Holy Spirit forms in our faith the hope that we shall return up above to our substance, into the power of Christ, increased and fulfilled through the Holy Spirit. So I understood that our sensuality is founded in nature, in mercy and in grace, and this foundation enables us to receive gifts which lead us to endless life. (55/286–87)

Julian is not afraid to reassure her audience that the Holy Spirit is indeed also working in her, allowing her to recount her visions accurately. They can trust that the God Julian met and describes is true and reliable (44/256). God says to her,

> Know it well, it was no hallucination which you saw today, but accept and believe it and hold firmly to it, and comfort yourself with it and trust in it, and you will not be overcome...and these words: You will not be overcome, were said very insistently and strongly, for certainty and strength against every tribulation which may come. He did not say: You will not be troubled, you will not be belaboured, you will not be disquieted; but he said: You will not be overcome. God wants us to pay attention to these words, and always to be strong in faith trust, in well-being and woe, for he loves and delights in us, and so he wishes us to love him and delight in him and trust greatly in him, and all will be well. (68/314–15)

Julian's understanding of the Holy Spirit's role is stated succinctly in chapter 58. The Spirit's realm is the active working of grace and mercy in the Christian community.

> And so our Mother works in mercy on all his beloved children who are docile and obedient to him, and grace works with mercy, and especially in two properties, as it was shown, which working belongs to the third person, the Holy Spirit. He works, rewarding and giving. Rewarding is a gift for our confidence which the Lord makes to those who have laboured; and giving is a courteous act which he does freely, by grace, fulfilling and surpassing all that creatures deserve. (58/294)

Julian assures her beleaguered readers that their lives of suffering are not without value and that God is one who gives gifts freely and endlessly, irrespective of their ability to earn or deserve it.

Julian's message of assurance involves the Holy Spirit in other ways as well. The Spirit assists us in both our understanding

and our affections. It is through the Holy Spirit that we understand that Christ is the church (34/236) and that God's judgment
can differ from that of the church (45/256). The Holy Spirit
teaches also that knowledge about ourselves and knowledge of
God is the same because we dwell in God (56/288). At one point,
Julian employs the contrasting images of light, cause of our life,
and darkness, cause of our pain. The light of clear vision is connected to all three persons. She says, "And at the end of woe, sud-
denly our eyes will be opened, and in the clearness of our sight our
light will be full, which light is God, our Creator, Father, and the
Holy Spirit, in Christ Jesus our saviour" (83/340).

The Spirit Helps Us Confront Sinfulness

From what we know about Julian's context and probable
intentions, it is understandable that she would not center her theology on sin. On the other hand, she does not soft-pedal or minimize sin. She calls Adam's sin "the greatest harm ever done or to
be done until the end of the world" (12/228). She laments that
human beings do nothing but sin (36/238–39). Sin is "so vile," she
says, and so much to be hated that it can be compared with no pain
which is not sin (40/247). Some deeds are so evil and lead to such
harm "that it seems impossible that any good result could ever
come of them" (32/232). Souls who truly accept the teaching of
the Holy Spirit hate sin more (76/328).

But given the blame church leaders are assigning to the
people, she is worried about obsessing over sin. She writes: "we
contemplate this [sin], and sorrow and mourn for it so that we cannot rest in the blessed contemplation of God as we ought to do"
(32/232). Julian's psychological perspicacity is visible in her realization of how easy it is, in troubled times, to get caught up in our
own darkness and that of others. Since God is always guiding us to
divine glory in this life and bliss in the next, we need to both know
this and pray for it. "For the one is not enough, for if we pray and
do not see that he does it, it makes us depressed and doubting; and
that is not to his glory. And if we see that he does it and do not
pray, we do not do our duty" (42/252). Preoccupation with sin is a
major obstacle to the goals of the spiritual life. It creates blindness,
preventing us from recognizing and trusting the wisdom, power,

and goodness of the Trinity. In her parable of the Lord and the servant, Julian lists not being able to see the loving face of the Lord as one of the most debilitating repercussions for the servant who fell into a ditch. With his body twisted away from the Lord, he was not able to know who he was. Hanging on to his true identity depended on his ability to see his own image reflected back to him through the loving gaze of the Lord.

For Julian, the Holy Spirit is directly implicated in our ability to face our sinfulness, own up to our selfish ways, and express contrition. It is the Spirit who leads the believer to sorrow for sin, confession, and penance (39/244). From contrition one is led to prayer and thus to soulful rest and an eased conscience. "So sins are forgiven by grace and mercy, and our soul is honourably received in joy, as it will be when it comes into heaven, as often as it comes by the operation of grace of the Holy Spirit, and the power of Christ's Passion" (40/246). In times of despair, the Spirit sheds light on our understanding so we are able to see God's loving, healing, and transforming grace at work in our lives.[31]

She encourages her readers by reminding them that sorrows, anguish, and trouble precede miracles. We need "to know our weakness and the harm that we have fallen into through sin" so that we can "cry to God for help and grace" (36/240). When we realize the enormity of our sin and see ourselves as fit for nothing but hell, the Spirit seizes us, turning "bitterness into hope of God's mercy" (39/244). The Spirit leads us to confess nakedly and truthfully with sorrow and shame that we have "befouled God's fair image" (39/244). Through penance, we are reunited with the community of faith in the body of Christ.

As a young girl, Julian prayed for the wounds of contrition, compassion, and longing for God (2/178). Contrition opens the floodgates to compassion and desire. For Julian, the Spirit's grace leads to an awareness of how God sees sin—wounds become honors and joys. Sin, no matter how vile, does not have the power to cut off God's love (39/245). Julian expresses the fruit of the Spirit's activity in us in terms of friendship.

> And then our courteous Lord shows himself to the soul,
> happily and with the gladdest countenance, welcoming it
> as a friend, as if it had been in pain and in prison, saying:

My dear darling, I am glad that you have come to me in all your woe. I have always been with you, and now you see me loving, and we are made one in bliss. So sins are forgiven by grace and mercy, and our soul is honorably received in joy...as often as it comes by the operation of the grace of the Holy Spirit and the power of Christ's passion (40/246).

With this kind of love, there is no room for blame in God (27/225–26; 50/266). We are never dead in the sight of God, nor does God ever depart from us (72/320).

The Spirit's Goodness

Julian identifies the quality of goodness, traditionally associated with the Spirit, as the most prominent aspect of God next to love. The attribution of goodness to God appears on almost every page. By emphasizing the Spirit's goodness and applying it to the entire Godhead, Julian works relentlessly to reverse the image of a wrathful God. At both literal and subliminal levels the reader is bombarded with the message that God's goodness is everywhere, eternally and generously offered to creation. She instructs us to pray for God's goodness, the source of God's flesh and blood, passion, death, and glorious wounds, nature and endless life, Mary's fiat, the help and strength we find in the cross, the precious love and friendship of the saints—all this is the fruit of God's goodness. "For the highest form of prayer is to the goodness of God, which comes down to us to our humblest needs" (6/185).

In five texts, Julian associates goodness explicitly with the Holy Spirit. She celebrates the "happy fault" of Adam and Eve, who in their resistance to God's goodness brought about the bliss, mercy, and grace of the incarnation. The goodness of mercy and grace opposed sin and turned everything into goodness (59/295; see also 54/285; 58/293; 58/295; 63/304). "For before he made us he loved us, and when we were made we loved him; and this is made only of the natural substantial goodness of the Holy Spirit, mighty by reason of the might of the Father, wise in mind of the wisdom of the Son" (53/283).

"Sweet Touchings"

Julian pictures the Holy Spirit's work in the faithful soul as "secret operations," "inward grace-giving operations" and "touchings of sweet spiritual sights and feelings."[32] Julian inherits the long tradition of the "spiritual senses" in which our five spiritual senses give rise to spiritual seeing, hearing, touching, smelling, and tasting. For Julian, the Spirit functions inwardly as the church functions outwardly (30/228). Interiorly, the Spirit kindles our desires to ask for and receive the gift of Godself. Julian counsels the simple soul to "come naked, openly and familiarly" to God. "For this is the loving yearning of the soul through the touch of the Holy Spirit" (5/184). She prays, "God, of your goodness give me yourself, for you are enough for me, and I can ask for nothing which is less which can pay you full worship" (5/184). Our true and gracious beseeching, our enduring will is united and joined to the Lord's will "by the sweet, secret operation of the Holy Spirit" (41/249). Until the day that we die, the Spirit's sweet grace infuses our prayer by "secret touchings of sweet spiritual sights and feelings" (43/255).

Desire is one of the most important elements of the spiritual life. It is the fuel, the "eros" the Spirit-power that enables us to reach out to God, each other, and the world. Christians who have inherited the faith but not yet appropriated it may not realize that they have the potential for an intense desire for God. This desire can be formed, developed, and directed. Others may be fully aware of their yearnings for God but afraid of where these desires might take them. Julian reminds her readers to pay attention to the Spirit's touch. "Marvelous and splendid is the place where the Lord dwells; and therefore he wants us promptly to attend to the touching of his grace, rejoicing more in his unbroken love than sorrowing over our frequent failings" (81/337).

According to Julian, the soul's job is to seek, suffer, and trust in faith, hope, and love—a job that can be accomplished only through the Spirit. Occasionally the Spirit illuminates the mind, bringing great joy to the seeker, but Julian's primary interest is in the will. Echoing the mystical thought of the Greek father of the church Gregory of Nyssa, Julian reminds us that seeking is as good as contemplating (10/195). It is clear that Julian is an idealist in the best sense. Trust and hope in God are a requirement for survival in a world of struggle. But she is also a realist. She knows all too well that life is a mix of "well-being and woe," made up of the risen Christ and Adam's sin. She writes: "Dying, we are constantly protected by Christ, and by the touching of his grace we are raised to true trust in salvation" (52/297).

In chapter 74, Julian offers an analysis of four kinds of fear: fear of assault, pain, doubt, and reverence. All of these fears are good because fear is the brother of love, leading the soul to repentance. Julian relates the Holy Spirit to the second of these four fears—the fear of pain. Anyone, she says, who is fast asleep in sin is not able "to receive the gentle strength of the Holy Spirit, until he has accepted this fear of pain from bodily death and from spiritual enemies." This fear moves us to seek the comfort and mercy of God by "the blessed touching of the Holy Spirit" (74/324).

We see again that Julian's message is not Pollyannish fantasy. She is realistic about what she sees as God's legitimate chastisement. The context for God's punishment is wisdom, goodness, and tenderness (77/330). Julian wants to infuse human suffering with sacred meaning. The Spirit's grace brings us to acknowledge sin, which, in turn, brings humility. And the more humble we are, the more good it does to touch the Lord. God told her nothing about self-imposed penance, only about the penance that life brings, which we should bear meekly and patiently in the memory of the cross. Julian's fourteenth-century "even-Christians" do not need to go to Lent; Lent had already more than come to them (77/330).

The Comforter

The Spirit's role as Advocate and Comforter runs like a leitmotif throughout Julian's text. Although she does not use the term *Paraclete* (John 14:16, 26; 15:26; 16:7), her text brings to mind the "Spirit of the Lord" of Isaiah (61:1–3), who comforts those who mourn, offering garlands instead of ashes, the oil of gladness instead of mourners' tears, and garments of splendor instead of a heavy heart. The Comforter ensures that the disciples are not left bereft. He dwells in them, teaches them all truth, witnesses to Jesus' teachings, and guides the proper discernment of right from wrong.

Julian's message of comfort is grounded in the meaning of her revelations, which she describes as love—love revealed by Love, for love (86/342). The God she meets offers comfort because this God is the personification of perfect goodness, a God whose promise of "all will be well" can be trusted (63/305). She counsels her readers that if they hold firmly to her message, comfort themselves with it, and trust in it, they will not be overcome (70/317). She says, "Therefore this is a supreme comfort and a blessed contemplation for a longing soul, that we shall be taken from pain. For in this promise I saw a merciful compassion which our Lord has for us because of our woe, and a courteous promise of a clean deliverance, for he wants us to be comforted in surpassing joy" (64/307).

Julian the Prophet

The voice of the mystic reminds us of the Spirit's freedom to blow where She will (John 3:8). Julian struggled with the tension between certain aspects of the church's doctrine and the God she experienced in her visions.[33] She comes very close to suggesting that salvation is universal (4/182; 8–10/190-93); she encountered a God who never blames (27/225; 28/227); and she puzzles about sin—is it more than the misguided enthusiasm of the servant desirous of serving his master (51/267)? In addition, Julian wrestled with issues of lower and higher authority (45/256–58).

We endure in this life, she says by three things: human reason, the common teaching of holy church, and the inward grace-giving operation of the Holy Spirit—different gifts, but all from the one God (80/336). The Spirit working in her over the years led her to a position of humble conviction about the truth of what God had revealed to her. She also realized that *all* revelation—her own as well as that of the institutional church—is always provisional: "we can have a little knowledge of that which we shall have the fullness in heaven" (80/335). She respects and defers to the church's teaching that sin must be punished, and yet she refuses to abandon God's message that God did not blame the sinner. She also wonders about the possible meaning of "all will be well" in the face of the church's teaching on hell. She credits her understanding and knowledge of these two judgments to "the gracious leading of the Holy Spirit" (45/257).

I admire Julian's ability to uphold the truth that the Spirit is present in *all* Christians and therefore functions both to legitimize and to limit the charism of office. With a reverent and holy fear, Julian spent a lifetime discerning the disturbing truths of her revelations. Her struggle included many moments of puzzlement and doubt (70/316–17). But in the end, she trusted the God she had seen, heard, and understood—she was committed to offering a word of "good news" to a suffering community whom she had to convince of hope against waves of depression and despair. God's compassion is the source of our compassion for others. Christ wants us to be aware of divine bliss, but God also wants to bring us consolation in our pain. We do not suffer alone but with Christ, whose suffering so exceeded ours that we cannot comprehend it. This knowledge "keeps us from lamenting and despairing as we experience our pains" (28/227; see also 39/245; 41/248; 42/251–52; 64/307; 69/315; 73/323; 74/324; 76/329; 77/331; 78/332; 79/334; 82/338).

Julian refused to engage in a mindless, "uncritical trust in the Church"—what Harding Meyer calls a "pneumatological maximalism" that turns a blind eye to the sins and errors in all human institutions.[34] She read the "signs of her times" and judged that a message of anger, threat, guilt, and damnation was *not* of God, and so she set out to correct it. Ideally we become attuned to the Spirit's voice in both individuals and institutions and realize that we must engage in discerning the meaning of the tensions and contractions that often arise within the church. Blind, absolute confidence in either the individual or the institution causes us to create false oppositions between these different charisms. Hans Küng—who speaks out of a lifetime of loyal ecclesial opposition— reminds us that there is but one Spirit—the Spirit of God, the Spirit of Jesus Christ, the Spirit of the church, and the Spirit of individual believers. To believe in the Spirit, he says, means to trust that God can be present in, and can seize hold of, our innermost selves. In the Spirit's freedom, we find "new courage, comfort and strength again and again in all the great and the small decisions, fears, danger, premonitions and expectations of life."[35]

Conclusion

Julian's Holy Spirit is a Spirit of truth, goodness, comfort, confidence, and intimate presence. Her message seems aimed at those who suffer from forces beyond their control—the simple, the powerless, the ordinary Christians of her day. It is a message spoken primarily to the marginalized and the oppressed. It does not address catastrophic evil—corporate greed, hate, unchecked egoism, genocide, deliberate starvation of the poor. And yet Julian does not back away from the universal need to confront our sinfulness, no matter who we are. In this task we are assisted by the grace of the Spirit. But her message of the "good news" of God's love is a universal one. She met the Trinity in whom dwells the Spirit of compassion, hope, and joy. By showering us with gifts and rewards, the Spirit builds up our confidence to face the heat of the day and trust in the promise of final bliss.

Through her trinitarian, christological, and pneumatological theology, Julian hopes to convince her readers that the Spirit's abundant gifts will comfort them (and herself) and ward off despair. "Therefore this is a supreme comfort and a blessed contemplation for a longing soul, that we shall be taken from pain. For in this promise I saw a merciful compassion which our Lord has for us because of our woe, and a courteous promise of a clean deliverance, for he wants us to be comforted in surpassing joy" (64/307; see also 69/316). In place of a wrathful God who punishes human sin, Julian describes a motherly, courteous, and familiar God, one who is easy to approach, who even stakes divine happiness on human satisfaction with redemption (22/216). It is only through the Spirit that we are able to discover and meet this courteous God (7/189). At the same time, Julian's most frequently used title for God is "Protector," that is, one who has the power, the love, and the will to guard us from the ravages of suffering and to ensure final beatitude. Julian repeats in diverse keys: you will not be overcome (68/314; 69/315; 70/317). Julian's "all will be well" is a fourteenth-century precursor of Martin Luther King's hope that "we shall overcome" the ravages of injustice.

Perhaps Julian's trust in this loving, forgiving God gave her the insight and the confidence to discern occasional discrepancies between God's judgment and that of an all-too-human church (45/256). Julian's mature faith provides a witness for those who struggle between the truth of their conscience and the rules of the institution. Julian reminds us that all revelation is provisional. Since charisms are given to individual Christians and church leaders, each functions to legitimize and limit the other. Julian also reminds us that when we are able to acknowledge our shortcomings, our neglect of others, our reluctance to share, our unwillingness to sacrifice for the other, we can be assured that the Spirit dwells within us, empowering us to respond in love, to give, share, comfort, heal. When we are a praying church, a church of honest self-reflection, the Spirit who forgives and heals will bring us to a deeper sense of the body of Christ.[36]

The good Lord answered Julian's doubts and questions with a most comforting message: "I may make all things well, and I can make all things well, and I shall make all things well, and I will make all things well; and you will see yourself that every kind of thing will be well" (31/229).[37] Julian associates the verb "may" with the Father; "can" with the son; "will" with the Holy Spirit; and "shall" with the Trinity. "You will see yourself that every kind of thing will be well." God's wish that we be enclosed in rest and peace is voiced in these five words (31/229). Julian invites us to speak with one voice: "Lord, blessed may you be, because it is so, it is well; and now we see truly that everything is done as it was ordained by you before anything was made" (85/341).

One of Julian's most important messages is to live in joy, to allow the Spirit's touch to create in us a deep and abiding sense of holy pleasure and delight. God's ability to make all things well results in a rich and multifaceted joy, and occasional laughter (13/201–2). This kind of joy contrasts dramatically with the surface pleasures of consumerism and the seemingly inexhaustible visual stimulation that bombards us. Julian describes divine and human joy in many ways—*bliss, happiness, rejoicing,* and *delight,* the word she most often associates with the Spirit. Julian's many triads point to both the persons of the Trinity and the trajectory of salvation history, beginning with creation, proceeding through the redemptive process and ending in heavenly bliss (58/294). In Julian's language, these triads include being/increasing/fulfillment; nature/mercy/grace; might/wisdom/love; pleasure and joy/honor and bliss/endless delight (23/218). Thus, the Spirit is often linked with the delight of the final consummation of the journey toward union with God (26/223; 41/249; 44/256).

But in spite of Julian's eschatological focus, the joy of heaven also breaks into the world of suffering.[38] Joy is the result of the human choice to live enclosed in God's goodness, to be like God in prayer, to possess God in the clarity of endless light, to feel God sweetly, and possess God in peace. Pain and sin are the opposite— blindness, mourning, hell, "dead to the true sight of our blessed life." But for Julian, we are never dead in the sight of God because God never departs from us. She holds out always the possibility of mutual love. "But [God] will never have his full joy in us until we have our full joy in him, truly seeing his fair, blessed face. For we are ordained to this by nature, and brought to it by grace" (72/320).[39] "And what can make us to rejoice more in God than to see in him that in us, of all his greatest works, he has joy?" (68/314).

One of the distinctive aspects of Julian's teaching is her portrayal of the joy the Trinity experiences in Christ's passion (see figs. 7, 15, 18). Julian recounts God's words to her about the passion.

> And in these three sayings: It is a joy, a bliss and an endless delight to me, there were shown to me three heavens, and in this way. By "joy" I understood that the Father was pleased, and by "bliss" that the Son was honoured, and by "endless delight" the Holy Spirit. The Father is pleased, the Son is honoured, the Holy Spirit takes delight. (23/218; see also 55/286)

The joy that Julian finds in God is infectious. We are right to ask how she musters so much joy in the midst of so much sorrow. Her answer of course is voiced in the final chapter. "What, do you wish to know your Lord's meaning in this thing? Know it well, love was his meaning. Who revealed it to you? Love. What did he reveal to you? Love. Why does he reveal it to you? For love. Remain in this, and you will know more of the same" (86/342). It is love that takes us from the cross to ecstatic joy.[40] Within the internal and external dynamics of trinitarian love, the Holy Spirit as Love provides the glue that binds and the eros that reaches out to touch each of us, the world, all our "even-Christians" (51/273–74).

⌒⁄⌒

Food For Thought

1. Have you ever experienced the Spirit as touching your inmost being? Reflect on the human experience of touching another person. How many types of touching can you name? Touch can be violent and invasive, nurturing and encouraging, reassuring and loving, passionate and freeing. Did you ever think that God might want to touch you? Imagine the Holy Spirit touching you in the ways Julian describes. What happens?

2. What is your image of the Trinity? How does it compare with Julian's? Is it helpful for you to think of yourself as enclosed in the Trinity or the Trinity enclosed in you? Do Julian's ideas of the Trinity as a community of love that includes all of creation make this doctrine more credible for you or more attractive to you?

3. Julian's text overflows with joy. God's primary interest is in comforting and loving humanity. There are few other authors in the Christian tradition who portray the Spirit as filled with delight as Julian does. Is this a God you have encountered before? Would you like to engage with this image of the Spirit in your own spiritual life? Are there things about a happy God that you don't like?

4. Julian's God is the antithesis of the God of "fire and brimstone"—angry, vengeful, demanding, punishing. Is it a good idea to think about God as not having any feelings of blame toward the human race? What are the advantages and drawbacks of this type of theology? Should one of God's roles be to punish? Why or why not?

CHAPTER 8

THE SPIRIT LIVES ON

In the northeast corner of France, early in the eighteenth century, Jean-Pierre de Caussade, S.J., gave a series of conferences on the spiritual life for a group of nuns. At the conclusion of these lectures, de Caussade reminded the nuns that through faith, Jesus continues to live and work among us through the Holy Spirit.

> We are in an age of faith; the Holy Spirit no longer writes gospels, except in our hearts; saintly souls are the pages, suffering and action the ink. The Holy Spirit is writing a living gospel with the pen of action, which we will only be able to read on the day of glory when, fresh from the presses of life, it will be published. O what a beautiful story! What a beautiful book the Holy Spirit is now writing! It is in press; not a day passes when the type is not being set, the ink not applied, the pages not being printed.[1]

With modifications to accommodate our computer age, de Caussade's analogy for the Holy Spirit as one who writes a living gospel reaches out to us across the centuries. Consciousness of the Spirit's lively presence grows slowly and in different ways: the Spirit visits in prayer; conversations about the Spirit take place; the Spirit is recognized in compassionate action for justice; sermons are heard; research is done; books and articles are written and read. The sheer variety of encounters with the Holy Spirit quickens us, first, to attend to the particular shape this holy power takes in our lives and world; and then to know about, and be accountable to, the long history of our ancestors' experience of Spirit. This book has been an attempt to keep these poles of past and present in creative dialogue.

We ponder old and new metaphors for the Spirit. Should we infuse new life into the image of the dove or imagine a whole new set of images for our time—force field, the green face of God, the One who lures? As citizens of the twenty-first century, what meaning do we want to attach to the Spirit as fire, light, gift, breath? Should we speak of the Spirit as "she" as well as "he"? How do we assist believers to link experiences of grace more explicitly with the Spirit's presence and power? Do we allow the Spirit to call us to voice a prophetic word? Do we limit the Spirit unnecessarily to personal and ecclesial life and neglect society and the cosmos?

The renewal of spirituality in our time has led us to reexamine the association of "spirit" with the dizzy heights of the spiritual mountaintop, the immaterial, and the exotic. The spiritual has taken on much more earthy, embodied, everyday qualities. One way to think about spirit is to see it as the innermost core of existence. As wonderful as scientific discoveries are, there is something in us that resists being reduced to DNA molecules or genes. Most of us are convinced that the meaning of our existence is somehow more than what appears on a genetic chart.[2] A further task involves linking what we understand as "spirit" with the Holy Spirit. We are also confronted with a new dichotomy between being "spiritual" and "religious." What happens when the spiritual life is set adrift from institutions, with their age-old language, symbol systems, and rituals?

Many of the Spirit metaphors we have examined have to do with life—wind, breath, water, fire, service, risk, reconciliation, love. To have, to be spirit means to be alive in every aspect of life— personal, professional, spiritual, intellectual, cultural, sexual, ecological. The human spirit marks the difference between rubbing horsehair over gut and Beethoven's Violin Concerto.[3] Spirituality has to do with the *eros* of the universe, the longing for more, the potential for power and presence beyond our finite existence. We are free to embrace and develop spirit, to detach our restlessness and anxiety from consumer instincts and reattach them to love. "Long before we do anything explicitly religious at all, we have to do something about the fire that burns within us. What we do with the fire, how we channel it, is our spirituality, whether we want one or not, whether we are religious or not."[4]

Christian believers are free to name the triune God as the source and goal of their ultimate desires. We can be grateful to our Jewish ancestors in the faith who left for our savoring the story of Genesis where we learn that all of creation is born of love, that we are made in the image and likeness of God, and that our destiny is to be caught up with all of reality in a divine community of love and joy. We are free to use the words *Holy Spirit* to name our deepest hopes and joys; our comfort in suffering and failure; the push to have courage and take risks. We have seen how the Spirit's presence and power lead us to know ourselves, the world, and God, and for God to know the world. Presupposing that we are made in God's trinitarian image, the Spirit names what we want for ourselves—who we want to become—in our most sane, honest, and loving moments. The Spirit provides the energy for action that has the common good of all in view, especially the poorest among us.

Image Language Revisited

The medieval religious literature we have examined offers a window into a theological tradition inspired by the Bible and expressed in metaphoric, analogical, and allegorical language. The return to the world of medieval images and metaphors not only has the potential to modify established ideas about the Spirit's identity but also to lead to creative new forms of more differentiated theological language.[5] For medieval writers, the Holy Spirit's presence is associated with an identifiable constellation of activities rooted in biblical language and imagery. This biblical imagery, deeply embedded in the consciousness of medieval authors and their communities, was reworked by each author in light of the needs of his or her particular historical setting.[6] The reigning historical-critical approach to the Bible has drawn criticism in recent years. On their own, these interpretive tools seem sterile, disconnected from the more fluid, poetic style of the Bible and the patristic and medieval traditions.

Many scholars and students of the Bible lament the narrow, negative attitudes toward medieval allegory and its creative multivocal approach to the biblical text.[7] Such a stance prematurely closes off this rich biblical tradition as a helpful resource and corrective to more rational methods employed in contemporary theology, spirituality, and biblical studies. Historical theologian Karl Froehlich notes the enormous influence of the Bible on Western categories of meaning. Biblical language has shaped so many aspects of human life and action.[8] The enormous variety of approaches to the biblical text helps us to keep its meaning alive, flourishing, and functional. For example, liberation and feminist hermeneutics are new lenses that have been added to more traditional methods of interpretation. But these innovations are not necessarily incompatible with the tools of allegory and free association that we have encountered in this study. All these styles and approaches to the scriptures complement each other and enrich the ways in which the text shapes Christian life today.[9]

We have encountered the wellsprings of biblical imagery linked to the Spirit: anointing (Luke 4:18; Acts 10:38); the variety of gifts within one spirit (1 Cor 1:7; Gal 5:22; Isa 11:2–3); the Holy Spirit as guide to truth (John 14:26; John 16:13); the Spirit being poured forth into our hearts (Rom 5:5); the Spirit as pledge of the future (2 Cor 5:5); as energizing fire (Acts 2); as source of vision and prophecy (2 Pet 1:21); as renewer of the earth (Ps 103:30); as the proof of God's presence within (1 John 4:13). Paul warns against quenching this abundant grace by grieving the Spirit (1 Thess 5:19; Eph 4:30).

Biblical scholar Walter Brueggemann comments that when the biblical stories are absent from our experience, everything is more likely to be "explained," and when all we have is explanation, new life is hard to imagine. Without the stories, we are not able to enter into the imagery: "thrones are never risked, songs are never sung, swords are never thrown, foreskins are never acquired, names are never precious."[10] As we have seen, scriptural stories and metaphors are the heart of medieval Spirit narratives. But medieval authors also felt free to go beyond the strict parameters of the biblical texts and to embellish them in tune with the dictates of their imaginations and pastoral needs. These stories have the potential to break open our flattened, one-dimensional lives. We think we have known the outcome of these stories, but they always await a new, surprising retelling, for the sake of life. When they are not retold, we must settle for things as they are, devoid of the renewal the Spirit offers us. We are ever in need of a new creation in which "God's providential care outruns both our remarkable personalities and our cunning, devastating power."[11]

A renewed appreciation of the medieval imagination challenges contemporary fears about the imagination generated by a fundamentalist, literalist orientation to religion in our own time. As we have seen, in many medieval texts, rigid lines of demarcation in our language about the Spirit give way to permeable borders, multileveled images, and fluid overlapping. If we allow ourselves to cross over into this material and allow the integrity of its form and feeling-tone to wash over us, we may discover insights about God and the human condition at deep, noncognitive levels. When theologians allow this kind of language to influence their work, the outcome may be a theology that is more capacious, more oriented toward reconciliation and renewal, more susceptible to honor and support the variety, elasticity, and developmental qualities of the Christian life. This medieval material can lead us to find ways for a theology of the Holy Spirit to embrace reasoned, academic aspects as well as spiritual, vocational, and ministerial dimensions. Barbara Newman compares the style of Bernard of Clairvaux with that of Hildegard in their penchant to employ a wide range of metaphors in a pattern that avoids conflation or confusion—light, food, oil, salt, honey, music, medicine. "The resultant sensual richness contributes to an impression of spiritual and intellectual richness"—a welcome alternative to our heavily cognitive, "bottom-line" thinking.[12]

Newman gathers a wide range of medieval texts under the rubric of what she calls "imaginative theology," which she defines as "the pursuit of serious religious and theological thought through the techniques of imaginative literature, especially vision, dialogue, and personification."[13] This is a welcome addition to the traditional, fourfold framework for interpreting medieval theology—monastic, scholastic, pastoral, mystical—and the more recent category of vernacular theology.[14] Philip Sheldrake iterates five ways in which the category of imaginative theology reconnects theology with spirituality—a goal of this book. Imaginative theology (1) uses images rather than propositions to show how spiritual texts work theologically as alternative ways of knowing;

(2) points to spiritual-theological authenticity beyond a one-dimensional sense of the "real"; (3) provides theological space that enables an expansion of Christian faith without rejecting classical doctrinal formulations; (4) challenges us to realize that formal theology needs to attend more carefully to piety, art, poetry, and contemplation; and (5) expands theology beyond an exclusivity that promotes good order at the expense of affective engagement.[15] Dwelling in the images of the Holy Spirit presented by our six authors is an invitation to meet the Spirit anew, to be moved by the Spirit to offer praise, and to reconceive our theological language about the Spirit in this spirit.

To Do Pneumatology Is to Do Trinity[16]

A prominent lesson from our journey into the writings of six medieval figures is the importance of locating all theologies of the Spirit within the context of the Trinity. We understand and celebrate the Spirit's being and power most fully only in light of the divine community. The church's affirmation of the triune God is a living phenomenon, expressed in a variety of ways that emerge from the lived faith experience of the Christian community. Medieval theologians' vibrant sense of the three divine persons in God offers us a way to renew our own consciousness of the trinitarian mystery and the important role the Spirit plays within it. Catherine LaCugna writes of the Trinity "for us":

> The life of God—precisely because God is triune—does not belong to God alone. God who dwells in inaccessible light and eternal glory comes to us in the face of Christ and the activity of the Holy Spirit. Because of God's outreach to the creature, God is said to be essentially relational, ecstatic, fecund, alive as passionate love. Divine life is also *our* life....The doctrine of the Trinity...is a teaching about God's life with us and our life with each other.[17]

In many ways our authors remind us that it is the Holy Spirit who makes it possible for the divine trinitarian life to be *our* life. Our

244

experience gives shape to the language we use to name God, and all Christians are implicated in this responsibility to name God in true and creative ways. Depending on the context and the needs at hand, some emphasize God the Creator/Father/ Mother/Flowing Fountain; others focus on God the Son/Redeemer/Savior/Friend; yet others are drawn to the Holy Spirit/Greenness/Lover/Sanctifier/Waiter. But in each case, we are reminded to celebrate each divine person as part of a community of a three-personed God. Each person, each metaphor provides a distinct path into the divine trinitarian center.

In significant ways, we limit God when we narrow the language we use to speak about God. The power of the Spirit can never be exhaustively grasped or domesticated.[18] Canadian Anglican theologian John Simons reminds us that when we stick to "correct" linguistic formulae to name the triune God, we not only fail to appreciate the generosity of God's self-communication but risk clinging to an abstract notion of the church's communion in the life of the Trinity. If we further fail to take into account the ministries of compassion and justice in our naming of God, we pose a threat to trinitarian orthodoxy greater than what we may fear by broadening our range of language for God. In either case, a church that fears to discover and use fresh names for God has failed to grasp something important about God.[19] Unless classical names for God are held within a wider repertoire of divine names, we risk idolatry.[20]

One example of a neglected image is that of God as *fons plenitudo*, and of the Holy Spirit as the fullness of that outpouring, seen most clearly in Bonaventure but present in many other medieval authors as well. Perhaps we have too precipitously jettisoned this dynamic way of speaking about the Spirit in the interest of an overly rational fear of subordinationism—placing the Spirit in third, and by implication, lower place.[21] Further, does the cluster of images that echoes the emanationism of Neoplatonism necessarily compromise God's freedom in creating the world?[22] I suggest that we are losing an important insight when we evaluate this tradition only as a primitive viewpoint that no longer offers any light. A renewed appreciation of this tradition, which Catherine LaCugna links with God's ecstasy[23] can enrich David Coffey's proposal that we add a "bestowal" or "mutual love" model to the "procession" model in our articulation of trinitarian theology.[24] Clearly the tradition has a substantial investment in this Neoplatonic viewpoint, and I suggest that these narratives remain suggestive and provocative for theology, spirituality, and ministry.

In addition to viewing the Spirit within the nexus of trinitarian life, several of our authors give the Trinity a more visible role in the process of redemption. In particular we meet the Trinity at the cross—an idea that is not prominent in the tradition (see figs. 17 and 18). Biblical texts likely to have inspired this material include John 7:38–39: "He who believes in me, as the scripture has said, 'Out of his heart shall flow rivers of living water.' Now this he said about the Spirit, which those who believed in him were to receive; for as yet the Spirit had not been given, because Jesus was not yet glorified"; John 19:34: "But one of the soldiers pierced his side with a spear, and at once there came out blood and water"; 1 John 5:6–8: "This is he who came by water and blood, Jesus Christ, not with the water only but with the water and the blood. And the Spirit is the witness, because the Spirit is the truth. There are three witnesses, the Spirit, the water, and the blood; and these three agree"; Acts 2:14–36, citing Joel 2:28–32: "And in the last days it shall be, God declares, that I will pour out my Spirit upon all flesh, and your sons and your daughters shall prophesy, and your young men shall see visions, and your old men shall dream dreams; yea, and on my menservants and my maidservants in those days I will pour out my Spirit; and they shall prophesy." The tradition that the church was born from the blood poured forth from Jesus' side on the cross is well established.

The soaring poetry of the final chapter in Bonaventure's *The Soul's Journey into God* helps us imagine the goal of our own lives in terms of a mystical death on the cross and challenges us to imagine the cross in terms of a paroxysm of love, the fruit of divine–human collaboration in virtue and love of others. Catherine of Siena offers perhaps the most startling images juxtaposing the Spirit and the cross. In a letter to Angelo da Riscasoli, Catherine describes how the Holy Spirit taps the cask of Jesus' body to set his blood flowing for us: "His humanity is the cask that enclosed the divine nature, and the cellarer, the fire and hand that is the Holy Spirit, tapped that cask on the wood of the most holy cross" (LT136). We note again Catherine's letter to Bartolomeo Dominici in which she imagines the Holy Spirit holding Christ so that he will stay affixed to the cross.

246

The Holy Spirit is the light that banishes all darkness, the hand that upholds the whole world. In that vein I recall his saying not long ago, "I am the One who upholds and sustains the whole world. It was through me that the divine and human natures were brought together. I am the mighty hand that holds up the standard of the cross; of that cross I made a bed and held the God-Man nailed fast to it." He was so strong that if the bond of charity, the fire of the Holy Spirit, had not held him, the nails could never have held him. (L29/103)

Thus, Catherine extends the image of the Spirit as the bond of love within the Trinity by giving the Spirit a direct and powerful role in the crucifixion. The implement of cruel punishment becomes the marriage bed. She shares with us her insight that only an unimaginable love could bring this gesture of salvation to completion.

Finally, we saw how Julian developed a theology out of her vision of the face of the crucified Jesus. These powerful representations that place the Spirit and the Father/Mother at the cross invite us to *sense the texts* as well as analyze them, to wonder at God's loving Mystery as well as understand it. This imagery invites us to read these mystics as we would view and appreciate a mosaic, a painting, or a musical composition.[25]

Prophetic Voice

The Spirit has traditionally been connected with eschatological vision and with prophecy, that divinely inspired energy that confronts sinfulness and ecclesial abuse. The Spirit has also been invoked to defend innovative movements (that are able to ensnare emotional women, we are frequently reminded). Some of these developments have later been deemed heterodox, while others have provided fresh and productive institutional alternatives.[26] When Christians are disturbed about the sin or mediocrity in the church, they often turn to the Spirit for inspiration, wisdom, and courage. Some who enlist the Spirit steer a steady course that genuinely renews the church—often at great cost; others are persecuted and driven out unjustly in the interest of an order that smacks of "power-over" and control. Still others abuse the Spirit in frivolous and scandalously destructive ways. The stories of prophets inevitably include an initial response of fear to the Spirit's call.

Many of the texts we have studied dwell on the Pentecost story, especially the Spirit's ability to cast out fear—a gift that remains crucial to maintaining a spiritually vibrant church today (see figs. 19, 20, and 21). They are astute in their portrayal of fear as a killer of the spiritual life. They invite us to examine our fears and to let the breath of the Spirit blow through them. Fear can take the form of self-protection. Prophets usually end up badly. We don't want to put ourselves in harm's way. Others will not like us if we have the courage to speak the truth to power. Fear of losing status, power, possessions, or reputation can also block the Spirit. We will go to great lengths to preserve illusions that we know well and know how to negotiate. But the image of the apostles transformed by the Spirit from fear, timidity, and hiding into confident preachers of the gospel stands like a beacon, beckoning us to pray for courage, to discern, and to become a voice for justice, freedom, and truth.

Our authors dedicated themselves to preserving and renewing the Spirit traditions they inherited. Augustine, Bernard, and Bonaventure held offices that required them to be stewards of the tradition, and in some cases they felt threatened by new, untried ideas. Hildegard was innovative on many fronts, assuming roles rarely open to women in the twelfth century. Catherine was seen as a prophet in her own time, and Julian's theology clearly pushed the boundaries of accepted understandings of the doctrines of God and grace. But all six figures functioned as prophets in their efforts to open themselves to the Spirit, name the sin of the church, preach reform, and voice a clarion call to holiness of life.

We need to continue to investigate the contours and motives of prophetic voices. We know how easily ideas and actions that confront and challenge established powers are stereotyped and demonized. Throughout the Christian tradition, prophetic groups linked with the Spirit have been silenced. Some of these groups warned of the imminent arrival of the end time, understanding themselves as inheritors of the prophetic and apocalyptic traditions of the Bible. Hallmarks include a call to a rigorous purity of Christian life; a belief in an imminent eschaton; visible gifts such as prophesying and tongues; direct access to the Spirit's power (which can raise questions about institutional mediation); and female leadership.

Examples include Montanism in the second century; the medieval Joachites[27] and Spiritual Franciscans; the Brethren of the Free Spirit;[28] Anabaptism in the sixteenth century;[29] the nineteenth-century Shakers;[30] and various forms of Pentecostalism emerging continuously from the turn of the twentieth century until the present.[31] In many of these groups, specific individuals were believed to have been touched by the Holy Spirit in extraordinary ways. It is possible that some, even many, Christians were reluctant to speak as frequently or as expansively about the Spirit because marginal groups called on the Spirit for their energy and validation.

Women played a prominent role in some of these Spirit-inspired movements. For example, in her book *From Virile Woman to WomanChrist*, Barbara Newman examines two medieval groups who, inspired by Joachite teaching, believed that the third age of the Spirit involved an incarnation of the Spirit in female persons, namely, Bohemian princess Guglielma of Milan (d. 1282) and Na Prous Boneta (d. 1328). One of Guglielma's followers, Maifreda of Pirovano, a member of the Umiliati, who lived in northern Italy in the early fourteenth century, was granted the title of pope, vicar of the Holy Spirit, by a small heretical sect. She was to have celebrated Mass at Santa Maria Maggiore on Pentecost when the Holy Spirit would rise from the dead—incarnate in Guglielma—to confer blessings on her people. She and at least two other women of her congregation ended up at the stake.[32]

Many such groups and individuals have been dismissed as extreme, dangerously anarchic, and heretical, not worthy of serious historical examination. But a more careful probing of the historical record usually reveals a more complex picture. Barbara Newman reminds us that recent research on medieval women's piety has led to a reconsideration of esoteric motifs of a feminine Holy Spirit that may have functioned to criticize the established church.

Beyond the Middle Ages, one must consider the effects on pneumatology of the Reformation and Counter-Reformation, as well as of various other social and cultural developments. Catholics reacted to Protestant trust in the Spirit's empowerment of the laity. Protestants reacted to the spawning of fringe movements that looked to the Spirit for legitimation. But an attentive reading of the political situation in Calvin's Geneva, of Anabaptist letters from prison, or later developments such as Zinzendorf's doctrine of the motherly office of the Spirit quickly lead one away from wholesale dismissal or condemnation. All of these more radical "Spirit" movements need to be revisited by social and theological historians. The Christian church is responsible to be vigilant, to safeguard the integrity and continuity of the tradition. But when thoughtful voices are silenced or the demand for order and unity becomes inordinate or rigid, we need to assess the motives for cutting off voices that may emerge from the Spirit's promptings to the community.[33] The Spirit Herself is available to help us discern when the need to control or the discomfort of fear, change, or upset have won out over the freedom to trust and test the Spirit's presence with love and patience.

Discernment

In conversations about the Holy Spirit, the issue of discernment inevitably arises. We may find on our own lips a version of Karl Barth's response to Friedrich Schleiermacher: "But are you sure you are speaking of the *Holy* Spirit?" In particular, fainting in the Spirit, speaking in tongues, and prophesying are foreign territory for most North Americans born of northern European, Puritan stock.[34] Another source of unease about the Spirit is the claim that the Spirit communicates divine truth in an unmediated fashion. The Holy Spirit has been named as the source of visions, direct divine inspiration, and insight into the scriptures and tradition by both the unlettered and official church leaders. Spirit-inspiration has a long pedigree in Christianity: the Bible itself, the prophets, the gift of tongues at Pentecost, some saints' miraculous understanding of the Scriptures. But in all cases, we must ask the question: Whose spirit are we talking about? Is it the Spirit of God or something else (1 John 4:2)?

Each one of our authors struggled mightily with discernment. In spite of, and at times, because of, their deep commitment to gospel living, they had to face conflict, difference of opinion, and inner doubt. We are not alone in our struggle to discern genuine grace from pseudo grace. Judging the authenticity of the Spirit's presence is quite a bit easier when done from the vantage point of history, when the fruits of a given message or action have become clear. Prophets like American Quaker John Woolman, who spoke out against slavery in the seventeenth century, suffered constant disapproval, harassment, and condemnation. Prophets who were banished from their faith communities may be viewed today as purveyors of wisdom, known for the genuine Spirit presence they embodied.

Much more challenging is the necessary work of discernment in the present, when we do not have the certitude that will be available to our distant future descendants. And yet we must engage in this process, especially when prophetic Christians speak out against the status quo, condemn abuses in church and society, or offer untested solutions. Since this work is fraught with challenges, it requires at least four important dispositions: trust, humility, patience, and love. A necessary prerequisite is a willingness to trust that the Spirit desires to speak to us. But this trust has to be infused with a profound sense of our own sin that leads to humility and genuine, committed, dispassionate openness. Knowing that even when we put forth our best effort, we may make mistakes and even fail is simply the truth that keeps us modest and should not be used as an excuse not to try.

Catherine especially counseled patience. Waiting on the Spirit is a hallmark of a serious spiritual life. Trust and humility lead to a willingness to bide our time in anticipation of the Spirit's presence and to discern the difference between waiting that is filled with possibility and waiting that signals procrastination in the face of the Spirit's bidding. But the most difficult disposition involves making sure that our judgments about good or evil are motivated as much as possible by loving hearts. Brutal honesty about our motives is at the heart of the process of genuine discernment.

Libraries are filled with tomes delineating the different patterns, rules, and spirit of the discernment process, many of which have provided the Christian community with invaluable wisdom and direction. Quaker and Jesuit discernment rules are among the most well known and successful. Rules or patterns for discerning good from bad spirits can be taught and learned, and it is incumbent on every Christian to have in place some pattern, some personal effective mix of tools for discernment. The alternative to engaging regularly in discernment is a mindless, directionless Christian existence, aping a toy figure that is wound up, lurches in one direction or another, and does not change course until it hits a wall.

But if we want to "cut to the chase" in the process of discernment, the biblical accounts of the fruits and gifts of the Holy Spirit (and the virtues) are the surest and simplest tests. Those of us Roman Catholics who grew up in a pre–Vatican II church memorized the fruits and gifts with more or less diligence, and many can still recite them today. For others who have forgotten or never knew them, here they are:

Theological virtues: faith, hope, and charity;

Cardinal moral virtues: prudence, justice, fortitude, and temperance;

Gifts of the Holy Spirit: wisdom, understanding, counsel, fortitude, knowledge, piety, and fear of the Lord;[35]

Fruits of the Holy Spirit: love, joy, peace, patience, kindness, goodness, long-suffering/generosity, gentleness/humility, faithfulness, modesty, self-control, chastity.[36]

The gifts of the Spirit are understood as established habits that develop over time through faithful practice—like practicing a sport or an instrument. The skills become "second nature" to us—we execute the moves with a certain ease and grace, without having to exert ourselves or think about every step. The fruits are the result of living this kind of life—we become more patient, more kind, more gentle in our dealings with God, ourselves, the world, and others. Bernard's reference to the Spirit as the "condiment" that makes it easier for food to be digested captures this dynamic movement of the gifts and fruits of the Spirit. They help us to be open to and follow the Spirit's promptings. When we ask whether something is genuinely "of the Spirit" we look for the results of the experience. Does the person live with more patience, love, gentleness? Is she faithful to God and to others in the long haul of life—which includes suffering and anguish as well as joy and pleasure?

Authentic discernment always takes place in some type of community setting. In addition to the community we form with God in private prayer, we need the benefit of others, without whom we run the risk of self-deception, calling on the Spirit in a kind of special pleading for our own agendas. Community might mean one other person or a small group—family, friends, church members, work colleagues, or a spiritual director. It might involve an entire religious community or parish. In faith communities, the Spirit is invoked and plays a central role as we prayerfully open ourselves to the Spirit's promptings. Discernment also involves trust that the Spirit does indeed desire to speak to us and through us. Bernard of Clairvaux reminds us that "the Spirit is always speaking in our thoughts so that we may hear what God speaks within us."[37]

In many first-world Western cultures, the experience of a community of faith is thin. Many Christian organizations are not prepared to practice discernment, lacking the skills and often the will, to understand the value and richness of this collaborative model of living in the Spirit. Claiming an exclusive lock on the Spirit; becoming deaf to the cries of the poor; condemning others because they are different, trying something new, or disturbing our comfort levels; rejecting the call to reconciliation; banning open and honest conversation about difficult topics—none of this honors the best of the Christian tradition on discerning the Spirit's presence. Bernard's description of the ideals of the Cistercian Order can be applied to all of us: "Our Order is lowliness, humility, voluntary poverty, obedience, peace and joy in the Holy Spirit....No words can express the mutual charity that exists between us and which works in a marvelous way by the pouring forth of the Spirit" (*Letter* 142.1, 3). Each of us can ask of the many communities to which we belong, How do the attitudes, values and behaviors of this community exhibit the presence of the Spirit?

Another test of the Spirit's genuine presence is openness to the diverse ways in which the Spirit might speak. Any group that claims a monopoly on the Spirit's voice is likely not listening to the Spirit. The Spirit works in ways that are as diverse as each member of a very broad Christian community. But no matter what form the Spirit takes—in the loud shout or the quiet whisper—discernment functions as a key "bottom line" in our experience of Spirit.

A yet more focused test of the Spirit's presence involves the cross. Theologian of the Holy Spirit Jürgen Moltmann suggests that it is the cross that tests true from false spirits. "What can endure in the face of the crucified Christ is from God; what cannot endure is not from God."[38] This test of the Spirit emerges out of a deep awareness of the profound suffering of most of our sisters and brothers across the planet. When we ask ourselves, as Christians, how we are doing, we must place the cross (and resurrection and ascension) at the center of the picture. Bonaventure's dramatic portrayal of mystical death on the cross at the finale of *The Soul's Journey into God* provides a powerful image that can guide us in our discernment of whether or not our spirits are in tune with the Holy Spirit of God.

Each of the authors we have examined relied on the virtues and gifts of the Holy Spirit to guide her or his spiritual journey. When we ask how well we are doing in love for God and neighbor, the gifts function as a litmus test. Even though our authors linked the gifts and fruits with their own religious or monastic callings, we are right to transcend these boundaries and apply this test universally to all members of the church. Life in the Spirit is not a private, isolated possession of those held up as public saints. Indeed, the Spirit's power is ordered toward the whole world, toward our neighbors and even our enemies. Just as the Spirit is ensconced in the loving community of the Trinity, so our Spirit-life is embedded in the life of the Christian community and of the world. Karl Rahner expresses this solidarity in a comment on prayer.

> If the one Holy Spirit is to move us all, and there is one body because we have been baptized by this Spirit into one body (1 Cor 12:13), and if we must therefore—because we are members of the one body of Christ—with one mind bear each others' anxieties, then everyone

ought to pray for everyone else. Apostolic prayer is a Christian duty.[39]

Silences of the Spirit

Silence can be a blessing or a curse. It can welcome us into its bosom or freeze us out. We trust that the Spirit has been present in the silences of the tradition, in the unspoken gesture or glance, between the lines of a sermon, a poem, or a treatise. The Spirit's power may marshal its forces in the fertile and quiet darkness of the soil in which seeds germinate and sprout in good time. We are accountable to trust these silences and to do what we can so that they will bear fruit, making all things new. There is also the silence that acknowledges that all language, imagery, symbols, and metaphors about God are inadequate. This is the apophatic or negative way that takes over when words fail, when we stand in silent awe at the mystery and majesty of God. At times, this blessed silence seems more truthful than a thousand words or images naming God. After thousands of words about metaphors of the Spirit, we must also remember that the Spirit is *not* "God," *not* a person, *not* Gift, *not* a waiter, *not* love pouring forth, *not* music, *not* Reconciler.

Negative silence about the Spirit signals incompleteness, hardness of heart, or simply undue preoccupation with other concerns. Medieval interest in the person of Christ accounts for some of the silences about the Spirit.[40] From Bernard's infatuation with Christ the Bridegroom to Bonaventure's Franciscan, Christ-centered spirituality and theology, this period reflects an intense Christ-consciousness that often places the Holy Spirit in the shadows. But medieval awareness of, and commitment to, a deeply trinitarian theology ensures that each divine person received attention. The Trinity is present in each divine person and each person represents the fullness of the Trinity.

Throughout the tradition, the Spirit has often been called upon to explain and defend ideas that "push the envelope." In retrospect, we see that many clearly transgressed the boundaries of the tradition. But we can only lament and ask forgiveness for others whose Spirit inspiration was wrongly declared heretical, bringing persecution, condemnation, and even death. As a result, we cannot but wonder about the Spirit-chaos that was ordered too soon and sometimes too harshly; about the Spirit-novelties that were not allowed to be born or to perdure; about the Spirit-silences that resulted in an impoverishment of the community's awareness of the infinite ways in which God pours out Godself into hearts and into a troubled world.

In the Middle Ages, innovation was suspect, and even when new ideas took root, as they inevitably did, arguments had to be made to ensure that the "new" emerged in an integral way from the "old." In a letter to Abbot Adelbert, Hildegard articulates this value explicitly. "Through the vain love of novelty and change, lies fly abroad, as if the people see God—and yet they know Him not."[41] It also makes sense that in times of decline and confusion, church leaders worked hard to reestablish order, not launch into the unknown deep of radical change. In our time, the situation is reversed. We take for granted and expect change and become impatient with earlier cultures that do not speak to our need that all things be made new in ecclesial culture or institutional organization. For Roman Catholics, Vatican II promised just such an about-face, a Spirit-filled turn toward the world, a stance that many now see jeopardized by a return to the status quo ante.

We also ask about awareness of the Spirit's presence in pastoral work and spirituality. To what extent is the Spirit silent and invisible in these arenas? How does discernment function on ministry teams and in parishes? It is important to find working models that provide for a maximum number of voices to be heard; that encourage power sharing; that find avenues to make the Spirit visible in the community. We can examine catechetical programs, liturgy, personal prayer, faith-sharing and study groups; work for justice, retreats, preaching, adult education, pastoral councils, diocesan offices and church documents for signs of the Spirit's presence. How deeply do we live and teach the truth that Baptism confers *the* distinctive hallmark of the Christian life—possession of the Spirit of Christ? Is confirmation the last time you learned something about how to pray in the Spirit, to invoke the Spirit's powers of healing and strength? If we do not have the tools or the will to allow the Spirit to operate in visible, explicitly named ways, the Spirit remains silent and invisible. Without the Spirit, our exercise of discipleship, leadership, and power remains hollow.

The Spirit's Voice and Power

Yet it is a pleasant surprise to discover the importance given to the Spirit in the tradition and in many Spirit-filled movements today. We have learned that medieval Christian thinkers were quite conscious of the Spirit's activity in individual lives and in the church. The Christian community set the course for many of the Spirit's functions early on in its history. In the fourth century, Athanasius describes the Spirit's activities as ordering, sanctifying, perfecting, illuminating, quickening, anointing, sealing, and divinizing.[42] The medieval texts we have examined reinforce this breadth of the Spirit's functions, revealing the wide range of ways in which different communities called upon and spoke of the Spirit out of their concrete experience in all its messiness and particularity.[43] We began with theological criticism about the poverty of Spirit-presence and with a sensed existential need to recover the Spirit's presence in theology and in faith communities. This historical excursion has allowed us to encounter a sampling of Spirit language from the past from which we return to the present with fresh ideas and new questions.

Most of us identify neither with those who study the past purely for its own sake (if this is even possible) nor with those who ignore or disregard the tradition altogether. More common is a tendency to rebel against a tradition that is judged oppressive, or dissent from a tradition that seems irrelevant, constricting, or simply wrong.[44] Whether we are aware of it or not, the past infuses the present. To know something of this tradition engages us in what Orthodox theologian Georges Florovsky calls "charismatic memory."[45] Knowledge of the Christian tradition helps us discover who we are and how we should proceed. It can protect us from negative, unconscious forces and wake us up through encounter with the strange and different. It reminds us that we are part of a long, sacred history in which our Christian sisters and brothers attended to how the Spirit was working in their time and place, linking us with them as we struggle to pay attention to God's presence in our lives and in our world. To cut ourselves off from the past, to retrieve only a narrow segment of it, or to succumb to its unexamined stereotypes is to deform our present relationships. Historical and contemporary social identities are not unrelated.

The medieval metaphors and images used to describe the Holy Spirit's work in the world can become a catalyst for reflection on our life in the Spirit in very concrete situations. In addition to being a resource for theology, the Spirit texts we have examined offer language, images, and stories to renew the life of faith. We experience specific occasions when we invoke the Spirit's presence. Many educational institutions begin the academic year with a liturgy of the Holy Spirit that points to the link between the Spirit and an intelligent faith. Some of us have witnessed the dramatic release of scores of doves at commemorations such as the fiftieth anniversary of the atomic bomb dropped at Hiroshima or at the World Special Olympics. In these settings, the doves symbolized the hunger for peace and pointed to the strength and courage of challenged athletes. We often call upon the Spirit at the beginning of meetings and as we undertake projects upon which we want the Spirit's presence and power to rest. Some of the faithful witness to the Spirit's presence in the gift of tongues. Others sit in quiet communal contemplation, awaiting an opening to the Spirit's presence and message. And still others call upon the Spirit in the secret recesses of their hearts to help them face anxiety or loneliness or suffering. Indeed, the term *Spirit* is itself a primal symbol or metaphor that points to many aspects of our existence.[46]

We also inquire about how the Spirit can enliven liturgy, preaching, and catechesis. We are called to help each other become more conscious of the Holy Spirit in our spiritualities, to call down the Spirit's power in our prayer and in the daily round of ordinary activities. We can learn more about discernment and grow in our ability to reflect together in groups, families, and church communities as we face significant decisions. It would be instructive to use the images we have explored as a structure for sacramental preparation for baptism, confirmation, matrimony, or orders. Awareness of the Spirit's presence in each person can only increase our appreciation of these sacraments; the care and respect we show each other; the courage we need to speak to others what the Spirit speaks in our hearts; the desire to grow in our ability to discern truth from falsity; the willingness to share power, since the Spirit speaks to high and low, rich and poor, educated and illiterate.

The hunger for the Spirit to bring unity to the church was a prominent theme in several of our authors—a hunger that perdures in our own time. We desire communion among the many branches of the Christian church. Neuralgic issues related to morality, gender, family, and politics continue to divide, creating deep animosities within the body of Christ. Augustine's vision of an inclusive church can continue to energize our own efforts to be of one heart and mind with all Christian peoples. In addition, we need the Spirit to help us counteract the rampant individualism that has seeped into every fiber of our culture. We can call upon the Spirit to sharpen our sensitivity to the common good, asking for the grace to set ourselves aside for the greater good of the whole. The Spirit also calls us to find a common heart among all the world's religions in spite of the violence and hatred that, at times, seem insurmountable. We need to find our way between a Pollyannish idealism and false, self-interested limits on the Spirit's power to draw us together.

This exposition of particular texts on the Spirit reveals how different medieval Europe was from twenty-first century North America. And yet, by lifting the veil from the faces of our medieval forebears, we release them from an anonymous, vague, or collective identity that is unrelated to the human condition and therefore inaccessible to our own times. I hope those who see the tradition primarily in a negative light as something to abandon will reconsider a fresh dialogue with the past. For it is only through this process of conversation that the tradition remains lively and useful. Knowing the past in the present allows us to contribute to the creation of a future pneumatology that is not a moribund "thing" incapable of touching the lives and particular contours of individuals and communities today. A sensitive reading of past encounters with the Spirit not only saves us from the arrogance of detached observers but invites us to new awareness of, and confidence in, the Christian community that is constituted by these stories of encounter with the trinitarian God.

Each of us is invited to reflect on how the images and metaphors we have examined might contribute to a renewed pneumatology and to a fresh, existential awareness of the Spirit's role in our lives and in the body of Christ. How is the Spirit calling the church in the twenty-first century? Since we find ourselves in situations that did not exist in the Middle Ages, we need to build on the tradition and use it to help us ask new questions, make new decisions, and engage in new actions. All of our authors lived within, and spoke to, the church. Each voiced concern for the church's health in protective yet challenging ways. As the divine power that makes all things new, the Spirit is an ever-present source of *aggiornamento*. The revitalization of our awareness of the Spirit goes hand in hand with a fresh appropriation of the Trinity in the life of the church—in faith, worship, preaching, institutional structures, patterns of relationships, spirituality, and mission.[47] Engagement with the Spirit tradition invites us not only to test, absorb, and make use of aspects of medieval pneumatology, but also demands that we explore the possibility of new language and imagery that resonate with the present ecclesial and social context.

A current concern in Western thought revolves around the uses of power. Suspicious of "business as usual" we ask about who benefits and why from social or ecclesial arrangements that have been in place for millennia or which are described as God-given. Inundated by the abuses of power in every sector of our society, we have understandably become jaded and skeptical about any kind of power. But power is a hallmark of the Holy Spirit. The need to discern between good and bad power is more incumbent upon us than ever before. The New Testament is filled with language about power, not power of rank and status, physical or intellectual prowess, but a transcendent power that comes from without and results in "wonders and signs" aimed at the internal transformation of human freedom.[48] New Testament texts about the Holy Spirit *(to pneuma to hagion)* refer to a "complex experiential field in which power is transmitted and exchanged. The *pneuma* is, precisely, active power."[49] It indwells, moves, transforms, gives life, is poured out, is drunk, fills. In these ways, "the symbol 'Holy Spirit' serves as the linguistic expression of the experience of power."[50]

One concrete example of the call to empowerment involves women. The texts of the three women in our sample invite us to attend to the Spirit's role in the empowerment of women and others held at the fringes of the church's life—persons of color, gay and lesbian Christians, the divorced. We marvel at the ways in which women "in the long history of the patriarchal Church were able again and again to breach the dominant structures in the power of the Holy Spirit," in spite of the church's distrust of both women and the Spirit's power.[51] Reflecting on the Spirit in the tradition can motivate us to reflect on power and authority, on hierarchical patterns of community, and on decision making as they relate to the presence of the Spirit throughout the church. These are not easy tasks.[52] But I am convinced that a critical appropriation of the tradition can help us shape pneumatologies that are "firmly grounded in the real world of faith today and related to the pressing concerns of persons and groups" who had no part in that tradition.[53]

Contemporary psychology has influenced us to name and use the gifts we have been given. Medieval and postmodern cultures view personal and communal charisms in different ways, and yet each acknowledges that the Spirit's gifts are gratuitously given. We do not "earn" them, but are commanded to use them for the glory of God. We may be more likely than medieval people to value our gifts as intrinsically good but less ready to understand them as bestowed by the Spirit to whom we are accountable. We also place freedom at the top of the list of human qualities that confer dignity and mark us as full human beings. The biblical maxim that the truth shall make us free means something quite different today than in the Middle Ages. Our authors did not emphasize freedom in ways that we do. But they can assist us to understand the freedom we value and seek as oriented toward the choice to love God and our neighbors. Catherine of Siena reminds us that "neither the devil nor anyone else can force us to a single deadly sin, since Christ has made us free and given us power over ourselves."[54] Gospel freedom has less to do with freedom of movement or endless options in the ways we structure our everyday lives than with the choice to be available, to radically dispose ourselves to cooperate with God's desires for the world. We can call on the Spirit's power to liberate us from the slavery of the law, compulsions, narcissism, self-image, and ideologies (2 Cor 3:17; Gal 5:18; 1 Cor 7:23; 9:19; Rom 6:20; John 8:34–36).

The task of being open to, and naming, the Spirit goes on. It is our task, our calling, our responsibility, our joy, to pray "Come, Holy Spirit"; to find new ways to know the Spirit; to experiment with new images and metaphors. Language itself, and our ability to interpret God's diverse communications to the world are gifts of the Spirit. Language reflects what already exists and simultaneously continues to call the Spirit's power and presence into newness of being. Because language conveys a sense of the structure of human community and the relationships of power within it, naming is important. The symbol of God functions.[55] False naming, refusing to name, and superficial naming constrict and damage, while true naming frees and empowers. It is the job of the community to sort through over and over again the difference between the two.[56]

Conclusion

Reflection on the medieval metaphors of the Spirit uncovered in these pages alerts us to the range of ways different communities called upon, and spoke of, the Spirit in their concrete life settings. The links between a community's experience of the Spirit, its choice of words and images to speak of that experience, and its more ordered, theological expression, continue to be forged. The faithful and theologians remain accountable to one another. In his book *We Drink from Our Own Wells* (whose title is taken from Bernard of Clairvaux's *On Consideration*), Gustavo Gutiérrez reminds us rather dramatically, "The solidity and energy of theological thought depend precisely on the spiritual experience that supports it. Any theological or religious reflection that does not help in living according to the Spirit is not a Christian theology."[57] By attending to the broad range of expressions in the tradition, the theologian can ensure that systematic and doctrinal statements take symbols and imagery into account and attend to how they give rise to concepts in every age.[58]

As individuals and as church we are never through with the task of discerning more carefully good and bad spirits. When does wise caution become irrational fear of the legitimate, freeing, renewing, and inevitably upsetting, power of the Spirit's presence? In what ways do we fear and block the Spirit's function as the guardian of the "divine madness"?[59] Hans Küng reminds us that there is but one Holy Spirit—the Spirit of God, the Spirit of Jesus Christ, the Spirit of the church and the Spirit of individual believers (and, I would add, the Spirit of the cosmos). To believe in the Spirit, he says, means to trust that God can be present in, and seize hold of, our inner-most selves. In the freedom of the Spirit, we find "new courage, comfort and strength again and again in all the great and the small decisions, fears, danger, premonitions and expectations of life."[60]

I suggest that the Spirit was neither absent nor lost in abstraction for our ancestors in the faith. Rather the Spirit was imagined, spoken about, called upon, resisted, depended upon, silenced, and celebrated with joy. And yet, consistently and in diverse ways, the Spirit brought the light of understanding, the oil of healing, the courage of prophecy, comfort to the afflicted, affliction to the comfortable, direction for a life of virtue, and most importantly the deep joy that is at the heart of Christian dis-cipleship. Surely engagement with these texts can contribute to the creation of constructive pneumatologies and to a livelier pres-ence of the Spirit among the faithful.

I close, as I began, with a prayer to the Holy Spirit—the sequence *Veni, Sancte Spiritus.*[61] We have uncovered a rich tradition of Spirit that continues to challenge us to rediscover in our own time and place the ever-old, ever-new power and presence of the Spirit. The experience, insights, language, and commitments of our ancestors in the faith; contemporary discussions of the Holy Spirit; and our own longings for holiness compel us to focus on the foundation of Spirit prayer—"Come!" This simple invocation carries within it a bountiful and complex history, opening us to an unknown future adventure in which the presence and power of the Spirit live and breathe and act within each of us (Luke 11:13). We ask the Spirit to come, to break through our blindness to the Spirit's presence, to take hold of our lives, to become real to our senses, our spirits, our friends, our families, and our world.[62]

> Come Creating Spirit,
> Enter the minds of those who are your own,
> Fill with grace from heaven
> The hearts you created.
>
> We call you Paraclete,
> Gift of God Most High,
> Living Spring, Fire, Love,
> And Inward Balm.

Touch of the Father's right hand,
You give seven gifts for us.
Truly, you are the Father's promise,
Gifting tongues with speech.

Flame into our senses,
Flood love into our hearts,
Fix in enduring power
Our frail bodies.

Drive our foes far off,
And give us a long peace;
With you to lead and guide us,
May we avoid all harm.

Grant us through you to know the Father,
And also to understand the Son,
That we may always believe you,
Who are the Spirit of them both.

To God the Father be glory,
And to God the Son, who rose
From the dead, and to God the Paraclete,
World without end, Amen.[63]

Food for Thought

1. What are your favorite images from those we have studied? Why do they appeal to you? Some examples include: force that fills breasts with the milk of sweetness, condiment, a melting fire, fearless power, teacher, God's breathing, the bridge, nursing mother, the cellarer, garment of love, nurse of souls, captain of a ship, servant/laborer, hand that holds the nails in Christ's hands on the cross, waiter, kiss. Are there modifications you might suggest that would make a given image more

relevant to the twenty-first century, or new images you might add?

2. The Spirit leads us in mission to the world, to compassionate and prophetic action. Where is the Spirit blowing and not blowing in the church? How do you know? What do you do about it? Can you identify ways in which you nurture or block the Spirit's power in the Christian community? How does our awareness of the Spirit move us beyond the walls of the church to the world, indeed to the cosmos?

3. Take a moment to create your own version of the prayer "Veni Creator Spiritus." Knowing how persons who respond to the Spirit are consumed (often painfully) by the Spirit's fire, do we dare to allow the mystics to influence us to pray "Come Holy Spirit" and mean it? Let your experience in today's world; encounters with, and learning about the Spirit; and your creative juices flow together. If you are in a group, discuss sections of your prayer with others in the group.

4. How has our study of the Holy Spirit affected your understanding of Trinity? Does father of the church Irenaeus's metaphor of the Son and Spirit as the "two hands of God" resonate with you? What would you suggest to help renew awareness of the Trinity for the person in the pew?

5. The older language of "Holy Ghost" to refer to the third person of the Trinity has given way to "Holy Spirit." What is your sense of the gains and losses of this change? Which do you prefer and why? Which title seems more meaningful in our pluralistic culture that runs the gamut from traditional churches to world religions to New Age?

NOTES

Preface

1. Almost fifty years ago, G. J. Sirks wrote an article entitled "The Cinderella of Theology: The Doctrine of the Holy Spirit," which is often referred to in recent literature on the Holy Spirit. *Harvard Theological Review* 50, no. 2 (1957): 77–89.

2. *Epiclesis* (Greek *invocation*) is the term assigned to a prayer in the liturgy that occurs after the words of institution. The prayer calls on the Spirit to be present in the transformation of the elements of bread and wine into the body and blood of Christ, and by extension, in the lives of all believers.

3. In the epilogue to the revised edition of his magisterial *Augustine of Hippo*, Peter Brown writes: "On looking back, I think that I had given undue weight to the formidable clarity of Augustine's formal theological works, and that I had not paid sufficient attention at the time to his sermons and letters." *Augustine of Hippo: A Biography* (Berkeley: University of California Press, 2000 [1967]), 446.

4. Three earlier studies on the Holy Spirit should be mentioned. Stanley M. Burgess used an approach similar to mine in *The Holy Spirit: Medieval Roman Catholic and Reformation Traditions (Sixth–Sixteenth Centuries)* (Peabody, MA: Hendrickson, 1997). Since Burgess includes twenty-four figures from Gregory the Great to the radical reformers (in two hundred pages), he was able to dedicate only five to six pages to each figure. He is thus unable to provide a broad sampling of primary texts, nor to situate them in their historical context. A second historical treatment, also published in 1997, is Gary D. Badcock's *Light of Truth and Fire of Love: A Theology of the Holy Spirit* (Grand Rapids: Eerdmans). Badcock treats biblical, patristic, Reformation, and contemporary authors, but omits any mention of medieval figures except to examine the filioque controversy. A third volume, *Come, Creator Spirit: Meditations on the "Veni Creator"* by Raniero Cantalamessa (Collegeville, MN: Liturgical Press, 2003), is structured around the themes found in the hymn *Veni Creator*

Spiritus and includes short excerpts from a wide range of authors throughout the Christian tradition.

5. Recent attention to the theology of the Holy Spirit has resulted in a number of substantive monographs from which the following is a sampling. G. W. H. Lampe, *God As Spirit* (Oxford: Clarendon, 1977); David Coffey, *Grace: The Gift of the Spirit* (Sydney: Catholic Institute of Sydney, 1979); Yves Congar, *I Believe in the Holy Spirit*, 3 vols. (New York: Seabury, 1983); J. Patout Burns and Gerald M. Fagin, *The Holy Spirit* (Wilmington, DE: Michael Glazier, 1984); Joseph Chinnici, ed., *Devotion to the Holy Spirit in American Catholicism* (New York and Mahwah, NJ: Paulist, 1985); José Comblin, *The Holy Spirit and Liberation* (Maryknoll, NY: Orbis Books, 1989); Michael Welker, *God the Spirit* (Minneapolis: Fortress, 1994); Eldin Villafañe, *The Liberating Spirit: Toward an Hispanic American Pentecostal Social Ethic* (Grand Rapids: Eerdmans, 1993); Hans Urs von Balthasar, *Explorations in Theology*, vol. 4, *Spirit and Institution* (San Francisco: Ignatius Press, 1995); Jürgen Moltmann, *The Source of Life: The Holy Spirit and the Theology of Life* (Minneapolis: Fortress, 1997); Mary Ann Fatula, T*he Holy Spirit: Unbounded Gift of Joy* (Collegeville, MN: Liturgical Press, 1998); Veli-Matti Kärkkäinen, *Pneumatology: The Holy Spirit in Ecumenical, International, and Contextual Perspective* (Grand Rapids: Baker Academic, 2002); Kilian McDonnell, *The Other Hand of God: The Holy Spirit as the Universal Touch and Goal* (Collegeville, MN: Liturgical Press, 2003); Bernard Cooke, *Power and the Spirit of God: Toward An Experienced-Based Pneumatology* (Oxford: Oxford University Press, 2004); Elizabeth Groppe, *Yves Congar's Theology of the Holy Spirit* (Chico, CA: American Academy of Religion, 2004); Mark I. Wallace, *Finding God in the Singing River: Christianity, Spirit, Nature* (Minneapolis: Fortress, 2005). Contributions to Spirit-Christology include Killian McDonnell, "Jesus' Baptism in the Jordan," *Theological Studies* 56, no. 2 (June 1995): 209–36; Roger Haight, "The Case for Spirit Christology," *Theological Studies* 53 (1992): 257–87; David Coffey, "The Gift of the Holy Spirit," *Irish Theological Quarterly* 38 (1971): 202–23; idem, *Grace: The Gift of the Holy Spirit* (Sydney: Catholic Institute of Sydney, 1979); idem, "The 'Incarnation' of the Holy Spirit in Christ," *Theological Studies* 45 (1984): 466–80; idem, "A Proper Mission of the Holy Spirit," *Theological Studies* 47 (1986): 227–50; idem, "The Holy Spirit as the Mutual Love of the Father and the Son," *Theological Studies* 51 (1990): 193–229; Ralph Del Colle, *Christ and the Spirit: Spirit-Christology in Trinitarian Perspective* (New York and Oxford: Oxford University Press, 1994).

6. Two exceptions are Raffaele Fassetta, "Le rôle de L'Esprit-Saint dans la Vie Spirituelle selon Bernard de Clairvaux," *Analecta Cisterciensia*

46 (1990): 349–89; and Kilian McDonnell, "Spirit and Experience in Bernard of Clairvaux," *Theological Studies* 58, no. 1 (1997): 3–18.

7. Information provided by Gretchen Pritchard, Children's Mission of St. Paul and St. James, New Haven, CT. For more information about the felt materials, see www.beulahenterprises.org/store/scripts/prodList.asp?idCategory=40.

8. A sampling of the many publications on Pentecostalism includes Allan Anderson, *An Introduction to Pentecostalism* (Cambridge: Cambridge University Press, 2004); Douglas Jacobsen, *Thinking in the Spirit: Theologies of the Early Pentecostal Movement* (Bloomington and Indianapolis: University of Indiana Press, 2003); Glenn Hinson, *Fire in My Bones: Transcendence and the Holy Spirit in African American Gospel* (Philadelphia: University of Pennsylvania Press, 2000); Eldin Villafañe, *The Liberating Spirit: Toward an Hispanic American Pentecostal Social Ethic* (Grand Rapids: Eerdmans, 1993); Harvey Cox, *Fire from Heaven: The Rise of Pentecostal Spirituality and the Reshaping of Religion in the Twenty-first Century* (London: Cassell, 1996); Donald W. Dayton, *Theological Roots of Pentecostalism* (Metuchen, NJ: Scarecrow, 1987).

9. Anderson, *Introduction to Pentecostalism*, 279.

Chapter 1: The Study of the Spirit
Context and Method

1. Some scholars attribute the text to Rhabanus Maurus (c. 780–856), abbot of Fulda and later archbishop of Mainz. Raniero Cantalamessa, *Come, Creator Spirit: Meditations on the "Veni Creator"* (Collegeville, MN: Liturgical Press, 2003), 1.

2. See Elizabeth A. Johnson, *She Who Is: The Mystery of God in Feminist Theological Discourse* (New York: Crossroad, 1992), 50; Sallie McFague, *Models of God: Theology for an Ecological, Nuclear Age* (Philadelphia: Fortress, 1987), 157–80, esp. 169–71; Walter Kasper, *God of Jesus Christ*, trans. V. Green (New York: Paulist, 1976), 223; Frederick Crowe, *The Doctrine of the Most Holy Trinity* (Willowdale: Regis College, 1970), 18, 69.

3. Kilian McDonnell summarizes highlights of this discussion in "A Trinitarian Theology of the Holy Spirit?" *Theological Studies* 46 (1985): 191–227. See also Ralph Del Colle, *Christ and the Spirit: Spirit-Christology in Trinitarian Perspective* (New York: Oxford University Press, 1994). McDonnell notes that Wolf-Dieter Hauschild has questioned assessments that pneumatology was lacking in the early theologians

(McDonnell, *Gottes Geist und der Mensch: Studien zur frühchristlichen Pneumatologie* [Munich: Kaiser, 1972], 11).

4. In 1921, Maurice Landrieux wrote *Le divin méconnu* (Paris: Beauchesne), translated by E. Leahy in 1924 as *The Forgotten Paraclete* (New York: Benziger Brothers). Cited in Charles E. Bouchard, "Recovering the Gifts of the Holy Spirit in Moral Theology," *Theological Studies* 63 (2002), 540 n. 6.

5. G. J. Sirks, "The Cinderella of Theology: The Doctrine of the Holy Spirit," *Harvard Theological Review* 50, no. 2 (1957): 77–89.

6. Kilian McDonnell, *The Other Hand of God: The Holy Spirit as the Universal Touch and Goal* (Collegeville, MN: Liturgical Press, 2003), 205. McDonnell notes that "pneumatological affirmative action" does not mean exalting the Spirit at the expense of Christology and the cross. They are not in competition (p. 206). See also his "Pneumatological Overview: Trinitarian Guidelines for Speaking about the Holy Spirit," *Catholic Theological Society of America, Proceedings* 51 (1996): 190–91.

7. McDonnell, "Trinitarian Theology of the Holy Spirit?" 194.

8. For a discussion of Orthdox criticism of Western pneumatology, see Del Colle, *Christ and the Spirit*, 8–33.

9. Louis Dupré, *The Common Life: The Origins of Trinitarian Mysticism and Its Development by Jan Ruusbroec* (New York: Crossroad, 1984), 10–11. He writes: "It would, of course, be absurd to claim that Western spiritual theology has ignored the Trinity....But the real question is, what the idea, so obviously present from the beginning of Western theology has *meant* to the spiritual life. While in the East the three Persons operate at once upon the soul, each one in a different mode, in the West God's operation in the soul appears as a single effect. All *we* know is one God. There is no *experience* of the distinctions he reveals about himself, nor is there any vital interest in them. This is not to say that the Trinity remains a purely abstract concept. St. Augustine, who is responsible for much of the later speculation, is deeply concerned with finding 'images' of the Trinity in human experience. But these images remain *external* analogies" (pp. 16–17).

10. Although from a poor family, Peter Lombard benefited from well-connected patrons (including Bernard of Clairvaux) who made it possible for him to study at Bologna, Reims, and Paris. In Paris, Peter taught theology in the cathedral school of Notre Dame, where he wrote his *Commentary on the Sentences* (composed between 1147 and 1150, although it may be dated as late as 1155). Nothing is known for certain of his later life except that he became bishop of Paris in 1159. This *Commentary* is a four-volume work that laid out the whole body of theological doctrine in a long series of questions organized by theme: (I) the

nature and attributes God, providence, predestination, and evil; (II) creation, angels, demons, the fall, grace, and sin; (III) the incarnation, redemption, virtues, and commandments; (IV) the sacraments and the last things.

11. Topics include: an introduction (dist. 1), the Trinity (dist 2), knowledge of God from creatures (dist. 3), generation of the Son (dist. 4–7), incommunicability and simplicity in God (dist. 8), distinction of persons (dist. 9), the Holy Spirit (dist. 10–18), other aspects of the Trinity, especially the way we speak about the persons (dist. 19–34).

12. Catherine LaCugna suggests further that Augustine's theology was largely cut off from the economy of salvation and that his obvious love of metaphysical speculation caused him to neglect the scriptures. *God for Us: The Trinity and Christian Life* (San Francisco: HarperSanFrancisco, 1991), 102–3. Critical statements about early pneumatology are not limited to Roman Catholic theologians. Protestant process theologian David Griffin laments the loss of Paul's awareness of the Spirit's presence. "But it was not long before the experience of being guided by the Spirit waned. A Christian was increasingly defined in terms of certain doctrinal beliefs, and these were beliefs that did not concern the relation of God's Spirit to the actual experiences of daily life....The sense of a present experience of God that characterized Jesus and the early Church was largely gone." Cited in "Holy Spirit: Compassion and Reverence for Being," in *Religious Experience and Process Theology: The Pastoral Implications of a Major Modern Movement*, ed. Harry James Cargas and Bernard Lee (New York: Paulist, 1976), 109.

13. Elizabeth A. Johnson attributes a less than vibrant trinitarian theology to the fact that "over time the triune symbol has been divorced from the original multifaceted, life-giving experiences that gave it birth in human understanding." *She Who Is: The Mystery of God in Feminist Theological Discourse* (New York: Crossroad, 1992), 192.

14. Bernard Cooke, *Power and the Spirit of God* (Oxford and New York: Oxford University Press, 2004), v.

15. The challenge is to engage in these corrections without obliterating what we are trying to correct. Focus on history, the affections, and action needs to be kept in creative tension with the general, the abstract, the intellectual, reason, and theory. The point is not to knock one perspective off the pedestal, creating a new hegemony in the process.

16. Television interview on PBS in 1996.

17. Ethicist Charles Bouchard identifies what he calls the "intellectual fallacy" in ethics and decries its "narrowly and nudely rationalist, analytic and intellectualist approach." The animating affective formation of moral knowledge found in the mystical and contemplative aspects of

moral consciousness is ignored. "Recovering the Gifts of the Holy Spirit in Moral Theology," *Theological Studies* 63 (2002), 541.

18. Pierre Hadot, *Philosophy as a Way of Life*, edited and introduced by Arnold I. Davidson (Oxford: Basil Blackwell, 1995); based on the second edition of *Exercices spirituels et philosophie antique* (Paris,1987).

19. Ibid., 281.

20. Ibid., 279.

21. Ibid., 284.

22. Pierre Hadot, "La philosophie antique: une éthique ou une pratique?" in *Problèmes de la morale antique*, ed. Paul Demont (Amiens: Université de Picardie-Jules Verne, 1993), 11; cited by Davidson in *Philosophy as a Way of Life*, 21.

23. Davidson, *Philosophy as a Way of Life*, 21.

24. Michel René Barnes, "Augustine in Contemporary Trinitarian Theology," *Theological Studies* 56, no. 2 (June 1995): 237–50.

25. Théodore de Regnon, *Études de théologie positive sur la Sainte Trinité*, 4 vols. in 3 (Paris: Victor Retaux, 1892/1898).

26. Barnes, "Augustine," 241.

27. Ibid., 245. In his criticism, Barnes includes Bertrand de Margerie, *La Trinité chrétienne dans l'histoire* (Paris: Beauchesne, 1975); LaCugna, *God for Us*; David Brown, *The Divine Trinity* (La Salle, IL: Open Court, 1985); James Mackey, *The Christian Experience of God as Trinity* (London: SCM, 1983); John J. O'Donnell, *Trinity and Temporality: The Christian Doctrine of God in the Light of Process Theology and the Theology of Hope* (Oxford: Oxford University Press, 1983); and Jürgen Moltmann, *History and the Triune God* (London: SCM, 1991).

28. David Tracy, *The Analogical Imagination: Christian Theology and the Culture of Pluralism* (New York: Crossroad, 1981), 102.

29. Michael Welker, *God the Spirit*, trans. John F. Hoffmeyer (Minneapolis: Fortress, 1995), 6, 21, 27.

30. Ibid., 132–33. Welker cites Moltmann's *Theology of Hope: On the Ground and the Implications of a Christian Eschatology* (Minneapolis: Fortress, 1993 [1964]); Elisabeth Schüssler-Fiorenza's *In Memory of Her: A Feminist Theological Reconstruction of Christian Origins*, 10th anniversary ed. (1983; New York: Herder and Herder, 1994); and James Cone's *Black Theology: A Documentary History*, 2nd ed. (Maryknoll, NY: Orbis Books, 1993) as examples of theologians who engage the biblical tradition in a "thick way."

31. "'Why Are You So Interested in the Wandering People of God?': Michael Welker on Theology and Common Sense," *Soundings* 79, nos. 1–2(Spring/Summer 1996): 128. See also Colin Gunton, *The One, The Three and The Many: God, Creation, and the Culture of Modernity*,

(Cambridge: Cambridge University Press, 1993), 181. Gunton suggests that a theology that resists the pressures of the modern cultural tendency toward homogeneity by giving due weight to the particular should begin with a theology of the Spirit.

32. Ibid., 131.

33. Langdon Gilkey calls for a better appreciation of the creative possibilities embedded in the tension between particularity, or the language of story, and universality, or the language of ontology. *Catholicism Confronts Modernity: A Protestant View* (New York: Seabury, 1975).

34. Jürgen Moltmann, *The Source of Life: The Holy Spirit and the Theology of Life* (Minneapolis: Fortress, 1997), 57.

35. Welker, *God the Spirit*, 132.

36. Ibid.

37. See, e.g., Philip Endean, "Theology out of Spirituality: The Approach of Karl Rahner"; Mark McIntosh, "Lover without a Name: Spirituality and Constructive Christology Today"; idem, "The Turn to Spirituality? The Relationship Between Theology and Spirituality"; Anne M. Clifford "Re-membering the Spiritual Core of Theology: A Response," in *Christian Spirituality Bulletin* 3, no. 2 (Fall 1995): 6–21; William M. Thompson, *Christology and Theology* (New York: Crossroad, 1991).

38. In discussing the relationship between theology and spirituality, Rowan Williams criticizes a theology that seeks to ape scientific method. He locates theological method within the humanities rather than the sciences and turns to patristic theology for insight into the nature of a unity theology has lost. He suggests that allegory, which has been jettisoned by much contemporary theology, is one resource that draws us back to liturgy and the spiritual life, disclosing a unity between theology and prayer/worship that is not always evident in the theology of more recent times. *Discerning the Mystery: An Essay on the Nature of Theology* (Oxford: Clarendon, 1983), 132–33.

39. One specific aspect of this *rapprochement* is the conversation about the relationship between spirituality and ethics. See William C. Spohn, "Spirituality and Ethics: Exploring the Connections," *Theological Studies* 58, no. 1 (1996): 109–23; Mark O'Keefe, *Becoming Good, Becoming Holy: On the Relationship of Christian Ethics and Spirituality* (New York: Paulist, 1995); Michael K. Duffey, *Be Blessed in What You Do: The Unity of Christian Ethics and Spirituality* (New York: Paulist, 1988); Dennis J. Billy and Donna L. Orsuto, eds. *Spirituality and Morality: Integrating Prayer and Action* (New York: Paulist, 1996).

40. See Walter Principe, "Toward Defining Spirituality," *Sciences Religieuses* 12, no. 2 (1983): 127–41; Sandra Schneiders, "Theology and

Spirituality: Strangers, Rivals or Partners?" *Horizons* 13 (Fall 1986): 253–74; idem, "Spirituality in the Academy," *Theological Studies* 50 (1989): 676–697; and idem, "Spirituality as an Academic Discipline: Reflections from Experience," *Christian Spirituality Bulletin* 1, no. 2 (Fall 1993): 10–15; Bernard McGinn, "The Letter and the Spirit: Spirituality as an Academic Discipline," *Christian Spirituality Bulletin* 1, no. 2 (Fall 1993): 1–10. Key essays dealing with method in the academic study of Christian spirituality can be found in *Minding the Spirit: The Study of Christian Spirituality*, ed. Elizabeth A. Dreyer and Mark S. Burrows (Baltimore: Johns Hopkins University Press, 2005), parts 1–3.

41. Karl Rahner, *The Trinity*, trans. Joseph Donceel (New York: Herder & Herder, 1970), 10, 14–15, 39.

42. See Leonardo Boff, *Trinity and Society* (Maryknoll, NY: Orbis Books, 1986), 100.

43. Endean, "Theology out of Spirituality," 6–8.

44. Ibid.

45. See Annice Callahan, "The Relationship Between Spirituality and Theology," *Horizons* 16, no. 2 (1989): 266–74; Micheline Lague, "Spiritualité et théologie: d'une même bouche," *Église et théologie* 20 (1989): 333–51; Jon Sobrino, "Spirituality and Theology," chapter 3 in *Spirituality of Liberation: Toward Political Holiness*, trans. Robert R. Barr (Maryknoll, NY: Orbis Books, 1988 [1985]), 46–79; Gregory S. Clapper, "Relations Between Spirituality and Theology: Kierkegaard's Model," *Studies in Formative Spirituality* 9 (1988): 161–67; David L. Schindler, "Catholicity and the State of Contemporary Theology: The Need for an Onto-logic of Holiness," *Communio* 14 (1987): 426–50; William M. Thompson, *Fire & Light: The Saints and Theology* (New York: Paulist, 1987); Schneiders, "Theology and Spirituality," 253–74; Daniel A. Helminiak, "Lonergan and Systematic Spiritual Theology," *New Blackfriars* 67 (February 1986): 78–92; Simon Tugwell, "Scholarship, Sanctity and Spirituality," *Communio* 11 (1984): 46–59; Roch Kereszty, "Theology and Spirituality: The Task of Synthesis," *Communio* 10 (1983): 314–31; Dermot A. Lane, *The Experience of God: An Invitation to Do Theology* (New York: Paulist, 1981); David Willis, "Contemporary Theology and Prayer," *Interpretation* (July 1980): 250–64; Ewert Cousins, "Spirituality: A Resource for Theology," *Proceedings of the Catholic Theological Society of America* 35 (1980): 124–37; Alan Jones, "Spirituality and Theology," *Review for Religious* 39 (March 1980): 161–76; Antonio Queralt, "La 'Espiritualidad' como disciplina teologica," *Gregorianum* 60 (1979): 321–76; Andrew Louth, *Theology and Spirituality* (Oxford, 1976); William Johnston, *The Inner Eye of Love: Mysticism and Religion* (London: Collins, 1978); Carl-A. Keller, "La théologie et la recherche spirituelle de

l'homme moderne," *Revue de théologie et de philosophie* 25 (1975): 1–11; Mary McDermott Shideler, "The Mystic and the Theologian," *Theology Today* 32 (1975): 252–62; Dom Fr. Vandenbroucke, "Le divorce entre théologie et mystique," *Nouvelle revue théologique* 72 (1950): 372–89.

46. Michael Buckley, "The Rise of Modern Atheism and the Religious *Epoche*," in *The Catholic Theological Society of America: Proceedings of the Forty-seventh Annual Convention*, ed. Paul Crowley (Santa Clara, CA: Catholic University of America, 1992), 77.

47. Ibid., 80, 83.

48. See Marigwen Schumacher, "Mysticism in Metaphor," in *S. Bonaventura 1274–1974* (Grottaferrata [Rome]: Collegio San Bonaventura, 1973), 2:362.

49. Edmund J. Dobbin, "Towards a Theology of the Holy Spirit," *Heythrop Journal* 17 (1976): 5–19, 129–49, here 141. Dobbin suggests that the symbol "Father" evokes the transcendent dimension of God—that which is most unlike us (*dissimilis nobis*); the "Son" is Jesus as the embodied likeness of God (the "real symbol"); the Holy Spirit reveals the gifted (donative) nature of the immanent dimension of the divine presence—the ways in which creation images God (*similis nobis*) (pp. 141–42). Dobbin builds his case by appropriating from Paul Ricoeur (1913–2005) the rationale for why Ricoeur's starting point in the discussion of evil is not the developed doctrine of original sin but the mythic and spontaneous symbolic expressions behind the doctrine. Paul Ricoeur, *The Symbolism of Evil*, trans. Emerson Buchanan (1960; New York: Harper & Row, 1967).

50. Examples include Ernst Cassirer, *The Philosophy of Symbolic Forms*, 3 vols. (New Haven: Yale University Press, 1955); Karl Rahner, "The Theology of Symbol," in *Theological Investigations*, vol. 4 (Baltimore: 1966): 221–52; Mircea Eliade, *Images and Symbols* (New York, 1961); Susanne K. Langer, *Philosophy in a New Key: A Study in the Symbolism of Reason, Rite and Art* (Cambridge, MA: Harvard University Press, 1969); Ricoeur, *Symbolism of Evil*.

51. Stephen Happel, "Symbol," in *The New Dictionary of Theology*, ed. J. A. Komonchak, M. Collins, and D. Lane (Collegeville, MN: Michael Glazier, 1987), 997.

52. Bernard Lonergan, *Method in Theology* (London: Darton, Longman & Todd, 1972), 66.

53. Michael Downey, *Understanding Christian Spirituality* (New York: Paulist, 1997), 39–40.

54. Gerhart Ladner, *God, Cosmos, and Humankind: The World of Early Christian Symbolism*, trans. Thomas Dunlop (Berkeley: University of California Press, 1995), 2.

55. Gerhart Ladner, "Medieval and Modern Understanding of Symbolism: A Comparison" (1979); reprinted in Ladner, *Images and Ideas in the Middle Ages: Selected Studies in History and Art*, 2 vols. (Rome, 1983), 245. See also Johan Chydenius, *The Theory of Medieval Symbolism* (Helsingfors, 1960); Robert Kaske, *Medieval Christian Literary Images* (Toronto and Buffalo: University of Toronto Press, 1988); Anna C. Esmeijer, *Divina quaternitas: A Preliminary Study in the Method and Application of Visual Exegesis* (Assen: Van Gorcum, 1978).

56. Marie-Dominique Chenu, *Nature, Man and Society in the Twelfth Century*, ed. and trans. Jerome Taylor and Lester Little (Chicago: University of Chicago Press, 1968), 103.

57. John C. Hirsh, "Religious Attitudes and Mystical Language in Medieval Literary Texts: An Essay in Methodology," in *Vox Mystica: Essays on Medieval Mysticism in Honor of Professor Valerie M. Lagorio* (Cambridge: D. S. Brewer, 1995), 17.

58. Margot Fassler, *Gothic Song: Victorine Sequences and Augustinian Reform in Twelfth-Century Paris* (Cambridge: Cambridge University Press, 1993), 13. Fassler cites Marcia Colish, *The Mirror of Language: A Study in the Medieval Theory of Knowledge*, 2nd ed. (Lincoln: University of Nebraska Press, 1983), 5.

59. Fassler, *Gothic Song*, 13.

60. Margaret Miles, *Image as Insight: Visual Understanding in Western Christianity and Secular Culture* (Boston: Beacon, 1985), xi. See also Erwin Panofsyk, *Gothic Architecture and Scholasticism* (Latrobe, PA: Archabbey Press, 1948).

61. Miles, *Image as Insight*, 143, citing Thomas Aquinas, *Opusc.* 16; *de Trinitate* 6.2 ad 5.

62. The use of the dove as a symbol of the Holy Spirit was formally approved by a local council of Constantinople in 536.

63. During the tenth century, the Holy Spirit was sometimes represented as a man—of every age, from earliest to latest years of life. Images include the Spirit floating on water as a little child; as a young child in the arms of the Father. Among the legendary pictures in which the Spirit was thus represented is an image of Christ received into heaven after his earthly mission. The Holy Spirit is seated near the Father, holding a book symbolizing wisdom. The Spirit blesses Jesus, as does the Father. The Spirit is also portrayed as assisting at the coronation of the Virgin. In some instances representations of the Spirit as man and dove were combined in the figure of a man with a dove on his head or hand. Use of anthropomorphic images of the Spirit declined after the Middle Ages and were declared unacceptable in a decree by Benedict XIV on October 1, 1745.

64. The three persons are seated on a gold bench under a red canopy. All three have gold nimbuses surrounding their heads. Christ holds a commanding position in the center, clothed only in a white loincloth, his wounds visible. His right arm and left arm are held up by the Father and Spirit respectively. They are clothed in ornate vestments, the Father in a full chasuble as the main celebrant; the Holy Spirit as a deacon with cope and stole crossed on his breast. Christ's eyes are cast downward; the bodies of the Father and Holy Spirit are turned inward toward Christ, their eyes gazing past him into the distance. Two female angels in green robes stand sentinel on either side, one holding lilies, the other a sword. The male trio sends a clear message about how God is imagined in terms of gender and hierarchy, but the painting also suggests a rather dramatic contrast between the gentle, vulnerable, almost naked Christ at the center and the richly robed Father and Spirit, who, while clearly not equal to each other, share, more or less, the same dress and priestly role.

65. In Bertrand de Margerie's *The Christian Trinity in History*, trans. Edmund J. Fortman. Studies in Historical Theology, I (Still River, Mass.: St. Bede's Publications, 1982 [1975]), 314.

66. The Father resembles a kingly figure wearing a jeweled crown, not unlike the crown being placed on Mary's head. The Son and Spirit are portrayed as younger men, almost identical in visage, long hair, no crowns, and wearing similar but differently colored clothing. Reproduced in Barbara Newman, *From Virile Woman to WomanChrist: Studies in Medieval Religion and Literature* (Philadelphia: University of Pennsylvania Press, 1995), 201.

67. In this painting, the artist symbolizes the unity of the persons: the three are separated above the waist and joined below; their three halos share parts of one cross. To the right is the gray-bearded Father; to the left the golden-haired Son; and in the middle, a smiling Holy Spirit whom some art critics identify as a younger male figure, but who clearly bears the features of a woman. Father and Son rest their hands on the shoulders of the Spirit figure to signify the procession from both. Father and Son share a single white garment, while the Spirit figure wears a pleated rose-colored gown. See Newman, *From Virile Woman to WomanChrist*, 198–99.

68. Mary Ann Fatula, *The Holy Spirit: Unbounded Gift of Joy* (Collegeville, MN: Liturgical Press, 1998), 24–25. Fatula notes a contrary position in the work of Brian Gaybba, who speaks of the Holy Spirit not as a divine person with a unique identity but as love, which has no identity except to be unity. The Spirit is thus the "way" we experience the presence of the Father and Son. (*The Spirit of Love: Theology of the Holy Spirit* [London: Geoffrey Chapman, 1987], 94–95, 123, 136–37).

69. Gen 8:8, 10, 12; Ps 54:7; 67:14; Song 2:10, 14; 5:2; 6:8; Isa 38:14; Jer 25:38; 46:16; 48:28; 50:16; Hos 7:11; 11:11; Matt 3:16; Mark 1:10; Luke 3:22; John 2:14, 16.

70. Two examples of miniscule-sized doves include a portrayal of the celestial court in the Book of Hours of John the Fearless, Duke of Burgundy (duke 1404–1419), reproduced in Newman, *From Virile Woman to WomanChrist*, 204; and *The Man of Sorrows*, painted about 1510 by Jacob Cornelisz, reproduced in Caroline Walker Bynum, *Holy Feast, Holy Fast: The Religious Significance of Food to Medieval Women* (Berkeley: University of California Press, 1987), plate 27 (after p. 302).

71. Philo, *Questions and Answers on Genesis*, 2.39–44; 3.3.

72. See Mircea Eliade, ed., *The Encyclopedia of Religion* (New York: Macmillan, 1987), 224; and *The Interpreter's Dictionary of the Bible*, vol. 1, ed. George A. Buttrick et al. (New York/Nashville: Abingdon, 1962), 866–67.

73. An example of this image is Athenagoras, *Supplication for the Christians* 7.2; 9.1, cited in J. N. D. Kelly, *Early Christian Doctrines*, rev. ed. (San Francisco: Harper & Row, 1978 [1960]), 102.

74. Alluding to Ps 45:2, Bonaventure wrote, "For the Father speaks through the Son or Tongue, but that which fulfills and commits to memory is the Pen of the Scribe." *Collations on the Six Days*, 12.17 (V, 385).

75. Ignatius of Antioch, *To the Ephesians*. 9.1; *To the Magnesians*. 13.1–2, cited in Kelly, *Early Christian Doctrines*, 92.

76. In a variation, the rod is the flesh of the Lord, raising up to heaven, bearing to the whole world the sweet-smelling fruits of religion.

77. The Latin reads "laeti bibamus sobriam/ebrietatem Spiritus." Hymn 3: *Splendor paternae gloriae*, in A. S. Walpole, *Early Latin Hymns* (Cambridge: Cambridge University Press, 1922), 38. An example from the Middle Ages is Jean Gerson (1363–1429): "In him [Christ] is the true vine, whose wine generates virgins and not only generates them but impregnates them. Let him give that wine, let him give the sober inebriation of the Spirit as drink." *Collectorium super Magnificat*, Treatise 9, in John Gerson, *Oeuvres complètes*, ed. Palemon Glorieux, vol. 8, *L'oeuvre spirituelle et pastorale* (Paris: Desclée, 1971), 397–98, cited in Bynum, *Holy Feast*, 32, 80.

78. Rosemary Drage Hale, "'Taste and See, For God is Sweet': Sensory Perception and Memory in Medieval Mystical Experience," in *Vox Mystica*, 14.

79. British author Sara Maitland suggests that we follow Roland Barthes's invitation to take pleasure (*jouissance*) in the unresolved text, the ending that opens up rather than closes down. *A Big-Enough God: A Feminist's Search for a Joyful Theology* (New York: Henry Holt, 1995), 111.

80. Edith Wyschogrod, *Saints and Postmodernism: Revisioning Moral Philosophy* (Chicago and London: University of Chicago Press, 1990), xxiii.

81. Miles, *Image as Insight*, 7.

82. Gilkey, *Catholicism Confronts Modernity*, 102.

83. Miles, *Image as Insight*, 30.

84. Jaroslav Pelikan, *The Vindication of Tradition* (New Haven: Yale University Press, 1984), 65. This approach needs to be complemented with a contemporary, sociotheological methodology, e.g., ascertaining how Christians in North America experience and talk about the Spirit in their lives. A further extension of this study would be to explore how "spirit" functions in the other major religious systems such as Hinduism, Buddhism, Judaism, and Islam.

85. Mikhail Bakhtin, *The Bakhtin Reader: Selected Writings of Bakhtin, Medvedev, Voloshinov*, ed. Pam Morris (London: Edward Arnold, 1944), ix.

86. Ibid.

87. In this regard, we have already noted the work of Pierre Hadot. Another example is the way Peter Brown has affected our understanding of virginity, sexuality, and holiness in early Latin Christianity. See *The World of Late Antiquity, AD 150–750* (New York: Harcourt Brace Jovanovich, 1971); idem, *The Cult of the Saints: Its Rise and Function in Latin Christianity* (Chicago: University of Chicago Press, 1981); idem, *Society and the Holy in Late Antiquity* (Berkeley: University of California Press, 1982); idem, *The Body and Society: Men, Women, and Sexual Renunciation in Early Christianity*, Lectures on the History of Religion sponsored by the American Council of Learned Societies, n.s. 13 (New York: Columbia University Press, 1988).

88. In 1974, Luis Alonso Schökel, the dean of the Pontifical Biblical Institute, noted that doctrinal studies on the exegesis of the church fathers or medieval theologians had disappeared from the agendas of Catholic theological faculties. Even the imposing work of Henri de Lubac on medieval exegesis, published on the eve of Vatican II, had only a tenuous impact on biblical studies and hermeneutics. Denis Farkasfalvy, "Bernard the Theologian: Forty Years of Research," *Communio* 17 (Winter 1990): 589.

89. Newman, *From Virile Woman to WomanChrist*, 16.

90. Columba Stewart, "Reimagining Early Monastic Spirituality," *Christian Spirituality Bulletin* 5, no. 1 (Spring 1997): 25.

91. McDonnell, "Trinitarian Theology of the Holy Spirit?" 206, 208.

92. Theologian Serene Jones identifies a similar methodology in a review essay of nine feminist works. Jones identifies five methodological approaches to the concept of "experience," one of which she labels "lit-

erary/textual." In this method, scholars view experience in the context of historically variant narratives rather than in the context of philosophical analysis. She offers as examples the work of Delores Williams and Sallie McFague. "'Women's Experience' Between A Rock and A Hard Place: Feminist, Womanist and Mujerista Theologies in North America," *Religious Studies Review* 21, no. 3 (July 1995): 175.

93. My methodology finds resonance with Bernard McGinn's concluding comments in the second volume of his history of Western Christian mysticism where he describes his method as one that does not criticize by measuring the gap between ideals and reality or by judging the legitimacy of the ideals. Rather he seeks to identify the spiritual values that various mystical authors said they were trying to inculcate in their lives and societies. That they no doubt often failed or deluded themselves about their intentions does not necessarily falsify the values at which they aimed. *The Growth of Mysticism: Gregory the Great through the 12th Century*, vol. 2 of *The Presence of God: A History of Western Christian Mysticism* (New York: Crossroad, 1994), 420. See also Roger Haight, "The Case for Spirit Christology," *Theological Studies* 53 (1992): 260.

94. Yves Congar, *I Believe in the Holy Spirit*, vol. 2, *Lord and Giver of Life* (New York: Seabury, 1983 [1979]), 153–54. See Elizabeth Teresa Groppe, *Yves Congar's Theology of the Holy Spirit*, American Academy of Religion Series (Oxford: Oxford University Press, 2004).

Chapter 2: Augustine of Hippo
The Spirit of Courage and Reconciliation

1. For a concise summary of the development of the role of the Spirit in the early creeds, see Joseph D. Small, "The Spirit and the Creed," in *Fire & Wind: The Holy Spirit in the Church Today*, ed. Joseph D. Small (Louisville: Geneva, 2002), 1–18. See also Robert Louis Wilken, *The Spirit of Early Christian Thought: Seeking the Face of God* (New Haven and London: Yale University Press, 2003), 80–93, 100–106.

2. There are several passages in the New Testament that suggest a hierarchy of persons (John 4:34; 5:30; 6:38; 14:10, 26; 15:26; 17:4, 7–8; 1 Cor 15:24). In the second century, Origen of Alexandria is an example of an early theologian who saw the Trinity in hierarchical terms. He spoke of the Son as divine in a derivative sense and the Spirit as the highest of creatures sent by God to sanctify believers.

3. For a discussion of these debates, see Kilian McDonnell, *The Other Hand of God: The Holy Spirit as the Universal Touch and Goal* (Collegeville, MN: Liturgical Press, 2003), 11–19.

4. Thomas Marsh, *The Triune God: A Biblical, Historical, and Theological Study* (Mystic, CT: Twenty-third Publications, 1994), 90.

5. Peter Brown, *Augustine of Hippo: A Biography*, revised ed. (1967; Berkeley: University of California Press, 2000), 9. Unless noted, subsequent references are to the 1967 edition.

6. Ibid., 24, citing B. H. Warmington, *The North African Provinces from Diocletian to the Vandal Conquest* (Cambridge: Cambridge University Press, 1954), 111.

7. Brown, *Augustine of Hippo*, 38.

8. Manichaeism was a religion founded by the Persian Mani in the latter half of the third century. Its tenets were drawn from Zoroastrian dualism, Babylonian folklore, Buddhist ethics, and some lesser Christian elements. Manichaeism is classified as a form of dualism that understands the world in terms of two opposing, eternal principles of good (spirit) and evil (matter).

9. James J. O'Donnell, *Augustine: A New Biography* (New York: HarperCollins, 2005), xiii.

10. Sermon 356.1 (*Patrologia cursus completus: Series latina*, ed. J. P. Migne, 221 vols. [Paris, 1844–64], 39:1574; hereafter PL, followed by volume and column number), cited in Brown, *Augustine of Hippo*, 224.

11. It is important to remember that during this period ordination to priesthood could take place simply through the acclamation of the community. Ambrose was called to ordination in this way before he was even baptized. F. Van der Meer notes that there were approximately seven hundred bishops in Africa, one consecrated, on average, every week. *Augustine the Bishop: The Life and Work of a Father of the Church*, trans. Brian Battershaw and G. R. Lamb (London: Sheed & Ward, 1961), 11, 225.

12. Brown, *Augustine of Hippo*, 207.

13. Ibid., 208.

14. Augustine, *Interpretations of the Psalms* (*Enarrationes in Psalmos*), 54.8.9 (PL 36:633–34), cited in Brown, *Augustine of Hippo*, 208.

15. Sermon 296 (PL 38:1352–59), cited in Brown, *Augustine of Hippo*, 293.

16. Sermon 22.7 (PL 38:152), cited in Brown, *Augustine of Hippo*, 262.

17. Brown, *Augustine of Hippo*, 162. See *Confessions* 11.2.2 (PL 32:675–76).

18. Letter 169.2.5 written to Bishop Evodius in 415 (PL 33:744; *Nicene and Post-Nicene Fathers*, First Series, ed. Philip Schaff [Peabody, MA: Hendrickson, 1994], 1:540; hereafter NPNF). See also *On the*

Trinity 4.21.30 (PL 42:909; NPNF 3:85–86), and Sermon 21 (PL 38:142–43; NPNF 6:324).

19. Letter 11.4 to Nebridius written in 389 (PL 33:76; NPNF 1:230).

20. *On Faith and the Creed* 9.19 (PL 40:191; NPNF 3:329).

21. *On the Trinity* 5.9.10 (PL 42:918; NPNF 1:92); 5.11.12 (PL 42:919; NPNF 3:93).

22. The first sending of the Spirit refers to Jesus' appearance on the evening of the resurrection (John 20:22).

23. *On the Trinity*, 4.20.29 (PL 42:908; NPNF 1:84–85).

24. Ibid., 5.14.15 (PL 42:921; NPNF 1:94–95).

25. Ibid.

26. William J. Collinge cites this sentence from a lecture given by Patout Burns at Yale University in 1973. "John Dunne's Journey of the Mind, Heart, and Soul," *Horizons* 16, no. 1 (1989): 35.

27. Yves Congar, *I Believe in the Holy Spirit*, 3 vols. (New York: Seabury; London: Geoffrey Chapman, 1979–80), 1:77.

28. *On Faith and the Creed* 9.18–19 (PL 40:190–91; NPNF 3:329).

29. The Donatists also called on the Spirit. W. H. C. Frend suggests that part of the Donatists' ability to survive was due to their ability to combine a hierarchically governed church with a nonhierarchical community devoted to the Spirit. Readers in their liturgies were thought to be transmitting the Spirit to the congregation. *The Donatist Church: A Movement of Protest in Roman North Africa* (1952; Oxford: Clarendon, 1971), 319–20.

30. Garry Wills compared the conflict to a family feud between two resentful twin brothers. *Saint Augustine* (New York: Penguin Group, 1999), 75.

31. Brown, *Augustine of Hippo*, 139.

32. Ibid., 141; see also Wills, *Saint Augustine*, 83.

33. *Interpretations of the Psalms*, 95.11 (PL 37.1234), cited in Brown, *Augustine of Hippo*, 221.

34. Brown, *Augustine of Hippo*, 214.

35. Ibid., 212–14.

36. Frend, *Donatist Church*, 238.

37. Brown, *Augustine of Hippo*, 212–14.

38. *On the Gospel of John*, Tractate 6.2 (PL 35:1425; NPNF 7:40).

39. Sermon 268.2; 269.2 (PL 38:1232, 1235).

40. Sermon 269.4 (PL 38:1237).

41. Letter 185.50 (PL 33:815; NPNF 4:651).

42. Sermon 271 (PL 38:1246).

43. Sermon 266.2 (PL 38:1225).

44. Sermon 267.3; 268.2 (PL 38:1230–31, 1232).

45. Sermon 267.4 (PL 38:1231).

46. "Haec dicuntur ut amemus unitatem, et timeamus separationem. Nihil enim sic debet formidare Christianus, quam separari a corpore Christi." *On the Gospel of St. John,* Tractate 27.6 (PL 35, 1618; NPNF VII, 176).

47. Wills, *Augustine of Hippo,* 100. Brown describes Augustine's age as harsh and prone to turn too easily to military discipline and uniformity. *Augustine of Hippo,* 224.

48. Sermon 112.8 (PL 38:647), cited in Wills, *Augustine of Hippo,* 103.

49. *Interpretations of the Psalms* 8.8 (PL 36:112; NPNF 8:30).

50. Sermon 21 (NPNF 6:318–32) [Sermon 71, PL 38:445–67]; Letter 185.49–50 (PL 33:814–15; NPNF 4:650–51).

51. Sermon 21.20 (NPNF 6:325 [Sermon 71, PL 38:455]).

52. *On Faith and the Creed* 9.19 (PL 40:191–92; NPNF 3:330).

53. Letter 185.50 (PL 33:815; NPNF 4:651).

54. John Cavadini, response given at CTSA Seminar, Annual Convention, New York, June 1995.

55. "Cur donum linguarum non modo conceditur numquid modo, fratres, non datur Spiritus sanctus? Quisquis hoc putat, non est dignus accipere. Datur et modo." Sermon 267.3 (PL 38:1230). In Sermon 269.1 (PL 38:1235) we read: "Can they [Donatists] possibly deny that even now the Holy Spirit comes upon Christians?"

56. Sermons 268.1; 268.4; 269.1 (PL 38:1232, 1233, 1234). "The reason, after all, why the Holy Spirit was prepared to demonstrate his presence in the tongues of all nations, was so that those who are included in the unity of the Church which speaks all languages might understand that they have the Holy Spirit." Sermon 268.2 (PL 38:1235).

57. Sermons 269.1, 2; 270.6; 271 (PL 38:1234–35, 1243, 1245).

58. Sermon 271 (PL 38:1245).

59. Sermons 266.2; 269.1 (PL 38:1225, 1234).

60. Sermon 71.12.18 (PL 38:454).

61. *On the Gospel of John,* Tractate 92.2 (PL 35:1863; NPNF 7:363). See also *Interpretations of the Psalms* 91.16 (NPNF 8:451 [Ps 90.8, PL 37:1167]). The root of our boldness and confidence is also attributed to Christ in Ephesians 3:11–13.

62. *On the Gospel of John,* Tractate 92.2 (PL 35:1863; NPNF 7:363).

63. *On the Catechizing of the Uninstructed* 2.3 (PL 40:311; NPNF 3:248).

64. The link between knowledge and the Holy Spirit runs throughout the tradition. In an article on the significance of Jesus' baptism in the

early church, Kilian McDonnell speaks of ways in which the Spirit affects knowledge. The Spirit's testimony allows the community to know the hidden cosmic vocation of the son (218) and that Jesus was the true Son of God (227). "To those who follow him down into the waters, Jesus imparts his quiet and the rest of the Spirit, a new way of knowing" (236). "Jesus' Baptism in the Jordan," *Theological Studies* 56 (1995): 209–36.

65. *On the Gospel of John,* Tractate 32.5 (PL 35:1614; NPNF 7:194).

66. Ibid., Tractate 6.7 (PL 35:1428; NPNF 7:41).

67. Ibid., Tractate 74.2 (PL 35:1827; NPNF 7:334).

68. *Our Lord's Sermon on the Mount,* 2.25.83 (PL 34:1307; NPNF 6:62).

69. Letter 169.1.4 (PL 33:744; NPNF 1:540).

70. Letter 118.5.32–33 (PL 33:447–49; NPNF 1:449–50), cited in Brown, *Augustine of Hippo,* 276.

71. Letter 130.15.28 (PL 33:506; NPNF 1:468).

72. Letter 120.3, 13 (PL 33:453), cited in Brown, *Augustine of Hippo,* 277.

73. At the end of the sermon, Augustine counsels meditation as perhaps a superior or supplemental route to understanding: "Let this suffice, Brethren; I know that I have said that which perhaps, if meditated upon, may develop itself to many, which oftentimes when expressed in words may chance to be obscured." Sermon 76.4, 15 (NPNF 6:482, 486 [Sermon 126.3.4 and 126.11.15, PL 38:699, 705]).

74. Kilian McDonnell traces the connection between knowledge and the Holy Spirit in the tradition in "A Trinitarian Theology of the Holy Spirit?" pp. 219–26.

75. For mention of Holy Spirit as "gift"—an idea closely connected for Augustine with love—see *On The Trinity* 5.15.16 (PL 42:921; NPNF 3:95); and 15.10.17–19 (PL 42:1069–71; NPNF 3:215–20). On the Holy Spirit as "breath," see *The City of God* 13:24 (PL 41:398–404; NPNF 2:259–61); and *Confessions* 13.6.6–10.10 (PL 32:827–30; NPNF 1:191–93).

76. *On the Trinity* 6.5.7; 10.8.11; 15.10.17–19 (PL 42:928, 979, 1069–71; NPNF 3:100, 140, 208–9). See William Hill, *The Three-Personed God: The Trinity as a Mystery of Salvation* (Washington, DC: Catholic University of America Press, 1982), 56, n. 12; and Bertrand de Margerie, *The Christian Trinity in History* (1975; Still River, MA: St. Bede's Publications, 1982), 110–21.

77. Gregory Anderson Love elaborates how this bond that creates union without erasing distinction extends into the world and history, enabling (1) God's will and human wills to come together; (2) the union

of the divine and the human in Jesus; (3) the correlation of divine transcendence and divine immanence; (4) God's redemptive care to embrace not only the human community, but all nonhuman creation as well; (5) the integrity of individual existence and life in communities of reciprocity and equality. Love also lists as a false choice the use of male language for the Spirit that excludes female images, pronouns, and metaphors. "Why the Holy Spirit Now: The Promise and Peril of Recent Interest in the Holy Spirit," in *Fire & Wind*, ed. Small, 80–83.

78. *On the Trinity* 15.19.37 (PL 42:1071; NPNF 3:219).

79. Sermon 21.18 (NPNF 6:325 [Sermon 71, PL 38:454]).

80. "Whence he says again, 'If any man have not the Spirit of Christ, he is none of His' (Rom 8.9). To which Person then in the Trinity could the communion of this fellowship peculiarly appertain, but to that Spirit which is common to Father and the Son?" Sermon 21.29 (NPNF 6:328; [Sermon 71.18.29, PL 38:461]). See also *On the Gospel of John*, Tractate 99.4–9 (PL 35:1887–90; NPNF 7:382–84); *On the Trinity* 5.10.11 (PL 42:918; NPNF 3:93); Letter 185.50 (PL 33:815; NPNF 4:651).

81. *On the Gospel of John*, Tractate 32.7 (PL 35:1615; NPNF 7:195).

82. *On the Catechising of the Uninstructed* 20.35 (PL 40:356; NPNF 3:305); see also Letter 55.16.29 (PL 33:219; NPNF 1:313); *Interpretations on the Psalms* 8.8 (PL 36:112; NPNF 7:29).

83. *On the Trinity* 15.10.17, 19 (PL 42:1069–71; NPNF 3:217). The Holy Spirit is given once upon earth (John 20:22) on account of the love of our neighbor and a second time from heaven, on account of the love of God (Acts 2:4). See also *On the Trinity* 15.16.26 (PL 42:1079; NPNF 3:224).

84. Augustine, *The Spirit and the Letter* (PL 44:201).

85. Augustine, *Handbook (Enchiridion)*, chapter 121 (Pl 40:288; NPNF 3:275–76).

86. *On the Catechising of the Uninstructed* 23.41 (PL 40:340; NPNF 3:308).

87. Letter 130.6.13 (PL 33:499; NPNF 1:463).

88. *On the Gospel of John*, Tractate 26.6 (PL 35:1609; NPNF 7:176).

89. Sermon 21.19 (PL 38:147–48; NPNF 6:324–25); see also *On the Gospel of John*, Tractate 6.2 (PL 35:1425; NPNF 7:40).

90. *On the Gospel of John*, Tractate 92.1 (PL 35:1862; NPNF 7:363).

91. Sermon 78.2.4 (NPNF 6:492 [Sermon 127.2.4, PL 38:715]).

92. *On the Gospel of John*, Tractate 6.2 (PL 35:1425; NPNF 7:39).

Those who groan for heavenly things are doves. Those who "clamor" for earthly things are ravens. There must be room in the church for both.

93. Letter 130 (PL 33:494–507; NPNF 1:459–69).

94. Letter 130.1.2; 130.2.5; and 130.3.7 (PL 33:494–97; NPNF 1:460–61).

95. Letter 130.10.20 (PL 33:502; NPNF 1:465).

96. Veli-Matti Kärkkäinen, *Pneumatology: The Holy Spirit in Ecumenical, International, and Contextual Perspective* (Grand Rapids: Baker Academic, 2002), 134.

97. Blair Reynolds, *Toward a Process Pneumatology* (London: Associated University Presses, 1990), 125, cited in Kärkkäinen, *Pneumatology*, 148–53.

98. I am reminded here of H. Richard Niebuhr's five paradigms depicting a range of stances between church and world in *Christ and Culture* (1951; New York: HarperCollins, 2001: Christ against culture; Christ of culture; Christ above culture; Christ and culture in paradox; Christ, the transformer of culture.

99. *Confessions* 13.7.8 (PL 32:847; NPNF 1:192).

100. *Confessions* 13.9.10 (PL 32:848–9; NPNF 1:193). Each of the last three books of the *Confessions* reflects on a person in the Trinity—book 11 on the Father; book 12 on the Son; and book 13 on the Holy Spirit.

Chapter 3: Hildegard of Bingen
The Spirit's "Greening" Power

1. Hildegard of Bingen, "Antiphon for the Holy Spirit," in Barbara Newman, *Saint Hildegard of Bingen: Symphonia* 2nd ed. (Ithaca and London: Cornell University Press, 1998), 140–41.

2. See Bernard McGinn, *The Presence of God: A History of Western Christian Mysticism*, vol. 2, *The Growth of Mysticism: Gregory the Great through the 12th Century* (New York: Crossroad, 1994), 149–57.

3. See Sister Edmée, SLG, "Bernard and Abelard," in *The Influence of Saint Bernard*, ed. Sister Benedicta Ward, SLG (Fairacres, Oxford: SLG Press, 1976), 92–95; and Marie-Dominique Chenu, *Nature, Man and Society in the Twelfth Century*, trans. Jerome Taylor and Lester K. Little (1957; Chicago: University of Chicago Press, 1968), 43–45.

4. Literature on the Crusades is vast. See Sylvia Schein, *Fideles Crucis: The Papacy, the West, and the Recovery of the Holy Land, 1274–1314* (Oxford: Clarendon; New York: Oxford University Press, 1991); Vladimir P. Goss, ed., *The Meeting of Two Worlds: Cultural Exchange between*

East and West during the Period of the Crusades (Kalamazoo, MI: Medieval Institute Publications, Western Michigan University, 1986); Malcolm Barber, *Crusaders and Heretics, 12th–14th Centuries* (Aldershot: Variorum, 1995); Jaroslav Folda, *The Art of the Crusaders in the Holy Land: 1098–1187* (Cambridge: Cambridge University Press, 1995); Alan Forey, *The Military Orders from the Twelfth to the Early Fourteenth Centuries* (Toronto: University of Toronto Press, 1992); Michael Gervers, ed., *The Second Crusade and the Cistercians* (New York: St. Martin's Press, 1992); Jonathan Riley-Smith, *The Crusades: A Short History* (New Haven and London: Yale University Press, 1987); idem, *The Oxford Illustrated History of the Crusades* (Oxford: Oxford University Press, 1995), idem, *What Were the Crusades?*, 2nd ed. (London: Macmillan, 1992); Sir Stephen Runciman, *A History of the Crusades*, 3 vols. (Cambridge: Cambridge University Press, 1951–54); Elizabeth Siberry, *Criticism of Crusading, 1095–1274* (Oxford: Clarendon, 1985).

5. The Waldensians, or the "poor of Lyons," were a group founded around 1173 by Peter Waldo, a wealthy man whose conversion to poverty imitated the spirit of Francis of Assisi. Given to poverty, vernacular translations of the Bible, and lay preaching, the adherents ran afoul of church authorities and were persecuted. *Humiliati* was a name given to a lay penitential order in Lombardy who, like the Waldensians, devoted themselves to works of charity and penance. With the advice of Bernard of Clairvaux, their first monastery was founded in 1134 in Milan. In 1201, Innocent III granted them a rule, adapted from the Rule of St. Benedict. When abuses developed, Charles Borromeo was appointed to investigate. A murderous assault was executed by a minority group that opposed reform. The group was suppressed by Pius V in 1571. The wives of Humiliati formed a community under Clara Blassoni, dedicated to caring for lepers. Their numbers increased, but the suppression of the male branch of the order had negative financial effects on the women's houses, causing many to close. There are still five independent houses of Humiliati in Italy.

6. Many movements identified by the church as heretical adhered to a dualistic view of the world that drew sharp lines between good and evil, spirit and matter, and asceticism and sexuality. This worldview appears regularly under a range of titles, going back to Zoroastrianism (a Persian religion founded by Zarathushtra, c. 1500–1000 BCE), Manichaeism (the group to which Augustine belonged in his youth), Albigensians, Cathars, and so on.

7. The Greek term *apocatastasis* means "restoration." Inspired by the text, "When all thing are subjected to him, then the Son himself will also be subjected to him who put all things under him, that God may be

everything to everyone" (1 Cor 15:28), this idea pointed to the final reconciliation of good and evil at the end of time. It was developed in the early church by Origen, Clement of Alexandria, and especially Gregory of Nyssa.

8. Chenu, *Nature, Man and Society*, 82.

9. Heinrich Schipperges, *The World of Hildegard of Bingen: Her Life, Times and Visions* (Collegeville, MN: Liturgical Press, 1998), 95. Images of nature and the cosmos can be found on pp. 83, 84, 91, 97, 104 in this volume.

10. Alan of Lille, *Contra Haeretico* 1.14.

11. Richard Payne, "A Mystical Body of Love" (paper delivered at the interreligious dialogue conference on the theme "The Spirituality of Love in the Twelfth Century and Today" held at Nantes, France, June 1-4, 1986), cited by Ewert Cousins, *Bernard of Clairvaux: Selected Works* (New York: Paulist, 1987), 6-9.

12. Chenu, *Nature, Man and Society*, 100-101.

13. Ibid., 101.

14. Ibid., 111. Symbolism was seen in the smallest details. For example, Chenu notes that Peter of Celle classified and interpreted allegorically all the biblical texts that mention bread.

15. Ibid., 113.

16. Letter 116 to Abbot Nicholas in *The Letters of Hildegard of Bingen*, 2 vols. trans. Joseph L. Baird and Radd K. Ehrman (New York: Oxford University Press, 1994), 2:61-62. In Letter 119 to a congregation of monks, Hildegard refers to those who row their boat "in the shipwreck of this world," a world that "has entered an age of injustice" (2:64).

17. Beginning in the fourth and fifth centuries, celibacy was seen as a value especially for the higher clergy. While documents show that celibacy was encouraged, evidence also reveals that it took centuries before the preponderance of behavior reflected injunctions against a married clergy. The Gregorian reform in the eleventh century and decrees at the First and Second Lateran Councils in the twelfth century, the Fourth Lateran Council in the thirteenth, and the Council of Trent in the sixteenth were important steps toward a more uniform enforcement of the celibacy laws.

18. Fiona Bowie and Oliver Davies, eds., *Hildegard of Bingen: Mystical Writings* (New York: Crossroad, 1990), 5.

19. Ibid., 22-24.

20. Peter Dronke, *Women Writers of the Middle Ages: A Critical Study of Texts from Perpetua (d. 203) to Marguerite Porete (d. 1310)* (Cambridge: Cambridge University Press, 1984), 144.

21. Bowies and Davies, *Hildegard of Bingen*, 8.

22. Hildegard's knowledge was often attributed to the Holy Spirit, but historical questions about the source of her knowledge of music, medicine, and theology are often raised. Without detailed historical records, it is difficult to identify with certainty what access she might have had to learning. As a member of the upper classes, Hildegard would likely have had access to books, conversations with educated males, not to mention her own innate intelligence, which seems to have been significant.

23. Hildegard benefited from the relationship between Bernard and Pope Eugenius III. Before his election to the papacy, Eugenius had been a Cistercian monk under Bernard of Clairvaux. This relationship perdured after Eugenius left the monastery to become pope. In fact, as his ever solicitous spiritual father, Bernard worried that the endless demands of the papacy might erode Eugenius's spiritual life. Bernard wrote a short treatise to him, entitled *De consideratione*, in which he outlines ways in which Eugenius should both attend to the legal, social, and business demands of the papacy and still retain the soul of a monk. Bernard wanted Eugenius to remain true to his monastic vows and commitments, especially since these might be threatened by his new existence. Thus, it is not hard to understand why Eugenius would have turned an open ear when Bernard placed Hildegard's situation before him.

24. The label "effeminate" in this context has nothing to do with sexual orientation. In the Middle Ages, the female sex was stereotypically associated with weakness and the male sex with strength. When men proved to be weak in virtue they were labeled "effeminate." Women who were strong in virtue were labeled "virile."

25. Scholars wonder if part of Hildegard's resistance to the exhumation might have been related to monetary contributions to the convent that this young gentleman had promised in return for being buried in Hildegard's cemetery. But the record is silent on this point.

26. Attempts to assess Hildegard's condition from a medical viewpoint suggest that she may have suffered from some form of congenital migraine headaches, a condition known as *scintilla scotoma*. See Charles Singer, "The Scientific Views and Visions of Saint Hildegard," in *Studies in the History and Method of Science* [Oxford] 1 (1917): 1–55.

27. Bowie and Davies, *Hildegard of Bingen*, 15.

28. Hildegard's interest in buildings is both theological and architectural. Building is a metaphor that evokes the human effort to build the City of God. It is an image of the moral life—the slow, steady creation of a life of virtue that reaches out from earth to the heavens and the communion of saints (Newman, *Symphonia*, 49–50). Hildegard scholars Fiona

Bowie and Oliver Davies comment, "It is no wonder that Hildegard's later visions are so full of images of buildings and craftsmen, and that the construction of the Kingdom of heaven was seen as analogous to a human building project. The Disibodenberg monastery and its women's cloister were in a state of continual development throughout her forty-four years there" (*Hildegard of Bingen*, 9).

29. Other works include a selection of readings from the Gospels, with allegorical commentary (*Expositiones evangeliorum*); commentaries on the Rule of St. Benedict (*Explanatio Regulae S. Benedicti*) and on the Athanasian Creed (*Explanatio Symboli S. Athanasii*); and two biographies—the *Life of St. Disibod* and the *Life of St. Rupert*, patrons of her two convents. There is also a work called *Solutions to Thirty-Eight Questions*, in which Hildegard attempted to solve theological problems put to her by the monks of Villers and Guibert of Gembloux; and two short pieces entitled the *Unknown Language* (*Lingua ignota*), which is a glossary created by Hildegard of some nine hundred words and arranged in thematic groups; and the *Unknown Writing* (*Litterae ignotae*).

30. Joseph McLellan, *Washington Post*, January 14, 1996.

31. Two accessible collections of colored reproductions are *Illuminations of Hildegard of Bingen* with commentary by Matthew Fox (Santa Fe, NM: Bear & Company, 1985); and Schipperges, *World of Hildegard of Bingen*.

32. Kathleen Norris, *The Cloister Walk* (New York: Riverhead Books, 1996), 9.

33. Ibid., 9–10.

34. Ibid., 10.

35. Dronke, *Medieval Women Writers*, 201.

36. All references to the *Scivias* in the text are from the translation in the volume in Classics of Western Spirituality, trans. Columba Hart and Jane Bishop (New York: Paulist, 1990).

37. Hildegard rivals Augustine in her description of the Trinity in various triads. Hildegard describes the Trinity as the three qualities in a stone—cool dampness (Father), solidity (Son), and sparkling fire (Spirit) (*Scivias* II.2.5); and as the three qualities in a word—sound (Father), force or meaning (Son), and breath (Spirit) (*Scivias* II.2.7).

38. Schipperges, *World of Hildegard of Bingen*, 72.

39. Letter 31 to Eberhard, bishop of Bamberg (Baird and Ehrman, *Letters*, 1:95–99).

40. Baird and Ehrman, *Letters*, 1:97. Kung Fu films such as *Crouching Tiger, Hidden Dragon* come to mind.

41. Hildegard of Bingen, "Antiphon for the Trinity," in Newman, *Symphonia*, 143.

42. McGinn, *Growth of Mysticism*, 333.
43. Cited in ibid., 230; see also 348.
44. Ibid., 349–50.
45. The term *forms* belongs to the thought world of Christian Platonism common to twelfth-century theologians. It refers to the exemplars of created beings that exist eternally in the mind of God. See "Poet: 'Where the Living Majesty Utters Mysteries,'" in *Voice of the Living Light: Hildegard of Bingen and Her World*, ed. Barbara Newman (Berkeley: University of California Press, 1998), 254 n. 42.
46. Ibid., 186–88. This sequence provides an excellent example of the ways in which medieval monastic writing arises out of an environment in which liturgy and Bible reading are the daily fare. Newman explains the liturgical and biblical associations of this sequence: the first two stanzas are a trope on the Sanctus of the Mass; stanzas 3 to 6 recall the "O" antiphons of Advent; stanzas 8 to 14 echo the story of creation in Genesis 1 and the image of Wisdom from Ecclesiasticus 24. For an alternate translation, see Newman, *Symphonia*, 148–51.
47. One example out of many is Letter 74 from Abbot Kuno (Baird and Ehrman, *Letters*, 1:158). See also *The Life of Holy Hildegard* (henceforth *The Life*) by the monks Gottfried and Theodoric, trans. Adelgundis Führkötter and James McGrath (Collegeville, MN: Liturgical Press, 1995), 39, 47, 54, and passim. In this text, Hildegard is compared to the apostle John, whose heart was inspired by the Holy Spirit at the breast of Jesus (pp. 47, 71).
48. Letter 16 from Philip, archbishop of Cologne (Baird and Ehrman, *Letters*, 1:65); see also Letter 22 from Conrad, archbishop of Mainz (ibid., 1:74); Letter 38 from Daniel, bishop of Prague (ibid., 1:106 and passim).
49. Baird and Ehrman, *Letters*, 1:71. Letter 20 from Arnold, archbishop of Mainz.
50. *The Life*, 48.
51. Letter 76 from Abbot Helengerus (Baird and Ehrman, *Letters*, 1:163).
52. Ibid., 1:166. Letter 77 from Abbot Helengerus.
53. Ibid.
54. *Scivias* 58; Fox, *Illuminations*, 26.
55. This image can found in Schipperges, *World of Hildegard of Bingen*, 50.
56. See *Scivias* III.7.1; Letter 66 to the Superior; Letter 84 to the Prior (Baird and Ehrman, *Letters*, 1:145, 183).
57. Baird and Ehrman, *Letters*, 1:56, 155, 157, 170, 137. Letter 15 to the Shepherds of the Church; Letter 70 to the Five Abbots; Letter 72

to the Abbot; Letter 77 to Abbot Helengerus; Letter 59 to the Congregation of Monks.

58. Two examples are Letter 53 to Canon Udalric and Letter 70 to the Five Abbots (Baird and Ehrman, *Letters*, 1:131, 155). Her contemporary William of St.-Thierry (d. 1148) has a developed theology of the healing power of the Spirit. See Mary Ellen O'Brien, "A Theology of Transformative Healing in the Monastic Teaching of William of St. Thierry," *Studies in Spirituality* 15 (2005): 71–89.

59. In chapter 6, we will see how Catherine of Siena reverses this metaphor of the Spirit. She writes to one of her disciples: "In him [the Word] all the dampness of selfishness is dried up, and we take on the likeness of the Holy Spirit's fire." Letter T228. *The Letters of Catherine of Siena*, vol. 2, trans. Suzanne Noffke (Tempe, AZ: Arizona Center for Medieval and Renaissance Studies, 2001), 15.

60. Baird, "Introduction," in *Letters*, 1:7. Hildegard connects *viriditas* with moisture (*humor, humiditas*). If the earth did not have moisture or greenness it would crumble like ashes. In the spiritual realm both *viriditas* and *humiditas* are "manifestations of God's power, qualities of the human soul, for 'the grace of God shines like the sun and sends its gifts in various ways; in wisdom, in greenness, in moisture.'" Letter 85 to Adam, the Abbot (Baird and Ehrman, *Letters*, 1:195). In the spiritual realm, a lack of moisture causes virtues to become dry as dust [*ariditas*]. Letter 85 to Abbot Adam (Baird and Ehrman, *Letters*, 1:194).

61. Letter 101 to the Abbess Adelheid (Baird and Ehrman, *Letters*, 2:16).

62. Barbara Newman, "Hildegard of Bingen" video (Washington, DC: The National Cathedral, 1989).

63. Hildegard of Bingen, "Song to the Virgin," in Newman, *Symphonia*, 36, 127.

64. Letter 38 to Daniel Bishop of Prague (Baird and Ehrman, *Letters*, 1:107).

65. Ibid. (Baird, "Introduction," in *Letters*, 1:7).

66. Hildegard describes the power of Antichrist as the ability to set the air in motion, bring forth fire and lightnings, raise thunders and hailstorms, uproot mountains, dry up water and take the greenness from forests (*Scivias* III.11.27).

67. Hildegard of Bingen, "Hymn to the Holy Spirit," in Newman, *Symphonia*, 143. In an article on music and creation, Peter J. Casarella, exploring the thought of Augustine, Bonaventure, and the British physicist-theologian, John Polkinghorne (1930–), cites Brian Greene on the conversation between theology and physics: "The universe—being composed of an enormous number of these vibrating strings—is akin to

a cosmic symphony," audible not to the naked ear but through mathe-matical physics. *The Elegant Universe* (New York: Vintage, 2000), 145–46, cited in Peter J. Casarella, "*Carmen Dei*: Music and Creation in Three Theologians," *Theology Today* 62 (2006): 499.

68. A selection of Hildegard's music: *The Origin of Fire*, Anonymous 4, 2005. *Saints*, Cologne Sequentia Ensemble for Medieval Music, 1998. *Canticles of Ecstasy*, Barbara Thornton, 1994. *Symphoniae (Spiritual Songs)*, 1985, Deutsche Harmonia Mundi 77020-2-RG. *Ordo Virtutum* (2 disks), 1998, Deutsche Harmonia Mundi 05472-77394-2. *11,000 Virgins*, Anonymous 4, 1997. *Heavenly Revelations*, Oxford Camerata, 1994. *O Vis Aeternitatis*, Schola of the Benedictine Abbey of St. Hildegard, 1997. *Hildegard—Celestial Stairs*, Augsburg Ensemble for Early Music, 1997.

69. Hildegard of Bingen, *Liber Vitae Meritorum* IV.59. Translation by Heinrich Schipperges, *World of Hildegard of Bingen*, 117.

70. Letter 140 to the Prioress (Baird and Ehrman, *Letters*, 2:80).

71. Dronke, *Women Writers of the Middle Ages*, 197. Heinrich Schipperges calls attention to the Pythagorean-Platonic tradition, in which music was seen as a fundamental regulative principle for the edu-cation of individuals and for the ordering of community life. In this social and also aesthetic sense, music was thought of as a therapeutic medium. In Hildegard's case, this musical therapy or ordering takes on theological and spiritual significance. The aim of the Christian life was to live a life of virtue open to the Spirit. The goal was to be in harmony with the celestial spheres (*World of Hildegard of Bingen*, 63).

72. Letter 23 to the prelates at Mainz (Baird and Ehrman, *Letters*, 1:77).

73. Ibid., 1:78.

74. Ibid.

75. Newman, *Symphonia*, 21. See also Letter 20 to Arnold, arch-bishop of Mainz (Baird and Ehrman, *Letters*, 1:72).

76. Hildegard of Bingen, "Hymn to the Holy Spirit," in Newman, *Symphonia*, 143. Guibert of Gembloux, a monk who would become Hildegard's secretary, wrote her a letter in which in a passage on Pentecost, he speaks of the relationship between the melodies Hildegard hears in her visions and the music she composes. Letter 104 from Guibert of Gembloux (Baird and Ehrman, *Letters*, 2:30).

77. Newman, *Symphonia*, 45.

78. Hildegard emphasizes the need to understand and administer the seven sacraments correctly. This concern is likely in response to posi-tions held by Cathars that disparaged the use of sacraments in favor of

direct, unmediated contact with God. Her interest focuses on the importance of tradition, orthodoxy, and orthopraxis.

79. Letter 15 to the Shepherds of the Church (Baird and Ehrman, *Letters*, 1:54).

80. Ibid., 1:61.

81. Letter 1 to Bernard, Abbot of Clairvaux (Baird and Ehrman, *Letters*, 1:27).

82. This human experience is wonderfully portrayed in the novel, *Zen and the Art of Motorcycle Maintenance: An Inquiry into Values*, by Robert Pirsig (New York: Bantam, 1984).

83. Preface to *Scivias*, trans. Columba Hart and Jane Bishop, introduction by Barbara J. Newman, Classics of Western Spirituality (New York: Paulist, 1990), 6.

84. Letter 40 to Odo, Master of the University of Paris (Baird and Ehrman, *Letters*, 1:112).

85. See Barbara Newman, *Sister of Wisdom: St. Hildegard's Theology of the Feminine* (Berkeley: University of California Press, 1987), 112ff; and, "Divine Power Made Perfect in Weakness," in *Peace Weavers*, ed. J. A. Nichols and L. T. Shank (Kalamazoo, MI: Cistercian Publications, 1987), 103–22.

86. Letter 104 from Guibert of Gembloux (Baird and Ehrman, *Letters*, 2:31–32).

87. Ibid. I wonder what female behavior Guibert had in mind when he speaks of haranguing the people?

88. Newman, *Symphonia*, 2–3, citing Hildegard, *Book of Divine Works* 3.10.38.

89. Barbara Newman, "Divine Power Made Perfect," 104–5.

90. Hildegard of Bingen, *Liber Vitae Meritorum*, trans. Bruce W. Hozeski (New York: Garland, 1994), 9–10.

91. Letter 18 to Heinrich, Archbishop of Mainz (Baird and Ehrman, *Letters*, 1:70).

92. Letter 45, cited in Newman, "Divine Power Made Perfect," 109.

93. Baird and Ehrman, *Letters*, 1:7; and Letter 2 to Pope Eugenius (written in 1148) *Letters*, 1:32–33). Hildegard also receives wings from the Spirit: "'O daughter, run! For the Most Powerful Giver whom no one can resist has given you wings to fly with. Therefore fly swiftly over all these obstacles!' And I, comforted with great consolation, took wing and passed swiftly over all those poisonous and deadly things" (*Scivias* I.4.2).

94. Colman O'Dell, "Elisabeth of Schönau and Hildegard of Bingen: Prophets of the Lord," in *Peace Weavers*, ed. Nichols and Shank, 85–102.

95. Abraham Heschel, *The Prophets: An Introduction* (San Francisco: Harper & Row, 1962), 12.

96. See O'Dell, "Elisabeth of Schönau and Hildegard of Bingen," 86–88, 94. O'Dell describes Hildegard as a "prophet of fire" because of her emphasis on fire and heat.

97. See Adam Zagajewski, "Try to Praise the Mutilated World," translated from the Polish by Clare Cavanagh, *The New Yorker*, September 24, 2001, 96.

98. Renate Craine, *Hildegard: Prophet of the Cosmic Christ* (New York: Crossroad, 1997), 153.

99. See Shipperges, *World of Hildegard of Bingen*, 148–50.

100. Hildegard of Bingen, "Antiphon for the Holy Spirit," in Newman, *Symphonia*, 140–41.

Chapter 4: Bernard of Clairvaux
The Spirit as Kiss

1. It can be argued that William of St.-Thierry is a better candidate for a study in pneumatology since he has a more highly developed theology of the Holy Spirit than Bernard. I chose Bernard because he is more well known and his works are more accessible to the wider Christian community.

2. The Cistercian Order was born out of a desire to follow the Rule of St. Benedict more fully. In 1098, the Benedictine abbot Robert of Molesme traveled to Cîteaux (in the Diocese of Langres in France) with twenty-one monks to found this new community. Subsequent abbots included Alberic and Stephen Harding.

3. In 1146 Pope Eugenius III asked Bernard to preach the Second Crusade, aimed at freeing the Holy Land from the Turks. This was the first crusade to be led by European forces—Germany (led by Conrad III) and France (led by Louis VII). The latter army departed for the Second Crusade on the feast of Pentecost. Bernard recruited for this crusade with great enthusiasm, but when both armies were defeated by the Seljuk Turks, Bernard was assigned part of the blame, which turned public opinion against him.

4. References in the text to Bernard's *Sermons on the Song of Songs* will be abbreviated SC followed by sermon and paragraph number. *Sermons on the Song of Songs*, trans. Kilian Walsh, 4 vols. (Kalamazoo, MI: Cistercian Publications, 1971 [Sermons 1–20], 1976 [Sermons 21–46], 1979 [Sermons 47–66], 1980 [Sermons 67–86]). The critical edition of Bernard's works is the *Sancti Bernardi Opera*, ed. J. Leclercq, C. H. Talbot

and H. M. Rochais, 9 vols. (Rome: Editiones Cistercienses, 1957–78, 1998). Because of the large number of references to *Sermons on the Song of Songs*, I have not included the Latin documentation, which can easily be found in the first volume of the *Opera*.

5. *Lectio divina* (sacred reading) is a slow, meditative reading of the scriptures or spiritual works in the context of silence and prayer. In the Middle Ages, this type of spiritual reading was often compared metaphorically with eating, chewing, tasting, and digesting food. Through this process, one *became* the Word of God, visible in a life of virtue.

6. The twelfth century set the stage for the use of logic and dialectic in the study of theology. Reason took on a new role at universities in France, Italy, and England during the thirteenth century.

7. Like many medieval authors, Bernard used metaphors in a very fluid way; for example, he links anointing with oil to the Spirit, but also associates oil with Christ, the Bridegroom (SC 14.8; 15.5).

8. During Bernard's abbacy (1115–53), monasteries directly affiliated with Clairvaux numbered sixty-nine. Seventy-five additional houses were founded from this group, and then an additional twenty-five—a total of 166 daughter houses of Clairvaux. For a detailed examination of the complex process by which this expansion took place, see Adriaan H. Bredero, "St. Bernard and the Historians," in *Saint Bernard of Clairvaux: Studies Commemorating the Eighth Centenary of His Canonization*, ed. Basil Pennington (Kalamazoo, MI: Cistercian Publications, 1977), 52–62.

9. Stephen Robson, *'With the Spirit and Power of Elijah' (Lk 1.17): The Prophetic-Reforming Spirituality of Bernard of Clairvaux as Evidenced Particularly in his Letters*, Analecta Gregoriana 293, Series Facultatis Theologiae (Rome: Pontifical Gregorian University Press, 2004), 163. B. P. McGuire titled his book on Bernard, *The Difficult Saint*, Cistercian Series 126 (Kalamazoo, MI: Cistercian Publications, 1991).

10. Bernard McGinn and Patricia Ferris McGinn, *Early Christian Mystics: The Divine Vision of the Spiritual Masters* (New York: Crossroad, 2003), 208.

11. Corroborating evidence of Bernard's celebrity in twelfth-century records of civil and ecclesiastical events is sparse. Bernard is rarely mentioned, suggesting that there is a divide between his importance in his own time and the subsequent attribution to him of fame as a major figure in European affairs. See P. Phillips, "The Presence—and Absence—of Bernard of Clairvaux in the Twelfth-Century Chronicles," in *Bernardus Magister: Papers Celebrating the Nonacentenary of the Birth of St. Bernard*, ed. John R. Sommerfeldt, Cistercian Studies 135 (Kalamazoo, MI: Cistercian Publications, 1992), 35–54.

12. Denis Farkasfalvy, "Bernard the Theologian: Forty Years of Research," *Communio* 17 (Winter 1990): 581. See Étienne Gilson, *The Mystical Theology of Saint Bernard*, trans. A. H. C. Downes (London and New York: Sheed & Ward, 1940; reprint, Cistercian Studies 120 [Kalamazoo, MI: Cistercian Publications, 1990]).

13. Callixtus II (1119–24); Honorius II (1124–30); Innocent II (1130–43) [Anacletus II (1130–38)]; Lucius II (1144–45); and Eugenius III (1145–53).

14. In 1130, Pope Honorius II died. An influential Roman family was grooming Peter Pierleone to become the next pope. An opposing group quickly elected Gregory Papareshi, who took the name Innocent II. Pierleone's supporters then declared the election invalid—it did not honor the required three-day waiting period after the death of a pope—and held their own election in which Pierleone became Anacletus II. Bernard put his energies into defending Innocent.

15. Bernard was known for many careful revisions of his writing. See Jean Leclercq, "The Making of a Masterpiece," in *Sermons on the Song of Songs*, trans. Walsh, 4:xvi–xxiii.

16. Jean Leclercq, *Bernard of Clairvaux: Selected Works* (New York and Mahwah, NJ: Paulist, 1987), 121–22.

17. *Sermon for Septuagesima* 1.2 (*Opera* 4:346).

18. In *On Grace and Free Choice*, Bernard writes of the Spirit's role in the exercise of freedom: "For in the first place, we were created with free will and willing freedom, a creature noble in God's eyes. Secondly, we are re-formed in innocence, a new creature in Christ: and thirdly, we are raised up to glory, a perfect creature in the Spirit" (3.7; *Opera* 3:171). Bernard later refers to the Spirit's role: "Able to go in either direction, [the will] is, as it were, on the sloping side of a fairly steep mountain. It is so weakened by its desires of the flesh that only with the Spirit constantly helping its infirmity through grace is it capable of righteousness" (12.41; *Opera* 3:195–96). Bernard sees human persons as fellow workers with God, cooperators with the Holy Spirit when they are united with God's will by their free consent (13.45). *On Grace and Free Choice*, trans. Daniel O'Donovan, *The Works of Bernard of Clairvaux*, vol. 7, *Treatises, III*, Cistercian Studies 19 (Kalamazoo, MI: Cistercian Publications, 1977), 51–111.

19. The editors of the *Opera Bernardi* note that this citation is part of an addition made c. 1180–90 (8:324).

20. *Vita sancti Malachiae* (*Opera* 3:295–378). English translation, *Bernard of Clairvaux: The Life and Death of Saint Malachy the Irishman*, trans. Robert T. Meyer (Kalamazoo, MI: Cistercian Publications, 1978). Hagiography is the name given to accounts of saints' lives in the

form of highly idealized and structured renderings of the individual's holiness. These texts often follow a predetermined pattern. For example, throughout the *Life of Malachy* Bernard places Malachy in a number of settings from the life of Christ in order to represent the saint as one who followed closely in the footsteps of Jesus. The aim of hagiography is not to render a historically accurate account but to inspire readers to imitate the saints' virtues, and in many cases the accounts were written with an eye to supporting the saint's canonization. Maedoc O'Morgair took the name Malachy when he was ordained five years in advance of the accepted age because the bishop wanted him as his vicar. Malachy went on to an illustrious career, was made bishop of Connor at age thirty, and brought order and renewal to the Irish church. On a trip to Rome in 1140, he stopped at Clairvaux, where he met Bernard. The visit made such an impression on him that when he got to Rome, he petitioned Innocent II to be relieved of his responsibilities so that he could become a monk. On a later trip, to meet with Eugenius III in 1148, Malachy again stopped at Clairvaux, where he became ill and died on November 2, surrounded by Bernard's community. In addition to Bernard's *Life of Malachy*, we have the sermons Bernard preached at his funeral and on the occasion of the first anniversary of his death.

21. There are more than one hundred manuscripts of Bernard's letters with a core of 310 letters. These can be found in volumes 7 and 8 of the *Opera*. The most frequent occurrence of references to the Spirit in a single letter (c. 1140) concerns a discussion of the feast of the Immaculate Conception of Mary—a feast that Bernard saw as a dangerous innovation. Bernard refers to the Spirit's activity in John the Baptist, Mary, and in Jesus (Luke 1:35). He maintained that Mary conceived *by* the Holy Spirit but was not herself conceived by the Spirit—a distinction, he said, that belongs to Jesus alone (*Letter* 174; *Opera* 7:388–92). Rarely does Bernard call on the Spirit for help. In one example in which he does, Bernard writes to King Louis of France in 1143, to complain of the king's warring behaviors. In what appears to be an intractable situation, Bernard does not despair because the Spirit, who smites the king's conscience, will come to their aid (*Letter* 226; *Opera* 8:96).

22. Most of the time, Bernard uses the term *spiritus* with an accompanying adjective to describe a human quality or disposition: *vitali spiritu, accediae spiritu, spiritu judicii, spiritu ardoris, spiritu sapientiae, spiritu de pace, spiritu fervens, spiritu ambulare, spiritu timoris, spiritu vehementi, inebriatio spiritus, turbulenti spiritus, reformatione spiritus,* and so on. Bernard often employs the phrase *unus spiritus* to refer to the unity and harmony of monastic life and the church.

23. The Song of Songs was very popular in the medieval period—commentaries on this text outnumbered those on any other book of the Bible.

24. See Thomas F. Ryan, "Sex, Spirituality, and Pre-Modern Readings of the Song of Songs," *Horizons* 28, no. 1 (2001): 86.

25. *On Loving God*, 35 (*Opera* 3:149), trans. Robert Walton, in *Bernard of Clairvaux, Treatises II*, Cistercian Fathers 13 (Kalamazoo: Mich.: Cistercian Publications, 1980), 127.

26. *Second Sermon for Pentecost*, 6 (*Opera* 5:169). English translation, *St. Bernard's Sermons for the Seasons and Principal Festivals of the Year*, translated by a priest of Mount Melleray, 3 vols. (Westminster, MD: Carroll, 1950), 2:287–88.

27. *Sermones de diversis* 88.1 (*Opera* 6:333–34).

28. Ibid. Bernard refers here to Augustine's analogy between the various human faculties (memory, intellect, and will) and the persons of the Trinity. In his analysis of the Holy Spirit as the kiss—kisser/kissed/kiss—Bernard reworks another of Augustine's triads: God lover/beloved/love.

29. *The Steps of Humility and Pride* 3.6 (*Opera* 3:20–21), trans. M. Ambrose Conway, *Treatises II*, Cistercian Fathers 13 (Kalamazoo, MI: Cistercian Publications, 1980), 34. Basil Pennington schematizes this threefold structure in his introduction to this volume (p. 11). See also Elizabeth Connor, "Saint Bernard's Three Steps of Truth and Saint Aelred of Rievaulx's Three Loves," in *Bernardus Magister*, ed. Sommerfeldt, 227–28.

30. *The Steps of Humility and Pride* 6.19–7.20 (*Opera* 3:30–31).

31. Ibid.

32. See Dante Alighieri, *The Divine Comedy*, vol. 3, *Paradise*, Cantos XXXI–XXXIII (Baltimore and New York: Penguin Books, 1975), 327–49.

33. Bill East and Jim Bugslag on the listserv Medieval Scholarly Discussion of Medieval Religious Culture. See also Thomas Austin, *Two Fifteenth-Century Cookery-Books*, Early English Text Society, Original Series no. 91 (1888; reprint, Oxford: Oxford University Press, 1964). Also Cristina Mazzoni, *The Women in God's Kitchen: Cooking, Eating, and Spiritual Writing* (New York: Continuum, 2005).

34. Walter Farrell and Dominic Huges, *Swift Victory: Essays on the Gifts of the Holy Spirit* (New York: Sheed & Ward, 1955), 181, cited in Charles Bouchard, "Recovering the Gifts of the Holy Spirit in Moral Theology," *Theological Studies* 63 (2002): 555.

35. *Fourth Sermon for the Feast of the Ascension* 9 (*Opera* 5:146).

36. *First Sermon for Pentecost* 2–4 (*Opera* 5:161–63).

37. Luke Anderson, "The Rhetorical Epistemology in Saint Bernard's *Super Cantica*," in *Bernardus Magister*, ed. Sommerfeldt, 107.

38. *First Sermon for Pentecost* 5–6 (*Opera* 5:161–63).

39. *Sixth Sermon for the Feast of the Ascension* 2 (*Opera* 5:152).

40. Dennis E. Tamburello, *Bernard of Clairvaux: Essential Writings* (New York: Crossroad, 2000), 107.

41. Pennington, *Saint Bernard of Clairvaux*, 131.

42. The *Vita Prima Bernardi* (henceforth *Vita*) is the oldest account of Bernard's life, compiled by three contemporaries and begun secretly while Bernard was still alive (PL 185:226–466). Geoffrey Webb and Adrian Walker have translated this text, *St. Bernard of Clairvaux* (London: A. R. Mowbray, 1960; Westminster, MD: Newman, 1960). A summary of the textual problems associated with this text can be found in Adriaan H. Bredero, *Bernard of Clairvaux: Between Cult and History* (Grand Rapids: Eerdmans, 1996), 25–29, 288–90. See also *Letter* 320.2 (*Opera* 8:254).

43. See Kilian McDonnell, "Spirit and Experience in Bernard of Clairvaux," *Theological Studies* 58 (1997): 3–18; P. Verdeyen, "Un Théologien de l'Expérience," in *Bernard de Clairvaux: Histoire, Mentalités, Spiritualité*, Sources Chrétiennes 380 (Paris: Éditions du Cerf, 1992), 557–78; G. R. Evans, *The Mind of St. Bernard of Clairvaux* (Oxford: Clarendon, 1983), 141; Ulrich Kopf, *Religiöse Erfahrung in der Theologie Bernhards von Clairvaux* (Tübingen: Mohr Siebeck, 1980); idem, "Die Rolle der Erfahrung im religiösen Leben nach dem heiligen Bernhard," *Analecta Cisterciensia* 46 (1990): 319; Dom Pierre Miquel, *Le vocabulaire latin de l'expérience spirituelle* (Paris: Beauchesne, 1989), 96–106.

44. McDonnell, "Spirit and Experience," 5.

45. Ibid., 6–7, 10.

46. Robson, *'With the Spirit and Power of Elijah,'* 119–20. A popular legend about Bernard found in the *Vita Prima* relates that as a boy, Bernard had a Christmas Eve dream of the Virgin giving birth to the Word-infant. Bernard noted that its vividness made the birth of Christ seem real and present to him a thousand years after the event.

47. In a sermon on the feast of the Ascension Bernard writes, "For at present, what labor it costs us to lift up our hearts! And that because— as each of us may read in the book of his own sad experience—the corruption of the body is a load upon them, and the earthly habitation presses them down" (Wis 9:15). *Sixth Sermon for the Feast of the Ascension* 2 (*Opera* 5:152). Visible in this citation are the heaviness and problematic nature of the body seen as an obstacle to the full realization of the spiritual life. In his theological treatise *On Grace and Free Will*, Bernard dis-

cusses at some length Paul's discussion of the tension between the human inclination to sin and the life of the Spirit in Romans 5–8. See Leclercq, *Bernard of Clairvaux*, 21.

48. *In Praise of the New Knighthood* 11.24 (*Opera* 3:233–34), trans. Conrad Greenia, in *The Works of Bernard of Clairvaux*, vol. 7, *Treatises III*, Cistercian Studies 19 (Kalamazoo, MI: Cistercian Publications, 1977), 158–59.

49. Leclercq, *Bernard of Clairvaux*, 30.

50. *Sermon for the Feast of Sts. Peter and Paul* (*Opera* 5:189–90).

51. Themes of confidence, optimism, and hope are especially prominent in the last volume of *Sermons on the Song of Songs* (Sermons 67.6; 68.4, 7; 69.1, 6–8; 70.4; 72.1; 74.4; 76.6).

52. In *Sermons on the Song of Songs*, Bernard cites the verse: "But he who is united to the Lord becomes one spirit with him" (1 Cor 6:17) fifty-four times—more than any other biblical verse.

53. *Sermones de diversis* 88.1 (*Opera* 6:333–34).

54. Andrew Louth, "Bernard and Affective Mysticism," in *The Influence of Saint Bernard*, ed. Sister Benedicta Ward, SLG (Fairacres, Oxford: SLG Press, 1976), 6.

55. Bernard cites Psalm 138:21: "Lord, do I not hate those who hate you, and loathe those who defy you?" as the lone exception to the otherwise universal love demanded by charity.

56. *The Steps of Humility and Pride* 3.6 (*Opera* 3:20–21).

57. *First Sermon for Pentecost* 1 (*Opera* 5:161).

58. It may be helpful to remind readers of two factors relevant to the use of erotic love language to describe the spiritual life. Courtly love literature was popular, inspiring even ordinary, educated people to write love poetry. Second, in the twelfth century a greater number of men entered monasteries later in life after having married and reared children. This change was an effort to correct the custom of enrolling children in monastic life at a very young age—with all of the problems attendant on this practice, especially the lack of freedom. The important point for our purposes is that many monks would have experienced physical as well as spiritual love, although Bernard himself was never married.

59. The Latin reads *Istiusmodi canticum sola unctio docet, sola addiscit experientia*. In *Sermons on the Song of Songs*, Bernard focuses especially on the Spirit in Sermons 8, 17, and 18. In this section on the Holy Spirit as "kiss," all references in parentheses are to *Sermons on the Song of Songs*, trans. Walsh (see n. 4 above).

60. Mention of the Spirit decreases toward the end of *Sermons on the Song of Songs*. In volume 4 of Walsh's translation, which covers ser-

mons 67–86, the term *Spirit* appears only twenty-five times, usually in contexts that lack significant theological import.

61. See Mark S. Burrows, "Foundations for an Erotic Christology: Bernard of Clairvaux on Jesus as 'Tender Lover,'" *Anglican Theological Review* 80, no. 4 (1998): 477–93.

62. *Sermones de diversis* 89.1 (*Opera* 6:335).

63. Ibid., 89.2 (*Opera* 6:336).

64. Ibid.

65. In *Sermons on the Song of Songs*, Bernard cites John 4:24: "God is spirit" eighteen times; he cites 1 John 4:8, "God is love" twelve times. Noted in Roch Kereszty, "'Bride' and 'Mother' in the *Super Cantica* of St. Bernard: An Ecclesiology for our Time?" *Communio* 20 (Summer 1993): 430.

66. *In Praise of the New Knighthood*, in *Works of Bernard of Clairvaux*, 7:158–59.

67. The traditional three stages of the spiritual life (purgation, illumination, and perfection) were traditionally associated with certain books of the Bible: Ecclesiastes for beginners; Proverbs for the advanced; and the Song of Songs for the perfect. Bernard refers to these books as loaves of bread, another example of his use of the metaphor of "eating" the Word of God in order to become holy (SC 1.4; see 1 Cor 3:1–2; Heb 5:12–14).

68. In *Sermons on the Song of* Songs, Bernard cites Galatians 5:17 twenty-three times: "For the desires of the flesh are against the Spirit and the desires of the Spirit are against the flesh; for these are opposed to each other; to prevent you from doing what you would." Cited in McDonnell, "Spirit and Experience," 8.

69. The choice to render the *s* of *spiritus* with upper- or lowercase is often left to the translator's discretion to give what she or he senses is the best rendering of Bernard's meaning.

70. In *Sermons on the Song of Songs*, Bernard cites 2 Cor 3:18 forty times: "And we all, with unveiled face, beholding the glory of the Lord, are being changed into his likeness from one degree of glory to another; for this comes from the Lord who is the Spirit." Cited in McDonnell, "Spirit and Experience," 10.

71. Catharism appeared in southern France between 1012 and 1020. The term likely originated from the Greek, *katharoi*, which means "pure ones." Their outlook on the world was deeply dualistic. They held that the spark of divine light in each person was held captive by darkness/material reality, which had been created by a demiurge called Satan, not the "True God." The Cathars proclaimed that the God worshiped by orthodox Christianity was an imposter, the church a corrupt abomination because of its associations with the material realm. They rejected the

sacraments, embraced a strict asceticism, advocated celibacy even within marriage, and minimized Christ's humanity. Several Cathars were executed in Toulouse in 1022. In 1147, Pope Eugenius III sent Bernard of Clairvaux to combat this movement, but it was too strongly entrenched to be easily eradicated.

72. See Mark S. Burrows, "Hunters, Hounds, and Allegorical Readers: The Body of the Text and the Text of the Body in Bernard of Clarivaux's *Sermons on the Song of Songs,*" *Studies in Spirituality* 14 (2004): 113–37.

73. *Homily on the Anniversary of the Death of Saint Malachy* 3 (*Opera* 5:419).

74. Leclercq, *Bernard of Clairvaux*, 38.

75. *Letter* 2.5; *Opera* 7:15; see also *Letter* 107.3; *Opera* 7:269.

76. Marsha L. Dutton, "The Face and the Feet of God: The Humanity of Christ in Bernard of Clairvaux and Aelred of Rievaulx." In *Bernardus Magister*, ed. Sommerfeldt, 205.

77. Michael Casey, *Athirst for God: Spiritual Desire in Bernard of Clairvaux's Sermons on the Song of Songs*, Cistercian Studies 77 (Kalamazoo, MI: Cistercian Publications, 1988), 204–5, citing P. Delfgaauw, "An Approach to St. Bernard's Sermons on the Song of Songs," Collectanea Ordinis Cisterciensium Reformatorum (COCR) #23 (1961): 148–61.

78. *Third Sermon for the Feast of the Ascension* 2 (*Opera* 5:132); see also *Sixth Sermon for the Feast of the Ascension* 12 (*Opera* 5:157).

79. See Cuthbert Butler, *Western Mysticism* (London: Constable, 1922), 118; Jean Leclercq, *Bernard of Clairvaux and the Cistercian Spirit*, trans. Claire Lavoie, Cistercian Studies 16 (Kalamazoo, MI: Cistercian Publications, 1976), 81–83; Gilson, *Mystical Theology of Saint Bernard*, 79.

80. *Third Sermon for the Feast of the Ascension* 8 (*Opera* 5:136).

81. *Sixth Sermon for the Feast of the Ascension* 13 (*Opera* 5:157).

82. Ibid., 14 (*Opera* 5:158).

83. Robson, '*With the Spirit and Power of Elijah,*' 161–62.

84. Pseudo-Dionysius is the "pen name" for an unknown Neoplatonic author of the late fifth century (possibly a Syrian priest). The name led subsequent readers of this text to identify him as the companion of Paul mentioned in the New Testament (Acts 17:34). Because of this misunderstanding, his work was highly revered in the Middle Ages. Two of his works, *The Celestial Hierarchy* and *The Ecclesiastical Hierarchy*, were very influential in medieval thought.

85. *Third Sermon for Pentecost* 8 (*Opera* 5:176).

86. See Conrad Rudolf, *Violence and Daily Life: Reading, Art and Polemics in the Cîteaux Moralia in Iob* (Princeton: Princeton University Press, 1997).

87. See also *Letter* 336 (*Opera* 8:275), in which Bernard accuses Abelard of preparing the way for the Antichrist by clinging to his false doctrine of the Trinity.

88. See Roch Kereszty, "The Significance of St. Bernard's Thought for Contemporary Theology," *Communio* 18 (Winter 1991): 574–89. Kereszty discusses six themes: process and feminist theologies; the universality of salvation in Christ; alienation from ourselves; the charismatic movement; and the theology of the body.

89. *Homily on the Anniversary of the Death of Saint Malachy* 8 (*Opera* 5:423).

90. A sampling of the abundant literature on this topic includes Paul Avis, *Eros and the Sacred* (London: SPCK, 1989); Sidney Callahan, "The Role of the Emotions in Moral Decision Making," *Hastings Center Report* (June/July 1988): 9–16; Rita N. Brock, *Journeys By Heart: A Christology of Erotic Power* (New York: Crossroad, 1988); Paula Cooey et al., *Embodied Love: Sensuality and Relationship as Feminist Values* (San Francisco: HarperCollins, 1988); Elizabeth Dreyer, *Passionate Spirituality: Hildegard of Bingen and Hadewijch of Brabant* (New York and Mahwah, NJ: Paulist, 2005); Carter Heyward, *Touching Our Strength: The Erotic Power and the Love of God* (San Francisco: Harper & Row, 1989); Alexander Irwin, *Eros Toward the World: Paul Tillich and the Theology of the Erotic* (Minneapolis: Fortress, 1991); E. Ann Matter, Discourses of Desire: Sexuality and Christian's Women's Visionary Narratives," *Journal of Homosexuality* 18 (1990): 119–31; Sallie McFague, *Models of God* (Philadelphia: Fortress, 1987); Bernard McGinn, "The Language of Love in Jewish and Christian Mysticism," in *Mysticism and Language*, ed. Steven Katz (London: Oxford University Press, 1990); idem, "Love, Knowledge and Mystical Union in the Western Christian Tradition," in *Mystical Union and Monotheistic Faith*, ed. M. Idel and B. McGinn (New York: Macmillan, 1989); Martha Nussbaum, *The Therapy of Desire* (Princeton: Princeton University Press, 1996); Catherine Osborne, *Eros Unveiled: Plato and the God of Love* (Oxford: Oxford University Press, 1995); Octavio Paz, *The Double Flame: Love and Eroticism* (New York: Harcourt Brace, 1995); Robert M. Polhemus, *Erotic Faith: Being in Love from Jane Austen to D.H. Lawrence* (Chicago: University of Chicago Press, 1990); Blair Reynolds with Patricia Heinicke, Jr., *The Naked Being of God: Making Sense of Love Mysticism* (Lanham, MD: University Press of America, 2000); Richard Rohr, "Pure Passion: The Holiness of Sexuality," *Sojourners* 11 (1982): 14–18; Joan Timmerman, *Sexuality and Spiritual Growth* (New York: Crossroad, 1993).

91. Jean Leclercq, *A Second Look at Bernard Of Clairvaux*, Cistercian Studies 105 (Kalamazoo, MI: Cistercian Publications, 1990), 94.

92. See Bredero, *Bernard of Clairvaux: Between Cult and History*, 14.
93. *Third Sermon for Pentecost*, 1 (*Opera* 5:171).

Chapter 5: Bonaventure of Bagnoregio
The Spirit of Divine Abundance

1. Bonaventure, *Major Life of Francis* (*Legenda maior*), Prol., 3. All references to Bonaventure's work (*Sancti Bonaventurae Opera Omnia*, 9 vols. [Quarrache: Collegium S. Bonaventurae, 1882–1902]) will use the following abbreviations: *Commentary on the Sentences* (*1–4 Sent.*); *The Reduction of the Arts to Theology/De reductione artium ad theologiam* (*De Reduc.*); *Major Life of Francis/Legenda maior* (*LM*); *Journey of the Soul Into God/Itinerarium mentis in deum* (*Itin.*); *A Brief Summary of True Theology/Breviloquium* (*Brev.*); *Collationes on the Six Days/Collationes in Hexaemeron* (*Hex.*); *Collations on the Seven Gifts of the Holy Spirit/Collationes de Septem donis Spiritus Sancti* (*Septem donis*); *The Triple Way/De Triplici Via* (*DTV*). Sermon translations from *Bonaventure: Rooted in Faith* (*RF*), trans. Marigwen Schumacher (Chicago: Franciscan Herald Press, 1974).

2. Frederick II negotiated control of Jerusalem in 1229, only to have it reconquered in 1244. The saintly Louis IX of France was taken prisoner in Egypt while leading a crusade from 1248 to 1254, and died in a second sortie in 1270. At century's close in 1291, Acre in Syria, the last foothold in the East, was lost to the Muslims.

3. In 1231 Gregory IX issued the bull *Excommunicamus* condemning heretics and established commissions of inquisition to be run by Dominican friars.

4. The Fourth Lateran Council in 1215 was the largest ecumenical gathering in the history of the church, with over four hundred bishops and eight hundred abbots and other clergy in attendance. The council was dominated by Innocent III's concerns about the Crusades and church reform. It was also at this council that Jews were required to wear special self-identifying garb, in part to guard against interfaith marriages.

5. An example is the Christmas crèche. Although Francis did not initiate this custom, he dramatized this piety in ways that became embedded in the community and eventually spread across the world.

6. C. Colt Anderson, *A Call to Piety: Saint Bonaventure's Collations on the Six Days* (Quincy, IL: Franciscan Press, 2002), 38.

7. In 1250, only twenty-four years after the death of Francis, there were over thirty thousand Franciscans.

8. The seriousness of the conflict between the Franciscans and the bishops is evidenced in the decision to call a special meeting prior to the Council of Lyons in 1274 in order to identify strategies to mollify bishops hostile to the order.

9. St. Francis of Assisi, "The Later Rule," in *Francis of Assisi: Early Documents*, vol. 1, ed. Regis J. Armstrong et al. (New York: New City Press, 1999), 100, cited in Anderson, *Call to Piety*, 35. At the Chapter meeting in 1266, Bonaventure responded to criticism that he had let the order slip into laxity by protesting that "there was no time since he became minister general when he would not have consented to be ground to dust if it would help the Order to reach the purity of St. Francis and his companions." David Burr, *Olivi and Franciscan Poverty: The Origin of the Usus Pauper Controversy* (Philadelphia: University of Pennsylvania Press, 1989), 78, cited in Anderson, *Call to Piety*, 36.

10. Anderson, *Call to Piety*, 7ff. John of Parma had been Minister General since 1247. Although he was admired for his personal and administrative gifts, he resigned in February of 1257 at the prompting of Pope Alexander IV because of his Spiritualist sympathies. Anderson labels Parma a "Moderate Joachite."

11. "Joachim of Flora," *Catholic Encyclopedia* online at http://www.newadvent.org. On apocalyptic movements, see David Burr, "Bonaventure, Olivi and Franciscan Eschatology," *Collectanea Franciscana* 53 (1983): 23–40; idem, "Franciscan Exegesis and Francis as Apocalyptic Figure," in *Monks, Nuns, and Friars in Medieval Society* (Sewanee, TN: 1989), 51–62; Bernard McGinn, "The Abbot and the Doctors: Scholastic Reactions to the Radical Eschatology of Joachim of Fiore," *Church History* 40 (1971): 30–47; Joseph Ratzinger, *The Theology of History in St. Bonaventure* (Chicago: Franciscan Herald Press, 1971), 104–8; 117–18.

12. Anderson, *Call to Piety*, 7.

13. See Marjorie Reeves, *Joachim of Fiore and the Prophetic Future* (New York: Harper & Row, 1976), 36–37; idem, *The Influence of Prophecy in the Later Middle Ages: A Study in Joachimism* (Oxford, 1969; Notre Dame, IN: University of Notre Dame Press, 1993); Bernard McGinn, *Visions of the End: Apocalyptic Traditions in the Middle Ages* (New York: Columbia University Press, 1979); idem, *Apocalyptic Spirituality* (New York: Paulist, 1979); idem, *The Calabrian Abbot: Joachim of Fiore in the History of Western Thought* (New York: Macmillan, 1985); Richard K. Emmerson and Bernard McGinn, eds., *The Apocalypse in the Middle Ages* (Ithaca and London: Cornell University Press, 1992); Malcolm Lambert, *Medieval Heresy: Popular Movements from the Gregorian Reform to the Reformation* (Oxford: Basil Blackwell, 1992), 189–214.

14. There were other conflicts involving the Holy Spirit. Gerard of Borgo San Donnino was a Sicilian Franciscan whose *Introductorius in Evangelium Aeternum* had been condemned by Alexander IV in 1255. In the Protocols of Anagni in 1255, Innocent charged San Donnino with heresy for interpreting scriptures according to senses not demanded by the Holy Spirit. This pronouncement naturally raised questions for exegetes of the twelfth and thirteenth centuries about how you know if your interpretation conforms to the Spirit's inspiration or not. Robert Lerner, "Ecstatic Dissent," *Speculum* 67 (1992): 33–57, cited in Anderson, *Call to Piety*, 123. In *Collationes on the Six Days* (12.17), Bonaventure turns to the Spirit as author of the scriptures to defend the legitimacy of multiple interpretations of biblical texts (Anderson, *Call to Piety*, 126).

15. *The Major Life of Francis* (*Opera* 8:504–49); *The Minor Life of Francis* (*Opera* 8:577–79); *Collationes on the Six Days* 16.16 (*Opera* 5:405). See also "The *Legenda Maior*: Bonaventure's Apocalyptic Francis," in *The Apocalyptic Imagination in Medieval Literature* by Richard K. Emmerson and Ronald B. Herzman (Philadelphia: University of Pennsylvania Press, 1992), 36–75; and S. Bihel, "S. Franciscus fuitne Angelus Sexti Sigilli?" *Antonianum* 2 (1927): 57–90.

16. *Hex.* 15.9, 20 (*Opera* 5:399, 401).

17. *Hex.* 1.6–9 (*Opera* 5:330). For Bonaventure, one negative eschatological sign was the presence of Aristotelian errors in theology. "False theologians and true spiritual men will be the opposed signs of the dawning age for the seraphic doctor." McGinn, "Abbot and the Doctors," 45.

18. Anderson, *Call to Piety*, 26, 44–47, 61, 72, passim.

19. Ibid., 39.

20. Ibid.

21. Ilia Delio, *Simply Bonaventure: An Introduction to His Life, Thought, and Writings* (New York: New City Press, 2001), 175–77.

22. These works include *Collations on the Ten Commandments* (*Collationes de decem preceptis*), *Defense of the Mendicants* (*Apologia Pauperum*), and *Collations on the Six Days* (*Collationes in Hexaemeron*).

23. *Commentary on John* 16.25 (*Opera* 7:461).

24. Zachary Hayes, trans., *Disputed Questions on the Mystery of the Trinity*, vol. 3 of *Works of Saint Bonaventure* (St. Bonaventure, NY: Franciscan Institute, 1979), 28. Bonaventure makes an exception to this tendency when he discusses whether the Son would have become incarnate if there had been no sin. To answer yes would provide a richness for piety, but he chooses to answer no because of his sense of God's

transcendence. He thinks the pious arguments might confine God or bring God within the sphere of this universe, so he rejects them.

25. See Optatus van Asseldonk, "The Spirit of the Lord and Its Holy Activity in the Writings of Francis," trans. Edward Hagman, *Greyfriars Review* 5, no. 1 (1991): 106; originally published in *Laurentianum* 23 (1982): 133–95.

26. *Hex.* 12.17 (*Opera* 5:387).

27. *Septem donis* 4.13 (*Opera* 5:476). In *Semiotics and the Philosophy of Language* (Bloomington: University of Indiana Press, 1984), 150, Umberto Eco cites Gilbert of Stanford (fl. c. 1200), who does not explicitly mention the Holy Spirit but speaks of the multiple meanings of scripture in terms of a flowing river: "Imitating the action of the swiftest of rivers, Holy Scripture fills up the depths of the human mind and yet always overflows, quenches the thirsty and yet remains inexhaustible. Bountiful streams of spiritual sense gush out from it and, merging into others, make still others spring up—or rather (since 'wisdom is undying'), they do not merge but *emerge* and, showing their beauty to others, cause these others not to replace them as they fail but to succeed them as they remain" (*In Cant.* 20.225).

28. Marigwen Schumacher, "Mysticism in Metaphor," in *S. Bonaventura 1274–1974* (Grottaferrata [Rome]: Collegio San Bonaventura, 1973), 2:361–86.

29. Ibid., 366. See *Dictionnaire de Spiritualité* (Paris: Beauchesne, 1936–), vol. 1, col. 1842.

30. Schumacher, "Mysticism in Metaphor," 362.

31. Ibid., p. 365. Schumacher goes on to link Bonaventure's poetic and harmonious expression to the joy of Francis, the wandering troubadour of mystic rapture. Francis was clearly endowed with what some have called "enthusiasm"—Bonaventure often used the term *fervor*—a gift Bonaventure admired, possessed, and in his own literary-mystical way, expressed. Schumacher describes it as the gift of being God-inspired, touched, attuned, gifted with that rare ability to "see" the direct equation between the divine and the human and express it in words both powerfully taut and simply clear.

32. Ilia Delio, "Bonaventure and Bernard: On Human Image and Mystical Union," *Cistercian Studies Quarterly* 34, no. 2 (December 1999): 251–63.

33. I am indebted in this section to Zachary Hayes's introduction to his translation of Bonaventure's *Disputed Questions on the Mystery of the Trinity.* Bonaventure also treats the Holy Spirit in *1 Sent.* dist. 10–18 (*Opera* 1:194–335).

34. Delio, *Simply Bonaventure*, 40.

35. An anonymous author, possibly a Syrian priest writing about 500 signed his name Dionysius, leading subsequent theologians to believe that he was the Dionysius mentioned by Paul in Acts 17:34. As a result, his thought greatly influenced medieval theology.

36. Richard of St. Victor, a Scottish-born theologian, was prior of the monastery of St. Victor in Paris from 1162 until his death in 1173. He wrote two treatises on the stages of the contemplative life entitled *Benjamin major* and *Benjamin minor*. These works have been translated by Grover A. Zinn as *The Mystical Ark* and *The Twelve Patriarchs* (New York and Mahwah, NJ: Paulist, 1979).

37. Bonaventure uses the phrase *bonum diffusivum sui* 240 times; 140 of them in the *Sentences*.

38. Hayes, *Disputed Questions on the Mystery of the Trinity*, 41.

39. See John F. Quinn, "The Role of the Holy Spirit in St. Bonaventure's Theology," *Franciscan Studies* 33 (1973): 275–76.

40. Hayes, *Disputed Questions on the Mystery of the Trinity*, 32.

41. *1 Sent.* d. 1, a. 3, q. 2, fund. 3 (*Opera* 1:40); *4 Sent.* d. 49, p.1, a.1, q.1, fund. 1 (*Opera* 4:1000); see also *Brev.* 5.1.3 and 7.7.3 (*Opera* 5:252, 289).

42. *1 Sent.* d. 2, q. 4 (*Opera* 1:56–58) and *Brev.* 1.3 (*Opera* 5:211–12).

43. *1 Sent.* d. 10, a. 1, q. 2 (*Opera* 1:197–98). Walter Principe notes that theologians of the twelfth and thirteenth centuries placed the idea of the Spirit as mutual bond of the Father and the Son at the center of their theologies of the Holy Spirit. "St. Bonaventure's Theology of the Holy Spirit With Reference to the Expression *Pater et Filius Diligunt se Spiritu Sancto*," in *S. Bonaventura 1274–1974*, 5 vols. (Grottaferrata [Rome]: Collegio San Bonaventura, 1974), 4:243–69.

44. *1 Sent.* d. 11, q. 1 (*Opera* 1:209–13).

45. *1 Sent.* d. 15, p. 1, q. 3 (*Opera* 1:262–63) and *Brev.* 1.5 (*Opera* 5:213–14).

46. *1 Sent.* d. 6, a.u., q. 2, resp (*Opera* 1:128).

47. Hayes, *Disputed Questions on the Mystery of the Trinity*, 59.

48. Ibid., 66.

49. Anderson, *Call to Piety*, 166.

50. *Second Sermon for Pentecost* (*Opera* 9:333–34); henceforth *Pent. I, II, III*, etc.

51. *Pent. I* (*Opera* 9:332); *Sermon on the Trinity* (*Opera* 9:354).

52. *Pent. I* (*Opera* 9:331): "Et haec tria [infallibilis veritas, liberalis caritas, insuperabilis potestas] sunt necessaria ad salutem omni conditione, sexui et aetati."

53. *Hex.* 2.1 (*Opera* 5:336), cited in Anderson, *Call to Piety*, 92.

54. *Pent. I* (*Opera* 9:332): "Quia Apostoli non extollebantur in superbiam, licet essent positi rectores totius orbis a Spiritu sancto."

55. *Pent. IX* (*Opera* 9:345).

56. *Pent. I* (*Opera* 9:331–32). In *Pent. X*, Bonaventure applies the gifts of the Spirit (Joel 2:28) in a particular fashion to the gift of preaching (*Opera* 9:345–46).

57. In this text, Bonaventure creates a schema in which each of the gifts corresponds to a virtue in the Beatitudes, to a vice, and to the seven petitions of the Lord's Prayer.

58. *3 Sent.* d. 34, p. 1, a. 1, q. 3, concl (*Opera* 3:746a).

59. *DTV* 1.13 (*Opera* 8:6).

60. *Hex.* 22.38 (*Opera* 5:443a).

61. *Septem donis* 1.7 (*Opera* 5:458).

62. Ibid., 3.9–12 (*Opera* 5:470–71).

63. Ibid., 3.13 (*Opera* 5:471).

64. Ibid., 5.8 (*Opera* 5:481).

65. Ibid., 7.16–19 (*Opera* 5:492–93).

66. Anderson, *Call to Piety*, 44–48.

67. *Septem donis* 9.3, 5, 10, 15 (*Opera* 5:499–502).

68. *Pent. VIII* (*Opera* 9:337, 339).

69. *Pent. VI* (*Opera* 9:337).

70. *LM*, Prologue (*Opera* 8:504–5).

71. Ibid., 1.2; 2.1; 3.2, 10; 4.10–11; 9.2; 11.14; 12.1, 7, 12 (*Opera* 8:506–8, 510, 512, 515–16, 530, 538–40, 542).

72. *Pent. VII* (*Opera* 9:338).

73. Ibid. (*Opera* 9:339).

74. *Itin.* 7.4, 5 (*Opera* 5:312–13); see also *DTV* 3.4.6 (*Opera* 8:14).

75. *Sermon on the Trinity* (*Opera* 9:351–57) and *Sermon on the Triple Witness of the Most Holy Trinity* (*Opera* 5:535–38).

76. Discussions of God's liberality can be found throughout Bonaventure's works, e.g., *Hex.* 3.19; 14.28 (*Opera* 5:346, 397); and *Brev.* 4.3.4; 5.2.2 (*Opera* 5:243, 253). Emphasis on God's overflowing goodness is also evident in the medieval emphasis on the gifts of the Spirit. William Hill notes that medieval theology of the Spirit was elaborated largely in terms of Paul's "gifts of the Spirit" (1 Cor 1:7), which point back to the gifts of Isaiah 11:2–3. The gifts were understood as concrete and specific examples of what Aquinas described as the more general grace of the Holy Spirit at the heart of the New Law. *The Three-Personed God: The Trinity as a Mystery of Salvation* (Washington, DC: Catholic University of America Press, 1982), 303. One example of this theology of the gifts can be found in Aquinas's "Explanation of the Lord's Prayer," in which he links the forgiveness of trespasses explicitly with the Spirit's gift of coun-

sel. *The Catechetical Instructions of St. Thomas Aquinas*, trans. J. B. Collins (New York: Joseph F. Wagner, 1939), 159.

77. Zachary Hayes captures this aspect of Bonaventure's conception of creation: "Flowing from that fountain as something willed and loved by God is the immense river of creation. The world of nature is a vast expression of a loving will. Such a world is not one-dimensional, but like water, it has many qualities and dimensions. Like the water of the ocean, the world has an overwhelming fullness as it flows from the depths of God...the river of creation circles back on its place of origin....Created existence, therefore, is a dynamic reality, directed in its inner core to a fulfillment and completion which is to be the mysterious fruit of its history." *The Hidden Center: Spirituality and Speculative Christology in St. Bonaventure* (New York: Paulist, 1981), 13.

78. *Hex.* 17.5 (*Opera* 5:410).

79. This reading of God's generosity is also visible in the Protestant theologies of Luther and Calvin. In his *Large Catechism*, Luther called God "an eternal fountain overflowing with sheer goodness; from him pours forth all that is good and is called good." See Brian A. Gerrish, *Grace and Gratitude: The Eucharistic Theology of John Calvin* (Minneapolis: Fortress, 1993), 31. For a historical survey of the development of the theme of plenitude in Western thought, see Arthur O. Lovejoy, *The Great Chain of Being* (Cambridge, MA: Harvard University Press, 1964).

80. In Jean-François Bonnefoy's analysis of Bonaventure's treatment of the gift of piety, the cross figures prominently. Bonaventure counsels novices to meditate always on the passion (*Regula novitiorum* 7.1–2 [*Opera* 8:483]). His response to a request for a letter of edification from the abbess of a monastery in Longchamp takes the form of a little treatise on Christian perfection in which one of the eight chapters is dedicated to the cross (*DPV* 6 [*Opera* 8:120ff.]). Bonaventure also recounts a personal story in which thoughts of the cross saved him from the devil's attacks (*Sermo II de Donis, XIII post Pent.* 1 [*Opera* 9:404]). Bonnefoy, *Le Saint-Esprit et ses dons selon Saint Bonaventure* (Paris: Librairie Philosophique J. Vrin, 1929), 150.

81. *Brev.* 3.1–11 (*Opera* 5:231–41).

82. In a sermon on the transfiguration preached in Paris on the Second Sunday of Lent in 1251, Bonaventure speaks of how mountains share generously by pouring the rain they receive onto the plains. Contemplatives should be "beacons of rain—fresh reflections or irrigation ditches for showers, or even dew-drops of charismatic gifts on Mount Sion to give to others through the word of witness and the model of dialogue" (*Opera* 9:217b).

83. *Pent.* IX (*Opera* 9:342).

84. *Pent.* X (*Opera* 9:345).

85. *Brev.* 1.1.9; 1.6.1; 5.1.4; 5.5.1 (*Opera* 5:210, 214, 252, 257).

86. Mechthild of Magdeburg, *The Flowing Light of the Godhead* (New York and Mahwah, NJ: Paulist, 1998), 2.6. Mechthild also links the metaphor of flowing liquids with the abundance of God's love. She speaks of the flood of love (5.31); the flowing fire of God's love (5.1); the great overflow of God's love that in its abundance and sweetness causes our small vessel to brim over (7.55); the playful flow of love flows in the Trinity, which love she desires to have released into her soul (3.1; 7.45). Oliver Davies comments, "The bewildering fertility of Mechthild's conception of the theme of 'flowing'…finds its centre in her understanding of the Christian Trinity. It is this which is the conceptual basis which underlies the unifying image of 'flowing' and which serves to unite the disparate themes of cosmic creation, Mechthild's own literary creation, the outflow of grace and God's gifts, as well as the soul's ecstatic *reditus* to God into a single integral vision of the dynamic fecundity of the Godhead….The Trinitarian dimension can be seen also in the fact that she frequently links the language of flowing with the Third Person, and also uses this term in order to speak of the generation of the Son from the Father." "Transformational Processes in the Work of Julian of Norwich and Mechthild of Magdeburg," in *The Medieval Mystical Tradition in England*, ed. Marion Glasscoe, Exeter Symposium 5 (Suffolk: D. S. Brewer, 1992), 49.

87. *Pent. II* (*Opera* 9:333).

88. Ibid. (*Opera* 9:335): "*quantum ad modum emanandi per nomen fluvii scaturientis, qui est ipse Spiritus.*" Speaking of the church: "*quantam ad receptaculum emanati per irrigationem paradisi, qui est ipse ecclesiasticus coetus.*" Water imagery is also prevalent in the more christological eighth sermon for Pentecost, in which Bonaventure offers the metaphorical similitude: "By 'living waters' is meant the Holy Spirit." This is so because of the properties of living water. It is living in its source (the Holy Spirit proceeds from Father and Son; Apoc 22:1 and John 5:26); in its continual flowing (the church is like a watered garden that will not fail because of the influence of the Holy Spirit in her sacraments and members; Isa 58:11 and Ps 45:4); and in the excellence of its effects (the twelve fruits of the Holy Spirit; Apoc 22:2 and Gal 5:22 and Ps 1:3) (*Opera* 9:340).

89. *Pent. VI* (*Opera* 9:337).

90. *Pent. IV* (*Opera* 9:335).

91. *Pent. V* (*Opera* 9:336).

92. Ibid.

93. *Pent. I* (*Opera* 9:330).

94. *Pent. X* (*Opera* 9:346).

95. *Pent. I* (*Opera* 9:330); see also *Pent. X* (*Opera* 9:346).

96. *Hex.* 14.8 (*Opera* 5:395–96).

97. *Pent. I* (*Opera* 9:331).

98. *Pent. IX* (*Opera* 9:345).

99. See also *Pent. IX* (*Opera* 9:342ff.) and *Sermo de trinitate* (*Opera* 9:354).

100. *Pent. VII* (*Opera* 9:339).

101. *Pent. VII* (*Opera* 9:337, 339).

102. *Pent. VIII* (*Opera* 9:340).

103. *Hex.* 18 (*Opera* 5:414–19).

104. *3 Sent.* 27.1.3 (*Opera* 3:597).

105. *Hex.* 18.25, 26 (*Opera* 5:418).

106. Bonnefoy, *Le Saint-Esprit et ses dons*, 89–91.

107. *3 Sent.* 34.1.1.3 (*Opera* 3:742).

108. Fear of the Lord and fortitude are located in the irascible faculty; wisdom and piety, in the concupiscible faculty; understanding, knowledge, and counsel, in the faculty of reason. Bonaventure holds that the gifts and beatitudes, while helpful to all, are not necessary for salvation. The virtues support the active life; the gifts, the contemplative life; and the beatitudes, the perfection of either. The gifts are obligatory for priest and bishop. Bonnefoy, *Le Saint-Esprit et ses dons*, 112–13.

109. Bonaventure speaks of experiential, affective knowledge of God in terms of sensation rather than knowing. The great contemplatives feel rather than know God: "magis sentiunt quam cognoscant" (*3 Sent.* 35, q. 1, ad 5 [*Opera* 3:775]; *Commentary on John* 1.43 [*Opera* 6:256]).

110. *Pent. IX* (*Opera* 9:341).

111. *Sermo de trinitate* (*Opera* 9:353).

112. Francis was known for his gift of insight into the hidden, spiritual meaning of the scriptures, a gift that Bonaventure links with prophecy. See *LM* 2.1; 11.2; 12.12 (*Opera* 8:507–8, 536, 542).

113. *Brev.* 5.6 (*Opera* 5:307). This tradition is traced back to Origen, who transposes the five physical senses onto a spiritual plane to describe the highest reaches of union with God in which the soul not only sees and hears God but also touches and tastes divinity metaphorically. See Karl Rahner, "The Doctrine of the 'Spiritual Senses' in the Middle Ages," in *Theological Investigations*, vol. 16, trans. David Morland (New York: Seabury, 1979), 104–34; and Hans Urs von Balthasar, *Studies in Theological Style: Clerical Styles*, trans. Andrew Louth, Francis McDonagh, and Brian McNeil, vol. 2 of *The Glory of the Lord: A Theological Aesthetics*,

ed. Joseph Fessio and John Riches (San Francisco: Ignatius Press, 1984), 329ff.

114. *DTV* 2.3, 12 (*Opera* 8:11).

115. It is interesting that in the invocation at the beginning of *The Soul's Journey into God*, the Holy Spirit is conspicuously absent. Bonaventure calls upon everyone but the Holy Spirit—the Father of Lights, the Lord Jesus Christ, through the intercession of Mary and the blessed Francis—to ensure that this work would inspire others into the way of peace, that is, contemplative mystical union (*Itin.*, Prol., 1 [*Opera* 5:295]). Since *The Soul's Journey into God* was written in 1259, two years after Bonaventure became Minister General in the midst of controversy over the Spiritualists, he may have been wary of beginning his text with a reference to the Spirit, but if so, this caution seems to have evaporated by the end of the text.

116. *Itin.* 7.4, 5 (*Opera* 5:312–13).

117. Ibid. 7.6 (*Opera* 5:313).

118. Ibid. 7.1 (*Opera* 5:312).

119. *Itin.* Prol., 4 (*Opera* 5:296).

120. *Brev* 7.7.4 (*Opera* 5:288–91): "*quod anima sit plene beata, nisi restituatur ei corpus, ad quod resumendum habet inclinationem naturaliter insertam; nec regiminis ordo sustinet, quod restituatur corpus spiritui beato nisi per omnia illi conforme et subiectum, quantum potest corpus spiritui conformari.*"

121. Ibid. 7.7 (*Opera* 5:290); see also *Pent. I* (*Opera* 9:333).

122. *DTV* 2.8 (*Opera* 8:9).

123. Ilia Delio, *Crucified Love: Bonaventure's Mysticism of the Crucified Christ* (Quincy, IL: Franciscan Press, 1998), 154, 160–61. Delio cites John Lakers, who develops the idea of intimacy as an antidote to a culture focused on power and judgment. In this view, individuals who do not live within the metaphor of intimacy become isolated and unable to engage in a fully human involvement with one another and God. The intimacy Bonaventure suggests at the end of *The Soul's Journey into God* is a clear invitation to imitate a God who is passionately involved in the world in all its joys and sufferings. John J. Lakers, *Christian Ethics: An Ethics of Intimacy* (Quincy, IL: Franciscan Press, 1996), 31.

124. *Pent. I* (*Opera* 9:331).

125. *LM* 8.1 (*Opera* 8:526). Ilia Delio comments on Richard of St. Victor's treatise on the degrees of love, in which he states that at the fourth and highest degree of love, the soul is transformed into a servant, following the humble Christ. At this stage the soul "begins to empty herself, taking the form of a servant" following Christ in his passion; "the soul goes forth on God's behalf and descends below herself...because of

her neighbor." Delio, *Crucified Love*, 66–67, 127; Richard of St. Victor, "Four Degrees of Passionate Charity," in *Selected Writings on Contemplation*, trans. Clare Kirchberger (London: Faber & Faber, 1957), 230.

126. *Sermo de trinitate* (*Opera* 9:353; *RF*, 64).

127. Ibid. (*RF*, 67).

128. *Septem donis* 1.15 (*Opera* 5:460–61).

129. Delio, *Crucified Love*, xxi.

130. Ibid., 127.

131. *Pent. IX* (*Opera* 9:341–42; *RF*, 27). Bonaventure cites Gregory, *In Evang.* II. hom. 30, n. 2.

132. Ibid.

133. *Sermo de trinitate* (*Opera* 9:357).

134. *3 Sent. d. 35, au., q. 6, concl* (*Opera* 3:786a).

135. Ibid., ad 1.2.3.4 (*Opera* 3:786b).

136. *Sermo de trinitate* (*Opera* 9:352, 356). In the *Nicomachean Ethics* (II.4) Aristotle names the three things necessary for virtue: to know, to choose, and to be active ceaselessly. Bonaventure also notes that it is more effective to draw persons from sin to the love of God by example than by words, citing Gregory: *"plus movet exemplum quam verbum"* (Homil, in evang. homil. 39, no. 10). *Pent. I* (*Opera* 9:332).

137. See *Septem donis* 9.6 (*Opera* 5:500).

138. *"amor enim…multo plus se extendit quam visio; et ubi deficit intellectus, ibi proficit affectus."* 2 Sent. d. 21, a. 2. q. 3 ad 4 (*Opera* 2:545); see also *Hex.* 2.30, 32 (*Opera* 5:341–42).

139. Bernard Cooke, *The Distancing of God: The Ambiguity of Symbol in History and Theology* (Minneapolis: Fortress, 1990), 163.

140. *Pent. X* (*Opera* 9:346).

141. *Itin.*, Prol. 1 and 7.1 (*Opera* 5:295, 312).

142. *Brev.* 5.6 (*Opera* 5:258–60).

143. *De Reduc.* 26 (*Opera* 5:325).

144. *Pent. I* (*Opera* 9:332): *"'Caeli enarrant gloriam Dei' (Ps 18:2), aeternam, sine inceptione et terminatione in incarnatione; magnam, sine diminutione in passione; et suavissimam, sine fastidione in Spiritus sancti missione."* See also *DTV* 3.7.12 (*Opera* 8:17); *Hex.* 21 (*Opera* 5:431–37). See Stephen F. Brown, trans., *The Journey of the Mind to God* (Indianapolis/Cambridge: Hackett, 1993), 70 n. 172.

145. Bonaventure was skilled at holding contrasting ideas in creative tension—a trait described by Ewert Cousins in his book *Bonaventure and the Coincidence of Opposites* (Quincy, IL: Quincy University Franciscan Press, 1978).

146. *Itin.* 7.6 (*Opera* 5:313).

Chapter 6: Catherine of Siena
The Spirit as Waiter

1. Bernard McGinn, *The Harvest of Mysticism in Medieval Germany*, vol. 4 of *The Presence of God: A History of Western Christian Mysticism* (New York: Herder & Herder, 2005), 48–79.

2. Suzanne Noffke, *Catherine of Siena: Vision through a Distant Eye* (Collegeville, MN: Liturgical Press, 1996), 7. See also Francis X. Newman, ed., *Social Unrest in the Late Middle Ages*, Medieval & Renaissance Texts and Studies 39 (Binghamton, NY: Medieval & Renaissance Texts and Studies, 1986); Richard Kieckhefer, *Unquiet Souls: Fourteenth Century Saints and Their Religious Milieu* (Chicago: University of Chicago Press, 1984); Barbara Tuchman, *A Distant Mirror: The Calamitous 14th Century* (New York: Knopf, 1984); Gordon Leff, *The Dissolution of the Medieval Outlook: An Essay on the Intellectual and Spiritual Change in the Fourteenth Century* (New York: Harper, 1976); Millard Meiss, *Painting in Florence and Siena after the Black Death: The Arts, Religion and Society in the Mid-Fourteenth Century* (New York: Harper, 1964); Denys Hay, *Europe in the Fourteenth and Fifteenth Centuries* (London: Longmans, 1966); Morton W. Bloomfield, *Piers Plowman as a Fourteenth-Century Apocalypse* (New Brunswick, NJ: Rutgers University Press, 1962); Johann Huizinga, *The Waning of the Middle Ages* (1949; New York: Doubleday, 1954).

3. Tuchman, *Distant Mirror*, xiii.

4. James Westfall Thompson, "The Aftermath of the Black Death and the Aftermath of the Great War," *American Journal of Sociology* (March 1920), cited in Tuchman, *Distant Mirror*, xiii–xiv.

5. Cited in Ellen Murray, "Tears: Symbol of Conversion in the Writings of Catherine of Siena" (Ph.D. diss., St. Louis University, 1996), 1.

6. An interdict, a common papal censure in the Middle Ages, prohibited the celebration of liturgy, sacraments, or Christian burial in a diocese or monastery.

7. Raymond of Capua, *The Life of Catherine of Siena*, trans. Conleth Kearns (Wilmington, DE: Michael Glazier, 1980), 385. Raymond of Capua (1330–99) was Catherine's advocate, friend, disciple and spiritual director. He was a Dominican priest who held a number of administrative offices, including that of Master General. He is known as the second founder of the Dominican Order and for his biography of Catherine.

8. Mary Ann Fatula, *Catherine of Siena's Way* (Wilmington, DE: Michael Glazier, 1987), 35.

9. Third orders were a lay branch of the Augustinians, Franciscans, Dominicans, and Carmelites. The first order is made up of ordained clergy; the second order, of enclosed contemplatives.

10. Fatula, *Catherine of Siena's Way*, 24.

11. Sigrid Undset, *Catherine of Siena* (New York: Sheed & Ward, 1954), 14.

12. Noffke, *Catherine of Siena*, 1–2.

13. Women in late medieval Italy had a variety of vocational options, allowing them to pursue an intentional religious life on their own or in various communal networks—enclosed canonical convents, third orders, religious guilds, communities of penance, and so on. In some arrangements, known as "open monasteries," women remained in the world, lived in their own homes and earned their own living. They might be wealthy widows, unmarried women who desired a contemplative existence or wished to endow religious projects, former prostitutes or concubines, or simply women whose lives had left them outside a clearly respectable category. "In both ecclesiastical Latin and local vernaculars, they went by many names: *mulieres religiosae, mulieres de penitentia, sorores, pinzochere, bizoke, mantellate, terziarie, monache di casa, monacelle, sante,* and *santarelle*. Sometimes women chose the life of a *pinzochera* in emulation of the monastic state, but women also chose it because they did not want to be enclosed." Katherine Gill, "Open Monasteries for Women in Late Medieval and Early Modern Italy: Two Roman Examples," http://matrix.divinity.yale.edu/MatrixWebData/KGILL-2.txt.

14. References to Catherine's letters in the text include "L" followed by the number of the letter and page numbers in *The Letters of St. Catherine of Siena*, vol. 1, ed. Suzanne Noffke, Medieval & Renaissance Texts and Studies 52 (Binghamton, NY: Medieval & Renaissance Text and Studies, 1988). References to vol. 2, *The Letters of Catherine of Siena*, ed. Suzanne Noffke, Medieval & Renaissance Texts and Studies 203 (Tempe, AZ: Arizona Center for Medieval and Renaissance Studies, 2001), include "LT," followed by the number of the letter and the page numbers in accord with Noffke's identification of the letters from the collection by Dupré Theseider. Letters cited that are not found in either of these volumes will be identified simply as "LT" with letter number only.

15. References to Catherine's prayers in the text include "P," prayer number, and page number in *The Prayers of Catherine of Siena*, ed. Suzanne Noffke (New York: Paulist, 1983).

16. The spontaneous and vivid character of Catherine of Siena's writing stems in part from her penchant to express herself in images. Mary T. O'Driscoll comments, "Metaphor trips over metaphor; one image barely formed, gives way to another." Recent, renewed apprecia-

tion of the role of image and metaphor in literature can lead us to a greater appreciation of Catherine's use of this literary device even though her context and ours differ considerably. While we do not share the Neoplatonic worldview of the Middle Ages, in which the divine lurks in every corner of reality, we can relate to the way symbols and images allow us to develop a sacramental consciousness that sees the world as more than simply a physical reality. Mary T. O'Driscoll, "St. Catherine of Siena: Life and Spirituality," *Angelicum* 57 (1980): 311.

17. Marie Walter Flood, "St. Thomas's Thought in the *Dialogue* of St. Catherine," *Spirituality Today* 32, no. 1 (March 1980): 27.

18. All references to *The Dialogue* in the text include "D," section number, and page numbers in Catherine of Siena, *The Dialogue*, ed. Suzanne Noffke (New York: Paulist, 1980).

19. It is interesting to note that there is no reference to the Holy Spirit in the section of the *Dialogue* entitled "Truth."

20. See, for example, Ralph Del Colle, *Christ and the Spirit: Spirit-Christology in Trinitarian Perspective* (Oxford: Oxford University Press, 1994).

21. Suzanne Noffke, "Catherine of Siena: The Responsive Heart," In *Spiritualities of the Heart*, ed. Annice Callahan (New York: Paulist, 1990), 67.

22. Ibid., 69, 74–75.

23. Catherine often refers to the Holy Spirit as the one who recruits individuals into religious life and away from life in the world (L84/255). Catherine believes that religious life maintains its holiness because it is founded in the Holy Spirit and thus will always produce upright members—in spite of some "bad seeds" (D125/242). Catherine also calls on the Spirit to counsel Monna Giovanna, a laywoman of Lucca, to live a life of sexual abstinence within her marriage. "And when does the Holy Spirit call you? When he sends you good holy inspirations; when he lets you recognize our human weakness and the wretched instability and fickleness of the world. Oh, let our hearts not become lukewarm, but let them rise up to respond to the Holy Spirit who is calling, and follow the way of perfection! And see to it, my daughter, if you hear the Holy Spirit calling you—both within yourself and within your husband—that you pay no attention to what other people say or to what the devil may suggest. No, act courageously, not like a child, and with the lamp of fortitude follow the light of the Holy Spirit" (LT1/51).

24. Raymond's text is an example of the exaggerated, idealized style of hagiography, whose aim is not to inform readers of historical information related to Catherine's life but to inspire them to holiness by praising Catherine's virtues.

25. Frequency in the reception of the Eucharist has varied over the course of Christian history. A number of factors led to infrequent reception of the Eucharist in the Middle Ages. Christian communities and the churches that housed them grew larger and more impersonal. Converts lacked adequate catechesis about the meaning of the Eucharist, leading them to pray on their own as silent spectators of a distant host elevated by the priest. An image of God as distant, removed from everyday life, and fearfully awesome led people to fear intimate contact. In special cases, holy individuals considered to be especially gifted requested more frequent reception. During this period, theologians debated the meaning of the Eucharist and how it should function in the liturgy.

26. Raymond also turns to the Spirit to legitimize Catherine's followers' custom of calling her "mother"—a custom that was likely criticized by some. He writes, "And indeed all of us, as if impelled to do so by the Spirit of God, habitually called Catherine 'mother'" (Life/II.11.300).

27. In human experience gentleness is often associated with mercy. Catherine often uses the term "gentle" (Italian *dolce*) to speak of the triune God. See Sheila Galligan, "Sheltered by the Mercy: St. Catherine's Gentle Way," *Spirituality Today* 42 (Spring 1990): 15–36.

28. Mary O'Driscoll links God's mercy for the world to Catherine's view of petitionary prayer. See "Mercy for the World: St. Catherine's View of Intercessory Prayer," *Spirituality Today* 32, no. 1 (March 1980): 36–45.

29. The following prayer is an example of the fluidity of Catherine's trinitarian theology. "Eternal Godhead, O high eternal Godhead! O supreme eternal Father! O fire ever blazing! You, eternal Father, high eternal Trinity, you are the measureless fire of charity. O Godhead, Godhead!" (P12/99).

30. The metaphor of clothing is found in the works of several medieval women mystics. Throughout history, women have engaged in weaving and making clothing. Julian of Norwich uses this metaphor to great advantage to speak of the intimacy between God and humans. Her familiarity with color and texture even suggest that she may have been from a family with a connection to the wool trade. Catherine's father was a dyer of wool.

31. In one letter, Catherine refers to the Holy Spirit as medicine, which is a fire that God never takes away from us (L84/255).

32. See Acts 7:51: "You stiff-necked people, uncircumcised in heart and ears, you always resist the Holy Spirit." See also Exodus 6:12 and Jeremiah 6:10.

33. See Ellen Murray, "Tears: Symbol of Conversion in the Writing of Catherine of Siena" (Ph.D. diss., St. Louis University, 1996).

34. O'Driscoll, "Mercy for the World," 39.

35. Catherine also refers to Christ's body (LT210/237) and pierced side (LT208/87) as a table.

36. The story of St. Lucy, virgin and martyr (c. 283–303) recounts that she was beheaded for the faith during the persecution of Diocletian. There is evidence that she was an object of great veneration in the early church. Her feast day is celebrated on December 13.

37. Catherine also imagines the Father and the cross as a bed (LT38/549).

38. George Herbert was from a large, eminent seventeenth-century English family. His mother was a patron of the poet John Donne. Herbert established himself in a successful career as poet and orator at Cambridge University and later as a member of Parliament. In 1630 he was ordained a priest in the Anglican Church, becoming rector in rural Bemerton for three years until he died of consumption. His poetry is filled with imagery, in the style of the metaphysical poets of the period, relating in a precise, at times humorous, and musical style the ways of God's love.

39. George Herbert, "Love III," in *George Herbert: The Country Parson, The Temple*, ed. John N. Wall, Jr., Classics of Western Spirituality (New York and Mahwah, NJ: Paulist, 1981), 316. I am grateful to Gretchen Pritchard for calling the connections between these two texts to my attention.

40. I cannot help but wonder if contemporary spiritual books that employ the metaphor of "chicken soup for the soul" would hold up to the demands and complexity of Catherine's spirituality. See *Chicken Soup for the Soul: 101 Stories to Open the Heart and Rekindle the Spirit*, ed. Jack Canfield and Mark Victor Hansen (Deerfield Beach, FL: Health Communications, 1993).

41. Suzanne Noffke suggests that Catherine may have encountered this idea in Domenico Cavalca's *Specchio di croce*: "No bond of iron could have held Christ nailed or bound—only charity, the bond of perfection." Domenico Cavalca, *Specchio di croce* (Brescia: Moro e Falsina, 1822), 41, cited in Noffke, *Letters of Catherine of Siena*, 2:161 n. 8. This concept is also found in other authors such as Ludolphus of Saxony and Feo Belcari, who writes "Not all the wood that ever was cut in this world, nor all the nails ever made, could have held Christ on the cross. No, only love for our salvation held him." Feo Belcari, *Parte della vita di alcuni Gesuati* (Milan: G. Silvestri, 1832), 131, cited in Noffke, *Letters of Catherine of Siena*, 2:176 n. 6.

42. This prayer, written during Catherine's stay at Rocca d'Orcia in 1377, was given to Frate Jeronimo da Siena, an Augustinian, who passed it on to another preacher in Venice who gave it to Caffarini, who in turn gave it to the Mantellate of Venice. Noffke, *Letters of Catherine of Siena*, 2:119 n.3.

Chapter 7: Julian of Norwich
"Sweet Touchings": The Spirit and Grace

1. For additional information on the fourteenth century, see Suzanne Noffke, *Catherine of Siena: Vision through a Distant Eye* (Collegeville, MN: Liturgical Press, 1996), 1–2. See also Francis X. Newman, ed., *Social Unrest in the Late Middle Ages*, Medieval & Renaissance Texts and Studies 39 (Binghamton, NY: Medieval & Renaissance Texts and Studies, 1986); Richard Kieckhefer, *Unquiet Souls: Fourteenth Century Saints and Their Religious Milieu* (Chicago: University of Chicago Press, 1984); Barbara Tuchman, *A Distant Mirror: The Calamitous 14th Century* (New York: Knopf, 1984); Gordon Leff, *The Dissolution of the Medieval Outlook: An Essay on the Intellectual and Spiritual Change in the Fourteenth Century* (New York: Harper, 1976); Millard Meiss, *Painting in Florence and Siena after the Black Death: The Arts, Religion and Society in the Mid-Fourteenth Century* (New York: Harper, 1964); Dennis Hay, *Europe in the Fourteenth and Fifteenth Centuries*, 2nd ed. (London: Longman, 1986); Morton W. Bloomfield, *Piers Plowman as a Fourteenth-Century Apocalypse* (New Brunswick, NJ: Rutgers University Press, 1962); Johann Huizinga, *The Waning of the Middle Ages* (1949; New York: Doubleday, 1954).

2. Thomas Brinton, *The Sermons of Thomas Brinton, Bishop of Rochester (1373–1389)*, ed. Mary Aquinas Devlin (London, 1954), vol. 2, sermon 70, 323, cited in John B. Friedman, "'He Hath a Thousand Slayn this Pestilence': The Iconography of the Plague in the Late Middle Ages," in *Social Unrest in the Late Middle Ages*, ed. Newman, 76, 82–83.

3. This development partially explains Julian's concern with orthodoxy in the Long Text, but the Short Text predates these events.

4. Joan Nuth notes the Council of Vienne decree *Cum de quibusdam mulieribus*, cited throughout the fourteenth century as the "authoritative document legitimizing investigations of women 'commonly known as beguines' who dared to 'discourse on the Trinity and the divine essence'..." *Wisdom's Daughter: The Theology of Julian of Norwich* (New York: Crossroad, 1991), 19–21.

5. Nuth thinks it likely that Julian knew about the persecution of the so-called Free Spirit heresy. Even the most orthodox mystics or any female who presumed to teach or preach could be suspect. *Wisdom's Daughter*, 19–20. See also Malcolm Lambert, *Medieval Heresy: Popular Movements from the Gregorian Reform to the Reformation*, 2nd ed. (Oxford: Basil Blackwell, 1992); R. I. Moore, *The Origins of European Dissent* (New York: St. Martin's Press, 1977); Eleanor McLaughlin, "Les femmes et l'hérésie médiévale," *Concilium* 111 (1976): 73–90; Robert E. Lerner, *The Heresy of the Free Spirit in the Later Middle Ages* (Berkeley: University of California Press, 1972).

6. An example of political violence is found in the situation of the ruling monarch in England, Edward III (d. 1375), who came to power as a young man in 1330 by way of the scandalous intrigues of his mother, Isabella, and her lover, Mortimer, who toppled Isabella's husband. Not long after, Mortimer was executed and Isabella went to live in Kings' Lynn near where Julian probably grew up. At first Isabella lived in luxury, at the expense of the people, but after a conversion, she began to help the poor and entered a Poor Clare Monastery. Edward III ruled till Julian was thirty-five, when Richard II became king.

7. See J. P. H. Clark, "Late Fourteenth-Century Cambridge Theology and the English Contemplative Tradition," in *The Medieval Mystical Tradition in England* (Cambridge: D. S. Brewer, n.d.), 5:13.

8. See Oliver Davies, *God Within: The Mystical Tradition of Northern Europe* (New York: Paulist, 1988); Bernard McGinn, "The English Mystics," in *Christian Spirituality*, vol. 2, *High Middle Ages and Reformation*, ed. Jill Raitt, World Spirituality 17 (New York: Crossroad, 1987); James Walsh, ed., *Pre-Reformation English Spirituality* (London, 1965); Martin Thornton, *English Spirituality* (London: SPCK, 1963); Eric Colledge, ed., *The Mediaeval Mystics of England* (London: Murray, 1962); David Knowles, *The English Mystical Tradition* (New York: Harper Brothers, 1961); Conrad Pepler, *The English Religious Heritage* (St. Louis: B. Herder, 1958); Gerard Bullet, *The English Mystics* (London: Michael Joseph, 1950); William R. Inge, *Studies of English Mystics*, St. Margaret's Lectures (London: John Murray, 1906).

9. See the introduction to the critical edition, *A Book of Showings to the Anchoress, Julian of Norwich*, ed. E. Colledge and J. Walsh, 2 vols. (Toronto: Pontifical Institute of Mediaeval Studies, 1978).

10. For background on Julian's life and times, see Grace M. Jantzen, *Julian of Norwich: Mystic and Theologian* (New York and Mahwah, NJ: Paulist, 1988), 3–50; Kerrie Hide, *Gifted Origins to Graced Fulfillment: The Soteriology of Julian of Norwich* (Collegeville, MN: Liturgical Press, 2001), 3–13; Nuth, *Wisdom's Daughter,* 7–22; Ritamary Bradley, *Julian's*

Way: A Practical Commentary on Julian of Norwich (London: HarperCollins, 1992), 1–59.

11. *The Book of Margery Kempe*, ed. William Butler-Bowdon (Oxford: Oxford University Press, 1944), 54–56. See also Maureen Fries, "Margery Kempe," in Paul Szarmach, *An Introduction to the Medieval Mystics of Europe* (Albany: SUNY Press, 1984), 217–35; and Clarissa W. Atkinson, *Mystic and Pilgrim: The "Book" and the World of Margery Kempe* (Ithaca and London: Cornell University Press, 1983).

12. References in the text indicate the chapter and page number from the Short and Long Texts of the volume *Julian of Norwich: Showings*, Classics of Western Spirituality (New York and Mahwah, NJ: Paulist, 1978).

13. For a detailed analysis of Julian's illness and the visions that accompanied it, see Jantzen, *Julian of Norwich*, 74–85.

14. See the introduction by Edmund Colledge and James Walsh in *Julian of Norwich: Showings*, 21–22; and Nicholas Watson, "The Composition of Julian of Norwich's *Revelation of Love*," *Speculum* 68 (July 1993): 638. Julian's text seems not to have been received with the same acclaim as those of her peers, Richard Rolle, Walter Hilton, and the anonymous author of *The Cloud of Unknowing*. In contrast to the plethora of surviving manuscripts of these latter writers, there is only one copy of Julian's short text, dated between 1450 and 1500. The long text survives from the Middle Ages only in extract, and in complete form in two seventeenth-century manuscripts. English Benedictine Serenus Cressy published a modern version of the long text in 1670, which was translated into French by Pierre Poiret. The one manuscript of the short text, now housed in the British Library, had been passed from one private owner to another, as a result of the British dissolution of the monasteries. Colledge and Walsh attribute Julian's unpopularity to the difficulty of her text, but her willingness to raise questions about church teaching might also have been a factor. *Book of Showings*, 17.

15. Jantzen, *Julian of Norwich*, 74–75.

16. Ibid., 25 n. 7.

17. This form of life can be traced back to the desert fathers and mothers who retreated to the wilderness in the fourth century as a protest against Constantine's edict that made Christianity the religion of the empire.

18. We know of a number of Rules for anchoresses that existed during Julian's time. Some would have followed the Rule of the religious order to which they had previously belonged, such as the Cistercians or Benedictines. There was also a rule written around 891 by a monk named Grimlaic entitled *Regula Solitariorum*. Aelred of Rievaulx wrote a rule

around 1160 for his anchoress sister. An anonymous text from the early thirteenth century, *Ancrene Riwle*, was written for three sisters who had become anchoresses.

19. Hide, *Gifted Origins*, 199–200, 212.

20. Jantzen, *Julian of Norwich*, 108.

21. Vincent Gillespie and Maggie Ross call attention to this stylistic element in Julian's text: "trinitarian functions are denied exact demarcation in terms of earthly activity or theological convention." "The Apophatic Image: The Poetics of Effacement in Julian of Norwich," in *Medieval Mystical Tradition in England*, 5:67.

22. Jantzen, *Julian of Norwich*, 114.

23. See Short Text, x–xi, 141–44.

24. Hide, *Gifted Origins*, 136.

25. Ibid., 155.

26. Ibid., 155 n. 1. Hide writes: "Though Julian has difficulty in defining the reality meant by the Holy Spirit, she grounds her understanding of the Spirit in the triune symbol of God and identifies the Holy Spirit with the love within the Trinity."

27. Ibid., 156.

28. Nicholas Watson, "The Trinitarian Hermeneutic in Julian of Norwich's *Revelation of Love*, in *Medieval Mystical Tradition in England*, 5:99.

29. See Gillespie and Ross, "Apophatic Image," 75.

30. It is likely that Julian's use of the term *Lord* to refer to the Holy Spirit has its source in the creed she would have recited at liturgy: "I believe in the Holy Spirit, Lord and Giver of life" and Paul's second letter to the Corinthians (3:17).

31. Hide, *Gifted Origins*, 170.

32. For a discussion of the Holy Spirit as the "touch of God," see Kilian McDonnell, *The Other Hand of God: The Holy Spirit as the Universal Touch and Goal* (Collegeville, MN: Liturgical Press, 2003), 109–20.

33. See Nuth, *Wisdom's Daughter*, 16–22.

34. Harding Meyer, "A Protestant Attitude," in *Conflicts about the Holy Spirit, Concilium* 128, ed. Hans Küng and Jürgen Moltmann (New York: Seabury, 1979), 85–86.

35. Hans Küng, "Epilogue: How Should We Speak Today about the Holy Spirit?" in *Conflicts about the Holy Spirit*, ed. Küng and Moltmann, 115–16.

36. I am grateful to Jane Ferreira for this application of Julian's message to the contemporary church.

37. The Middle English *shal* contains the meanings of obligation or necessity not present in contemporary usage of *shall*, which is more

limited to the idea of futurity. A better translation might be "all things must inevitably come to good." See Alexander Barratt, "How Many Children Had Julian of Norwich?" in *Vox Mystica: Essays on Medieval Mysticism in Honour of Professor Valerie M. Lagorio*, ed. Anne Clark Bartlett, with Thomas Bestul, Janet Goebel, and William F. Pollard (Cambridge: D. S. Brewer, 1995), 36, cited in Hide, *Gifted Origins*, 159.

38. Nuth, *Wisdom's Daughter*, 151–58.

39. Ibid., 82–83, 148–51.

40. Ibid., 85.

Chapter 8: The Spirit Lives On

1. Jean-Pierre de Caussade, *The Sacrament of the Present Moment* (1867; San Francisco: HarperSanFrancisco, 1982), 101.

2. Ronald Modras, *Ignatian Humanism: A Dynamic Spirituality for the 21st Century* (Chicago: Loyola Press, 2004), ix.

3. Ibid., x.

4. Ronald Rolheiser, *The Holy Longing: The Search for Christian Spirituality* (New York: Doubleday, 1999), 7, cited in Modras, *Ignatian Humanism*, x–xi.

5. Bernard McGinn, *The Harvest of Mysticism in Medieval Germany*, vol. 4 of *The Presence of God: A History of Western Christian Mysticism* (New York: Herder & Herder, 2005), 85. Kilian McDonnell suggests that the retrieval of the biblical and liturgical experience of the early church would help restore trinitarian theology and pneumatology to its role as a normal preparation for contemplation. He advocates the addition of aesthetic, hymnodic, and doxological images to philosophical categories and argumentation in theology so that we can better pray, preach, and celebrate our theology. *The Other Hand of God: The Holy Spirit as the Universal Touch and Goal* (Collegeville, MN: Liturgical Press, 2003), 31.

6. Margaret Miles quotes a very modern-sounding Thomas Aquinas: "The image is the starting point of our knowledge. It is that from which our intellectual activity begins, not as a passing stimulus, but as an enduring foundation." Thomas Aquinas, *Opusc.* 16, de Trinitate 6.2 ad 5, cited in Margaret Miles, *Image as Insight: Visual Understanding in Western Christianity and Secular Culture* (Boston: Beacon, 1985), 143.

7. Karl Froehlich, "Church History and the Bible," *Lutheran Quarterly* 5 (Summer 1991): 127–42.

8. Ibid., 139.

9. Ibid., 135.

10. Walter Brueggemann, *Power, Providence and Personality* (Louisville: Westminster/John Knox, 1990), 48.

11. Ibid.

12. Barbara Newman, *Saint Hildegard of Bingen: Symphonia* (Ithaca and London: Cornell University Press, 1988), 41, 51.

13. Barbara Newman, *God and the Goddesses: Vision, Poetry, and Belief in the Middle Ages* (Philadelphia: University of Pennsylvania Press, 2003), 292. See review symposium of this volume in *Spiritus* 5, no. 2 (Fall 2005): 203–20.

14. Bernard McGinn develops this idea in *The Flowering of Mysticism: Men and Women in the New Mysticism—1200–1350*, vol. 3 of *The Presence of God: A History of Western Christian Mysticism* (New York: Crossroad, 1998), 18–24.

15. Philip Sheldrake, "Imaginative Theology: A Strategy of Subversion," *Spiritus* 5, no. 2 (Fall 2005): 212–13.

16. This is the title of the first chapter in Kilian McDonnell's *The Other Hand of God* (p. 1). McDonnell notes that "the health of pneumatology is in Trinity." At this moment in history, McDonnell prefers to emphasize a Christology dependent on pneumatology to correct the dominance in the West of a pneumatology dependent on Christology (pp. 155, 193–94). He goes on, "In the broad central tradition, the significance of the person and mission of the Son is rarely impoverished, but we cannot say this of the Spirit, because pneumatology has not been integrated in an organic way into the whole theological process" (p. 205).

17. Catherine Mowry LaCugna, *God for Us: The Trinity and Christian Life* (New York: HarperCollins, 1991), 1.

18. McDonnell, *Other Hand of God*, 61.

19. John Simons, "Naming and Glorifying the Trinity," in *The Challenge of Tradition: Discerning the Future of Anglicanism*, ed. John Simons (Toronto: Anglican Book Center, 1997), 27.

20. Ibid., 28.

21. William Hill, *The Three-Personed God: The Trinity as a Mystery of Salvation* (Washington, D.C.: Catholic University of America Press, 1982), 16, 37, 142, 235, 278. Maria Calisi has done important work using Bonaventure's doctrine of the good as self-diffusive as a resource for a more gender-inclusive theology of the Trinity. "Bonaventure's Trinitarian Theology as a Feminist Resource," *Spirit and Life* 8 (1999): 117–32.

22. Stephen H. Webb, *The Gifting God: A Trinitarian Ethics of Excess* (New York: Oxford University Press, 1998), 86.

23. LaCugna, *God for Us*, 351–53.

24. David Coffey, *Grace the Gift of the Holy Spirit* (Manly NSW, Australia: Catholic Institute of Sydney, 1979); "The 'Incarnation' of the

Holy Spirit in Christ," *Theological Studies* 45 (1984): 466–80; "A Proper Mission of the Holy Spirit," *Theological Studies* 47 (1986): 227–50; "The Holy Spirit as the Mutual Love of the Father and the Son," *Theological Studies* 51 (1990): 193–229. See also Ralph Del Colle, *Christ and the Spirit: Spirit-Christology in Trinitarian Perspective* (New York and Oxford: Oxford University Press, 1994), 91–140.

25. I recall again here Rosemary Drage Hale's invitation to explore the role of sensory perception and memory in medieval mystical experience. When we read medieval mystical texts, she writes, "We miss something of the sensory dynamic of the world or culture of medieval mystics if we persist in interpreting their experience solely as 'visions.'...perhaps we can begin to do more than translate the words if we take a 'hermeneutical turn'—instead of reading the texts, we could be learning to sense them." In "'Taste and See, For God is Sweet': Sensory Perception and Memory in Medieval Mystical Experience," in *Vox Mystica: Essays on Medieval Mysticism in Honor of Professor Valerie M. Lagorio*, ed. Anne Clark Bartlett, with Thomas Bestul, Janet Goebel, and William F. Pollard (Cambridge: D. S. Brewer, 1995), 14.

26. Abraham J. Heschel describes the prophet as one who intensifies responsibility; who is impatient of excuse and contemptuous of pretense and self-pity. He calls them exegetes "of existence from a divine perspective." The prophet is one who is sensitive to evil and who feels fiercely. *The Prophets: An Introduction* (San Francisco: Harper & Row, 1962), xiv, 3, 5, 7. David Tracy names as the two principal foci of his theology a hermeneutics in which the "other," not the "self," is the dominant focus. He finds a prophetic-mystical form of theology for naming God as most helpful today. In "God, Dialogue and Solidarity: A Theologian's Refrain," *The Christian Century* 107, no. 20 (October 10, 1990): 902.

27. See Yves Congar, *I Believe in the Holy Spirit*, vol. 1, *The Experience of the Spirit* (New York: Seabury, 1983), 126–37.

28. See Robert Lerner, *The Heresy of the Free Spirit in the Later Middle Ages* (Berkeley: University of California Press, 1972).

29. See *Early Anabaptist Spirituality: Selected Writings*, trans. Daniel Liechty (New York/Mahwah, NJ: Paulist, 1994).

30. See *The Shakers: Two Centuries of Spiritual Reflection*, ed. Robley Edward Whitson (New York/Mahwah, NJ: Paulist, 1983).

31. Harvey Cox, *Fire from Heaven: The Rise of Pentecostal Spirituality and the Reshaping of Religion in the Twenty-first Century* (New York: Addison-Wesley, 1995).

32. See Barbara Newman, *From Virile Woman to WomanChrist*, Studies in Medieval Religion and Literature (Philadelphia: University of

Pennsylvania Press, 1995), 182. See also Stephen Wessley, "The Thirteenth-Century Guglielmites: Salvation through Women," in Derek Baker, *Medieval Women* (Oxford: Oxford University Press, 1978), 289–303; and Felice Tocco, ed., "Il Processo dei Guglielmiti," *Rendiconti della Reale Accademia dei Lincei: Classe di Scienze Morali, Storiche e Filologiche*, ser. 5, vol. 8 (Rome, 1899) 309–42; 351–84, 407–32, 437–69, cited in Newman, *From Virile Woman*, 295. Yves Congar also addresses the "femininity" of the Holy Spirit in *I Believe in the Holy Spirit*, vol. 3, *The River of Life Flows in the East and in the West* (New York: Seabury, 1983), 155–64.

33. See Todd Breyfogle and Thomas Levergood, "Conversation with David Tracy," *Cross Currents* (Fall 1994): 293–98.

34. Joseph Chinnici notes the disappearance of citations referring to the Holy Spirit from mystical texts between 1620 and 1680 in England, France, and Italy, and suggests that appeal to the Holy Spirit became associated with the forces of anarchy. He also notes that the rise of science with its effects on epistemology removed the Holy Spirit from the language field into the realm of the unknowable, mysterious, emotional, and enthusiastic. Later choices to speak of the church as the perfect society rather than as the Mystical Body no doubt helped move the Spirit further onto the sidelines. "'Have you seen the one whom my heart loves? Contemplative Prayer and the Ambiguities of History," and "The Politics of Mysticism: Church, State, and the Carmelite Tradition" (unpublished papers, 1994).

35. The biblical references are to Isaiah 11:2: "The Spirit of the Lord shall rest upon him, the spirit of wisdom and understanding, the spirit of counsel and might, the spirit of knowledge and the fear of the Lord."

36. The biblical reference is to Galatians 5:22: "But the fruit of the Spirit is love, joy, peace, patience, kindness, goodness, faithfulness, gentleness, self-control."

37. Bernard of Clairvaux, *First Sermon for Pentecost*, 2–4.

38. Jürgen Moltmann, *The Source of Life: The Holy Spirit and the Theology of Life*, trans. Margaret Kohl (Minneapolis, MN: Fortress, 1997), 18.

39. Karl Rahner, "The Apostolate of Prayer," in *Theological Investigations*, vol. 3 (New York: Crossroad, 1982), 218–19.

40. Gerhart Ladner, *Ad Imaginem Dei: The Image of Man in Mediaeval Art* (Latrobe, PA: Archabbey Press, 1965), 42, 108–9.

41. Letter 91r to Abbot Adelbert, in *The Letters of Hildegard of Bingen*, 2 vols., trans. Joseph L. Baird and Radd K. Ehrman (New York: Oxford University Press, 1994), 2:6.

42. Athanasius, *Letters to Serapion, in Letters of Saint Athanasius concerning the Holy Spirit*, trans. C. R. B. Shapland (London, 1951), cited in R. P. C. Hanson, *The Search for the Christian Doctrine of God: The Arian Controversy, 318–381* (Edinburgh: T. & T. Clark, 1988), 751.

43. For an exposition of the importance of context in the study of spirituality, see Philip Sheldrake, *Spirituality and History* (New York: Crossroad, 1992); and Walter Principe, "Broadening the Focus: Context as a Corrective Lens in Reading Historical Works in Spirituality," *Christian Spirituality Bulletin* 2, no. 1 (Spring 1994): 1–5.

44. Alisdair MacIntyre, *After Virtue: A Study in Moral Theory* (London: Duckworth, 1981), 205.

45. Georges Florovsky, "The Work of the Holy Spirit in Revelation," *The Christian East* 13, no. 2 (1932): 49–64, cited in Rowan Williams, *Why Study the Past: The Quest for the Historical Church* (Grand Rapids: Eerdmans, 2005), 92.

46. William M. Thompson, *Christology and Spirituality* (New York: Crossroad, 1991), 5.

47. See Francine Cardman, "The Holy Spirit and the Apostolic Faith: A Roman Catholic Response," *Greek Orthodox Theological Review* 31, nos. 3–4 (1986): 292–93.

48. Luke Timothy Johnson, *Religious Experience in Earliest Christianity: A Missing Dimension in New Testament Studies* (Minneapolis: Fortress, 1998), 7. Greek words denoting power include *exousia*, with its connotations of freedom and authority (John 1:12; 1 Cor 6:12; 8:9; 9:4; 2 Cor 10:8; 13:10; 2 Thess 3:9; Heb 13:10; Rev 2:26); *energeia* with its suggestion of efficacy and energy (1 Cor 12:6, 11; 1 Thess 2:13; Gal 3:5; 5:6; Col 1:20; Eph 3:20–21); and most frequently *dynamis* (Rom 1:16; 15:13, 19; 1 Cor 1:18; 6:14; 12:3; 12:28; 14:31; 15:50; 2 Cor 1:4; 6:7; 8:3; 10:4; 12:9–10; 13:4, 9; Gal 3:5; Eph 3:20; 6:10; Phil 3:10, 21; 4:13; Col 1:29, etc.) (p. 6 n. 12).

49. Johnson, *Religious Experience*, 8. See Luke 24:49; Acts 1:8; 8:18–19; 10:38; Rom 1:4; 8:26; 15:13, 19; 1 Cor 2:4; 5:3–4; 12:11; 2 Cor 4:13; Gal 3:1–5; Eph 2:2; 3:16; 6:18–20; 1 Thess 1:5; Heb 2:4.

50. Ibid., 9.

51. Elisabeth Moltmann-Wendel, "Becoming Human in New Community," in *The Community of Women and Men in the Church*, ed. Constance Parvey (Philadelphia: Fortress, 1983), 41, cited in Cardman, "Holy Spirit," 309.

52. Cardman, "Holy Spirit," 300–305. Women (and some men) theologians who address this issue in specific ways include Elizabeth A. Johnson, *She Who Is: The Mystery of God in Feminist Theological Discourse* (New York: Crossroad, 1992); Newman, *God and the Goddesses*; Elisabeth

Schüssler Fiorenza, ed., *The Power of Naming: A Concilium Reader in Feminist Liberation Theology* (Maryknoll, NY: Orbis Books, 1997); Kari Elisabeth Borresen, ed., *The Image of God: Gender Models in Judaeo-Christian Tradition* (Minneapolis: Fortress, 1995); Mary Daly, *Beyond God the Father: Toward a Philosophy of Women's Liberation* (Boston: Beacon, 1973); Margaret Farley, "New Patterns of Relationship: Beginnings of a Moral Revolution," *Theological Studies* 36, no. 4 (1975): 643; Mary Rose D'Angelo, "Beyond Father and Son," in *Justice as Mission: An Agenda for the Church*, ed. T. Brown and C. Lind (Burlington, ON: Trinity, 1985), 107–18; Othmar Keel and C. Uehlinger, *Gods, Goddesses, and Images of God in Ancient Israel* (Minneapolis: Augsburg Fortress, 1998); Sallie McFague, *Metaphorical Theology: Models of God in Religious Language* (Philadelphia: Fortress, 1982); Carol Ochs, *Behind the Sex of God* (Boston: Beacon, 1977); Eleanor Rae, *Women, the Earth, the Divine* (Maryknoll, NY: Orbis Books, 1994); Laurel C. Schneider, *Re-Imagining the Divine: Confronting the Backlash against Feminist Theology* (Cleveland: Pilgrim, 1998).

53. Cardman, "Holy Spirit," 294.

54. *The Letters of Catherine of Siena*, trans. Suzanne Noffke, Medieval & Renaissance Texts and Studies (Tempe, AZ: Arizona Center for Medieval and Renaissance Studies, 2001), 99.

55. Johnson, *She Who Is*, 5.

56. Cardman, "Holy Spirit," 304.

57. Gustavo Gutiérrez, *We Drink from Our Own Wells: The Spiritual Journey of a People*, trans. Matthew O'Connell (Maryknoll, NY: Orbis Books, 1984), 37. Gutiérrez cites Marie-Dominique Chenu's sentiment that the interest and grandeur of theological systems lie in their being expressions of a spirituality. One gets to the heart of a theology by grasping it in its origins "via that fundamental intuition that serves to guide a spiritual life and provides the intellectual regimen proper to that life." Chenu, *Le Saulchoir: Una Scuola de teologia* (1937; Casale Monferrato: Marietti, 1982), 59, cited in Gutiérrez, *We Drink from Our Own Wells*, 147 n. 2.

58. See LaCugna, *God for Us*, 359.

59. See Breyfogle and Levergood, "Conversation with David Tracy," 293–98.

60. Hans Küng, "Epilogue: How Should We Speak Today About the Holy Spirit?" In *Conflicts about the Holy Spirit*, ed. Hans Küng and Jürgen Moltmann, *Concilium* 128 (New York: Seabury, 1979), 115–16.

61. *A Scholastic Miscellany: Anselm to Ockham*, ed. and trans. Eugene R. Fairweather, Library of Christian Classics 10 (Philadelphia: Westminster, 1956), 359–60. Also cited in Congar, *I Believe in the Holy Spirit*, 1.109–10.

62. See Tom Stella, *A Faith Worth Believing* (New York: HarperCollins, 2004).

63. *Come Holy Spirit*, trans. Eleonore Stump and Kilian McDonnell, in McDonnell, *Other Hand of God*, xvii–xviii.

ILLUSTRATION CREDITS

Cover Art: Jean Poyet, *The Pentecost*. French, c. 1500. Miniature from a Book of Hours. Photo © The Cleveland Museum of Art.

1. Duccio (di Buoninsegna) (c. 1260–1319), *Pentecost*. From the upper section of the Maesta altarpiece. Photo Museo dell'Opera Metropolitana, Siena, Italy/Art Resource, New York.

2. Andrea Orcagna (c. 1308–c. 1368), *Pentecost*. Accademia, Florence, Italy. Photo Alinari/Art Resource, New York.

3. El Greco (1541–1614), *The Pentecost*. Museo del Prado, Madrid, Spain. Photo Scala/Art Resource, New York.

4. *Holy Trinity*. Mexico, n.d. Peters Collection, St. Joseph's University, Philadelphia. Photo © Laird Bindrim, St. Joseph's University.

5. Andrei Rublev (1360–c. 1430), *Trinity of Uglic*. Russian icon. Rubliev Museum, Moscow, Russia. Photo Scala/Art Resource, New York.

6. Rubielos Master, *The Coronation of the Virgin with the Trinity*. Spanish, c. 1400. Oil on panel. Photo © The Cleveland Museum of Art.

7. Jean Malouel (c. 1370–1415), *Pietà with God the Father*. Louvre, Paris, France. Photo Scala/Art Resource, New York.

8. Hildegard of Bingen (1098–1179), *Trinity*, in a rendition by Mother Placid Dempsey, OSB. From Hildegard of Bingen, *Scivias*, Classics of Western Spirituality (New York and Mahwah, NJ: Paulist, 1990), 409.

9. Hildegard of Bingen (1098–1179), *The Blue Christ*, in a rendition by Mother Placid Dempsey, OSB. From Hildegard of Bingen, *Scivias*, Classics of Western Spirituality (New York and Mahwah, NJ: Paulist, 1990), 159.

10. Hildegard of Bingen (1098–1179), *Hildegard Inspired by the Spirit*, in a rendition by Mother Placid Dempsey, OSB. From Hildegard of Bingen, *Scivias*, Classics of Western Spirituality (New York and Mahwah, NJ: Paulist, 1990), 58.

11. Hildegard of Bingen (1098–1179), *Confirmation*, in a rendition by Mother Placid Dempsey, OSB. From Hildegard of Bingen, *Scivias*, Classics of Western Spirituality (New York and Mahwah, NJ: Paulist, 1990), 187.

12. Laurent Girardin, *The Trinity*. French, c. 1460. Oil on wood. Photo © The Cleveland Museum of Art.

13. Jean Fouquet (c. 1420–c. 1480), *The Hours of the Holy Ghost: Pentecost (Prime)*. 1450–1455. From the Hours of Etienne Chevalier, Ms.71, folio 21. Musée Condé, Chantilly, France. Photo Réunion des Musées Nationaux/Art Resource, New York.
14. Nicholas of Verdun (1130–1205), *Pentecost*. Detail from Klosterneuburg Altar, 1181. Gold and enamel. Sammlungen des Stiftes, Klosterneuburg Abbey, Austria. Photo Erich Lessing/Art Resource, New York.
15. José de Ribera (1588?–1652), *Holy Trinity*. 1635-36. Oil on canvas. Photo Museo del Prado, Spain/Art Resource, New York.
16. *The Trinity*. Bohemia, Prague, c. 1410. Cutting from an Antiphonary: Initial "G"[loria tibi Trinitas]. Photo © The Cleveland Museum of Art.
17. Masaccio (1401–28), *The Holy Trinity*. Fresco. S. Maria Novella, Florence, Italy. Photo Scala/Art Resource, New York.
18. Albrecht Dürer (1471–1528), *The Holy Trinity*. German, 1511. Woodcut. Photo © The Cleveland Museum of Art.
19. Limbourg Brothers, *Pentecost*. Fifteenth century. From The Hours of the Holy Spirit. Les Très Riches Heures du Duc de Berry. Musée Condé, Chantilly, France. Photo Réunion des Musées Nationaux/Art Resource, New York.
20. *Pentecost*. c. 1200. From the Psalter of Ingeborg of Denmark, Queen of France. Ms. 1695, fol 32b. Musée Condé, Chantilly, France. Photo Réunion des Musées Nationaux/Art Resource, New York.
21. *The Pentecost*. Flemish/Liege, c. 1260. Leaf Excised from a Psalter. Photo © The Cleveland Museum of Art.

INDEX

95, 164, 249, 250, 258,
264; and touch, 215,
231–32, 236, 238, 264,
324; and tradition, 15–16
(*see also* Tradition); and
unity, 51, 57–63, 82, 83,
123–24, 134, 155, 195,
284–85 (*see also* Trinity);
and vocation, 133–36,
190–94, 227, 243, 318; as
waiter, 33, 164, 190, 192,
203–11, 212, 255, 264;
and water, 31, 41, 81–82,
85–86, 89, 103, 164–68,
191, 223–24, 242, 246; as
weight, 194; in the
Western tradition, 1, 3,
6, 14, 17, 270

Ignatius of Antioch, 31, 278
Imagery. *See* Symbol
Imagination, 17, 243
Irenaeus, 41, 204, 265

Jesus. *See* Christ
Joachim of Fiore, 71, 153–54,
170, 306
Johnson, Elizabeth, 269, 271,
329, 330
Julian of Norwich, 3, 7, 165,
179, 182, 187, 215–38,
248, 312, 319; anchoress,
218–19, 323–24; English
school, 217, 322, 323; life
of, 215–19; grace, 215,
224–28, 233; Holy Spirit
and sin, 228–30;
metaphoric style of writing,
223–28; motherhood of

God, 222–23, 227, 235;
as prophet, 233–35;
Spirit and goodness, 230;
Spirit's touch, 215,
231–32, 324; works, 3,
216, 218, 323

Küng, Hans, 234, 262–63,
324, 330

LaCugna, Catherine, 14–15,
244, 245, 271, 326, 330
Ladner, Gerhart, 27, 275, 276,
328
Laity, 66–67, 70, 73, 74, 132,
175–76, 193, 250, 287
Leclercq, Jean, 120, 129, 138,
297, 301, 303, 304
Lectio divina, 5, 105, 296
Liturgy, 41, 75, 76, 80, 86,
108, 113, 196, 218, 219,
256, 258, 273, 290, 291,
319, 325
Lombard, Peter (*Sentences*),
14, 155, 270–71
Luther, Martin, 14, 311

Manichaeism, 41–42, 281
Mary, 4, 29, 31, 35, 85, 143,
162–63, 186, 226, 230,
276, 277, 298, 300, 332
McDonnell, Kilian, 13,
268–70, 279, 280, 284,
300, 302, 325, 326, 331
McGinn, Bernard, 80, 274,
280, 286, 291, 296, 304,
306, 316, 322, 325, 326
Metaphor. *See* Symbol
Methodology, 4–6, 13, 34–36;